Herbert A. Howe

Elements of descriptive Astronomy

Herbert A. Howe

Elements of descriptive Astronomy

ISBN/EAN: 9783743343498

Manufactured in Europe, USA, Canada, Australia, Japa

Cover: Foto ©ninafisch / pixelio.de

Manufactured and distributed by brebook publishing software (www.brebook.com)

Herbert A. Howe

Elements of descriptive Astronomy

TO

MR. HUMPHREY B. CHAMBERLIN,

TO WHOSE MUNIFICENCE

THE AUTHOR IS DEEPLY INDEBTED,

This Book

IS GRATEFULLY DEDICATED.

INTRODUCTION.

THIS book is intended for the use of students who have a fair knowledge of elementary algebra and plane geometry, and is the outcome of several years of experience with classes of this sort. The author hopes that the volume will also be acceptable to more advanced scholars.

The teacher may here be reminded of the fact that among the most urgent needs in the study of astronomy is the exercise of the geometric imagination; that is, the faculty which forms mental pictures of the relative positions of planes and circles, and of the motions, real and apparent, of the celestial bodies. The initial step in astronomical instruction is to teach pupils the use of their eyes, — to insist that they observe the heavens and watch the celestial motions. Though they may be bewildered by such work at first, they will soon learn to delight in it, and will derive much profit from it. The earliest work in the line of observation is the study of the constellations. Acquaintance with the principal stars of the chief constellations visible in his latitude will prove a source of lifelong enjoyment to the pupil. Each student should keep a small blank book in which to make sketches, and to record the results of observations.

The Star Maps, at the end of the volume, are on a generous scale, and include all stars not fainter than the fifth magnitude, from the north pole to 40° of south declination. By the use of these maps and star groups drawn on the blackboard, the teacher may greatly aid his pupils, who should copy the pictures and then find the corresponding objects in the sky.

The use of a telescope adds much of interest to this study, especially if the students are taught to manipulate it themselves, and to find by its aid the telescopic objects mentioned in Chapter XIV. Even a good opera-glass is very serviceable. The observation exercises given at times will be found very helpful, and will assist in the cultivation of the geometric imagination. A globe, with blackboard surface, may be useful in various ways, but as soon as the pupils have derived a geometric conception by its aid they should be led at once to transfer the mental picture to the heavens.

It is also recommended that constant recourse be had to such periodicals as "Popular Astronomy," "Knowledge," etc., in order to follow the progress of astronomical research, month by month, and thus to supplement the text-book. The list of works, given in Appendix VII., is intended as a guide in the selection of an astronomical library.

The optical principles of the telescope and spectroscope have been explained very simply, for students not familiar with descriptions of them in elementary text-books on physics. Especial attention has been paid to the Meridian Circle and to the Equatorial, because accurate knowledge of the positions and motions of the heavenly bodies depends chiefly on observations made with these instruments.

The purely descriptive matter about the sun, moon, planets, etc., has been kept quite free from such statistics as the values of the masses of the planets, and the intensity of the pull of gravitation at the surface of each. The student should, however, learn the distance, diameter, time of revolution, and time of rotation of each planet. More extended data for purposes of reference are to be found in the Appendices.

In this edition the results of the latest important investigations and discoveries have been stated. The work of the Lick Observatory, as set forth in the publications of the Astronomical Society of the Pacific, merits and has received much attention. The columns of astronomical periodicals have furnished a large amount of reliable information.[1] The author will welcome for a second edition any suggestions or corrections.

The Exercises, which are a special feature of this book, and are placed at the end of each chapter, will be of great help to the pupils

---

[1] A good Star Atlas is a desideratum. Almost every school-book publishing house can furnish one. It will supplement the Star Maps at the end of this volume.

in reviewing the lessons, and also to the teacher in the work of the class-room.

The Appendices contain, along with other useful material, questions for examination, topics for essays, and short reviews of a number of valuable works on Astronomy suitable for reference and general reading.

A large number of the illustrations have never before appeared in any text-book. For many of the finer ones the author is indebted to Prof. E. S. Holden, Prof. Wm. W. Payne, Mr. A. Cowper Ranyard, and Dr. E. E. Barnard. Prof. E. C. Pickering kindly furnished a fine set of lithographs, made from observations at Harvard College Observatory, many of which have been reproduced. Prof. G. E. Hale has contributed photographs of the solar disturbance of July 15, 1892. Messrs. G. W. Saegmuller, of Washington, D. C., and J. A. Brashear, of Allegheny, Pa., supplied the pictures of some of the instruments. The author desires to state that he is specially indebted to his wife, Fannie Shattuck Howe, for her assistance in the preparation of the manuscript.

UNIVERSITY PARK, COLORADO,
1896.

CONTENTS.

CHAPTER I.

GENERAL SURVEY OF THE HEAVENS.

	PAGE

Celestial Objects classified; the Star Maps explained; Names of the Constellations; how to find the Constellations; Hints on Constellation Study 1

CHAPTER II.

APPARENT DAILY MOTION OF THE STARS.

The Daily Motion; the Celestial Sphere; the Celestial Equator and Horizon; Exercises 6

CHAPTER III.

THE TELESCOPE.

Reflection and Refraction of Light; Lenses; Formation of an Image; Object-glass and Eyepieces; Dispersion of Light; Achromatism; Refractors and Reflectors; Equatorial Mountings; Exercises 19

CHAPTER IV.

THE SUN.

Its Distance and Diameter; how to Observe it with a Small Telescope; Photosphere; Faculæ; Spots; Solar Disturbances; Magnetic Storms; the Spectroscope; Laws of Spectrum Analysis; the Chromosphere; Prominences; the Corona; Light and Heat; Constitution; Exercises . 36

CONTENTS.

CHAPTER V.

THE EARTH.

PAGE

Dimensions; Latitude and Longitude; its Orbit; the Ecliptic; the Equinox and Solstices; the Zodiac; the Day; the Seasons; Precession and the Calendar; Aberration; Atmospheric Refraction; Twilight; Exercises 64

CHAPTER VI.

CELESTIAL MEASUREMENTS.

Circles of Reference; Parallax; Time; Solar and Sidereal Days; Civil and Astronomical Days; Mean Solar and Sidereal Time; Standard Time, and its Determination by Means of a Meridian Circle and a Chronograph; Determination of Latitude and Longitude; Exercises 87

CHAPTER VII.

THE MOON AND ECLIPSES.

Distance; Diameter; Orbit; Period; Rotation; Librations; Phases; Plains; Craters; Mountains; Water and Air; Light and Heat; Effect on the Weather; Eclipses, Solar and Lunar; Exercises 108

CHAPTER VIII.

MOTIONS OF THE PLANETS.

Their Orbits; Newton's and Kepler's Laws; Aspects; Periods; Exercises. 133

CHAPTER IX.

MERCURY, VENUS, MARS, THE ASTEROIDS.

Their Distance; Diameter; Revolution; Rotation; Phases; Satellites; Atmosphere; Telescopic Appearance; Physical Condition; Exercises. 143

CHAPTER X.

JUPITER, SATURN, URANUS, NEPTUNE.

Their Distance; Diameter; Revolution; Rotation; Discovery; Satellites; Atmosphere; Telescopic Appearance; Physical Condition; Exercises. 164

CONTENTS.

CHAPTER XI.

COMETS AND METEORS.

                                                                                               PAGE

Comets, their Discovery; Designation; Parts; Orbits; Appearances; Tails; Mass; Light; Spectra; Fate. — Meteors, their Classes; Paths; Light and Heat; Constituents; Showers; Orbits. — Exercises 186

CHAPTER XII.

THE FIXED STARS.

Number; Milky Way; Constellations; Names; Magnitudes; Dimensions; Distances; Clusters; Parallax; Spectra; Motions; Double and Multiple; Variable; Exercises 225

CHAPTER XIII.

THE NEBULÆ.

Various Forms; Spectra; Notable Ones; the Nebular Hypothesis; the Future of the Visible Universe 257

CHAPTER XIV.

THE CONSTELLATIONS IN DETAIL.

The Greek Alphabet; Detailed Descriptions of the Constellations visible in the United States, with Tabular Lists of Prominent Double Stars, Clusters, Nebulæ, Colored and Variable Stars 272

APPENDICES.

I. Names of Stars 303
II. Astronomical Constants 304
III. Planetary Data 305
IV. Landmarks in the History of Astronomy 307
V. Topics for Essays 313
VI. Queries for Use in Reviews and Examinations 315
VII. List of Reference Books 320

INDEX 327
STAR MAPS 342

LIST OF ILLUSTRATIONS.

	PAGE
FRONTISPIECE. Spectra of Different Types	
Fig. 1. Solar Prominences . . *opposite*	1
" 2. Revolution of the Sphere . .	7
" 3. The Great Dipper and Polaris .	8
Figs. 4-6. Diagrams illustrating Definitions	9
" 7, 8. Apparent Daily Motion of the Stars	16
Fig. 9. Apparent Daily Motion of the Stars	17
" 10. Reflection by a Plane Mirror . .	19
" 11. Reflection by a Concave Mirror .	20
" 12. Refraction	20
" 13. Refraction by Prisms	20
" 14. Lenses	21
" 15. Rays made Divergent	21
" 16. Visual Angle	21
" 17. Object and Image	22
" 18. Lens as Eyepiece	23
" 19. Object-Glass and Eyepiece . .	23
" 20. Dispersion	25
" 21. Dispersion Corrected	25
" 22. Achromatic Object-Glass . . .	26
" 23. Portrait of Alvan Clark . . .	26
" 24. Eyepieces	27
" 25. Path of Rays of Light in a Reflector	27
" 26. A Newtonian Reflector made by Brashear	28
" 27. Lord Rosse's Six-foot Reflector .	29
" 28. Scheme of an Equatorial Mounting	30
" 29. A German Equatorial	31
" 30. The Lick Telescope	32
" 31. The Sun's Image on a Screen .	37
" 32. Absorption of Light by the Sun's Atmosphere	37
" 33. Faculæ observed Visually . . .	38
" 34. Sun Spot	40
" 35. Large Sun Spot	41
" 36. The Sun at the Time of a Spot Maximum	42
" 37. Photographs of the Disturbance of July 15, 1892	43

	PAGE
Fig. 38. Cyclonic Motion	44
" 39. A Spectroscope made by Brashear	47
" 40. Plan of a Spectroscope	47
" 41. Slit of a Spectroscope	48
" 42. Production of Spectra	49
" 43. Spectra	49
" 44. Protrait of Kirchhoff	50
" 45. A Geissler's Tube	50
" 46. A Portion of the Solar Spectrum	51
" 47. Correspondence of Bright and Dark Lines in Two Spectra .	51
" 48. Solar Prominences . . *opposite*	53
" 49. A Spectroscope attached to a Telescope	54
" 50. The Corona on July 29, 1878 . .	55
" 51. The Corona, photographed on December 21, 1889	56
" 52. Illustrations of Schaeberle's Theory of the Corona	57
" 53a. A Drawing of the Corona . .	57
Figs. 53b, 53c. Drawings of the Corona	58
Fig. 53d. A Photograph of the Inner Corona	58
" 54. Electrical Appearances similar to the Corona	59
" 55. Production of Heat by the Action of Gravity	61
" 56. Direction of the Plumb-line . .	65
" 57. How to find the Earth's Diameter	66
" 58. Latitude and Longitude . . .	66
" 59. The Astronomical Latitude . .	67
" 60. An Ellipse	68
" 61. Illustration of the Ecliptic . .	69
" 62. The Obliquity of the Ecliptic .	70
" 63. The Ecliptic and the Equator .	70
" 64. The Sun's Daily Motion among the Stars	71
" 65. A Spinning Top	71
" 66. Successive Positions of the Earth's Equator	72
" 67. An Orange Half Submerged . .	72

LIST OF ILLUSTRATIONS.

		PAGE
Fig. 68.	Locating the North Pole	74
" 69.	The Midnight Sun	74
" 70.	Effect of the Slant of the Sun's Rays	75
" 71.	The Earth's Equatorial Ring	75
" 72.	A Leaning Top	76
" 73.	Positions of the Axis of the Top	76
" 74.	The Precessional Motion of the Earth's Equator	77
" 75.	Path of North Celestial Pole among the Stars	78
" 76.	Different Kinds of Years	79
" 77.	Illustration of Aberration	81
" 78.	Refraction	82
" 79.	Gravity and the Earth's Rotation	82
Figs. 80–83.	Illumination of the Earth by the Sun	85
Fig. 84.	Circles of Reference	87
" 85.	Equator, Horizon, Meridian, etc.	89
" 86.	Parallax	90
" 87.	Unequal Lengths of Apparent Solar Days	91
" 88.	Variable Motion in Hour Angle	92
" 89.	A Standard Clock	95
" 90.	A Portable Meridian Circle	96
" 91.	A Reticle	97
" 92.	Motion of a Star's Image	97
" 93.	A Chronograph	99
" 94.	A Chronographic Record	100
" 95.	Determination of Latitude	100
" 96.	Latitude found by Observation of Polaris	101
" 97.	An Engineer's Transit	102
" 98.	A Chronometer	103
" 99.	A Sextant	104
" 100.	Orbits of the Earth and Moon	108
" 101.	Sidereal and Synodic Periods	109
" 102.	Illustration of the Moon's Rotation	109
Figs. 103, 104.	Libration	110
Fig. 105.	The Moon Illuminated	111
" 106.	The Moon's Phases	111
" 107.	The Moon: Photographed at Lick Observatory	112
" 108.	Skeleton Map of the Moon	114
" 109.	Conspicuous Craters of the Moon	115
" 110.	The Crater Copernicus	116
" 111.	Portrait of Copernicus	117
" 112.	The Terrestrial Crater Vesuvius	118
" 113.	The Lunar Apennines	119
" 114.	The Crater Vendelinus: From Photograph	120
" 115.	Umbra and Penumbra of the Earth's Shadow	125
" 116.	Umbra and Penumbra of the Moon's Shadow	125

		PAGE
Fig. 117.	Cross-section of a Shadow	125
" 118.	Beginning of a Total Lunar Eclipse	126
" 119.	Lunar Eclipse, Jan. 1888	opp. 126
" 120.	Path of Central Line of Eclipse, May 27, 1900	127
" 121.	Cause of Annular Eclipse	128
" 122.	Appearance of Sun during an Annular Eclipse	128
" 123.	Portrait of Sir Isaac Newton	134
" 124.	Portrait of Kepler	135
" 125.	Equal Areas in Equal Times	136
" 126.	Aspects of the Planets	137
" 127.	Apparent Movement of a Superior Planet	139
" 128.	Relative Sizes of the Planets	143
" 129.	A Transit of Venus	147
" 130.	The Black Drop	147
" 131.	Portrait of Galileo	148
" 132.	The Ring of Light	149
" 133.	Mars: Drawn by Barnard	151
" 134.	The Canals of Mars	155
" 135.	The Zone of Asteroids	160
" 136.	Telescopic Experiment	163
" 137.	Jupiter, as seen with the Lick Telescope	166
" 138.	Orbits of the Major Satellites	168
" 139.	Phenomena of the Satellites	169
" 140.	Markings seen with the Lick Telescope	169
" 141.	Jupiter and the Orbit of the Fifth Satellite	170
" 142.	Saturn, as seen with the Lick Telescope	172
" 143.	Different Positions of the Rings	174
" 144.	Old Drawing of Saturn	175
" 145.	Portrait of Sir William Herschel	177
" 146.	Portrait of John Couch Adams	180
" 147.	Conic Sections	189
" 148.	Varieties of Orbits	189
" 149.	Orbits of some Comets of Jupiter's Family	191
" 150.	A Jet	192
" 151.	Companions of Brooks's Comet	193
" 152.	Development of a Tail	194
" 153.	Comet's Tail. Type I.	195
" 154.	Comet's Tail. Type II.	195
" 155.	Comet's Tail. Type III.	195
" 156.	Comet of 1528	198
" 157.	Comet of 1861	200
" 158.	The Great Comet of 1882	203
" 159.	Nucleus of the Great Comet of 1882	204
" 160.	Swift's Comet: Photographed by Barnard	205
" 161.	Brooks's Comet: Photographed by Barnard	207

LIST OF ILLUSTRATIONS.

Fig.		Page
162.	Meteor seen at Bassein, Burmah	210
163.	A Meteorite	212
164.	The Canyon Diablo Meteorite	213
165.	Relative Frequency of Meteors in the Morning and Evening	215
166.	The Radiant	216
167.	The Orbit of the August Shower	218
168.	Capture of the Leonids	220
169.	Stars Visible to the Naked Eye	224
170.	The Yerkes Telescope at the World's Fair, 1893	226
171.	A Portion of the Milky Way	227
172.	Plant-like Structure	228
173.	The Great Cluster in Hercules	232
174.	The Cluster Omega Centauri: Photographed by Dr. Gill at the Cape of Good Hope	233
175.	Stellar Parallax	234
176.	Method of observing Stellar Parallax	234
177.	Relation of Parallax to Distance	235
178.	Proper Motions of the Pleiades	240
179.	Double Stars	242
180.	A Spectroscopic Binary	244
181.	Multiple Stars	245
182.	Portrait of Tycho Brahe	247
183.	Tycho's Star in Cassiopeia	248
184.	How to find Algol	249
185.	Y Cygni	250
186.	Real Velocity of a Star	254
187.	The Pleiades: Photographed by Roberts	258
188.	The Trifid Nebula	260
189.	The Nebula in Andromeda: Photographed by Roberts	261
190.	The Nebula in Orion: Drawn by Bond	262
191.	The Ring Nebula in Lyra: Drawn by Bond	264
192.	The Spiral Nebula in Canes Venatici: Photographed by Roberts	265
193.	Portrait of La Place	266
194.	The Star Finder	295
195.	The Declination Circle	295

THE SUN

SOLAR PROMINENCES.

ELEMENTS

OF

DESCRIPTIVE ASTRONOMY.

CHAPTER I.

GENERAL SURVEY OF THE HEAVENS.

> " The sky
> Spreads like an ocean hung on high,
> Bespangled with those isles of light
> So wildly, spiritually bright.
> Who ever gazed upon them shining,
> And turned to earth without repining,
> Nor wished for wings to flee away,
> And mix with their eternal ray?"
>   BYRON.

1. The Fixed Stars. — The fixed stars are points of light, of various degrees of brightness, which bestrew the sky. They are called fixed, because, as seen with the naked eye, they do not change their relative positions from year to year.

In the earliest ages men divided them into various groups, which we call constellations; the appearance of each of these constellations is almost the same to-day as when it was named by the ancients.

A star just visible to an average eye is said to be of the sixth magnitude; one a little brighter is said to be of the fifth magnitude, and so on, a few of the brightest being called first magnitude stars. All fixed stars are at inconceivably great distances from us.

2. The Planets. — The word planet is derived from a Greek word meaning "a wanderer." The designation is applied to certain star-like objects which appear to move among the fixed stars. The brightest ones have received the names of ancient divinities, as Jupiter, Saturn, and Venus. They revolve about the sun in paths nearly circular; the earth is considered one of them.

3. The Moon. — This familiar object revolves about the earth in $27\frac{1}{3}$ days. It is the nearest of the celestial bodies, being a little less than a quarter of a million of miles away. It belongs to the class of objects known as satellites, which revolve about the planets, held fast by their attractive force.

4. The Sun. — The sun, like the moon, is so familiar that no particular description of it is needed here. Though its distance from the earth is nearly 93,000000 miles, it is very much nearer to us than any one of the fixed stars. To its abounding light and heat we owe the preservation of our lives, the maintenance of our vigor, the physical comforts which we enjoy, and the marvellous beauties of nature.

5. Comets. — The word "comet" is derived from a Greek word meaning "long-haired." Comets are usually invisible to the naked eye, but sometimes attain great splendor and beauty. In ancient and mediæval times their appearance was usually regarded as a dire omen. Even in 1861 it was rumored in Italy that the great comet of that year presaged the death of Pope Pius IX.

6. Meteors. — These are evanescent objects which flash across the sky, and usually fade from sight in a few seconds. Occasionally they are so brilliant as to be seen in broad daylight, and are accompanied by terrific detonations.

7. Nebulæ. — Nebulæ, as their name implies, are cloudlike in appearance. A few of them are conspicuous enough to be faintly seen without telescopic aid, and appear as feeble patches of light on the dark background of the sky. They are large and diffuse masses of matter, at vast distances from us.

8. The Star Maps. — In the maps at the end of this book, the magnitudes are indicated very simply; especial care has been taken in drawing the dotted lines connecting the stars in the constellations, so that figures easily remembered may be obtained. Careful directions are given for learning the constellations, together with lists of telescopic objects, most of which are within the power of a three-inch telescope. Stars of the first magnitude are indicated by heavy black dots. Those of the fifth magnitude are represented by small dots. A star of the second magnitude has two short arms projecting from a central dot. Stars of the third and fourth magnitude have, respectively, three and four projecting arms. The figures at the top and bottom of each map, except the first, denote the right ascensions of the stars; those at the sides indicate the declinations. On Map I. right ascensions are given around the circumference, declinations along a diameter. These terms are explained in § 122. They are not needed in learning the constellations. Each constellation is bounded by a heavy dotted line, and its name is printed in large letters. The proper names of the brightest stars, such as Sirius, Vega, etc., are given. Most of the stars are marked by letters or numbers. The name of such a star is formed by adding to its letter the Latin genitive of the name of the constellation in which it lies. Thus the star *m* in Orion is called *m* Orionis.

9. Names of the Constellations. — The names of the constellations shown on the Star Maps are given in the table below. The Greek alphabet is found in § 405.

LATIN (Nominative)	LATIN (Genitive)	ENGLISH
An-drom'-e-da	Andromedæ	Andromeda
A-quā'-ri-us	Aquarii	The Water Carrier
Aquila (Ak'-wi-la)	Aquilæ	The Eagle
Ar-go Nā-vis	Argus	The Ship
Aries (A'-ri-ēz)	Arietis	The Ram
Au-rī'-ga	Aurigæ	The Charioteer
Boötes (Bo-ō'-tēz)	Boötis	The Bear Keeper
Cam-el-o-par'-dus	Camelopardi	The Camelopard
Can-cer	Cancri	The Crab
Canes Venatici (Kā'-nēz Ve-nat'-i-si)	Can. Ven.	The Hunting Dogs
Cā-nis Mā-jor	Canis Majō'ris	The Great Dog
Cā-nis Mī-nor	Canis Minō'ris	The Little Dog
Cap-ri-cor'-nus	Capricorni	The Goat
Cassiopeia (Kas-si-ō-pē'-ya)	Cassiope'iæ	The Lady in the Chair
Centaurus (Sen-taw'-rus)	Centau'ri	The Centaur
Cē'-phe-us	Cephei	Cepheus
Cē-tus	Ceti	The Whale
Co-lum'ba	Columbæ	The Dove
Coma Berenī'ces	Comæ Berenī'ces	The Hair of Berenice
Co-rō'-na Bo-re-ā'-lis	Coronæ Boreā'lis	The Northern Crown
Corvus	Corvi	The Crow
Crā-ter	Crā'teris	The Cup
Cyg'-nus	Cygni	The Swan
Del-phī'-nus	Delphini	The Dolphin
Drā-co	Dracō'nis	The Dragon

Latin (Nominative)	Latin (Genitive)	English
Equuleus (E-kwū'-lē-us)	Equu'lei	The Little Horse
E-rĭd'-a-nus	Eridani	The River
Gem'-i-nī	Geminō'rum	The Twins
Her'-cu-les	Herculis	Hercules
Hy'-dra	Hydræ	The Snake
La-cer'-ta	Lacertæ	The Lizard
Lē-o	Leō'nis	The Lion
Lē-o Mī-nor	Leō'nis Minō'ris	The Little Lion
Lē-pus	Lep'-ŏ-ris	The Hare
Lī-bra	Libræ	The Scales
Lū-pus	Lupi	The Wolf
Lynx	Lyncis	The Lynx
Ly'-ra	Lyræ	The Harp
Monoceros (Mŏ-nos'-e-ros)	Monocerō'tis	The Unicorn
Oph-i-ū'-chus	Ophiuchi	The Serpent Bearer
O-rī'-on	Oriŏnis	Orion
Peg'-ă-sus	Pegasi	The Winged Horse
Per'-se-us	Persei	Perseus
Pisces (Pis'-sēz)	Piscium	The Fishes
Pis'-cis Aus-trā'-lis	Piscis Austr.	The Southern Fish
Sagitta (Sa-jit'-ta)	Sagittæ	The Arrow
Sagittarius (Saj-i-tā'-ri-us)	Sagittarii	The Archer
Scor'-pi-ō	Scorpii	The Scorpion
Sculp-tor	Sculptō'ris	The Sculptor
Scū-tum	Scuti	The Shield
Serpens (Ser'-penz)	Serpentis	The Serpent
Sextans (Seks'-tanz)	Sextantis	The Sextant
Taurus (Taw'-rus)	Tauri	The Bull
Triangulum (Tri-ang'-gu-lum)	Trianguli	The Triangle
Ur'-sa Mă-jor	Ursæ Majō'ris	The Great Bear
Ur'-sa Mī-nor	Ursæ Minō'ris	The Little Bear
Vir'-go	Vir'-gĭnis	The Virgin
Vul-pec'-u-la	Vulpeculæ	The Fox

10. How to Find the Northern Constellations. — The constellations visible in the northern sky are to be found on Map I. The appearance of these constellations at 8 o'clock on any evening may be found by using the dates around the circumference of the map. If the aspect of the northern sky on April 1st, for instance, is desired, hold the map so that the date April 1st shall be uppermost. Face the north and hold the map up toward the sky.

The Great Dipper, which is a portion of the constellation of the Great Bear (Ursa Major), can then be found readily.

After the Great Dipper has been fixed in mind, the Pole Star can be located by the help of Fig. 3. Cassiopeia is on the opposite side of the Pole Star from the Great Dipper, and at about the same distance from it. The five brightest stars in this constellation form a straggling W and are quickly discovered.

Beginning at the Pole Star, one can then trace out the Little Bear (Ursa Minor) with the assistance of the map.

When the outlines of these constellations have been learned thoroughly, there will be very little difficulty in becoming acquainted with the adjacent ones.

11. How to Find the Constellations in the South. — These constellations are pictured on Maps II.–V.

The stars underneath any particular date at the top of the map are to be seen in the south at 8 P. M. on that date. For example, Map II. shows that on February 16th Orion is in the south at 8 P. M. In winter, Orion is the best southern constellation to learn first, because of its conspicuousness.

In spring, Leo (see Map III.) is recommended as a starting point; in summer, Scorpio (see Map IV.) will answer the same purpose; it will be seen low down in the south. For autumn, Pegasus (see Map V.) is available. Four of the principal stars of this constellation form a large square.

12. Hints on Constellation Study. — When trying to learn any particular constellation, the student should find from the maps about half a dozen or a dozen of its principal stars. The configuration of these should be impressed upon the mind so thoroughly that a drawing showing their relative positions can be made without looking at the maps. With this picture well in mind, the student may confront the sky. It is well to note the brightness and color of any first magnitude star in the constellation, and to learn its name. In many cases one can trace in a constellation a resemblance to the object after which it is named. Orion, for instance, resembles the figure of a man. The best way to secure a thorough acquaintance with the constellations which have been learned is to draw them from memory frequently, and to look at the heavens whenever occasion offers.

The descriptive matter in Chapter XIV. will be found useful in this work.

CHAPTER II.

APPARENT DAILY MOTION OF THE STARS.

> "The sad and solemn night
> Hath yet her multitude of cheerful fires;
> The glorious host of light
> Walk the dark hemisphere till she retires;
> All through her silent watches, gliding slow,
> Her constellations come, and climb the heavens, and go."
>
> BRYANT.

13. The Daily Motion. — The most casual observer cannot fail to notice that the majority of the visible stars daily rise, travel across the sky, and set.

The Greek philosopher, Pythagoras, is said to have taught that the thousands of fixed stars which stud the sky were set in a crystal sphere, which, by its daily revolution, carried them around the earth as a centre.

By this theory the apparent daily motion of the stars was explained very simply and accurately, so far as the unassisted eye could judge.

14. Cause of the Motion. — When a passenger train, which has been standing near a motionless freight train, starts without perceptible jar, a passenger looking at the freight train has the impression at first that the latter train is moving, and his own standing still. A person on the deck of a steamer, which is slowly turning about in a harbor, sees the objects on shore apparently revolving about him. If a visitor to an astronomical observatory looks upward at the dome while it is being turned, the floor on which he stands seems to be revolving. Similarly, the apparent daily revolution of the heavens is an illusion.

The earth turns upon its axis once a day, but makes the rotation without noise or jar, so that the observer is unconscious of it, and is led to think that the earth is at rest, and that the sky moves.

15. The Celestial Sphere. — As one looks by night at the heavenly bodies, they all seem to lie on the surface of an immense dome.

Were the earth to vanish suddenly, the observer would seem to be in the centre of a hollow star-spangled sphere.

The distance from his eye to any celestial object he could not tell. But his reason would quickly declare that the stars might *really* be at widely different distances from him, while they *appeared* to be upon a spherical surface which lay beyond them all. Each star would seem to be situated where a straight line drawn from his eye through the star, met the spherical surface. This imaginary spherical surface is called the celestial sphere.

16. Radius of the Celestial Sphere. — Astronomers find it convenient to assume that the radius of the celestial sphere is infinite, that is, too great for human comprehension. Were it possible for a man to take his stand upon the celestial sphere and look back at the vast assemblage of worlds which we call the physical universe, their combined mass would appear to him to be a mere point of light, which would be situated at the centre of the sphere. Hence it is evident that the observer's eye, or any point on the earth's surface, or the earth's centre, or the sun's centre, may be considered without palpable error as the centre of the celestial sphere.

17. Revolution of the Sphere. The Poles. — Imagine that the earth's axis is prolonged until it strikes the celestial sphere at two opposite points, called the north and south celestial poles, respectively. The heavens appear to revolve about an axis drawn from one celestial pole to the other.

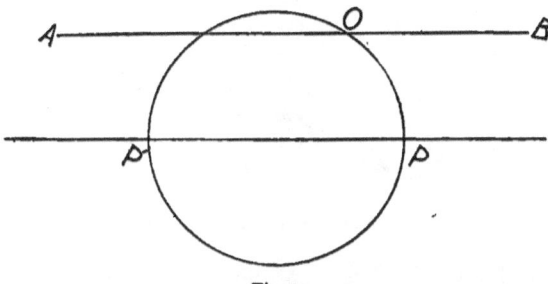

Fig. 2.

In Fig. 2, P is the north pole of the earth and P' the south pole; O is the position of an observer upon its surface; AB is drawn through O parallel to PP'. Now there is no fixed star which is known to be nearer to us than 20,000,000,000000 miles. To give greater definiteness to our ideas, conceive the radius of the celestial sphere to be 20,000000,000000 miles, and its centre to be at the earth's centre. Prolong AB and PP', until they strike the surface of the sphere: suppose the places where they strike to be marked by brilliant points of light. So enormous is the radius of the sphere when compared with the distance between AB and PP', that to an observer on the earth an extremity of AB would seem to coincide with the corresponding extremity of PP', even if the observer's eye were assisted by the most powerful telescope of modern times.

We may therefore consider the sky as revolving on AB as an axis, and may state the following principle.

The celestial sphere appears to revolve on an axis drawn from the eye of the observer to either pole of the celestial sphere.

18. Location of the North Celestial Pole. — Nearly every one is familiar with the configuration of seven bright stars which is called

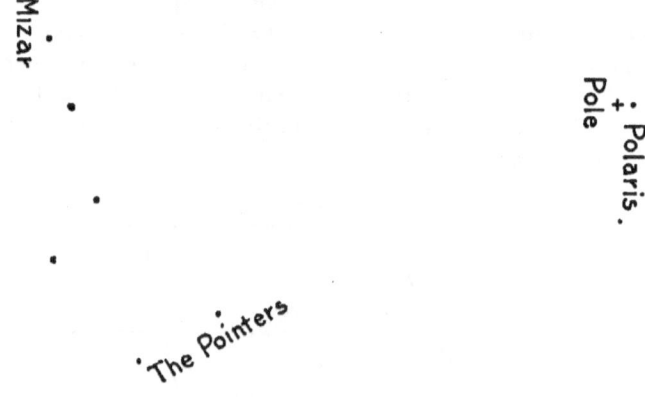

Fig. 3. — THE GREAT DIPPER AND POLARIS.

"The Great Dipper." It is represented in Fig. 3. The two stars in the bowl of the dipper which point nearly to the Pole Star (Polaris) are called "The Pointers." The distance from Polaris to the nearer one of the Pointers is about five times the distance between the latter. The position of the pole is shown in the figure;

it lies very near a line drawn from Polaris to Mizar; its distance from Polaris is one fourth of the distance between the Pointers.

19. Definitions. — If a straight line does not lie in a plane, but meets it at some point, the point is called the *foot* of the line. A straight line is perpendicular to a plane when it is perpendicular to every straight line that can be drawn in the plane through its foot.

The corner of a room, where two walls meet, is a line perpendicular to the plane of the ceiling, or of the floor.

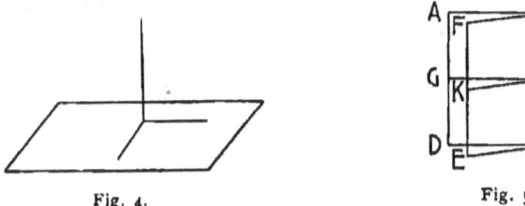

Fig. 4.   Fig. 5.

A straight line is parallel to a plane when they cannot meet, however far they may be extended.

When two planes meet, their line of intersection is called the *edge* of the angle which they make with each other. The planes AC and CF meet in the edge BC. At any point, H, in the edge, two perpendiculars to the edge are drawn, one lying in each plane. The angle GHK made by these perpendiculars measures the angle between the planes.

To find the angle which a line, prolonged if necessary, makes with a plane which it meets, a perpendicular to the plane is dropped from some point A in the line: the foot of the perpendicular is then joined with the foot of the original line. The angle which the last line drawn makes with the original line is the angle sought. In the figure, AB is the original line, AC the perpendicular, BC the joining line, and ABC the angle.

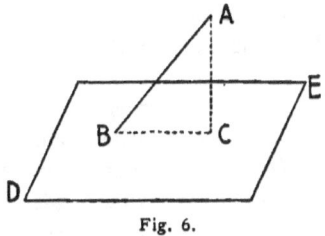

Fig. 6.

20. The Celestial Equator. — The equator of the earth is an imaginary line encircling it, midway between the poles. The plane of the equator extended indefinitely cuts the celestial sphere in a circle, which is called the *celestial equator*. Since the plane of the terrestrial equator is perpendicular to the earth's axis, the plane of the celestial equator is perpendicular to the axis of the celestial sphere.

21. The Horizon. — The word "horizon" is commonly used to designate the line where the earth and sky appear to meet. But astronomers use the word in a different sense. If the observer holds a plumb-line so that it hangs vertically, any plane surface, like a book-cover, when held so that it is perpendicular to the plumb-line, will represent a portion of the plane of the horizon of the place of observation. If the flat surface of the book-cover be extended horizontally in all directions until it reaches the sky, the plane thus formed is called the plane of the horizon. This plane cuts the celestial sphere in a circle called the horizon.

22. The Zenith, for any place on the earth, is the point where a plumb-line prolonged upward strikes the celestial sphere.

23. The Nadir is the point where the plumb-line prolonged downward strikes the celestial sphere.

The zenith and nadir are those points on the celestial sphere which are most remote from the horizon.

In the language of geometry, they are called the *poles of the horizon*.

EXERCISES.

24. 1. Narrate some personal experience of illusory motion similar to those mentioned in § 14.

2. The diameter of the earth is about eight thousand miles. What is the greatest possible distance between AB and PP′ in Fig. 2?

3. The observer is on the terrestrial equator.

(*a*) What is the distance in miles between AB and PP′ in Fig. 2?

(*b*) If he walked toward either pole, and the earth were a perfect sphere, would this distance increase or decrease?

4. If another line were drawn through O in Fig. 2, making an angle of 10° (one ninth of a right angle) with AB, would AB and the new line, when prolonged, meet the celestial sphere at the same points apparently?

APPARENT DAILY MOTION OF THE STARS.   11

[If there be any doubt in the student's mind concerning this, he should take two straight sticks, and put an end of one in contact with an end of the other, so that the sticks make an angle of 10° with each other. Then, placing his eye near the vertex of the angle, he can look along each stick at the sky.]

5. If the nearest fixed star were 20,000000,000000 miles from us, how many years would it take its light, travelling 186,330 miles per second, to reach us? Ans. 3.4+ years.

6. Look at the Great Dipper and Polaris in the sky, and draw a map of them; first make a dot for Polaris and draw a line below it to represent the horizon. Draw another line through Polaris perpendicular to the horizon line. Draw the Dipper, showing its position with reference to these lines, and state the hour at which your observation was made.

7. The observer, facing north, notices that the Dipper is below the pole.

(*a*) Will the Dipper appear, on account of the earth's rotation, to move towards his right hand, or towards his left?

(*b*) What would be the direction of motion of the Dipper if it were above the pole, near the zenith?

(*c*) What direction (up or down), if at the right of the pole?

(*d*) What direction, if at the left?

8. If a line be drawn from your eye to each of the two "Pointers" in the Dipper, the two lines make an angle of about 5°. Astronomers commonly say that the distance between the Pointers is 5°. Estimate the distance from the Pole Star to the Pointer nearest to it.

9. Suppose that the earth's centre is fixed in the centre of the celestial sphere, and that the earth rotates on its axis. Imagine all the stars to be fixed on the surface of the celestial sphere. If the earth's axis were then tipped a few degrees, would the north celestial pole remain at the same point among the stars as before? Would the position of the celestial equator be changed?

10. If, instead of tipping the axis of the earth, as in the preceding exercise, the earth were moved toward some point on the celestial equator and were placed 1,000000 miles away from its former position, the new direction of its axis being parallel to its former direction, would the new celestial poles appear coincident

with the former celestial poles? Would the old and new celestial equators coincide?

11. Conceive that the earth, in exercise 9, is rotating about a straight wire stretched from the north celestial pole to the south celestial pole. If it were slid along this wire to a place 10,000000 miles from its first position, would the new celestial equator appear to coincide with the old?

12. The earth makes its annual journey around the sun in a path nearly circular.

(*a*) If the earth's axis at every instant during the year were parallel to its position at every other instant, would the celestial poles change their position during the year?

(*b*) Would the celestial equator change its position?

[The earth's axis remains almost parallel to itself during a year. Its deviations will be explained later. So far as naked-eye observations are concerned, it may be considered as remaining parallel to itself.]

13. Take a ball or an orange to represent the earth. Mark on it the north and south poles and the equator. Find from a geography or other source the latitude of your place of observation to the nearest degree, and locate the place on the ball. (If the latitude were 45°, the place would be half way between the pole and the equator.) Take a flat stiff card, and lay one of its surfaces against the ball, at the point representing the place of observation. Fasten the card by a pin thrust through it into the ball at the point of contact. The pin should point toward the centre of the ball. The surface of the card will then represent the plane of the horizon of the place, and will be tangent to the spherical surface of the ball.

(*a*) Is your horizon parallel or perpendicular to the earth's axis?

(*b*) Is it parallel to the earth's equator?

(*c*) If you were at some point on the earth's equator, would your horizon plane be perpendicular to the earth's axis, or parallel to it?

(*d*) If you were at the north pole, would your horizon plane be parallel to the earth's axis, or perpendicular to it?

(*e*) As the earth turns on its axis, does the inclination of the axis to the plane of your horizon change?

14. If the polar axis of the ball in the last exercise be prolonged both ways, which prolongation (north or south) would pierce the plane of the card representing your horizon plane? If the ball be held so that the card is horizontal, what points on the celestial sphere would the pin strike if prolonged indefinitely each way?

REMARK. — In obtaining the answers to the following exercises, the apparatus described in exercise 13 can be used; *but it would be much better to imagine the earth itself, with its poles and equator, and with horizon planes touching it at different points. The student should make every endeavor to picture to himself the realities of nature, rather than the apparatus or the geometrical diagrams used to explain principles. Wherever possible, he should observe the celestial motions about which he studies.*

15. If you were at the north pole, would your horizon plane be parallel to the plane of the earth's equator, or perpendicular to it?

If you lived at the equator, would your horizon plane be parallel to the earth's equator, or perpendicular to it?

16. (*a*) If one man were at the north pole and another at the south, would their horizon planes be parallel?

(*b*) If one man were at the north pole and another at any point of the equator, would their horizon planes be perpendicular to each other?

(*c*) Could the horizon planes at two points on the equator be parallel?

(*d*) Could they be perpendicular to each other?

REMARK. — In answering questions about the rising and setting of the stars, the student should remember that the horizon of the place of observation seems motionless, while the heavens appear to revolve about a line drawn from the observer's eye to either celestial pole.

17. The radius of the celestial sphere is considered infinite. The observer is at the north pole.

(*a*) Does his horizon coincide with the celestial equator?

(*b*) Is the north celestial pole at his zenith?

(*c*) Could he see a star which lay between the south celestial pole and the equator?

(*d*) Would any star visible to him set within 24 hours?

(*e*) Every star in the sky would appear to describe a circle in

24 hours. Would the planes of these circles be parallel to his horizon?

(*f*) If the sun were always north of the celestial equator, would night ever come for him?

18. A man lives at some point on the equator.

(*a*) Does his horizon coincide with the celestial equator?

(*b*) Do the celestial poles lie on his horizon?

(*c*) Is the plane of the celestial equator perpendicular to the plane of his horizon?

(*d*) If the celestial equator were drawn as a line of light on the celestial sphere, would it pass through his zenith?

(*e*) Would the celestial equator cut his horizon?

(*f*) If so, at what points (north, south, east, or west)?

(*g*) How great a portion of the celestial equator would be visible at any instant?

(*h*) If a star rose at the east point of the horizon, at what point would it set?

(*i*) If a star rose a little north of the east point of the horizon, would it set a little north of the west point, or a little south of that point?

(*j*) If a star rose at a point half way between the south and east points of the horizon, where would it set?

(*k*) Where would Polaris rise and set?

(*l*) For how many hours would a star be above the horizon, and for how many below?

REMARK. — To assist in forming clear ideas about the answers to the questions in exercise 19, the scholar may take an orange, through which a knitting-needle has been thrust, to represent the celestial sphere; on it a circle may be drawn to represent the celestial equator; other circles may be drawn parallel to this one. The orange may then be half submerged in water, as shown in Fig. 67. The surface of the water will represent the plane of the observer's horizon, and the upper half of the orange the visible heavens, the observer being supposed to be at the centre of the orange.

19. The observer is located somewhere between the north pole and the equator, say at 40° north latitude.

(*a*) Is his horizon plane parallel or perpendicular to the celestial equator?

APPARENT DAILY MOTION OF THE STARS. 15

(*b*) Does the axis of the celestial sphere make an oblique angle with his horizon plane?

(*c*) Does a line from the north celestial pole to the observer's eye make a right angle with his horizon plane, or an acute angle?

(*d*) If a plane be passed through the observer's eye, perpendicular to the line last mentioned, will it be parallel to the plane of the earth's equator?

(*e*) The plane just passed through the observer's eye intersects the horizon in a line: what direction (north and south, or east and west) does that line have?

(*f*) The plane mentioned, when extended in all directions to the celestial sphere, will cut a circle on it, half of which is above the horizon; if this semicircle could be seen as a line of light on the celestial sphere, would it lie north of the zenith, or south of it?

(*g*) Would this semicircle coincide with half of the celestial equator?

(*h*) With extended arm and forefinger point to the east point of the horizon; swing your arm in such a way that your forefinger will point to the celestial equator, as it runs from the east point of the horizon to the west point.

(*i*) Similarly trace the circle which Polaris describes in a day.

(*j*) Similarly trace the circle which a star 10° from the north celestial pole would describe in a day.

(*k*) As seen from your home, does the bowl of the Great Dipper ever set?

(*l*) If a star rises half way between the north and east points of your horizon, at what point of the horizon will it set?

(*m*) If it could be watched for 24 hours, would it be above the horizon just 12 hours, or more, or less?

(*n*) If a star rose at the east point of the horizon, would it be above the horizon just 12 hours?

(*o*) If a star rose half way between the east and south points of the horizon, would it be above the horizon more or less than 12 hours?

(*p*) If a star is between the north celestial pole and the celestial equator, will it be above your horizon more or less than half a day at a time?

(*q*) If a star is between the south celestial pole and the celestial equator, will it be below your horizon more or less than half a day at a time?

(*r*) Point your finger at the south celestial pole.

(*s*) Could a star be so near the south celestial pole that it could not be seen from your home?

20. State which one of the following diagrams represents the apparent daily motion of the stars as seen from the north pole. Which, as seen from the equator. Which, as seen from a place in latitude 40° north.

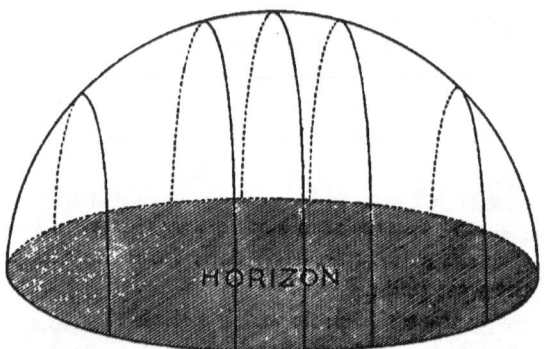

Fig. 7.

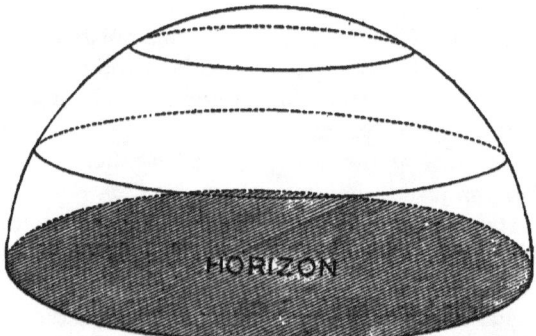

Fig. 8.

APPARENT DAILY MOTION OF THE STARS. 17

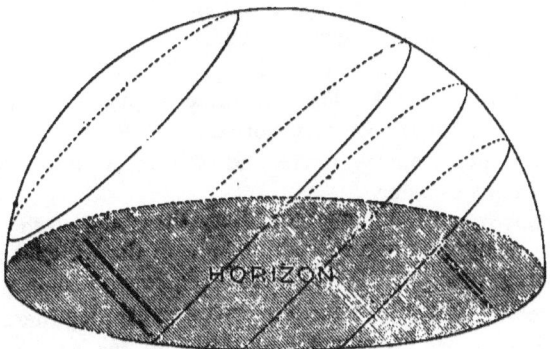

Fig. 9.

21. Find, with the teacher's aid if necessary, some bright planet, which will be visible during the time you expect to devote to the study of this book: on a moonless night, make a map showing its position with reference to the neighboring bright stars. Preserve the map, and note on it the planet's position among the stars from week to week.

22. Take your seat in a dark room, before a south window. Adjust your head so that by looking with one eye just past the western sash of the window you will see a star. Hold your head steady until you see the star disappear behind the sash. The farther you are from the window, the easier the observation will be. If you have a good opera-glass or spy-glass, by fastening it so that it will point to the southern portion of the sky, you can observe the motion of the stars more easily. Near the north celestial pole the apparent motions of the stars are too slow to be observed satisfactorily in this way.

23. At your first opportunity, early in the evening, draw a map similar to that required in exercise 6. Before retiring for the night, look again, and draw another map of the Dipper.

(*a*) Does a comparison of these maps show a movement of this group?

(*b*) If you look at the face of a watch held between your eye and the north celestial pole, will its minute hand move around in the same direction as the Dipper?

24. Some evening, notice the hour and minute when some star, easily recognized again, is near the eastern horizon. After about two weeks, at the same hour and minute, look for the star. Is it nearer the horizon than before? Try the same experiment, at the same time, with a star near the western horizon. From these observations determine whether a star will rise and set earlier than at present, a month from now, or later.

25. Find from an almanac or diary the date of the next new moon. An evening or two thereafter, look in the west for the moon, in the evening twilight. When first seen, draw a sketch of it and date the sketch. Sketch its form every clear evening thereafter until it does not rise before your bedtime: then look for it in the morning, and continue sketching it, if possible, until the next new moon.

(*a*) While making these sketches, did you notice that the moon moved westward among the stars?

(*b*) Did you see the dark part of the moon?

(*c*) When the moon was a slender crescent did the cusps or "horns" of the crescent point toward the sun?

(*d*) When the moon was full (a complete circle of light) did it rise at about the time of sunset?

(*e*) Did you ever see a star between the cusps of the moon?

(*f*) Did you ever see the moon occult a star, that is, hide it from view?

26. On some moonless night, find the Milky Way, which is a broad band of hazy light.

(*a*) Are there any dark places in it?

(*b*) Are there any brilliant spots in it?

(*c*) Does it run through the Great Dipper?

CHAPTER III.

THE TELESCOPE.[1]

"Through thee will Holy Science, putting off
Earth's dusty sandals from her radiant feet,
Survey God's beauteous firmament unrolled
Like to a book new-writ in golden words,
And turn the azure scroll with reverent hand,
And read to men the wonders God hath wrought."

ANON.

25. Refractors and Reflectors. — There are two kinds of telescopes, called respectively refractors and reflectors. Opera-glasses and spy-glasses belong to the former class.

Reflectors are rarely seen, except in connection with astronomical observatories. The principal portion of one of these is a large curved mirror, which reflects the rays of light coming from the object viewed, in a manner to be explained hereafter.

In order to understand the action of a telescope, one must be acquainted with a few elementary principles of optics, which we proceed to unfold.

26. Reflection by a Plane Mirror. — In the figure, DC is a ray of light striking the plane mirror AB at the point C; it is reflected along the line CF. EC is perpendicular to AB. The angle DCE, which the incident ray makes with the perpendicular to the mirror at C, the point of incidence, is *the angle of incidence*. Similarly ECF is *the angle of reflection*. The *angle of incidence is equal to the angle of reflection*.

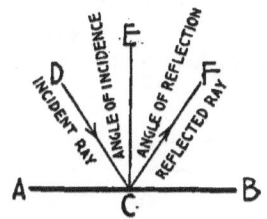

Fig. 10. — REFLECTION BY A PLANE MIRROR.

---

[1] It is well to illustrate this chapter as thoroughly as possible by experiments with lenses and mirrors. When a class is pressed for time, the more mathematical portions of the chapter may be omitted, or simply explained by the teacher. If an equatorially mounted telescope is not available, a rude wooden model of it may easily be made, and will be of service.

27. Reflection by a Concave Mirror. — A concave mirror may be considered as made up of a very large number of minute plane mirrors. If a system of parallel rays strikes the surface of a concave spherical mirror, each ray will be reflected at its point of incidence, in accordance with the principle of § 26. The reflected rays will converge and will meet (almost exactly) at a point called the focus (Fig. 11). Opticians make their mirrors deviate slightly from a true spherical form, in such a way that all rays are brought accurately to a focus.

NOTE. — In §§ 28-34 the dispersion of light is neglected; it is explained in §§ 37, 38.

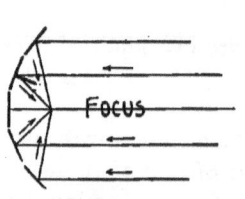

Fig. 11. — REFLECTION BY A CONCAVE MIRROR.

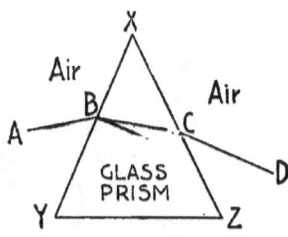

Fig. 12. — REFRACTION.

28. Refraction by a Prism. — A ray of light passing from one medium, as air, into another of a different density, as glass, is bent out of its course, unless it strikes the surface of the second medium perpendicularly. This bending is called *refraction*.

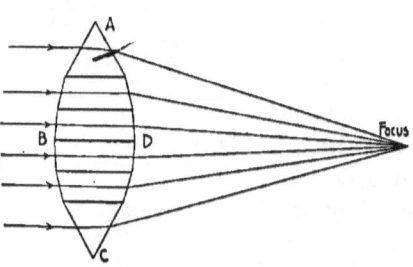

Fig. 13. — REFRACTION BY PRISMS.

The ray AB, striking obliquely on the surface XY of the glass prism XYZ, is refracted and travels along BC; at emergence, the ray is again refracted, taking the direction CD.

29. Action of a Number of Prisms. — By inspection of Fig. 13 we see that a number of pieces of glass may be so arranged that a system of parallel rays, in the plane of the paper, falling upon them will be converged to a common point. If the number of pieces of glass be largely increased, each piece being very small, the broken lines ABC and ADC will approach closely to arcs of circles. Hence, if a single piece of glass be so shaped that ABC and ADC will be nearly arcs of circles, the system of rays will be converged, as above, to a single point, called the *focus*.

30. Lenses. — A common burning glass is circular in form, and when looked at edgewise has the shape of (*a*) in Fig. 14. The two surfaces of the glass are portions of spherical surfaces. The sun's

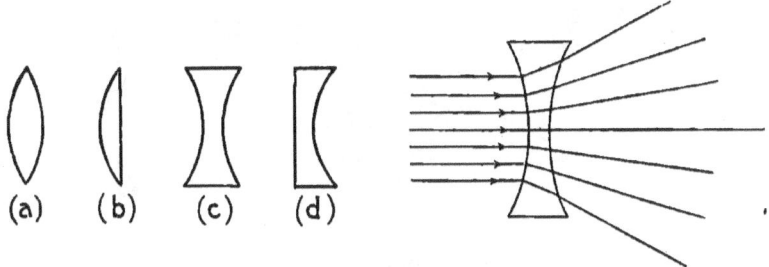

Fig. 14.—LENSES.   Fig. 15.—RAYS MADE DIVERGENT.

rays striking on the glass are converged to a focus. Such a glass is called a *double convex lens:* (*b*), one side of which is flat, is a plano-convex lens; (*c*) is double concave; (*d*) is plano-concave; (*c*) and (*d*), instead of bringing a system of parallel rays to a focus, make them diverge as shown in Fig. 15.

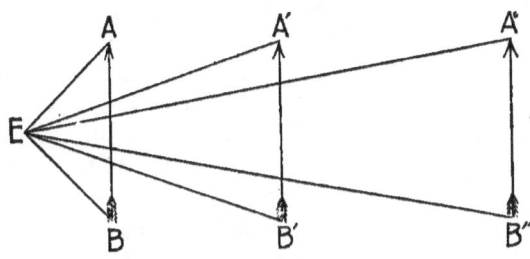

Fig. 16.—VISUAL ANGLE.

31. Visual Angle. — The visual angle of an object is the angle made by two lines drawn from the eye to the extremities of the object. In Fig. 16, the object AB is placed in three different positions AB, A' B', and A" B", the eye being at E. The visual angles are respectively AEB, A'E B', and A" E B". The nearer the object is to the eye, the greater is the visual angle, and the larger the object appears. If the object be carried away from the eye, the visual angle will become less, and the object will appear smaller.

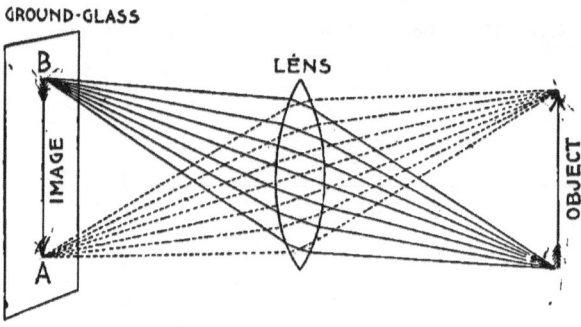

Fig. 17. — Object and Image.

32. Formation of an Image. — The action of a double convex lens in forming an image of an object may be easily seen in a photographic camera. Let the arrow in Fig. 17 represent a tree which is to be photographed. From the point of the arrow come innumerable rays of light, which strike the outer face of the lens, and are refracted by it to a common focus at A. Similarly the rays from the other end of the arrow are brought to a focus at B. When the photographer adjusts his ground-glass so that the points A and B lie on its surface, an image of each of these points is formed on the glass. Every other point of the arrow images itself on the glass, in like manner. The *object-glass* of a telescope is the large lens at the end farthest from the eye: its function is, like the photographer's lens, to form an image of the object viewed.

33. Action of the Eyepiece. — In a telescope there is no ground-glass to receive the image formed by the object-glass, but the rays of light pass on through another lens, called the eyepiece, before reaching the eye. The three rays shown in Fig. 18 as diverging from the point A in the image are rendered more nearly parallel to each other in passing through the eyepiece, and are sharply bent. The rays diverging from B are bent in the same fashion. Prolong the central one of the rays coming from A backward to any convenient point, Y, and the central ray from B to X, and draw the arrow XY. AB seen through the eyepiece looks as large as XY would without the eyepiece, XEY being the common visual angle.

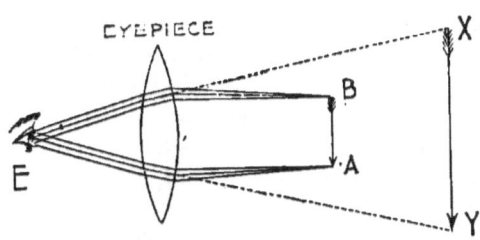

Fig. 18. — Lens as Eyepiece.

34. A Simple Refracting Telescope. — Placing the object-glass and eyepiece at opposite ends of a tube, we have a telescope. In Fig. 19, suppose the telescope to be pointed at a distant tree: the rays A', A, A'', coming from the top of the tree, meet at the focus a, and, passing on through the eyepiece, enter the observer's eye. The rays B', B, B'', coming from the bottom of the

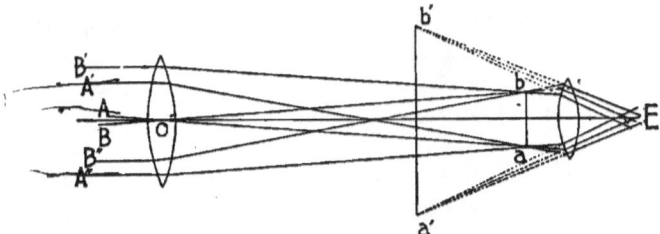

Fig. 19. — Object-glass and Eyepiece.

tree, meet at the focus b, and pass on through the eyepiece to enter the observer's eye. The central rays, A and B, of the two systems meet at E, and to the observer the tree appears to subtend a visual angle b'E a'. If the object-glass be now removed, and the observer, placing his eye at O, where the centre of the object-glass was, looks at the tree, it will subtend a visual angle of AOB. If he were to stand near the eyepiece, the visual angle would be a trifle smaller than AOB, since he is a little farther from the tree. But when he looked through the telescope, the tree appeared to subtend the angle b'E a', which is much larger than AOB. This explains why a telescope magnifies an object.

35. Object-glasses of Various Sizes. — When one looks at a star, only those rays which fall upon the pupil enter the eye. Were the pupil larger, more rays would enter, and the star would appear more brilliant. If the area of the object-glass of a telescope is one hundred times the area of the pupil of the eye, one hundred times as much light will fall upon it as upon the unaided eye. The pupil of a human eye, when not exposed to a bright light, has on the average a diameter of one fifth of an inch. An object-glass one inch in *aperture* (as its diameter is called) has a diameter five times as great as that of the pupil of the eye. A twenty-inch object-glass has a diameter one hundred times as great. Geometry teaches that the areas of two circles are to each other as the squares of their diameters: hence a one-inch object-glass collects not merely five times as much light as the pupil of the eye, but 5^2, or 25 times as much. A twenty-inch "objective" collects 100^2, or 10,000 times as much light from any star, as the unassisted eye does. About 18 per cent of this light is lost in passing through the object-glass and eyepiece.

36. Magnifying Power of Eyepieces. — After the object-glass has made a brilliant image of an object, at the focus, the eyepiece magnifies the image, as shown in § 34. By using lenses of different degrees of curvature, different "magnifying powers" are obtained.

If the apparent diameter of the planet Jupiter, for instance, were increased sixteen fold by a telescope armed with a certain eyepiece, the magnifying power of that eyepiece would be *sixteen diameters*. Very high magnifying powers cannot be used advantageously, because of the disturbances continually going on in our atmosphere. The rays of light from a star, coming through various disturbed strata of air of different densities, are bent hither and thither, so that the image of the star in the telescope dances about, and looks blurred. The higher the magnifying power employed, the worse the blur. Ordinarily, an eyepiece the magnifying power of which is more than twenty times the aperture of the object-glass (in inches), cannot be used to advantage. But when the atmosphere is exceedingly calm, a power of one hundred times the aperture may be used on a bright object. A glass six inches in aperture would then bear a power of six hundred diameters.

37. Dispersion of Light. — When a beam of sunlight is passed through a prism, and then allowed to fall on a screen, a colored spot is seen where the light strikes the screen. The spot is red at

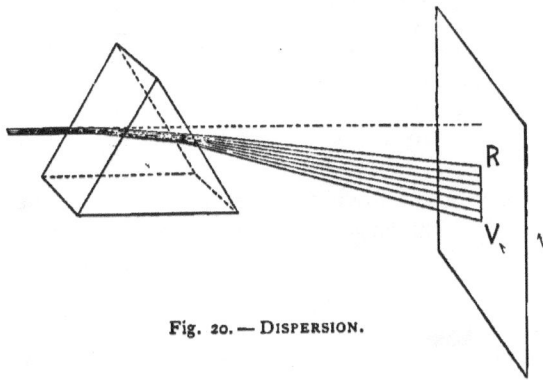

Fig. 20. — DISPERSION.

one end and violet at the other. Careful experiments show that sunlight, when passed through a prism, is decomposed into the following colors: *red, orange, yellow, green, cyan-blue, ultramarine blue,* and *violet.* The light thus decomposed is said to be *dispersed.* The figure shows that the red rays are not refracted (deviated from their original direction) as much as the violet rays. A prism of flint glass separates the red rays from the violet more widely than a prism of crown glass.

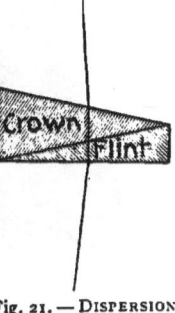

Fig. 21. — DISPERSION CORRECTED.

38. Correction of Dispersion. — The dispersion caused by one prism may be counteracted by passing the dispersed beam through a similar inverted prism. The final emergent beam is parallel to the original beam. By passing a beam through two prisms of different angles, one being of crown glass, and the other of flint, it is possible to correct the dispersion very nearly, and at the same time to alter the direction of the beam.

39. An Achromatic Object-glass. — This is shown in Fig. 22. Almost all object-glasses are made of two lenses: the outer lens is of crown glass, and is double convex; the inner is of flint glass, and is

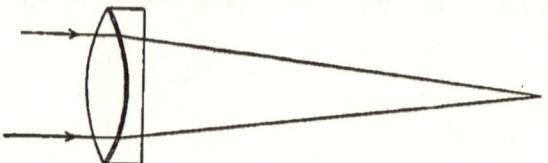

Fig. 22. — ACHROMATIC OBJECT-GLASS.

nearly plano-concave. Such an object-glass is said to be *achromatic* (without color). The largest and finest object-glasses in the world have been ground by the firm of Alvan Clark and Sons of Cambridge, Mass. In 1881, Prof. Abbe and Dr. Schott, of Jena, Germany, began a series of experiments which have resulted in the manufacture of lenses of various refractive and dispersive powers, combinations of which give almost perfect achromatism. Some of these lenses, however, tarnish in time.[1]

Fig. 23. — ALVAN CLARK.

40. Achromatic Eyepieces. — Eyepieces are made achromatic also, for a bad eyepiece undoes the work of a good object-glass. There are two common forms, the Huyghenian, or negative, and the Ramsden, or positive: the former is more achromatic than the latter. The large lens of the negative eyepiece receives the rays from the

---

[1] Mr. J. A. Brashear, the well known optician, of Allegheny, Pa., makes a specialty of grinding lenses of the new glass.

object-glass just before they come to a focus; the focus is formed between the two lenses of the eyepiece. In the case of the positive

Fig. 24. — EYEPIECES.

eyepiece, the rays come to a focus before they reach the eyepiece. A positive eyepiece can be used as a hand magnifying glass, but a negative cannot.

41. The Reflector. — A reflector, or reflecting telescope, receives its name from the fact that, instead of an object-glass, it has a large concave mirror, which reflects to a focus the rays from a celestial

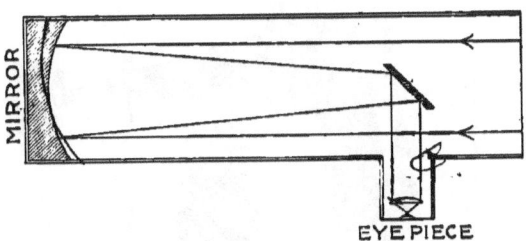

Fig. 25. — PATH OF RAYS OF LIGHT IN A REFLECTOR.

object. Reflectors have many forms, differing in minor particulars. The form most used is the Newtonian, devised by Sir Isaac Newton, which is shown in Fig. 26.

The mirror is now made of glass, on which a thin film of silver is deposited by a chemical process.

42. Comparison of Refractors and Reflectors. — The silver makes a brilliant reflecting surface, and there is no trouble from dispersion of light, as in the case of a refractor. This gives a reflector an advantage for photographic and spectroscopic work. But a large reflector has many disadvantages when compared with a refractor of equal power. The silver film tarnishes, and must be renewed periodically. Slight deformations of the concave surface, caused by

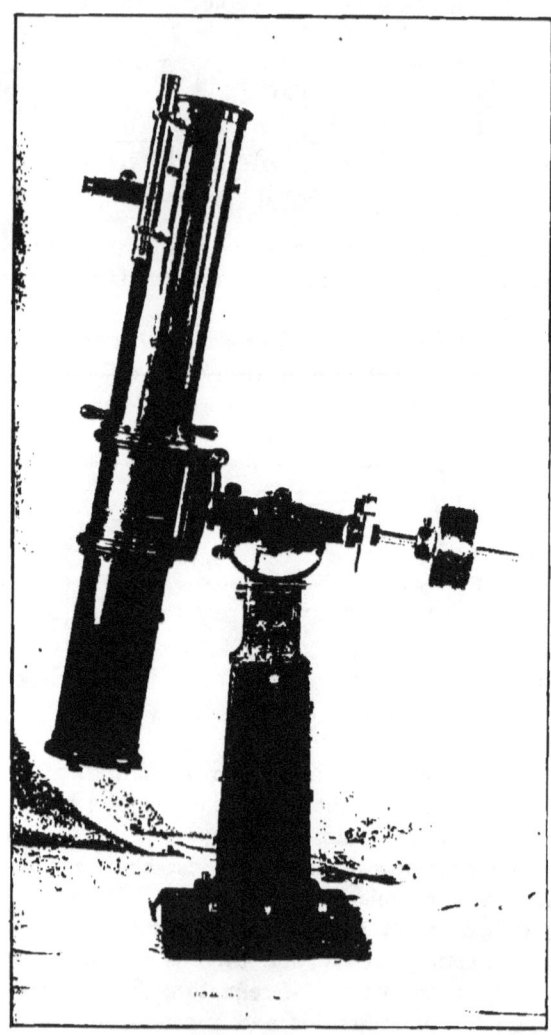

Fig. 26. — A Newtonian Reflector made by Brashear.

Fig. 27.—Lord Rosse's Six-foot Reflector
(From Scribner's Magazine, by permission.)

a difference in temperature between the front and the back of the mirror, or by sagging because of its own weight, distort the image of the object looked at.

43. Some Noted Reflectors. — Lord Rosse has at Parsonstown, Ireland, the largest reflector ever built. The mirror, which consists of an alloy of copper and tin, is six feet in diameter. Mr. A. A. Common, a wealthy English amateur, has made a silver on glass reflector, sixty-two inches in aperture, which is more efficient than any other ever constructed. Such an instrument is capable of marvellous work in photographing faint objects like nebulæ. Fig. 27 represents Lord Rosse's six-foot reflector. There is no reflector in America which approaches these in power.

44. An Equatorial Mounting. — Though a large telescope be well-nigh perfect optically, it will be practically useless unless well

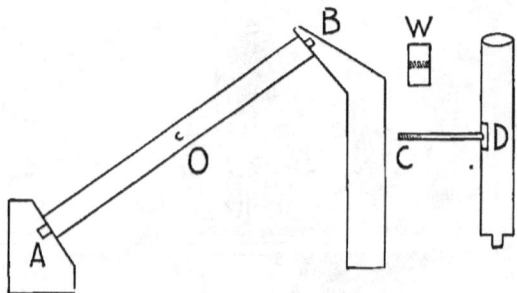

Fig. 28. — Scheme of an Equatorial Mounting.

mounted. On account of the diurnal motion of the stars, if the telescope is pointed at one, and is motionless, the star will quickly pass out of the field of view. The best mounting, when an object is to be watched for some time, is therefore one which will enable the telescope to follow the object most easily. It has been shown (§ 17) that the heavens appear to rotate daily about an axis drawn from the north celestial pole through the observer. Let a strong steel axis, AB, be supported at each end on pivots A and B, on which it may turn, and let it point to the north celestial pole. This steel axis may then be considered as a portion of the axis about which the celestial sphere appears to rotate. Through the hole O let the axis CD, to which the telescope is fastened, be thrust, and the weight W be placed at C, to balance the telescope. Let the telescope be pointed to any star, and the axis AB be turned by suitable clockwork, so that it will make one revolution in twenty-four hours. Then the telescope will move just as it would if it were actually fastened to the axis of the celestial sphere, and will continue to point to the star.

45. Illustration of the Principle of an Equatorial Mounting. — To get a clearer idea of this, one may imagine that the earth's axis is a wooden pole running through it; further, that a person in the interior of the earth nails a lath to this pole in such a way that the lath points to the city of Boston. The lath will continue to point to Boston as the earth rotates. If the lath had originally pointed to any other city, it would continue to do so, whether the city were near the equator or in the vicinity of one of the poles. The lath represents the telescope, and the city, a star.

46. The German Form of an Equatorial Mounting. — The form of mounting just described is not suited to a large refractor, because the axis AB would necessarily be very large and cumbrous. In Fig. 29, AB is parallel to the earth's axis, and is called the *polar axis*. CD, the *declination axis* (§ 122), runs through the "sleeve" EF, which is bolted to the top of the polar axis. The telescope tube is fastened to the declination axis. W is a counterpoise, to balance the weight of the telescope, so that the whole mechanism will be nicely poised on the polar axis. The German form of mounting is shown in Fig. 30.

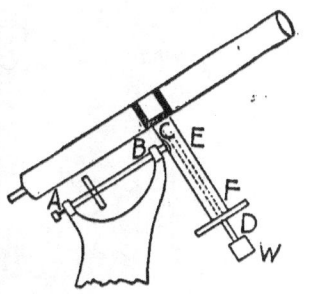

Fig. 29. — A German Equatorial.

47. Management of a Telescope. — The following directions are for inexperienced observers using small telescopes.

1. Do not look through a closed window; the irregularities of the pane of glass will distort objects.

2. Do not point the telescope out of an open window, in a room warmer than the external air; the warm air currents rushing from the room cause the images of objects to waver.

Fig. 30.—The Lick Telescope.

3. If a telescope has several eyepieces, use the one of lowest power first; if the object appears distinct, you may try a higher power.

4. For comets and nebulæ use low powers.

5. In general, avoid touching the telescope when looking through; you may shake it.

6. Focus carefully, by sliding the eyepiece in or out, until the view is most distinct. Different eyes frequently require different adjustments of the eyepiece.

7. Clean the object-glass rarely, and carefully. A little dust on it will be of no appreciable detriment. Dust may be removed with a camel's-hair brush. Never *rub* the glass with any material.

8. Keep the eyepieces clean.

EXERCISES.

48. 1. If an incident ray be perpendicular to the surface of a plane mirror, what direction will the reflected ray take?

2. Is the image on the ground-glass of a photographer's camera upright or inverted? Does an object which is at the right of another, as seen with the naked eye, appear at the right of it on the ground-glass?

3. If you look through the wrong end of a telescope, are objects magnified, or are they minified?

4. The object-glass of the Lick telescope is 36 inches in diameter. If the diameter of the pupil of one's eye be one fifth of an inch, how many times as much light as the unaided eye does the Lick glass receive from a star?

5. When looking across a landscape at a distant fixed object, did you ever notice that the object trembled slightly, or had a wavy appearance?

Explain the cause of this appearance.

6. Draw a circle having a radius of two inches. With the same centre draw another having a radius of $2\frac{1}{8}$ inches. At some point of the inner circle draw a line about three inches long, tangent to it. From the same point draw outward a perpendicular to the tangent, and two oblique lines, making respectively angles of 45° and 10° with the tangent. The smaller circle represents the earth, and

the space between the circles the atmosphere. The tangent is the observer's horizon. When a man looks straight up at the heavens, does he look through more atmosphere, or less, than when he looks nearly horizontally?

7. On a given night does the moon appear more brilliant when in mid-heaven than when rising or setting? Give a reason for your reply.

8. On a clear, moonless night, do stars near the zenith twinkle more violently, or less, than those near the horizon? Why?

9. Did you ever see a fixed star set? Would the observation of its setting be difficult at sea?

10. Which rays are the more refrangible, the red or the violet?

11. When a person is looking through a telescope, if you hold your finger in front of the object-glass and near it, will he see it?

12. If a person were looking through a telescope at the full moon, and another suddenly covered up one half of the object-glass, how would the appearance of the moon be changed?

13. In an equatorial mounting, what angle does the declination axis make with the sight line? What angle does the declination axis make with the polar axis?

14. If one takes hold of the telescope at the eye end and moves it about its axes into various positions, will the angle between the declination axis and the sight line change? Will the angle between the declination axis and the polar axis change?

15. An astronomer using an *equatorial* (as the whole instrument is usually designated) in a fixed observatory points the telescope to various parts of the sky.

(*a*) Does the polar axis turn?

(*b*) Does the polar axis point to different points on the celestial sphere?

(*c*) Does the declination axis point toward different points on the celestial sphere?

16. (*a*) Does the declination axis ever lie in a plane perpendicular to the polar axis?

(*b*) Does the declination axis always lie in a plane perpendicular to the polar axis?

(*c*) If the polar axis be turned through one revolution, what circle would the declination axis, prolonged to the celestial sphere, trace on it?

REMARK. — In answering the following exercises, scholars may obtain assistance by using a pair of shears. Let the cutting edge of one blade represent the sight line, the edge of the other the polar axis, and the rivet holding the blades together the declination axis. The shears should be so held in the hand that the blade representing the polar axis points to the north celestial pole.

17. If the sight line of a telescope equatorially mounted be placed (by turning the telescope about the declination axis) perpendicular to the polar axis (see Fig. 28), it will be parallel to the plane of a well known circle. What is the name of the circle?

18. When the sight line of an equatorial telescope has been placed perpendicular to the polar axis, if the latter be rotated by the clockwork, what circle will the sight line, prolonged to the celestial sphere, trace upon it?

19. If the sight line of an equatorial be placed parallel to the polar axis, toward what point on the celestial sphere will the telescope point?

20. The telescope, placed as in the preceding exercise, is rotated on its polar axis.

(*a*) Will the sight line continue to be parallel to the polar axis?

(*b*) What sort of a geometrical figure will the sight line, prolonged, trace on the celestial sphere?

(*c*) Would that figure, if it could be seen from the earth, appear large or small?

21. If the sight line of an equatorial be placed at an oblique angle with the polar axis, and the instrument be rotated on that axis, will the sight line describe a circle on the celestial sphere?

22. Do stars near the celestial equator seem to move across the sky more swiftly than those near the pole, or more slowly? Will the clockwork of an equatorial (when so rated that a star near the celestial equator will be kept in the field of the telescope) need a special adjustment, to enable it to keep a star near the pole in the field?

CHAPTER IV.

THE SUN.

> "But yonder comes the powerful king of day,
> Rejoicing in the east. The lessening cloud,
> The kindling azure, and the mountain's brow,
> Illumed with fluid gold, his near approach
> Betoken glad."
>
> THOMSON.

49. Distance and Diameter. — The average distance of the earth from the sun is 92,900,000 miles.

Prof. Mendenhall has said that, if a babe could instantaneously reach across this stupendous gulf and touch the glowing surface of the sun, he would never realize that his hand was burned, for, though the nerves transmit sensations to the brain with great rapidity, over one hundred years would be required for this message.

The sun's diameter is 866,500 miles, 109.5 times as great as that of the earth. Were the earth to swell to the size of the sun, and were men to increase in the same ratio, an average man would be 625 feet tall. Since he would also be 109.5 times as broad and 109.5 times as thick as at present, his bulk would become $109.5 \times 109.5 \times 109.5$, or more than 1,300,000 times as great as now.

The force of gravity at the sun's surface being 27.6 times as powerful as at the surface of the earth, our giant, if transported to the sun, would weigh 2,750,000 tons, if of ordinary build.

50. How to View the Sun through a Small Telescope. — The sun may be viewed, *for a moment*, through a pinhole in a card, without injury to the eye, but the observation is not to be recommended.

A small telescope may be directed toward the sun by moving it until its shadow, thrown on a book held near the lower end, is as small as it can be made, and a dazzling light issues from the eyepiece. A dark shade glass may then be held close to the eyepiece, and one may look through. Great care should be taken to avoid getting the full blaze of sunlight into the eye, and one should not continue looking through a dark glass, if the sun is uncomfortably bright.

The dark glass and eyepiece soon become hot, and may break if the telescope is kept pointed at the sun too long. The amount of light and heat may be much diminished by covering the object-glass with a piece of paper having a circle an inch or more in diameter cut in it, but one will not be able to see the more delicate details of the sun's surface quite as well.

51. Use of a Screen. — If a piece of white paper be held about a foot from the eyepiece, and the eyepiece pulled out a fraction of an inch beyond its proper focal position, an image of the sun will be formed on the screen. By careful adjustment of the eyepiece, the sun spots will usually be well seen.

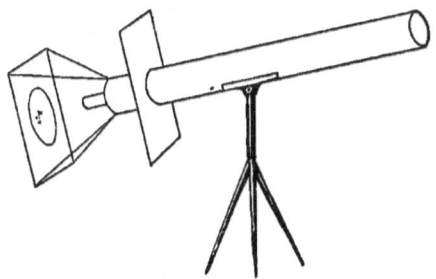

Fig. 31. — THE SUN'S IMAGE ON A SCREEN.

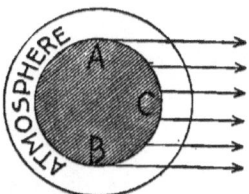

Fig. 32. — ABSORPTION OF LIGHT BY THE SUN'S ATMOSPHERE.

Another screen fastened to the telescope, as shown in Fig. 31, so as to throw its shadow on the first screen, will improve the view. Several persons can thus view the sun at once. The telescope, unless equatorially mounted and driven by clockwork, must be moved about every minute in order to keep the sun's image on the screen. If the eyepiece be of high magnifying power, the entire sun cannot be seen at once. Special eyepieces are made for solar work, which obviate, in large measure, the inconveniences rising from its intense light and heat.

52. The Photosphere. — The name photosphere (sphere of light) is given to the brilliant surface of the sun. This surface, as seen through a telescope, has a grayish cast. It is brighter at the centre than near the edge. The cause of this is shown in Fig. 32. To an observer situated at the right of the figure, rays coming from A or B, which would be at the edge of the sun, pass through more of the sun's atmosphere than those coming from C; thus they suffer a greater absorption, and appear fainter. The photosphere corresponds to the crust of the earth, but it is far from solid: it is to be regarded as a cloud-like shell of intensely heated vapors. As water

Fig. 33. — FACULÆ OBSERVED VISUALLY.

on the earth, when evaporated, rises and condenses in the upper air into clouds, so the vapors of metals, rising from the interior of the sun, condense into drops and form the photospheric clouds.

53. Rice Grains. — The photosphere, when viewed under favorable conditions, is seen to be mottled with small bright objects, which have been likened to rice grains floating in a plate of soup, or snowflakes on a gray cloth. To an observer situated a few thousand miles from the earth, the cloud forms on a cloudy day might exhibit much the same appearance. The cloud formation which navigators call a mackerel sky is suggestive of it.

54. Faculæ. — Faculæ (from the Latin word *facula*, a small torch) are shown in Fig. 33. They are best seen near the limb[1] of the sun, and are especially abundant in the neighborhood of spots. The photosphere is agitated by such furious storms that its outer surface rises in mountain-like ridges, or crests, like the waves of a raging sea; these, projecting upward through the lower part of the solar atmosphere, look brighter than the general background.

A man standing on the summit of Pike's Peak on a clear night would see the moon through much less of our light-absorbing atmosphere than if he were at sea level. Hence the moon would appear more glorious.

In like manner, an observer on the moon could see high terrestrial mountains better than the low level of the plains. The faculæ are more distinct near the limb of the sun, because the general background is darker there. Recent photographs, however, show them well near the centre of the sun's disk. They are sometimes 20,000 miles long, and more than 200 miles high. The faculæ seem to form an irregular network over the entire surface of the sun.

SUN SPOTS.

55. General Appearance of a Spot. — Sun spots reside in the photosphere. In looking at the sun with a telescope, specks of dust on the eyepiece are seen as black spots on its face. But a true sun spot is distinguished from these by the fact that it has a dark central portion surrounded by a lighter border. The dark central part is called the *umbra;* the border is the *penumbra*. Some portions of the umbra are frequently darker than others. The impression given to an observer is that these dark places are deep holes. The penumbra is composed of filaments which point inward toward the umbra. Sometimes bridges of light cross the umbra from side to side, or, if too short, seem to project out over it, as a fishing rod hangs over a pool.

[1] The word "limb" is used by astronomers to denote the edge of the disk.

40   DESCRIPTIVE ASTRONOMY.

Occasionally, when a spot is just on the edge of the sun, it is seen as a notch in its smooth periphery. Hence spots are thought to be saucer-like depressions below the general level.

Fig. 34. — Sun Spot.
(From Langley's "New Astronomy," by permission.)

56. Changes in Appearance. — These objects are not of fixed form, like mountains or lakes, but change continually. The change in a day is usually very marked. Bridges may form or disappear; the spot may grow or diminish very perceptibly, may break into two or more spots, or may even vanish altogether. The changes are on some occasions so rapid as to make it impossible to sketch the spot. An area as large as the United States may vanish in a quarter of an hour. The lifetime of a spot averages three or four weeks; one has been known to last a year and a half.

57. Dimensions. — The smallest ones observed with large telescopes have umbræ 500 miles in diameter. In a large spot the diameter of the umbra may reach 50,000 miles. The largest group in recent years was visible during Feb. 5-17, 1892. It was 150,000 miles long and 75,000 miles broad, the central spot of the group being 100,000 miles long, and half as broad. Such a group may be seen without a telescope, by looking through a colored or smoked glass, or even through a bank of haze when the sun is near the horizon.

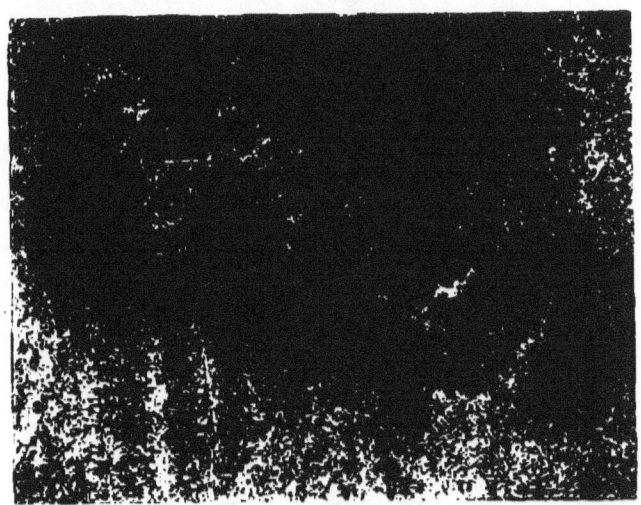

Fig. 35. — LARGE SUN SPOT.

58. Movements: Rotation of the Sun. — If a spot be seen at noon of a certain day in the centre of the sun's disk, at the next noonday it will appear at the right of its former position. In a week it will have passed the western limb, and in two weeks thereafter it will emerge into view on the eastern limb, if still in existence. This shows that the sun rotates on an axis, as the earth does. Careful observations made on spots show that different portions of the sun rotate in different times. Near the solar equator spots make their circuit in twenty-five days, but spots situated half way from the equator to the poles consume twenty-seven days in a like journey.

Spots are rarely seen at the solar equator, and never more than half way to the poles. No one has yet explained satisfactorily this distribution of the spots, or the irregularity of the rotation time of different portions of the sun's surface.

59. Periodicity. — In 1826, Schwabe, a magistrate in the little German town of Dessau, began for his own pleasure to count the number of sun spots visible in his telescope each day. After twenty-five years of patient endeavor he found that he had been, like Saul,

Fig. 36. — THE SUN AT THE TIME OF A SPOT MAXIMUM.

"going out to seek his father's asses, and finding a kingdom." For he discovered that spots were much more numerous in some years than in others, and that the numbers changed with considerable regularity. Later investigations have fixed the average period as being 11.1 years. A maximum of spottedness occurred in 1893, but was not very pronounced. After that the spot activity gradually lessened, and is expected to be feeblest about 1900. Then for weeks at a time no spot may be visible; after the minimum, the spotted area will increase until about 1905, when another maximum is due; at a time of maximum the sun is never free from spots. Times of maxima and minima may vary a year or two from those predicted. The cause of this periodicity is unknown; it has been surmised to be due in some way to planetary influences.

60. Observations by Carrington and Hodgson. — Very violent disturbances are at times noted in the neighborhood of spots. The

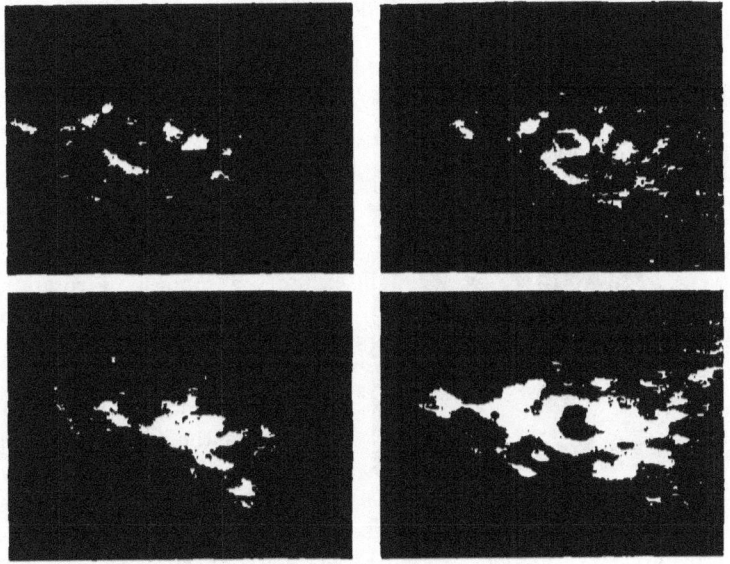

Fig. 37. — PHOTOGRAPHS OF THE DISTURBANCE OF JULY 15, 1892.

classic observation of Carrington and Hodgson, two English observers, was made on Sept. 1, 1859. Near the edge of a great spot there suddenly appeared two luminous masses, the length of each of which was equal to the earth's diameter. So dazzling were they that they were estimated to be five times as brilliant as the general surface of the sun. They moved side by side across the spot with a velocity of over 100 miles a second, growing fainter; in five minutes they had faded from view. These were probably the product of an eruption of marvellous energy.

61. Disturbance on July 15, 1892. — On this date Prof. George E. Hale[1] took a photograph of a large spot which had two umbræ separated by a bright bridge of light. Another photograph, taken twelve minutes after, showed an exceedingly bright object, shaped somewhat like a fish-hook, the hook end being baited with a brilliant ball which was near the centre of the umbra. In half an hour thereafter, the region of the spot was completely covered with brilliant outbursts, so that the umbræ were no longer visible in the photograph. Two hours later, the disturbance, which extended over an area of four billion square miles, had disappeared entirely. It seems to have been high above the spots, which were unchanged by these terrific outbursts.

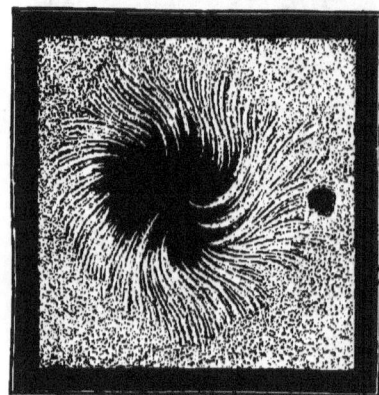

Fig. 38. — Cyclonic Motion in a Spot.

62. Cyclonic Motion. — On rare occasions a spot is found which exhibits a motion of rotation; sometimes an entire revolution is accomplished in a few days, but usually only a portion of a revolution is accomplished. In such spots the filaments of the penumbra are curved, as shown in Fig. 38. The motion of these spots is analogous to that of whirlwinds and cyclones upon the earth. But the analogy must not be pressed too far, for terrestrial cyclones in the northern hemisphere always rotate in a left-handed direction (opposite to that of the hands of a watch). Sun spots have no regularity of rotation.

63. Nature of Sun Spots. — Upon this there has been much speculation. No theory has yet been found which accounts for the

[1] Director of the Yerkes Observatory.

observed appearances fully. Prof. Young's[1] theory is given in substance below.

When the fiery gases imprisoned beneath the photospheric cloud-shell burst forth at any weak place in the shell, there is a temporary diminution of the upward pressure against the photosphere in that locality. Hence the photosphere sinks somewhere in the neighborhood, an irregular shallow cavity being formed. The materials thrown out by the eruption are cooled in the upper regions of the sun's atmosphere, and fall back into the cavity. The light from below, struggling up through this mass of comparatively cool vapors, is dimmed by absorption. Hence the umbra, though really intensely luminous, sends to us less light than the surrounding photosphere, and looks black by contrast with it.

The filaments of the penumbra are supposed to be long drawn out rice grains (§ 53).

64. Sun Spots as Causes of Changes of the Weather, etc. — Many have been the attempts to show that the maxima and minima of spots affect the meteorological conditions. One investigator discovers that years when sun spots are at a maximum are more rainy than the average, and that cyclones and other violent storms are then most prevalent. Another concludes that such years are hotter than the average, while a third finds them to be cooler. Others attribute the recurrence of Asiatic cholera, variations in the amount of atmospheric ozone, or the prevalence of commercial panics, to the direful spots. The data on which these conclusions are based are, in general, so conflicting as to produce, in one who examines them, much weariness of the flesh and little satisfaction of the spirit.

65. Magnetic Storms. — A compass needle does not always point in the same direction. One of the large and accurate ones used in magnetic observatories shifts in direction a few minutes of arc every day, vibrating to and fro. Sometimes these oscillations are greatly increased, and are subject to no perceptible law; the needles seem fairly beside themselves with magnetic excitement.

Powerful currents traverse the telegraph wires, and send messages in an unknown tongue; private lines are temporarily worked in the nervous systems of the operators; the regular electrical

---

[1] C. A. Young, Professor of Astronomy in Princeton University, one of the most distinguished students of the sun.

apparatus is set on fire at times. At night the weird auroral beams execute their most fantastic dances.

66. Connection of these Storms with Solar Outbursts. — The singular event mentioned in § 60 took place during a great magnetic storm, which was raging upon the earth. In Washington and Philadelphia the telegraph operators were severely shocked. At Boston a flame of fire followed the pen of a recording telegraphic instrument.

There were fine auroral displays in all parts of the world; even countries near the equator enjoyed the spectacle, to them almost unknown. During the years 1873 to 1892 there were three especially severe magnetic storms on the earth. There were also three very notable displays of sun spots. The magnetic storms occurred at the times of the greatest development of the spots.

67. The Storm of February, 1892. The great spot of Feb. 5-17, 1892 (§ 57), was accompanied by a magnetic storm which raged on Feb. 13 and 14, when the spot group had attained its maximum dimensions, covering $\frac{1}{860}$ of the sun's visible hemisphere. Fine auroras flashed out during this storm. Magnetic recording instruments were more violently disturbed than for ten years previously. An earth current awakened a sleeping operator, in France, by ringing his signal bell. Nearly a month afterwards, when the spot, much enfeebled, came by reason of the sun's rotation into the same apparent position on its disk, another bright aurora accompanied by a magnetic storm occurred.

68. Frequency of Magnetic Storms. — An examination of the records of these storms shows that they too have times of maximum and minimum, and that these times correspond closely with those for sun spots. That there is some connection between the two is no longer doubtful, though the most distinguished physicists are unable to explain the nature of the relation. Conspicuous sun spots, or other solar disturbances, are not always accompanied by magnetic storms on the earth. This is not astonishing, however; for terrestrial storms often occur in which there is no special display of electrical phenomena.

Some are of the opinion that, when a solar storm is associated with electrical disturbance there, the disturbance is propagated with the speed of light through the ether to the earth, which is thrilled responsively.

THE SUN. 47

THE SPECTROSCOPE.

69. Description of the Instrument. — We learned in § 37, that white light might be resolved into its component colors by pass-

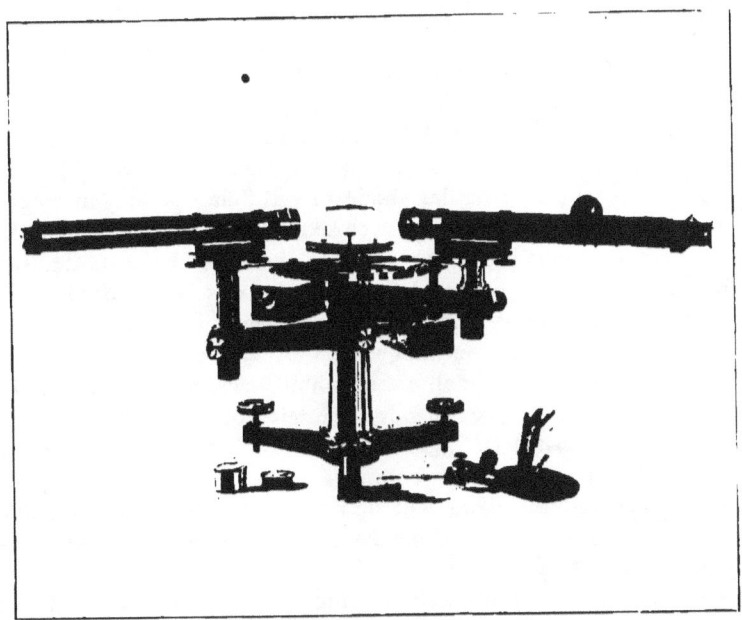

Fig. 39. — A Spectroscope (made by Brashear).

ing it through a prism. The peculiarities of light thus dispersed are conveniently studied by means of the spectroscope; the action

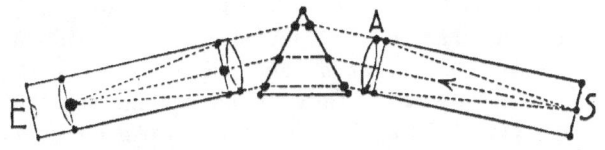

Fig. 40. — Plan of a Spectroscope.

of a simple form of this instrument is shown by Fig. 40. At the point S is a slit, shown in Fig. 41. It is a straight narrow opening between two pieces of metal, *x* and *y*, shown in the cut; *x* is movable by the screw *a*, so that the width of the slit may be altered at pleasure. S is put at such a distance from the lens A that the rays of light coming from S are rendered parallel by passing through A. These rays then strike the prism, are refracted by it, enter the telescope, and come through to the eye at E.

Fig. 41. — SLIT OF A SPECTROSCOPE.

70. Slit Illuminated by Red Light. — Suppose that in front of the slit we could burn some substance which gave out a red light, *no other color* except a particular shade of red being given out by the substance. Let the slit be almost closed. On looking through the telescope one would see a fine red line, just the shape of the slit. If half the slit were covered by a card, the observer would see a line only half as long as before; if the slit were widened by turning the screw *a* (Fig. 41), the image seen by the observer would be widened likewise. If a small circular hole were put in place of the slit, the observer would see through the telescope a red circle.

71. Slit Illuminated by Lights of Different Colors. — The flame of an alcohol lamp is almost colorless. Place on the wick some common salt and the flame will be colored yellow, this hue being due to sodium. Put the yellow flame in front of the slit, and the observer will see a yellow line, the image of the slit. Try a similar experiment with a salt of thallium, and a green slit image will be seen. Next lay on the wick of the lamp both common salt and a salt of thallium. Both yellow and green light will enter the slit, but in passing through the prism the yellow rays will not be bent out of their course as much as the green rays. Therefore, if the slit be nearly closed, the observer will see two fine lines, one yellow and the other green, standing side by side. If any number of colors be admitted at once, there will be the same number of slit images standing side by side. When a candle, which gives a light composed of a great number of tints, illuminates the slit, the images are so closely crowded together that they form a continuous band of color from red to violet (§ 37). This is called a *continuous spectrum*. Were the candle capable of giving out all colors but green, there would be in the ribbon of light or spectrum a dark gap between cyan-blue and yellow.

THE SUN.   49

72. White Light shining through an Incandescent Gas. — Arrange the apparatus as shown in Fig. 42. Let the sodium and thallium be giving in the spectroscope their yellow and green lines. Lift up the screen so that the calcium light[1] shines through the glowing gases in the flame of the spirit lamp into the instrument.

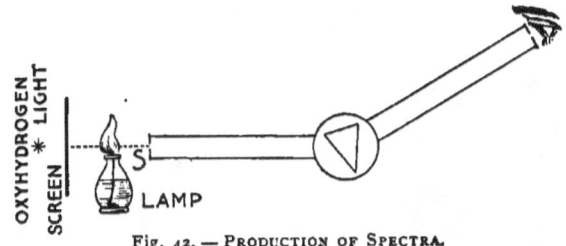

Fig. 42. — PRODUCTION OF SPECTRA.

Instantly, the spectrum will change to a many-colored ribbon, like that caused by a candle, except that, where the bright lines due to sodium and thallium formerly were, the spectrum will be crossed by dark lines. Such a spectrum is called an absorption spectrum. The two spectra are shown without the colors in Fig. 43. Put the

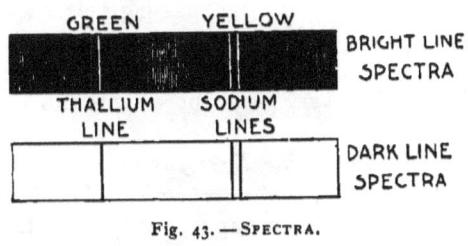

Fig. 43. — SPECTRA.

screen in place again, so as to cut off the rays from the calcium light, and the bright lines will reappear. Remove the alcohol lamp and the screen, and the calcium light will produce a continuous spectrum.

[1] The calcium light is produced by introducing a piece of lime into a flame caused by burning oxygen and hydrogen gases together. Such a light has been seen over one hundred miles in full daylight.

73. Laws of Spectrum Analysis. — By an exhaustive series of experiments similar to the preceding, the following laws have been discovered. They are called Kirchhoff's laws.

1. *An incandescent solid, or liquid, or even gas under high pressure, gives a continuous spectrum.*

A candle or kerosene lamp gives a continuous spectrum because nearly all of its light comes from glowing particles of solid carbon (which when cooled form soot).

Fig. 44. — Kirchhoff, the Discoverer of the Laws of Spectrum Analysis.

2. *A glowing gas, unless condensed by high pressure, gives a discontinuous spectrum made up of bright lines or bands.*

The spectrum of iron vapor consists of hundreds of bright lines. Sodium vapor gives a small number of lines, the most conspicuous of which has been mentioned; with a spectroscope of high dispersive power, such as one in which the light is passed through several prisms, this line is seen double. The spectrum of a gas is usually obtained by passing electrical discharges through a Geissler's tube containing the gas. The narrow portion of the tube has a very small bore, and the gas in it glows brightly.

3. *A gas absorbs from white light passing through it those rays which the gas itself when incandescent emits.* This law explains absorption spectra. When sodium vapor in the flame of the spirit lamp

Fig. 45. — A Geissler's Tube.

is interposed between the slit of the spectroscope and the calcium light, it absorbs much of the yellow light coming from the lamp which would otherwise have fallen upon that place in the spectrum where the main sodium line is located. This place in the spectrum is therefore lighted up only by the light coming from the sodium vapor and a *portion* of the yellow light coming from the lime. Hence it looks dark by contrast with the rest of the spectrum which is brightly illuminated by the lime light.

It is found that the heated vapor of any elementary substance,[1] (like sodium, iron, aluminum, oxygen, etc.,) when at a given temperature and pressure, has for its spectrum a particular group of bright lines by which it is distinguished from other elements.

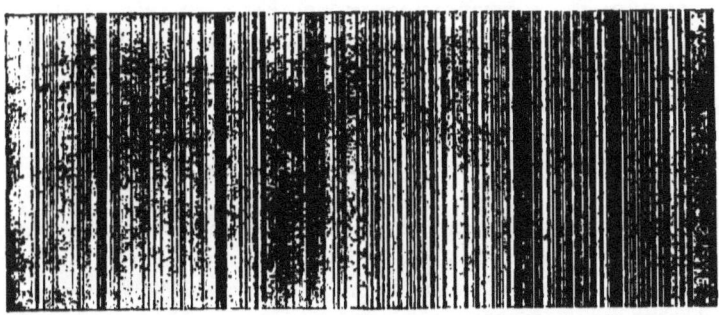

Fig. 46. — A Portion of the Solar Spectrum.

74. The Solar Spectrum. — When sunlight is admitted through the slit of a spectroscope, it gives an absorption spectrum, the lines being very numerous; a number of them are shown in Fig. 46.

Fig. 47. — Correspondence of Bright and Dark Lines in Two Spectra.

From the third law we conclude that the light coming from the photosphere has passed through some gas or gases on its way to us. In order to find out what these gases are, we compare the solar spectrum with the bright line spectra of various gases. This is done by admitting sunlight through one half of the slit, while the

[1] For a list of the elements, consult any work on chemistry.

light from some glowing gas is admitted through the other half. One who looks through the telescope sees one spectrum above the other, as shown in Fig. 47, which exhibits the correspondence between bright and dark lines in portions of two spectra.

We conclude that whenever the bright lines in the spectrum of some particular glowing gas correspond to certain dark lines in the solar spectrum, that gas is present in the atmosphere of the sun.

75. Constituents of the Sun: Telluric Lines. — By comparison of the spectra of various vapors with that of the sun, it has been shown that many of the substances found on the earth exist in the sun also. Some of the most commonly known of these are iron, carbon, hydrogen, nickel, and copper. No trace has been found of such important elements as chlorine, nitrogen, and mercury. But the spectra of these, when heated to an enormous temperature, as at the sun's surface, may be very different from those produced in our laboratories.

Lockyer[1] has advanced the theory that substances regarded as elements are really compounds which are separated into their constituents by the intense heat at the sun, so that their spectra are much changed.

Many of the dark lines in the solar spectrum are caused by absorption in passing through our atmosphere. These are called telluric (*tellus*, the earth) lines.

THE SUN'S SURROUNDINGS.

76. The Chromosphere. — The chromosphere is that portion of the sun's "atmosphere" which lies next to the photosphere. It is visible during a total solar eclipse, when the moon has hidden the photosphere from view; its color is scarlet. It is composed of upright filaments, and has the appearance of a stubble-field, the "stubble" averaging over five thousand miles in height. Hydrogen, helium, and calcium are its principal constituents.

Helium received its name from the Greek word *helios* (the sun), because it was supposed to exist in the sun only. But when Dr. Ramsey[2] was examining a specimen of a species of pitchblende in

---

[1] J. Norman Lockyer, an English astronomer, who is among the foremost of living spectroscopists.

[2] An English physicist, one of the discoverers of argon.

Fig. 48.

SOLAR PROMINENCES.

1895, he detected helium in it. It has since been found in certain mineral springs in Europe, and in several rare minerals, though always in small quantities. It is now known to be widely distributed throughout the universe, for lines due to it are in the spectra of stars and nebulæ.

77. Prominences or Protuberances. — At the time of a solar eclipse many fantastic crimson objects are seen jutting out from the chromosphere at the sun's limb. They are divided into two classes, the *cloudlike* or *quiescent*, and the *eruptive*.

They are shown in Figs. 1 and 48.

The former are immense irregular masses which overhang the chromosphere, looking like the thunder-heads which lazily bask in the sunshine on a quiet summer afternoon. Usually they are connected with the chromosphere by columns which remind one of pictures of terrestrial water-spouts. Sometimes they last a month. One has been seen which was 475,000 miles high: its extreme apparent breadth was about the same. They are of the same composition as the chromosphere.

Eruptive prominences are fiery fountains of gas which spurt out from the chromosphere. Some fine specimens are shown in Fig. 1. One has been known to rise to a height of 350,000 miles. In these prominences not only chromospheric matter, but some of the vapors of the photosphere are carried up, with velocities which baffle comprehension. On May 5, 1892, a velocity of 323 miles per second was measured. This eruption probably hurled masses of glowing gas entirely away from the sun.

78. Prominences seen with the Spectroscope. — Prominences are not visible with a simple telescope except at the time of an eclipse. But if a spectroscope of good dispersive power be attached at the eye-end and properly adjusted, one may study the prominences on any clear day. (See Fig. 49.) The explanation of this may be found in large works on astronomy.[1]

Prominences are distributed all over the sun, but are seen only at its limb. Those upon its face are invisible because the photosphere back of them is so bright.

79. Prominences and Magnetic Storms. — Prominences, like sun spots, are periodic; their times of maximum and minimum coincid-

---

[1] See Young's General Astronomy, Art. 324.

ing with those of the spots. Like the spots, they are associated with magnetic storms.

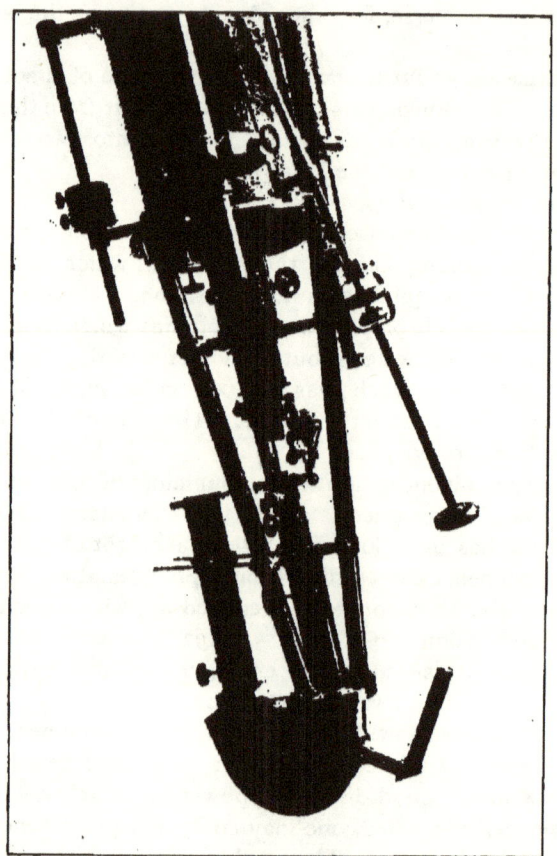

Fig. 49.—A Spectroscope attached to a Telescope.

Prof. Young, when observing at a mountain station during the forenoon of August 3, 1872, noticed especial activity of prominences, jets of unusual brightness being ejected. At dinner time one of the party, who had been taking magnetic observations, and who did not know what Prof. Young had seen, said that he had been obliged to desist, because the magnet had swung clear off the scale. Three times during the forenoon especially violent disturbances were observed, and at those times the magnetic needles in English observatories exhibited great fluctuations.

80. Appearance of the Corona. — At the moment when the last ray of sunlight vanishes, in a solar eclipse, there bursts upon the vision a pearly radiance of wonderful beauty, which is shown in Fig. 50. This is the corona, so called because it is a crown upon the King of Day.

Fig. 50. — THE CORONA ON JULY 29, 1878.

Near the sun it is almost dazzling in brightness, but it fades away into faint streamers and tufts of light which sometimes extend to great distances. Observers on the summit of Pike's Peak, in 1878, saw streamers 9,000000 miles in length. In the telescope the inner bright part of the corona is seen to be composed of innumerable fine filaments, like the dishevelled blonde tresses of some mountain nymph. Fig. 51 is from a photograph of the corona. The corona differs widely in appearance at different eclipses.

During 1895, Mr. D. E. Packer [1] made the capital discovery that

---

[1] Of South Birmingham, England.

56 DESCRIPTIVE ASTRONOMY.

the corona could be photographed on any clear day through a thin metallic screen. Coronal light, like the Röntgen rays, penetrates such screens. The photographs show that there is an intimate connection between the corona and active sun spots, as every promi-

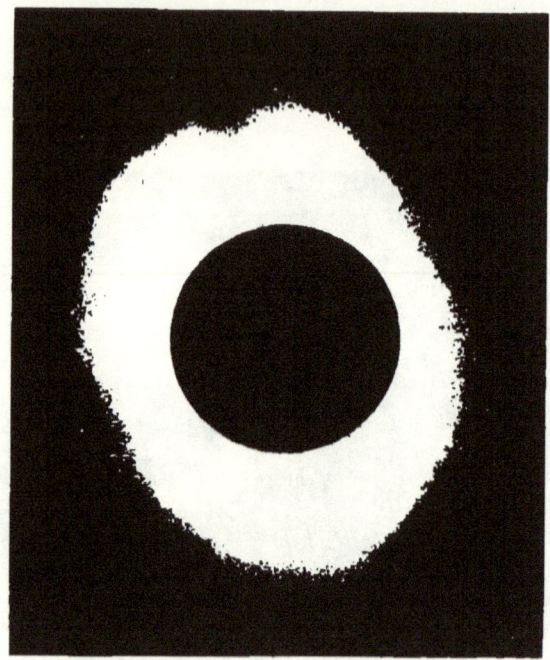

Fig. 51. — THE CORONA, PHOTOGRAPHED ON DEC. 21, 1889.

nent filament points toward some spot. Many of the filaments are twisted, like a corkscrew.[1]

81. Schaeberle's Theory of the Corona. — Prof. Schaeberle[2] has advanced a theory that the corona is caused by the ejection of numerous streams of matter, driven by forces which are most active near the centre of the zones in which spots are found. Owing to the sun's rotation these streams are curvilinear, and appear to interlace.

---

[1] Mr. Packer's work still (July, 1896) awaits confirmation by other astronomers, and may prove to be illusory.
[2] J. M. Schaeberle, Astronomer at the Lick Observatory, Mt. Hamilton, Cal.

THE SUN. 57

The variations in the form of the corona at various eclipses are partially explained by the fact that our point of view is continually changing, as the earth pursues its annual journey about the sun.

Fig. 52. — ILLUSTRATIONS OF SCHAEBERLE'S THEORY OF THE CORONA.

Prof. Schaeberle took a ball to represent the sun, and thrust into it a large number of needles, in the regions corresponding to those where spots on the sun are most numerous. The ball was then placed in several positions, and photographed: two of the results are shown in Fig. 52.

Fig. 53a. — A DRAWING OF THE CORONA.

The photographs of the eclipse of April 16, 1893, are thought by Prof. Schaeberle to confirm his theory.

82. Nature of The Corona. — The corona gives two spectra, one made up of bright lines, the other continuous. The bright line spectrum comes from a glowing gas. The continuous spectrum may come from incandescent solid or liquid particles scattered through the corona, or from the light of the photosphere reflected from the materials of the corona.

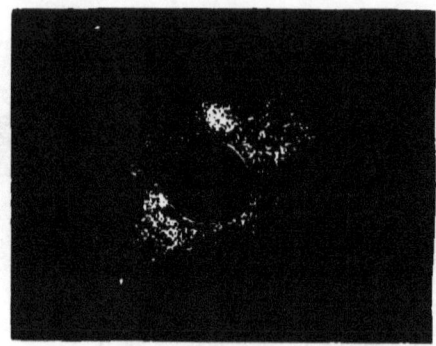

Fig. 53*b*. — A Drawing of the Corona.

The bright line spectrum, when carefully examined, reveals the presence of an unknown element, which has been called coronium; hydrogen is also found. No complete explanation of the phenomena

Fig. 53*c*. — A Drawing of the Corona.

Fig. 53*d*. — A Photograph of the Inner Corona.

exhibited by the corona has yet been found, but it is not improbable that electrical action may account for many of them. Fig. 54 shows some effects produced by Dr. Pupin,[1] by electrical discharges around

[1] M. I. Pupin, Columbia College, New York.

a brass sphere placed in a globe from which the air was largely exhausted. They are strikingly like coronal forms. Similar experiments have been made in Germany by Dr. Ebert and Prof. Wiedemann. These experiments show the raylike structure and silvery light of the corona, the dark rifts which are frequently seen extending from the sun's limb to the limit of the corona, and the abnormally long streamers which have graced the sun during certain eclipses.

Fig. 54. — ELECTRICAL APPEARANCES SIMILAR TO THE CORONA.

83. Light of the Sun. — Under the clear sky of Colorado, a newspaper may be read by any person of normal eyesight by the light of the full moon. How 100,000 full moons, crowding the vault of the heavens would blind us by their radiance! Yet the sun gives us six times as much light. If an electric arc light be placed between the eye and the sun, and both be viewed through a dark glass, the arc light will appear as a dark spot on the face of the sun. Since the earth receives only $\frac{1}{2,200,000,000}$ of the light radiated by the sun, the amount of light radiated in all directions by the sun is 2,200,000000 times as great as that which the earth receives. (See exercise 3, at the end of this chapter.) This inconceivable quantity of light is shot through space with a velocity of 186,330 miles per second. Were the sun divested of its atmosphere, it would probably be three times as bright, and blue in color. The blue rays are now strongly absorbed by its atmosphere.

84. Heat of the Sun. — By letting the sun shine for a given length of time upon the blackened cover of a box filled with a known quantity of water, and by noting the rise of temperature in the water, it is possible to find approximately the amount of heat received by the earth from the sun. Calculation based on such measurements has shown that the sun sends to the earth every second enough heat to raise 600,000000 tons of ice water to the boiling point.

Imagine that a gigantic fire-engine was throwing at the sun a stream of water 75,000 miles in cross section, at the rate of 1,000 miles a second. The water would be turned into steam as fast as it advanced, if the entire heat of the sun were concentrated upon it. Stationary engines have been run by concentrating the sun's heat by means of huge reflectors. In case some economical way of storing and distributing heat energy were discovered, solar engines might take the place of coal-burning ones.

Langley[1] says that, "even on such a little area as the island of Manhattan, or that occupied by the city of London, the noontide heat is enough, could it all be utilized, to drive all the steam engines in the world."

85. Causes of the Sun's Radiation: Combustion: Meteoric Theory. — It is certain that the outpour of heat and light is not kept up by mere combustion. Had the sun been a solid mass of the best anthracite, burning swiftly enough to produce the known supply of heat, less than 6,000 years would have been required for its complete consumption.

There has been a theory that a continual rain of small bodies falling upon the sun from adjacent space keeps up the supply of heat. We see evidences of such production of heat, when a cannon

---

[1] Dr. S. P. Langley, Secretary of the Smithsonian Institution, Washington, D. C.

ball strikes an armor plate, and both are heated by the impact. This is known as the "meteoric theory." While the sun doubtless receives some of its heat from such a pelting, the most careful investigations show that only a minute fraction of its heat can come from such a source. For if the sun be thus bombarded, why not the earth, though to a much less degree, on account of its smaller size and feebler attraction?

Calculation has shown that, upon this theory, each square mile of the earth would be bombarded by fifty tons of missiles every day.

86. The Contraction Theory. — If a body be dropped from the top of a high tower, heat will be produced when its motion is arrested

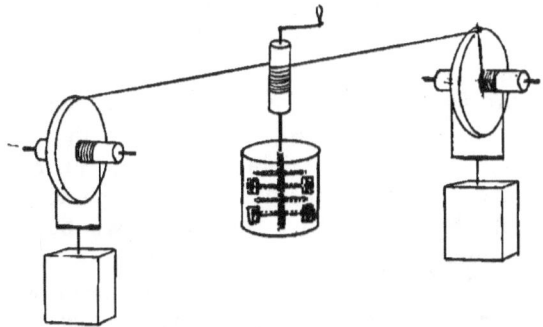

Fig. 55. — Production of Heat by the Action of Gravity.

by striking the earth. If it be made to fall slowly, by being used as a weight to drive a machine, as in Fig. 55, heat will still be produced. In the machine shown in the cut, the revolution of the paddles heats the water. Now, we conceive that the entire mass of the sun is shrinking slowly, each particle (except the one at the centre) gradually falling inward. This process will generate heat. So enormous is the sun's mass that the rate of contraction necessary to keep up the supply of heat is very slow, being only ten inches a day. The amount of contraction during the past 6,000 years would not be noticeable, even with the best modern telescope. This theory is generally accepted by astronomers as the best which has been advanced.

87. Past and Future of the Sun. — If the sun has been radiating heat uniformly in all directions, at the same rate as now, during its entire past, and if the heat has been kept up by contraction alone, however large it may originally have been, in less than 18,000,000 years it would have shrunk to its present dimensions. Since the time when its diameter was equal to that of the orbit of Mercury, it has radiated over eighty times as much heat as previously, according to this theory. By the use of similar assumptions it has been guessed that the sun will not give enough light and heat to supply the needs of man for more than 10,000,000 years hence. These figures might be awe-inspiring, if the foundations on which they rest were more substantial than "the baseless fabric of a vision." For it is extremely improbable that we can reason with any approach to exactness from the slender data at our disposal. The sun may be much older or younger. As Sir William Thomson[1] once said, in a lecture on this subject, "After all, we don't know anything about it."

88. The Sun's Constitution. — The interior of the sun is supposed to be gaseous on account of the intense heat, the gases being extremely compressed by the weight of the huge solar bulk.

Surrounding this interior is the photosphere, a cloud shell formed of vapors which, though they have been condensed by exposure to the cold of surrounding space, are yet very hot.

The chromosphere comes next, composed of gases not so easily condensed as the materials of the photosphere; chief among these is hydrogen.

Mingled with the chromosphere, but extending to vastly higher elevations, is the mysterious corona, made up of rare gases, through which are scattered finely divided particles of matter, which might remind us (if we could see them) of motes floating in a sunbeam.

EXERCISES.

89. 1. If light travelling 186,330 miles per second consumes 8 m. 19 sec. in coming from the sun to us, find the sun's distance from the earth.

2. In § 83 it is estimated that 100,000 full moons would more than fill the visible hemisphere of the sky. Let us find out how the

---

[1] Now Lord Kelvin, the great mathematical physicist.

THE SUN.

number was computed. The moon is 240,000 miles from us, and its radius is 1,080 miles. Imagine that the visible sky is a hemispherical surface, the radius of which is 240,000 miles, and that the moon is a circle, the radius of which is 1,080 miles, located on the hemispherical surface. The area of a hemisphere $= 2 \times 3.1416 \times$ the square of its radius. The area of a circle $= 3.1416 \times$ the square of its radius. How many times the area of the circle is the area of the hemisphere?

3. In § 83 it is stated that the earth receives only $\frac{1}{2,200,000000}$ of the light and heat sent out by the sun. Imagine a huge soap-bubble, the centre of which is at the sun, its radius being the distance from the sun to the earth, 93,000000 miles. Change the film to a thin crystal shell in which an emerald 8,000 miles in diameter is set, to represent the earth. Remove the emerald, leaving a circular hole 8,000 miles across. The light which strikes the crystal sphere in one second equals the total light emitted by the sun in one second. The light which streams through the hole in one second equals the amount received by the earth in one second. Hence, as the area of the hole is to the area of the sphere, so is the amount of light the earth receives in one second to the total light given out by the sun in one second.

The area of the surface of a sphere $= 4 \times 3.1416 \times$ the square of its radius. The area of a circle $= 3.1416 \times$ the square of its radius. Compute the fractional part of the sun's radiation which strikes the earth.

4. Why cannot the prominences and corona be seen with a good telescope on any bright day?

5. What change does the vapor which is shot off from the sun (§ 77) undergo, in passing through space?

CHAPTER V.

THE EARTH.

> "The earth,
> Though in comparison of heaven so small,
> Nor glistering, may of solid good contain
> More plenty than the sun that barren shines,
> Whose virtue in itself works no effect,
> But in the fruitful earth; there first received
> His beams, inactive else, their vigor find."
>
> MILTON.

90. Dimensions and Shape. — The earth is a globular body, nearly 8,000 miles in diameter. The surface of the ocean is not truly spherical, but bulges at the equator. If a soft rubber ball be spun rapidly on an uncarpeted floor, it will assume a form like that of the earth: its shortest diameter will be that on which, as an axis, it rotates. This is due to the tendency of every particle of matter which is whirling around a centre to fly away from it. Mathematicians call the earth an *oblate spheroid*. Such a solid is formed by revolving an ellipse (§ 96) about its shortest diameter as an axis.

91. Direction of the Plumb-line. — A string, at the lower end of which a plumb-bob hangs, is a *plumb-line*. If the earth were truly spherical and homogeneous, and did not rotate, its attraction for the bob would cause the line to point directly to its centre. In Fig. 56, PP' is the earth's axis, and EQ its equator. When the earth whirls, the plumb-bob at Q tends to fly directly away from C, in the direction of the line CQ prolonged. But gravity pulls the bob directly toward C, and overcomes its tendency to fly away. At D, on account of the earth's rotation, the bob tends to fly away from the axis PP', in the direction indicated by the arrow A. This tendency causes the plumb-line, instead of pointing toward C, to swing a trifle, taking the position shown. At P, since the plumb-line is in the prolongation of the earth's axis, the rotation causes no sidewise swing. Hence, *at the poles and at any point on the equator the* *plumb-line points towards the earth's centre (if the earth be homogeneous); at other places it does not point quite towards the centre.* The plumb-line is perpendicular to the surface of still water.

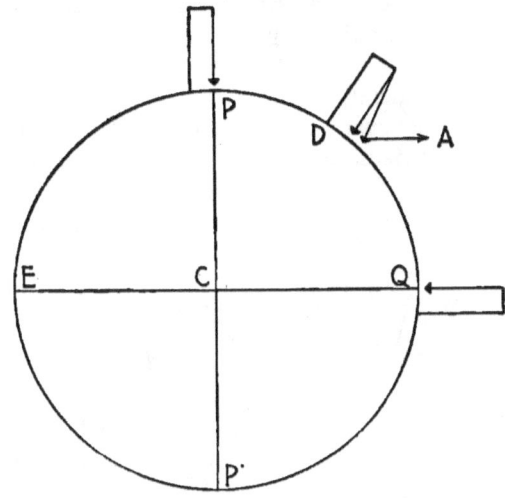

Fig. 56.—Direction of the Plumb-line.

92. How the Earth's Diameter is Found. — While the details of this process are too difficult for us to understand at this stage of our progress, we may get a notion of the principles involved by assuming that the earth is a perfect sphere, and that a plumb-line points toward its centre. In Fig. 57, C is the earth's centre, and AB an arc of a meridian. At A, AP is drawn toward the north celestial pole, and AZ in the direction of the plumb-line. At B, BZ' is drawn "plumb," and BD is made parallel to AP. BE is parallel to AZ. Now the angle PAZ = DBE, because their sides are parallel. For the same reason, —

$$EBZ' = ACB.$$
Then $\quad ACB = EBZ',$
$\qquad\quad = DBZ' - DBE,$
$\qquad\quad = DBZ' - PAZ.$

An astronomer at B measures the angle DBZ'; then, using his utmost skill and refined apparatus, he determines the length of AB in feet or meters. On arriving at A, he measures the angle PAZ. Subtracting one of these angles from the other, he gets the value of ACB, as explained above. If ACB were one degree, the circumference of the sphere would be 360 times the length of AB in feet or meters. Geometry teaches that the circumference divided by 3.1416 gives the diameter.

The real spheroidal shape and the lengths of the polar and equatorial diameters are deduced from measurements made in various parts of the world.[1]

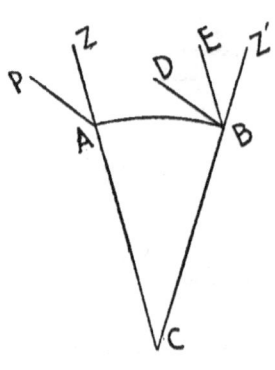

Fig. 57.

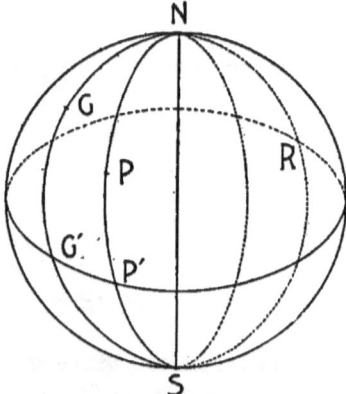

Fig. 58. — LATITUDE AND LONGITUDE.

93. Latitude and Longitude, if the Earth were a Perfect Sphere. — Assuming for a moment that the earth is a perfect sphere, we get the following definitions.

The terrestrial *meridian* of any point on the earth's surface is the circle drawn through the point and the poles. In Fig. 58, NGG'SR is the terrestrial meridian of Greenwich, if G represent that place.

The *latitude* of any point on the earth is the arc of its meridian, between the equator and the point. The arc is measured in degrees. A city in 30° north latitude is one third of the way from

---

[1] The lengths of the diameters are respectively : —
    Polar . . . . 7,901.476 miles.
    Equatorial . . . . 7,926.592 miles.

THE EARTH.   67

the equator to the north pole. A place in 45° south latitude is half way between the equator and the south pole.

The *longitude* (from Greenwich) of any point on the earth is the arc of the equator embraced between the meridian of the point and the meridian of Greenwich. It is reckoned either east or west of the Greenwich meridian. Sometimes it is expressed in degrees, but more often in hours, by putting 360° equal to 24 h. Thus 15° equals 1 h.; a place in longitude 105° west of Greenwich is said to be 7 h. west of Greenwich.

94. Latitude and Longitude accurately Defined. — Astronomers are accustomed to regard the earth as a perfect spheroid (§ 90), making allowances, when necessary, for the irregularities caused by the unevenness of its surface.

The *astronomical latitude* of any point on the earth's surface is the angle made by the plumb-line suspended at that point with the plane of the equator. In Fig. 59, the astronomical latitude of D is the angle DAE.

The *plane of the meridian* of any point on the earth's surface is the plane passing through the point and the poles. Any two meridian planes intersect,

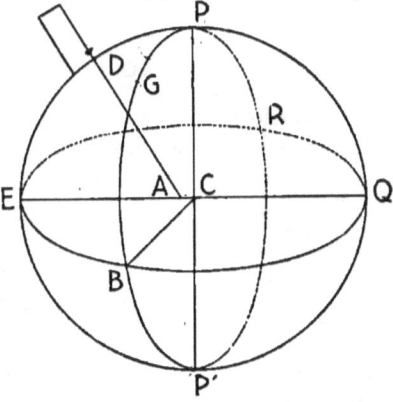

Fig. 59. — THE ASTRONOMICAL LATITUDE.

their line of intersection being the earth's axis. In Fig. 59, PP' is the line of intersection of the planes PGP' and PEP'. The angle between these planes is (§ 19) equal to ECB, because EC and BC are both perpendicular to PP'. The angle ECB is measured by the arc EB.

The *longitude* (from Greenwich) of any point on the earth's surface is the angle made by its meridian with the Greenwich meridian; or it is the arc of the equator lying between the two meridians. Thus, in Fig. 59, the longitude of D, reckoned from G, is the angle between the planes PGP' and PEP', which, as we have found, is measured by the arc EB.

Latitude is measured in degrees; longitude in degrees or hours, as stated in the last section.

95. Variation of Latitude. — During the past few years it has been shown that the latitudes of various observatories are not constant, but change by slight amounts, according to a law which has been pretty thoroughly determined by Dr. S. C. Chandler.[1] The change is due to a "wobbling" of the earth upon its axis, so that the north and south poles do not remain at the same points on the earth's surface. This movement of the poles amounts to a few yards in the course of a year, and takes place in a very sinuous path. It is believed to be due to slight changes in the earth's form, due to the varying forces which act upon it. A rude illustration is given by a base ball, which is usually rotating about some axis just before it is struck by a bat; immediately after the stroke, it commonly rotates about an entirely different axis.

THE ECLIPTIC AND THE ZODIAC.

96. The Orbit. — The earth completes its circuit about the sun in a year, moving in an ellipse. This curve may be drawn as shown in Fig. 60. A string runs from F around the pencil at P to F'. The pencil, being moved in such a way that the string slips around it and is continually kept taut, describes the curve. F and F' are the *foci.* AA' is the *major axis;* BB' is the *minor axis;* C is the centre The sun is not at the centre of the earth's orbit, but at one of the foci. When the earth is nearest the sun, it is said to be in *perihelion;* when farthest away, in *aphelion.* Half the major axis is called the *mean distance* (CA); the mean distance of the earth is 93,000000 miles. The earth travels most swiftly when in perihelion, and with the least velocity at aphelion.

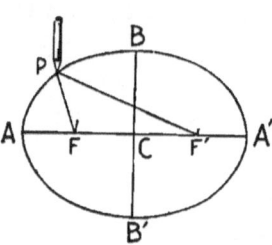

Fig. 60. — An Ellipse.

97. The Ecliptic. — If the plane of the earth's orbit be extended till it cuts the celestial sphere, their intersection will be a circle, known as *the ecliptic.* In Fig. 61 is a pond of water in which a

[1] Of Cambridge, Mass.

croquet ball is floating, half submerged. The surface of the water represents the plane of the ecliptic, and the croquet ball the earth, the centre of which is just in the plane. The point S, near the centre of the pond, represents the sun's centre.

If the earth's axis were perpendicular to the plane of its orbit, the planes of the equator and ecliptic would coincide. But the axis is tipped so as to make an angle of 23° 27′ with the perpen-

Fig. 61. — Illustration of the Ecliptic.

dicular. (See Fig. 62.) The plane of the equator, being perpendicular to the axis, is also tipped, and makes the same angle with the plane of the ecliptic. This angle has been named *the obliquity of the ecliptic*.

98. The Equinoxes. The Sun's Yearly Path. — The planes of the ecliptic and equator, when extended, cut the celestial sphere in two circles, which cross each other at two opposite points (A and B) in Fig. 63. The points are the *vernal* and *autumnal equinoxes* respectively. It is evident, from Fig. 61, that a straight line drawn from the earth's centre through that of the sun, and prolonged to meet the celestial sphere, will strike at some point of the ecliptic. As the earth moves in its orbit around the sun, the other end of this line moves along the ecliptic.

To an observer on the earth, the sun appears to be on the surface of the celestial sphere, at the end of the line just mentioned. Hence the sun seems to us to creep along the ecliptic, taking a year to make one complete circuit. On or near the 20th of March, the sun is at A; this point is called an equinox, because at that time the days and nights are equal, as will be demonstrated later. Six months afterwards, about September 22d, the sun is at B, the autumnal equinox.

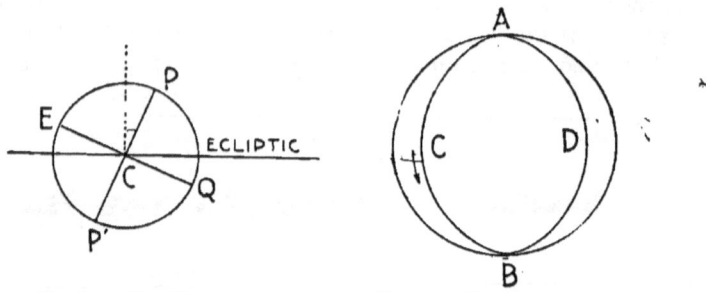

Fig. 62. — THE OBLIQUITY OF THE ECLIPTIC.

Fig. 63. — THE ECLIPTIC AND THE EQUATOR.

99. The Solstices: The Sun's Eastward Motion. — The point C in Fig. 63, midway between A and B, is the *summer solstice*. The sun is at this point about June 20th. In travelling from A, the vernal equinox, to C, the summer solstice, the sun keeps getting farther away from the celestial equator every day, and nearer to the north pole. While travelling from C to B, the sun continually lessens its distance from the celestial equator. After passing through the autumnal equinox, it is between the south celestial pole and the equator, and gets farther south of the equator every day until it reaches D, the *winter solstice*, about December 21st.

When going from D to A, it is approaching the equator every day. It must be diligently remembered that during the entire year, the sun, whether north or south of the celestial equator, is continually moving *eastward* along the sphere. If one could look right past the sun and see the stars beyond, the amount of the sun's motion among the stars in a day would be very plain to the naked eye. Fig. 64 shows such a view of the sun's daily motion.

100. The Zodiac. — The zodiac is a belt 16° broad, encircling the sky, like the colored band on a croquet ball. The ecliptic is its central line. Twelve constellations lie in this belt or zone. They are: Aries, Taurus, Gemini; Cancer, Leo, Virgo; Libra, Scorpio, Sagittarius; and Capricornus, Aquarius, Pisces. The moon and the planets are always to be found in the zodiac. The *signs* of the zodiac are twelve arbitrary divisions of it, each of which is 30° long. The first three of them stretch from the vernal equinox to the summer solstice. The signs have the same names as the constella-

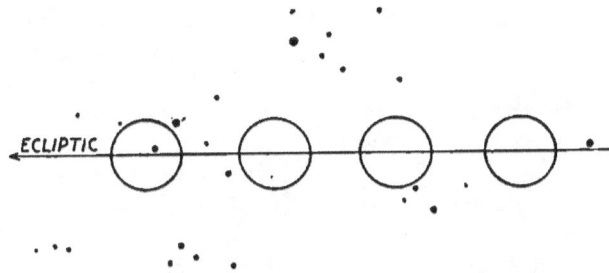

Fig. 64. — THE SUN'S DAILY MOTION AMONG THE STARS.

tions just mentioned, but do not coincide with them. The expression, "The sun enters Aries," found in almanacs, means that the sun passes the vernal equinox.

101. Is the North Celestial Pole Fixed? — When a heavy top spins rapidly on a smooth surface, its axis keeps the same direction, no matter how much the top wanders around. The successive positions taken by the axis of the top are parallel lines. As the earth goes spinning around the sun once a year, all the positions of its axis from moment to moment are parallel lines. We here neglect certain minute

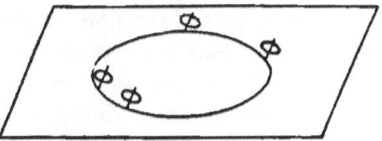

Fig. 65. — A SPINNING TOP.

tippings caused by the attraction of other bodies for the earth. These parallel lines when extended appear to strike the celestial sphere at the same point, because of the infinite distance of the sphere from us. This explains why the north celestial pole can be found at the same place among the stars (§ 18) during the entire year. It does not move enough during his lifetime to attract the attention of one observing with the naked eye.

102. Are the Celestial Equator and Ecliptic Fixed? — Since the plane of the earth's equator is perpendicular to its axis, all the positions

72   DESCRIPTIVE ASTRONOMY.

which it takes during a year will constitute a series of parallel planes. These planes, being extended to the celestial sphere, cut it in great circles, which appear to us to coincide on account of their infinite distance from us. Since the earth's axis is tipped a little this way and that, as mentioned in the last article, the equator suffers slight shiftings. But for purposes of naked eye observation, we regard the celestial equator as fixed among the stars. Its place among them is shown on the maps.

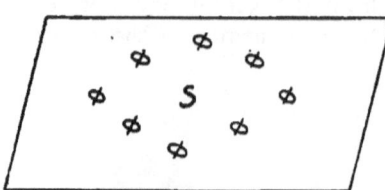

Fig. 66. — SUCCESSIVE POSITIONS OF THE EARTH'S EQUATOR.

Similarly the ecliptic is to be regarded as a circle practically fixed among the stars.

DAY AND NIGHT: THE SEASONS.

103. The Length of The Day. — Everybody knows that in summer the days are long and the nights short, and that the case is reversed in winter. We refer now to middle latitudes, leaving the polar regions and the equator out of consideration for the moment.

One may get a clear grasp of this matter by a simple experiment. Take an orange, with a knitting needle thrust through it to serve as an axis of rotation, and mark upon it with a penknife the equator, together with three or four circles on each side of the equator and parallel to it. Submerge half the orange in a basin of water in the position shown in Fig. 67. The surface of the water represents our horizon, and the upper part of the orange the half of the celestial sphere visible to us at any moment, PP' being its axis and EQ its equator. It is plain that just one half of the equator is below the horizon. Hence, if any celestial object is on the equator, as the sphere turns, the object will be above the horizon for twelve hours and below for the same length

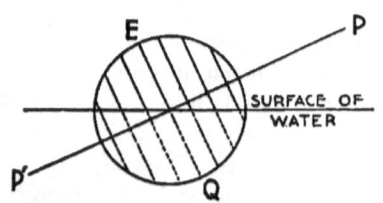

Fig. 67. — AN ORANGE HALF SUBMERGED.

of time. More than half of every circle between P and EQ is above the horizon. Therefore, if any celestial object be north of the equator, it will be above the horizon more than twelve hours out of the twenty-four. If it be near the north celestial pole, it will be above the horizon all the time. Less than half of every circle between P′ and EQ is above the horizon. Consequently any celestial object south of the equator is above the horizon less than twelve hours out of the twenty-four. If it be near the south celestial pole, it will never rise above the horizon.

On March 20th the sun is near the vernal equinox all day; and since this point is on the equator, it rises nearly at the east point of the horizon and sets nearly at the west point, so that both day and night are almost exactly twelve hours long. After March 20th the sun, creeping along the ecliptic, gets farther and farther north every day until June 20th, so that the days continue to grow longer and the nights shorter until that date, which is the longest day of the year.

After June 20th the sun approaches the equator and the days shorten and the nights lengthen until September 22d, when the sun reaches the autumnal equinox, and the days and nights are again equal. The sun then passes south of the equator, and the days grow shorter till December 21st, when the sun is farthest south. The sun approaches the equator during the next three months, so that the days continually lengthen until the days and nights again become equal.

104. Day and Night at the Equator. — In Chapter II. we learned that, if a man lived at the equator, the celestial poles would be on his horizon at the north and south points. The orange used in the last section is now to be placed in the water, with the knitting needle lying horizontal in the liquid surface. Then every circle marked on the orange, as previously described, will be half submerged, and the sun, wherever it may be on the sphere on any given day, will be above the horizon twelve hours, and below for the same number of hours.

105. Day and Night at the Poles. — The horizon of a man at the north pole would be parallel to the terrestrial equator. Both planes, when extended to the celestial sphere, would seem to cut it in the same circle, the celestial equator. The north celestial pole would be in the zenith. Therefore, if the sun were north of the equator it would be above the horizon, and if south of the equator it would be below the horizon. For the possible polar bears or seals in that locality there is continuous day from March to September, and night for the remaining months of the year. During much of the night there is a strong twilight, because the sun is not far below the horizon.

106. The Midnight Sun. — In Fig. 68, PP' is the earth's axis, and EQ is the equator. O is the situation of an observer who is in a high northern latitude. OA, drawn from the observer's position at O, parallel to the earth's axis, is directed toward the north celestial pole. OZ points toward the zenith, and NS represents the horizon. Suppose that the observer is in 70° north latitude, then the angle OCQ will be 70°, and OCP will be 20°. But OCP = AOZ. Since OA points to the pole and OZ to the zenith, and the angle AOZ is small, the pole is near the observer's zenith.

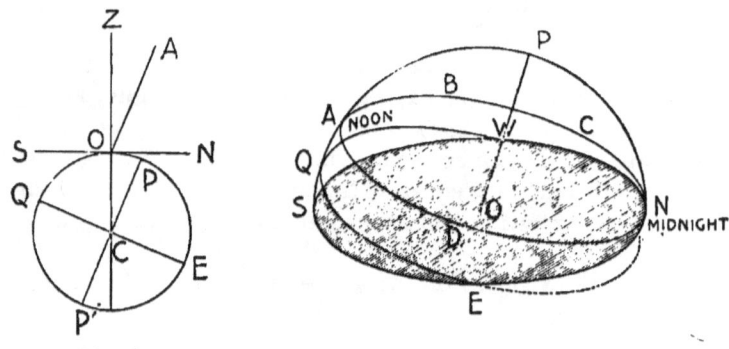

Fig. 68.

Fig. 69. — THE MIDNIGHT SUN.

The appearance of the celestial sphere, as seen by an observer at O is shown in Fig. 69. NESW is the horizon; EQW is half of the celestial equator; P is the north pole, and OP is the apparent rotation axis of the sphere. In June the sun is so far north of the equator that its daily path through the sky, ABCD, lies entirely above the horizon, so that it is visible even at midnight; this may be made very plain by using the orange of § 103.

107. The Seasons in Middle Latitudes. — We consider first a place at a north latitude of about 45°. The change of seasons is due principally to two causes. 1. The sun is above the horizon during more hours on a day in summer than on a day in winter. 2. The sun heats the earth's surface at any place the more powerfully the higher up it is in the sky. This is shown in Fig. 70, where a bundle of rays from the sun, coming nearly vertically downward, heats up a square foot, while an equal bundle, striking obliquely, spreads its heat out over a greater surface; consequently it heats each square inch of the surface less. The oblique rays also traverse a longer path in the atmosphere, and are more absorbed by it, before reaching the ground.

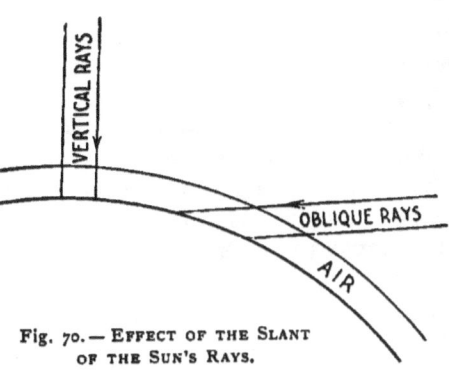

Fig. 70. — EFFECT OF THE SLANT OF THE SUN'S RAYS.

108. The Seasons at the Equator.—The change of seasons is much less marked than in middle latitudes: for the sun is above the horizon the same time (twelve hours) every day of the year, and its rays come down nearly vertically at noon, throughout the year.

THE PRECESSION OF THE EQUINOXES, AND THE CALENDAR.

109. Attraction of the Earth's Equatorial Ring.— Since the earth bulges at the equator, we may consider it as a true sphere, around the equatorial regions of which an extra ring of matter has been placed. This conception is rudely represented in Fig. 71. The attraction of the earth and moon upon this ring-like protuberance cause the precession, which we proceed to explain. Suppose the moon to lie in the direction of the arrows, and by its attractive force to be tugging away at the ring. Its pull on the half of the ring at the left (in the figure) of C tends to tip the earth, so that P will move

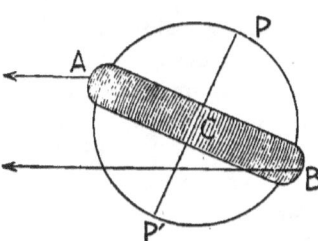

Fig. 71.— THE EARTH'S EQUATORIAL RING.

to the left. Its pull on the half of the ring at the right of C tends to tip the earth in the other direction, so that P will move to the right. But since the left half of the ring is nearer the moon than the right half, it is pulled the more strongly, and therefore P will move slowly toward the left. In consequence of this attraction, the earth will *tend* to turn slowly about an axis going through C, but perpendicular to the plane of the page on which Figure 71 is drawn. But meanwhile the earth is spinning with prodigious energy about the axis P P′, and the moon's attraction on the ring produces only a slight disturbance of this energetic rotation.

110. Illustration with a Top.—If a top, which is not spinning, be placed in a slanting position on a floor, the force of gravity pulling in the direction of the arrow in Fig. 72, will cause it to fall over; in falling it will move just as if it were turning about a line AB, drawn

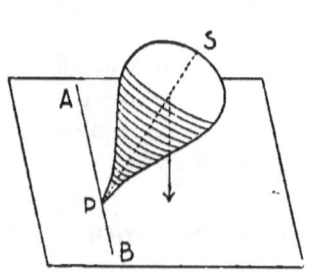 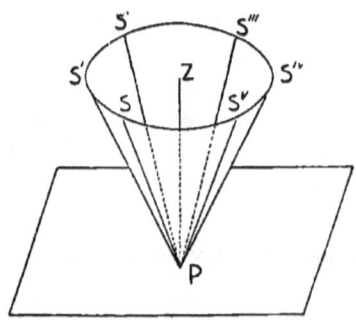

Fig. 72.—A Leaning Top.   Fig. 73.—Positions of the Axis of the Top.

on the floor, as an axis. When the top is spinning swiftly in an inclined position, it rotates about the axis PS, and gravity is at the same time trying to make it rotate about AB. Any one who has watched a top knows that, under these circumstances, the axis PS moves slowly around, taking the successive positions PS, PS′, PS″, etc., Fig. 73. PZ is perpendicular to the floor. The more swiftly the top spins, the slower is this motion of PS around PZ.

111. The Earth compared with the Top.—Both spin rapidly. The force of gravity attempts to tip the axis PS of the top. The pulls of the sun and moon on the equatorial protuberant ring of the earth tend to tip its axis, PP′. The axis of the top swings around PZ, a

THE EARTH. 77

perpendicular to the plane of the floor. The earth's axis swings around a perpendicular to the plane of the ecliptic, as shown in Fig. 74. CA is perpendicular to the ecliptic; PC, the earth's axis, takes successively the positions PC, P'C, P"C, etc., 25,800 years being required for a complete journey around the circle PP'P"P'''.

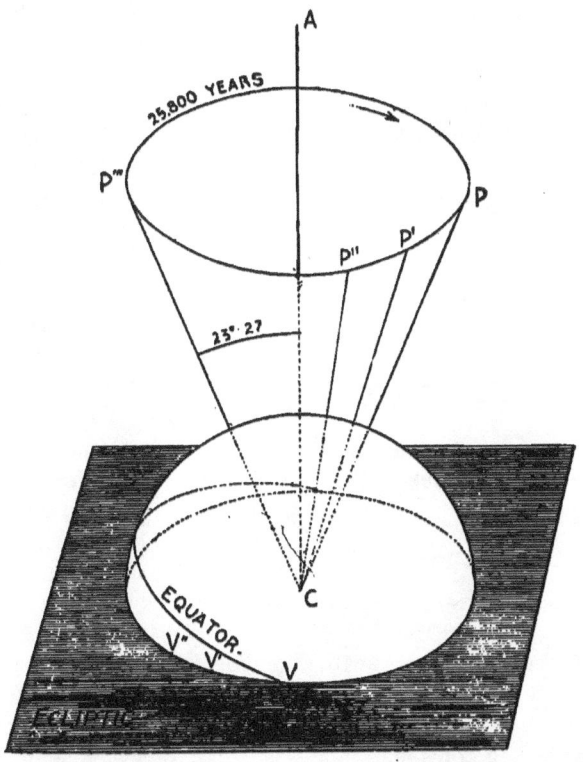

Fig. 74.—The Precessional Motion of the Earth's Equator.

The point where the equator cuts the plane of the ecliptic likewise moves around, taking the positions V' and V" successively. On extending the planes of the equator and the ecliptic to the sky, the point V, where the celestial equator and ecliptic intersect, becomes the vernal equinox.

Hence, *the vernal equinox moves slowly along the ecliptic, westward, taking 25,800 years for a complete revolution. The autumnal equinox does likewise.* This is the *precession of the equinoxes.*

This motion of the equinoxes may be made plain by using the orange described in § 103, and representing the ecliptic by a sheet of paper in which a circle a little larger than the orange has been cut. Then, by moving the orange in a way suggested by Fig. 74, the motion of the equinoxes becomes easily visible.

112. Some Effects of Precession. — On account of precession the north celestial pole, moving as described in the preceding section, comes near different stars as the centuries pass away. About twelve thousand years hence, the north pole will be so near the brilliant star Vega, in the constellation of the Lyre, that it will be called the pole star.

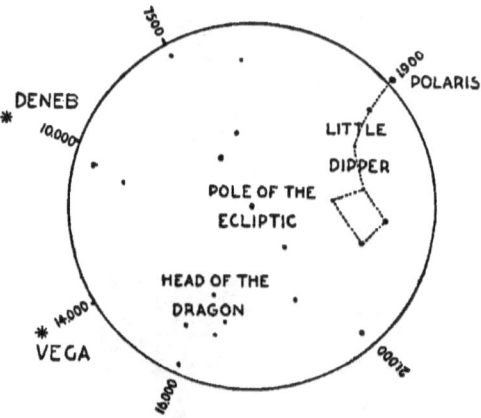

Fig. 75. — The Path of the North Celestial Pole among the Stars.

The path of the pole among the stars is shown in Fig. 75. Polaris will be only half a degree from the pole in the year 2000.

The non-coincidence of the sign Aries with the constellation Aries is due to precession. For the sign Aries begins at the vernal equinox, which, as we have seen, shifts slowly westward among the stars. It is now in the constellation Pisces. If Greenwich and its meridian moved perceptibly on the earth's surface, the longitudes of all other cities would be changed. If the earth's equator kept shifting its position on the surface, the latitudes of cities would keep changing. In the same way the shifting of the celestial equator and vernal equinox, by precession, causes changes in the right ascensions and declinations (which correspond to longitudes and latitudes of cities) of the stars.

Since the vernal equinox moves a little westward every year, the sun in his apparent annual march eastward reaches the vernal equinox sooner than if it were fixed. This makes the year twenty minutes shorter than it would be otherwise.

113. Different Kinds of Years.—The *sidereal* year is the time required for the earth to make a complete revolution about the sun. If the sun, as seen by us, is now in line with some fixed star, a sidereal year must elapse before it will get into line with the same star again. The length of the year is 365 d. 6 h. 9 m. 9 sec.

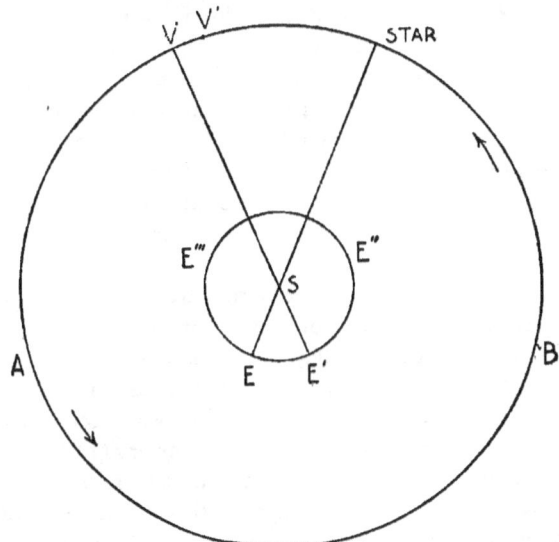

Fig. 76.—Different Kinds of Years.

The *tropical* year is the time which elapses between two successive passages of the sun through the vernal equinox. Suppose that the vernal equinox, when the sun appears to be in it, in March, 1900, is at V in Fig. 76. As the earth moves from E' to E", E''', etc., the sun appears to move from V through A to B, and so on. But meanwhile the vernal equinox, because of precession, has been moving westward a slight distance, so that the sun will meet it in March, 1901, at V'.

A *sidereal* year will be completed when the sun reaches ♈ again. A tropical year is therefore shorter than a sidereal year. Its length is 365 d. 5 h. 48 m. 46 sec.

114. The Julian Calendar. — Julius Cæsar found the Roman calendar in great confusion. It was decidedly complex, and the priests, whose duty it was to regulate the religious festivals in accordance with it, sometimes introduced alterations capriciously, to subserve their own interests. Matters had come to a pretty pass, in Roman eyes, when a festival of Bacchus must be celebrated while grapes were green. Acting upon the advice of Sosigenes, a noted Alexandrian astronomer, Cæsar ordained that three years out of every four consist of 365 days, the fourth being 366 days long. He did this because the year was known to be about $365\frac{1}{4}$ days in length. If the number of a year be divisible by 4 it is a leap year, and contains 366 days according to the Julian calendar. He also directed that the year begin on Jan. 1, instead of in March, as before.

This Julian calendar went into effect in 45 B. C., and is still employed in Russia. Dates reckoned according to it are now called "Old Style."

115. The Gregorian Calendar — The true tropical year being 365 d. 5 h. 48 m. 46 sec. in length, the Julian year of 365 d. 6 h. is too long by 11 m. 14 sec. This discrepancy amounts to over 3 days in 400 years. In 1582 Pope Gregory XIII. introduced a reform which dropped 3 days in every four centuries. This was accomplished by ordering that the year which rounds out each century (1300, 1800, etc.) should be a leap year *only when its date number is divisible by* 400. Thus 1600 was a leap year according to this calendar, while 1700 was not. Accordingly three out of every four century years are not reckoned as leap years, and 3 days are thus dropped from the Gregorian calendar which are retained in the Julian. At the time of the famous Council of Nice (A. D. 325) the sun was in the vernal equinox on March 21st; but in 1582 the same event happened on March 11th, because of the imperfection of the Julian calendar. The Pope therefore ordered that the 10 days lost should be made up by calling the day following October 4th October 15th.

The new calendar was at once adopted by all nations which recognized the Pope's authority. In England, the Old Style was used until 1752, when by act of Parliament the New Style was intro-

THE EARTH.

duced, in the face of opposition and rioting on the part of some of the people, who acted as though they believed that by the change of date from September 3d to September 14th, eleven days were to be stolen from them. It is now quite common in Russia to write a date according to both styles: thus, Mar. $^3/_{15}$.

ABERRATION AND REFRACTION.

116. Aberration of Light. — One who walks briskly along the street, when the rain is descending vertically, does not hold his umbrella straight up, but slants it forward. Were he to stand, holding a tube vertical, raindrops would pass through it without touching its sides. But if he walked briskly, still holding the tube upright, a drop of rain entering at the top would strike against the side. However, if he slanted the tube forward at the proper angle, drops would go through freely. While the drop was falling the distance AB in Fig. 77, the man would walk a distance equal to CB.

Fig. 77. — Illustration of Aberration.

In the same way, if the earth were still, and a man pointed a telescope *directly at* a fixed star, the rays from the star would come down through the telescope tube and emerge at the eyepiece. But since the earth moves, it is necessary to slant the telescope by a minute angle, so that rays from a star, after passing through the object-glass, may come out at the centre of the eyepiece. Now the star seems to us to lie in the direction in which the telescope points, and a ray which has the direction AB appears to have the direction AC. This apparent change in the direction of the ray is called its *aberration*. It is a quantity altogether too small to be detected with the naked eye.

117. Astronomical Refraction. — In § 28 we learned that a ray of light passing from one medium into another of different density is bent out of its course unless it strikes the surface of the new medium perpendicularly.

In Fig. 78 a ray coming from S through the earth's atmosphere is bent from its course. The air may be considered as made up of a large number of strata of different densities, the stratum nearest the surface of the earth having the greatest density, because it is compressed by the weight of all the air above it. Therefore the ray is being continually bent, coming through denser and denser strata, till, when it reaches the eye at E, it is coming in the direction S'E. The star appears to lie at S' instead of S. Since S' lies nearer the zenith than S, the effect of refraction is to make celestial objects appear nearer the zenith, or farther above the horizon, than they really are. When a star is in the zenith,

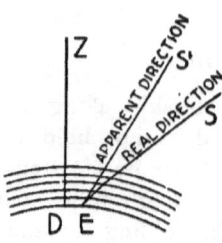

Fig. 78. — REFRACTION.

its rays strike perpendicularly on the atmosphere and suffer no deviation. The nearer the horizon a star is, the more its rays are refracted. The sun and the moon, when rising or setting, are elevated by refraction a little over half a degree, so that we see them when they are really just below the horizon.

118. Twilight. — In the air there are not only clouds, but also minute particles of dust and globules of water, which reflect the sunlight. For some time after the sun has set, he still shines on the clouds over our heads, and on the particles in the upper strata of the air. The light is reflected from these down to the ground, and thus produces twilight. When the sun gets about 18° below the horizon, his rays are shot above the clouds and other reflecting objects, so that they are no longer reflected to us, and twilight ceases. In England and other countries of like northern latitude, twilight lasts all night in midsummer, because the sun is less than 18° below the horizon, even at midnight.

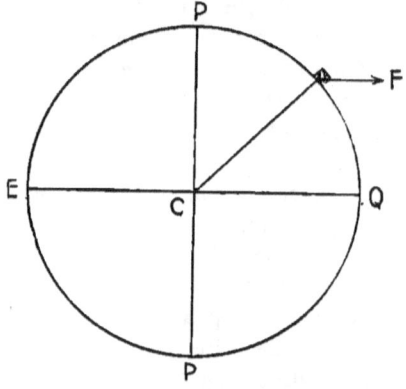

Fig. 79. — (See Exercise 1.)

EXERCISES.

119. 1. Suppose the earth to be a perfect and smooth sphere and a body to be placed on it, as shown in Fig. 79; gravity would pull it toward the centre, while it would tend to fly off in the direction of the arrow F, because of the earth's rotation.

(*a*) As a result of this state of affairs, would the body slide toward the equator?

(*b*) If the earth were a perfect sphere, would its rotation cause the water of the ocean to move toward the equator?

(*c*) Because of the bulge of the earth, is the surface of the water at the mouth of the Mississippi River nearer the earth's centre than at St. Paul, or farther from it?

(*d*) If the earth did not rotate, which way would gravity make the river flow?

(*e*) Why does the river run south?

(*f*) Why does not the water of the ocean leave the poles and rush to the equator?

(*g*) If the earth were composed entirely of water, and did not rotate, what would be its form?

2. If the earth were a sphere the diameter of which was 7,920 miles, what would its circumference be according to § 92? Ans. 24,881.472 miles.

3. In Fig. 60, if the sun be at F, what points are perihelion and aphelion?

4. In Fig. 60, the sun being at F, prove that the semi-major axis (AC) is half the sum of the greatest and least distances (A'F and AF) of the earth from the sun.

5. Why does the earth move most rapidly in its orbit when at perihelion?

6. Cut two equal circles out of stiff paper; in each cut a narrow slit from a point on the circumference to the centre. Then fit the circles together in such a way that they will represent the relative positions of the planes of the equator and ecliptic.

7. Let the surface of a small round body, like an apple or orange, represent the celestial sphere. On it mark in their proper positions the north and south celestial poles, the equator, the ecliptic, the

equinoxes, and the solstices. Also mark the circle in which the north celestial pole makes its precessional journey of 25,800 years. Does the south celestial pole describe a similar circle on the sphere?

8. The sun, when at C or D in Fig. 63, ceases to recede from the equator and begins to approach it. Show that this fact harmonizes with the derivation of the word " solstice."

9. Why is that equinox in which the sun is on March 20th called the vernal equinox?

10. If the earth's axis lay in the plane of the ecliptic, and always pointed directly at the sun, the north pole being toward the sun, in what portion of the earth would the sun never be visible?

11. If the earth's axis lay in the plane of the ecliptic, but always pointed toward one particular fixed star as the earth performed its yearly journey around the sun, in what part of the earth would the sun never be seen?

12. If the earth's axis were perpendicular to the plane of the ecliptic, and the earth were rotating on its axis and revolving about the sun as fast as at present, would *all* of that part of the earth which is in darkness at any instant be in the light twelve hours thereafter?

13. If the earth's axis made an angle of 70° with the plane of the ecliptic, and the earth rotated as at present, but did *not* revolve around the sun, is there any part of the earth in which there would be no night?

14. At the moment when the sun lies in the plane of the equator, about March 20th or September 22d, does its pull on the equatorial protuberance of the earth tend to tip the earth's axis?

15. When a common almanac makes the statement, "The sun enters Aries," does it refer to the sign or to the constellation?

16. From an almanac which gives the times of rising and setting of the sun, find out the number of hours of daylight on the longest day of the year, and also on the shortest, at the place for which the almanac is computed.

17. When it is summer in the northern hemisphere, what is the season in the southern hemisphere?

18. At the place where you live does the sun rise very near the east point of the horizon in midsummer (June 20th)? Answer the same question for Christmas time.

19. In each of the four figures here given, the earth is represented as illuminated by the sun at a certain time of the year. Determine the time of year which corresponds to each figure.

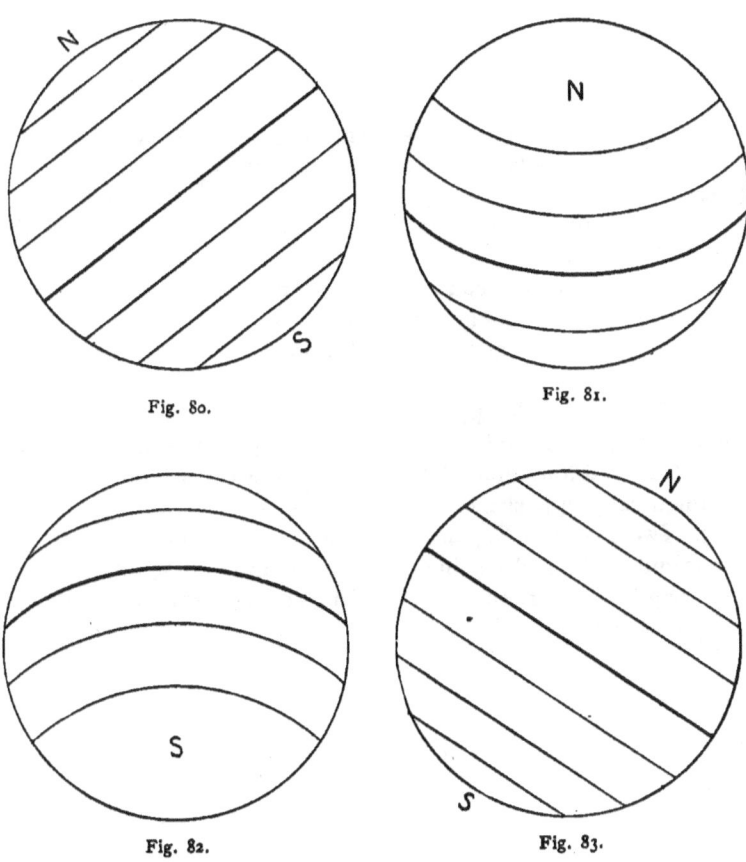

Fig. 80.   Fig. 81.

Fig. 82.   Fig. 83.

20. If a man were perched on the top of a balloon, which was rising straight up through a shower of rain falling vertically, in what position would he have to hold the glass tube of § 116 so that the raindrops would go straight through it, without touching the sides? If the earth be moving directly toward a certain star, would aberra-

tion cause a telescope pointed at a star to deviate a trifle from the real direction in which the star lay?

21. (*a*) Does refraction make sunrise come earlier than it otherwise would, or later?

(*b*) What is its effect on the time of sunset?

(*c*) Does it lengthen the number of hours of daylight, or shorten them?

22. (*a*) When the moon is seen near the horizon, which edge (or limb, as it is called) is lifted more by refraction, the upper or lower?

(*b*) What effect does this have on the apparent shape of the moon?

(*c*) Does *refraction* cause the moon to look larger, when near the horizon, than when high in the heavens?

23. At your home does twilight last longer in midsummer, or in midwinter?

24. Denver is in longitude 105° W. of Greenwich, and in north latitude 39° 40'. Considering the earth as a perfect sphere, what are the latitude and longitude of the point on the earth's surface which is diametrically opposite Denver?

25. Two places in England have the same latitude, and differ 1° in longitude. Two places in Ohio differ 1° in latitude, but have the same longitude. Are the places in England as many miles apart as those in Ohio?

CHAPTER VI.

CELESTIAL MEASUREMENTS.

"Snatch me to heaven; thy rolling wonders there,
World beyond world, in infinite extent,
Profusely scattered o'er the blue immense,
Show me : their motions, periods, and their laws,
Give me to scan."
                                        THOMSON.

120. Position of Points on a Sphere. — In describing the positions of points on the surface of a sphere, a fundamental circle is first assumed, bisecting the sphere. In Fig. 84, ABCD is the fundamental circle. *Great circles* are those whose planes pass through the centre of the sphere. All others drawn on the spherical surface are *small circles*. GPH is a small circle. *Secondary circles* are great circles which are perpendicular to the fundamental circle. All secondaries pass through two points called the *poles* of the fundamental circle. E and F are the poles of ABCD; AECF and EBFD are secondaries.

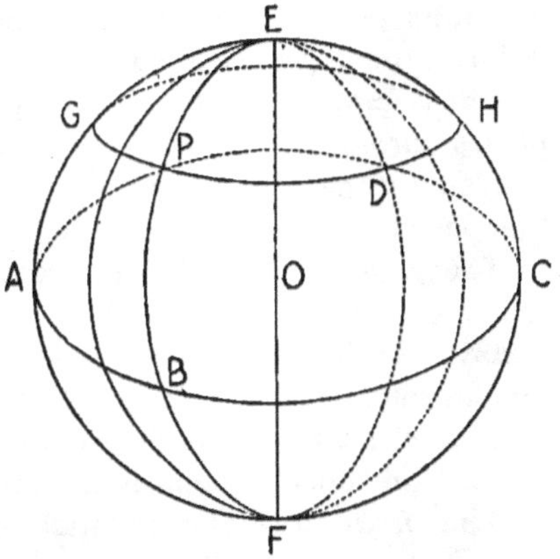

The *fundamental point* is a point of reference, which lies on the fundamental circle. In the figure, A is chosen as the fundamental point.

Fig. 84. — CIRCLES OF REFERENCE.

In finding the position of a point on a sphere, we first draw a secondary through the point. If P is the point, EPBFD is the secondary drawn. We then find out two things: first, how many degrees (measured on the secondary) the point is above or below the fundamental circle, that is, the length of PB; second, the number of degrees in that arc (AB) of the fundamental circle which lies between the fundamental point (A) and the secondary (EPBFD). This system has already been employed in defining the latitude and longitude of a place on the earth (§ 93).

121. The Horizon System. — In this system the horizon is the fundamental circle. As shown in § 21, the *horizon* of any place is the circle in which the celestial sphere is cut by a plane perpendicular to a plumb-line suspended at the place. The secondaries, being perpendicular to the horizon, are called *vertical circles*. All vertical circles pass through the *zenith* and *nadir* (§§ 22, 23).

The south point of the horizon is usually taken as the fundamental point.

The *altitude* of a celestial object is the portion of its vertical circle lying between it and the horizon.

Its *azimuth* is the arc of the horizon, measured from the south point around towards the west, to its vertical circle.

The *zenith distance* of a celestial object is the portion of its vertical circle lying between it and the zenith. In Fig. 84 the altitude of P is PB, its zenith distance is EP, and its azimuth (if A be the south point of the horizon) is ADCB.

The *celestial meridian* of any place is that vertical circle which passes through the north and south points of the horizon. It is divided by the poles into two equal *branches*; the *upper branch* is that in which the zenith lies.

The *prime vertical* is that vertical circle which passes through the east and west points of the horizon.

122. The Equator System. — Here the celestial equator is the fundamental circle. The secondaries are called *hour circles*; all hour circles pass through the celestial poles.

The fundamental point is the vernal equinox.

The *declination* of a celestial object is the portion of its hour circle between it and the celestial equator. When a star is north of the equator, it is in north declination; when south, it is in south declination. North declinations are accounted positive; south, negative.

The *right ascension* of a celestial object is the arc of the celestial equator, measured *eastward* from the vernal equinox to the hour circle on which the star lies.

CELESTIAL MEASUREMENTS. 89

Right ascension may be measured in degrees, but is usually reckoned in hours, like longitude, 15° being equivalent to one hour. The right ascensions and declinations of the *fixed stars* change very little from year to year.

The *north polar distance* of a celestial object is the portion of its hour circle lying between it and the north celestial pole.

Instead of the vernal equinox, another fundamental point is frequently taken, viz. the point where the celestial meridian of the place of observation cuts the celestial equator. Then the *hour angle* of a celestial object is the arc of the equator embraced between the meridian and the hour circle of the object. Hour angles are reckoned either east or west of the meridian, east hour angles being accounted negative: they are usually reckoned in hours.

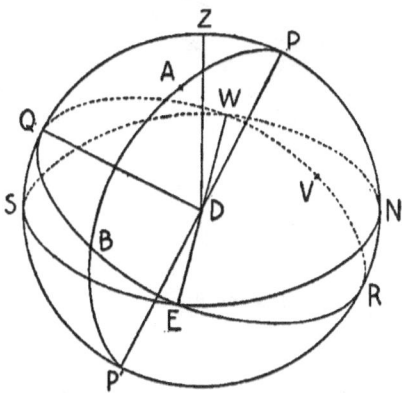

Fig. 85. — THE EQUATOR, HORIZON, MERIDIAN, ETC.

In Fig. 85, NESW is the horizon, EQWR the celestial equator, PABP' half of the hour circle of the star A, and V the vernal equinox. AB is the declination of A, VWQB its right ascension, and QB its east hour angle. The hour angle of W, the west point of the horizon, is QW, which equals +6 h.: that of the east point E is QE, which equals −6 h.

123. Parallax. — The word *parallax* is a broad term. In general, it means the difference in direction of an object when viewed from two different standpoints: it is the angle formed by two lines drawn from the object to the two standpoints respectively. Thus, the parallax of the moon, as seen from Boston and the Cape of Good Hope, is the angle between lines drawn from the moon's centre to these places.

Usually the earth's centre is regarded as one of the standpoints: then the parallax of Venus, for example, as seen from Denver at any instant, is the angle made at Venus by two lines drawn from its centre to Denver and the earth's centre respectively. It is the angle DVC in Fig. 86. If the object is in the plane of the horizon of the place of observation, its parallax is called the *horizontal parallax*. DV'C is the horizontal parallax of an object at V'. If we consider the earth as a perfect sphere, the angle V'DC is a right angle. We know the length of DC, the earth's radius. When the value of the angle V' is known, it is easy to compute the distance CV' by elementary trigonometry.

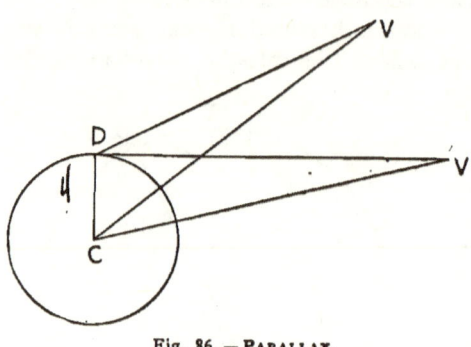

Fig. 86. — PARALLAX.

If D be a point on the earth's equator, CV'D is the *equatorial horizontal parallax* of an object situated at V'.

The parallaxes of the sun, moon, and planets are large enough to be measurable; but the fixed stars are so distant that the angle CV'D is too small to be measured. In getting the parallax of a fixed star, the two lines are drawn from the star to the earth and sun respectively. Stellar parallax is discussed in § 350.

TIME.

124. The Year. — The two principal kinds of years have been explained already in § 113. The principles of the Julian and Gregorian calendars have been set forth in §§ 114 and 115.

125. Solar Days. — There are two kinds of solar days, *apparent solar* and *mean solar*. An *apparent solar* day is the interval of time which elapses between two successive passages of the sun across the upper branch of the celestial meridian of any place. The earth rotates on its axis at a uniform rate, so that, if the sun were fixed on the celestial sphere, all solar days would be of equal length. But the sun appears to creep slowly eastward on the sphere, on account of the yearly revolution of the earth, and *at an irregular rate*, creeping more on some days than others, as will be explained in the next section. Hence apparent solar days vary in length, the greatest variation being nearly a minute.

The sun being so irregular a timekeeper, astronomers have devised a fictitious sun, called the *mean sun*, which moves in the equator at a *uniform rate*, completing its apparent journey around the celestial sphere in a year. The mean sun crosses the meridian sometimes a few minutes in advance of the true sun, at other times a few minutes behind it. The greatest difference is sixteen minutes. A *mean solar* day is the interval between two successive passages of the mean sun over the upper branch of the celestial meridian of any place.

All ordinary clocks and watches are regulated by mean solar time.

126. Causes of the Unequal Lengths of Apparent Solar Days. — There are two principal causes: —

I. The earth in travelling around the sun does not move at a uniform speed. When at perihelion it moves most swiftly; at aphelion, with the least velocity. Since the apparent motion of the sun eastward is due to the earth's revolution about it, the distance over which the sun creeps each day on the sphere varies, being greatest when the earth's motion is most rapid.

II. But even if the sun moved at a uniform rate in the ecliptic, apparent solar days would still vary in length. Suppose that the *mean* and *true* suns are together at the vernal equinox, V, in Fig. 87. After one fourth of a year has elapsed, each sun, if moving uniformly, will have

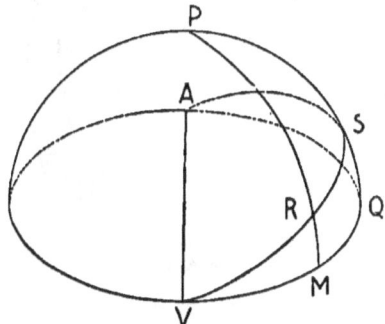

Fig. 87. — Unequal Lengths of Apparent Solar Days.

described an arc of 90°; the true sun will then be at S, the summer solstice, and the mean sun at Q, both lying on the same hour circle, PSQ.

Let M be the middle point of VQ, and draw the hour circle PM cutting the ecliptic at R. One easily sees that the arc VR is longer than VM, so that, when the mean sun arrived at M, the true sun had

92   DESCRIPTIVE ASTRONOMY.

not reached R. Hence the mean sun and the true sun, though together on the same hour circle at the beginning and at the end of their three months' race, did *not keep on the same hour circle during the race.* Now any celestial objects which are on the same hour circle cross the meridian at the same time. Hence, while the mean sun by its successive passages across any given meridian was marking off days of uniform length, those marked off by the true sun were not of uniform length.

127. Another Explanation. — On a sphere, (the larger the better,) draw the ecliptic and equator. Mark the summer solstice, and put another mark, a quarter of an inch away, on the ecliptic. Draw an hour circle through each. Place a mark on the ecliptic a quarter of an inch from the vernal equinox and draw hour circles through these two points. One sees at once that the first pair of hour circles make a larger angle with each other than the second pair. The quarter of an inch represents the amount that the sun creeps on the ecliptic in a day.

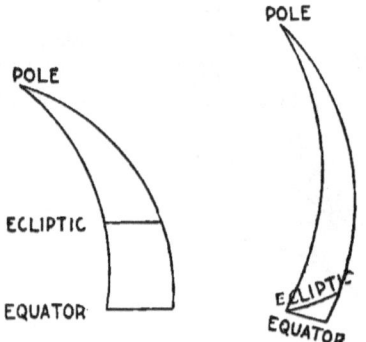

Fig. 88.—Variable Motion in Hour Angle.

At the time of the vernal equinox an apparent solar day would be the time of a rotation of the earth plus the time required for it to turn through the angle between the first pair of hour circles.

At the time of the summer solstice an apparent solar day would be the time of a rotation of the earth plus the time required for it to turn through the angle between the second pair of hour circles. Since the second angle is larger than the first, the two days would be of unequal length. Fig. 88 exhibits the arcs drawn as directed.

128. A Sidereal Day. — A sidereal day is the interval between two successive passages of the vernal equinox over the upper branch of the celestial meridian of any place. Since the apparent daily rotation of the celestial sphere is caused by the real rotation of the earth, sidereal days are of uniform length. The length of this day might be changed by various causes. A gradual shrinkage of the earth in cooling would make it rotate faster: the friction caused by the tidal movement of the water of the ocean tends to impede the rotation. However, no change in the length of a day has ever been detected by observations. It is considered certain that it has not changed a hundredth of a second in the past thirty centuries.

129. Civil Day and Astronomical Day. — Each of these days consists of 24 hours of mean solar time. The civil day, employed for the ordinary purposes of life, begins at midnight. The astronomical day begins 12 hours later than the civil day, at noon.

Thus, Sept. 3, 9 P. M. of civil time is equivalent to Sept. 3, 9 h. by astronomical time; but Sept. 3, 9 A. M. of civil time is Sept. 2, 21 h. by astronomical time. An astronomer when observing at night is saved the trouble of changing the date in his record-book when midnight comes. A movement is on foot to discontinue the use of the astronomical day at the end of the nineteenth century.

130. Mean Solar and Sidereal Time. — An astronomical clock keeping mean solar time at Denver, for instance, reads 0 h. 0 m. 0 sec., when the *mean sun* is on the upper branch of the meridian of Denver, at noon. Its face is graduated from 0 h. to 23 h., and the hour hand sweeps around the dial once in a mean solar day. Such a clock is said to keep "local" mean time.

A sidereal clock, on the other hand, reads 0 h. 0 m. 0 sec., when the vernal equinox is on the upper branch of the meridian. When it reads 10 h. 30 m. 0 sec., it shows that the vernal equinox crossed the meridian $10\frac{1}{2}$ sidereal hours ago. A reading 23 h. 0 m. 0 sec. indicates that the vernal equinox crossed the upper branch of the meridian 23 sidereal hours ago, and will cross again in an hour.

If the mean sun and the vernal equinox were together on the celestial meridian of a given place, both the sidereal and the mean time clock at that place should indicate 0 h. 0 m. 0 sec. After a lapse of 24 sidereal hours, the vernal equinox would be on the meridian again; but the mean sun, on account of its eastward motion on the sphere, would be east of the vernal equinox, and would cross the meridian a little while after it. A mean solar day is therefore longer than a sidereal day. As the mean sun travels entirely around the sphere in a year, in a day it moves about $\frac{1}{365}$ of the circumference of the sphere, making the mean solar day $\frac{24}{365}$ h., or nearly four minutes, longer than the sidereal day.

DESCRIPTIVE ASTRONOMY.

131. Right Ascension vs. Sidereal Time. — By the definition of right ascension (§ 122), we see that a star whose right ascension is 4 h. will cross the meridian of any place 4 h. after the vernal equinox has crossed the same meridian. But the sidereal clock will read 4 h. We therefore have the following principle.

The right ascension of any star is equal to the sidereal time at any place at the instant when the star is on the meridian of that place.

Thus when a star whose right ascension is exactly 16 h. is on the meridian of the U. S. Naval Observatory at Washington, the Washington sidereal clock should read 16 h. 0 m. 0 sec.

When the sidereal time is 13 h., the star mentioned has an east hour angle of 3 h., because 3 h. must elapse before it will reach the meridian. If the sidereal time be 18 h., the star crossed the meridian two hours before, and hence has a west hour angle of 2 h.

132. Relation between Longitude and Time. — If the longitude of a place is one hour west of Greenwich, the mean sun arrives at its meridian one hour after it has crossed the Greenwich meridian; hence at noontime at the place in question it is 1 P. M. at Greenwich. When a city is two hours east of Greenwich, the sun crosses its meridian two hours before it reaches the meridian of Greenwich; when it is 10 A. M. at Greenwich, it is noon at the city.

133. Where the Date Changes. — A place whose longitude is 180°, or 12 h. west of Greenwich, is also 12 h. east of Greenwich. Reckoning it as 12 h. west of Greenwich, its time will be 12 h. less than the Greenwich time; so that when it is 11 A. M. on July 4 at Greenwich, it will be 11 P. M. on July 3 at this place. But if we say that the place is 12 h. east of Greenwich, its time will be 12 h. more than the Greenwich time at the same instant, making 11 P. M. of July 4. Thus there is a discrepancy of one day, according as we count east or west from Greenwich. Mariners when crossing the 180th meridian change the date; in going west, an entry in the log-book just before crossing the line might be dated Wednesday, Sept. 12, 3 P. M. An entry made an hour afterward, if the ship had crossed the line meanwhile, would be dated Thursday, Sept. 13, 4 P. M. Similarly, in crossing from the west, Tuesday, October 9, would be changed to Monday, October 8.

134. Standard Time. — There is now in use throughout North America a system of standard time, which is a great boon to the business world. Five standard meridians have been adopted, west of Greenwich 4, 5, 6, 7, and 8 hours respectively. A city generally adopts the time of that standard meridian to which it is nearest. The standard times are called respectively Colonial, Eastern, Central, Mountain, and Pacific. In a few large cities there is still confusion. At Pittsburg both Eastern and Central times are in use. It would be well if all towns in the same State kept the same time. Several European countries have adopted standard times based upon the meridian of Greenwich.

135. Clocks and Watches. — Accurate time obtained from various astronomical observatories (chiefly from Washington) is telegraphed daily all over the United States. The clocks in the observatories are regulated with the greatest care, so that they are rarely over a second in error. The pendulum jar of the clock shown in Fig. 89 is nearly filled with mercury. In warm weather the pendulum rod lengthens because of the heat; this lengthening would make the clock go slow, but the mercury expanding rises in the jar, and thus counteracts the elongation of the rod. In cold weather there is a similar compensation: such a clock is said to be *compensated for temperature*.

Good watches should be wound regularly and kept in the same position by day and by night. When the second hand is at sixty, the minute hand should be over some minute mark. A sudden change of rate is not a sure sign that the regulator needs to be moved. The best watches exhibit anomalous variations at times, and frequently right themselves without being regulated anew.

Fig. 89.— A Standard Clock.

136. The Meridian Circle. — The telescope of this instrument is put in the middle of, and at right angles to, an axis which turns in

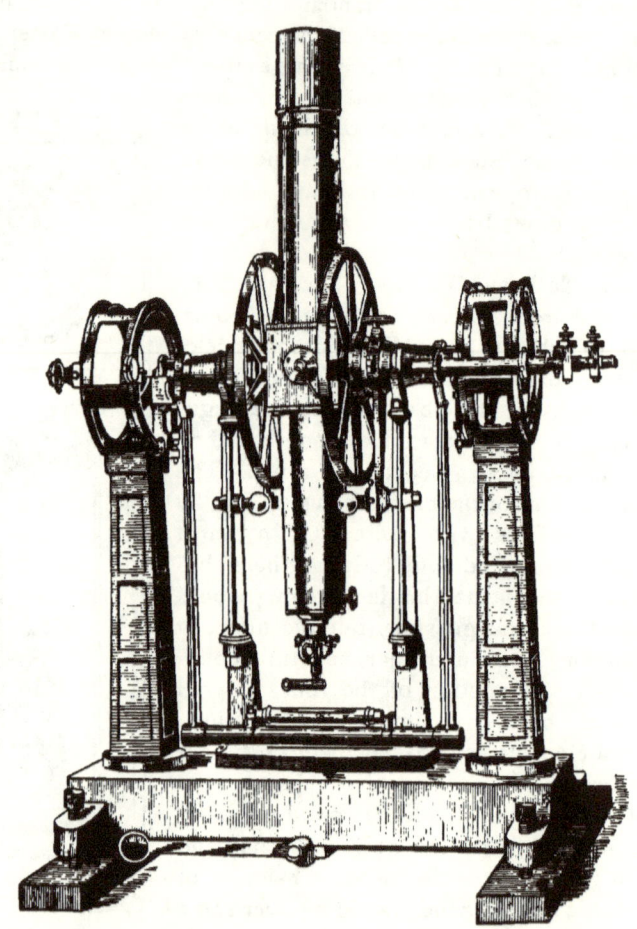

Fig. 90.—A Portable Meridian Circle.

CELESTIAL MEASUREMENTS. 97

a bearing at each end as shown in Fig. 90. The axis is horizontal, and points due east and west. Upon the axis are mounted a couple of graduated circles, which are used for finding the altitude of stars when they cross the meridian. At the focus of the object-glass near the eye-end of the telescope is the "reticle," which, as seen through the eyepiece, presents the appearance shown in Fig. 91. It is usually made of spider-webs, or of fine lines ruled on a thin piece of glass. The "wire" AB is parallel to the axis of the instrument.

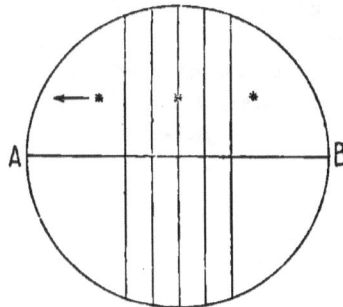

Fig. 91.— A Reticle.

137. A Star passes the Meridian. — If the telescope be pointed in the direction of a star just before it passes the meridian, it will be seen to move across the field of view in a path parallel to AB, crossing each of the five parallel wires. The reason for this is shown in Fig. 92. A line drawn from the star at S through the centre of the object-glass meets the star's image at I. As the star moves to S' and S'' its image moves to I' and I''. Therefore, the observer sees the star's image crossing the wires of the reticle.

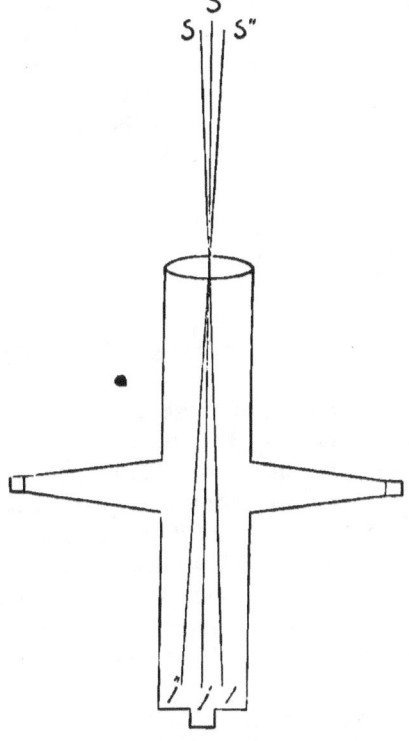

Fig. 92.—Motion of a Star's Image.

If S'I' is perpendicular to the rotation axis, it lies in the plane of the meridian, for the meridian plane is perpendicular to a horizontal east and west line. Therefore both the star S' and its image I' lie in the plane of the meridian. The reticle is so placed that the star's image when at I' lies on the middle wire in Fig. 91.

138. Determination of Clock Error. — In the Nautical Almanac,[1] which is issued yearly, is to be found an extensive list of bright stars, the right ascensions of which are given. The right ascension of any star, as we have learned, equals the sidereal time when that star crosses the observer's meridian. The astronomer who wishes to find the error of his sidereal clock selects from the list a star, Sirius, for example, and points the telescope of the meridian circle in such a direction that Sirius when it crosses the meridian will pass through the field of view. As it crosses each wire of the reticle he notes the reading of the clock as below: —

	h.	m.	sec.
	6	39	46.3
		39	56.2
		40	11.4
		40	26.6
		40	36.6
Average,	6	40	11.42

The average of these readings is a pretty accurate value of the clock reading when the star crossed the middle wire, which represents the meridian. Turning to the almanac, he finds that on the date of observation the right ascension of Sirius was 6 h. 40 m. 26.94 sec. Hence, if the instrument was in perfect adjustment, the error of the clock was 15.52 sec. Was the clock fast or slow?

To attain greater accuracy, the astronomer observes a number of stars. Four stars, after allowance had been made for errors in the position of the meridian circle, might give him for the clock error respectively 15.52 sec., 15.46 sec., 15.53 sec., and 15.45 sec. The average of these is 15.49 sec.

By comparing observations made on two dates, the amount that a clock gains or loses in a day can be found. This amount is the

[1] A copy of this work, if not obtained through a Senator or Representative, may be had by sending one dollar to the Nautical Almanac office, Washington, D. C. The British, German, French, and some other nations publish such almanacs.

CELESTIAL MEASUREMENTS.   99

daily rate. Sidereal time is easily reduced to mean time by tables given in the Nautical Almanac.

139. The Chronograph. — A chronograph is employed to facilitate noting the time when any phenomenon occurs. Its most common use is to record the reading of a timepiece at the instant when an astronomer sees a star cross a wire in the reticle of his meridian circle.

Fig. 93. — A Chronograph.

A sheet of paper is wrapped around the barrel, which is rotated once a minute by the mechanism, driven by a weight not shown in the figure. If this were the only motion, the pen which rests on the barrel would draw a circle around the cylinder in a minute, and repeat the same circle the next minute, and so on, as long as the mechanism ran. But the carriage which holds the pen is mounted on a long screw, shown in front of the barrel: the screw rotates once a minute, and continually moves the pen carriage, which is set near one end of the barrel at starting, toward the other end of the barrel. Consequently the pen, instead of making a single circle over and over, makes a long spiral line, like a screw thread, running from one end of the barrel to the other.

100   DESCRIPTIVE ASTRONOMY.

140. Records of a Clock and Key. — By suitable electrical connections, which cannot well be explained here, a clock causes the pen to give a quick vibration each second, so that a series of notches are made in the line, as shown in Fig. 94. No notch is made at the

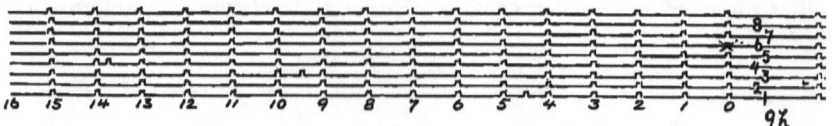

Fig. 94. — A Chronographic Record.

fifty-ninth second of each minute: the first notch thereafter marks the beginning of a new minute. The observer notes the time which the clock read when some particular notch was made, and marks that notch. In Fig. 94 the notch for 9 h. 6 m. 0 sec. was thus marked: from this record he can tell the time when any other notch was made by the clock.

The astronomer, when observing, has at his side a telegraph key, connected with the chronograph: when he wishes to note the time, he presses the key quickly, and the pen makes a notch at that instant. Fig. 94 shows some records made between 9 h. 1 m. and 9 h. 6 m., on a small portion of a sheet. In the place where the fifty-ninth second of each minute is omitted, the observer has written on the lines the numbers of the successive minutes. The numbers of the seconds of each minute are written along one of the lines. There are three extra marks, made when the observer pressed his key. One of the marks was made at 9 h. 1 m. 4.5 sec., another at 9 h. 3 m. 9.4 sec., and the third at 9 h. 4 m. 13.8 sec.

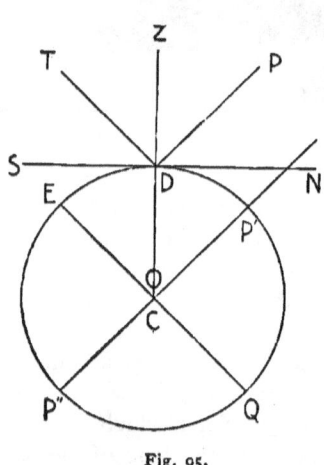

Fig. 95.

141. Determination of Latitude. — Let D in Fig. 95 be a point on the earth's surface, NS its horizon, P'P'' the earth's axis, and EQ the equator. ZDO is perpendicular to NS. PD is parallel to P'P", and therefore points to the north pole of the celestial sphere. DT is parallel to EQ. PDT is a right angle. By definition (§ 94) the latitude of D is DOE. This equals $ZDT = 90° - ZDP = PDN$, which by definition (§ 121) equals the altitude of the celestial pole. Hence the *latitude of the place of observation equals the altitude of the pole.* Though an astronomer cannot see the north celestial pole, he can find its altitude by observing the Pole Star when it is on the meridian. In Fig. 96, D is the place of observation, NS the horizon, NZS the meridian, P the north celestial pole, P' and P" the two positions of the Pole Star when it crosses the meridian. By

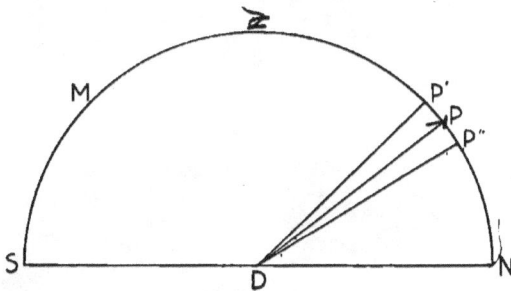

Fig. 96. — LATITUDE FOUND BY OBSERVATION OF POLARIS.

means of the divided circle on the axis of the meridian circle, the astronomer measures the angle P'DN, the altitude of the Pole Star when it is on the meridian above the pole. Twelve hours later he measures P"DN.

$$P'DN = PDN + PDP'$$
$$P''DN = PDN - PDP''$$
$$P'DN + P''DN = 2\ PDN + PDP' - PDP''.$$

But $\qquad PDP' = PDP''.$

Therefore $\qquad P'DN + P''DN = 2\ PDN$
$\qquad\qquad PDN = \tfrac{1}{2}\ (P'DN + P''DN).$
$\qquad\qquad$ PDN is the latitude required.

The method by which the angles P'DN and P"DN are measured will be understood readily by examining an engineer's transit, such as is shown in Fig. 97.

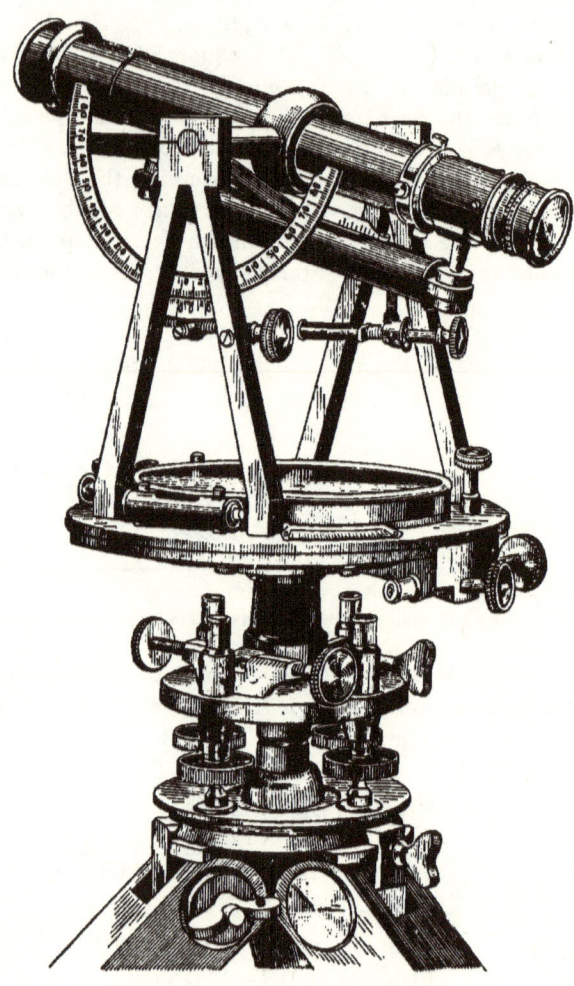

Fig. 97.—An Engineer's Transit.

142. Determination of Longitude. — We have seen (§ 132) that the difference in longitude between two places, such as Washington and Chicago, is equal to the difference at any instant between the readings of two clocks, one of which keeps correct Washington time, while the other keeps Chicago time. If a chronometer keeping Washington time be carried to Chicago and compared with the Chicago clock, the difference between their readings, if both are

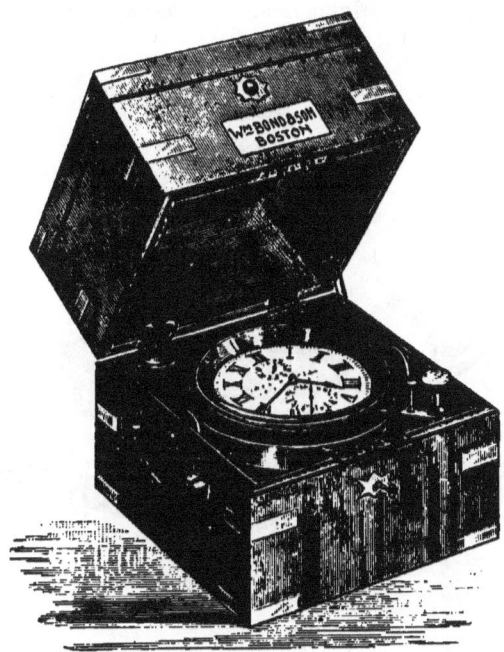

Fig. 98. — A Chronometer.

correct, is the difference of longitude sought. In practice several chronometers are used, the errors of which — for no chronometer or clock runs exactly right — are very carefully determined by observations of the stars. The electric telegraph, however, furnishes a much more accurate method. By quite simple mechanism the Washington clock, as it ticks, makes a telegraphic sounder at Chicago click, so that an astronomer at Chicago can compare the telegraphic beats of the Washington clock with his own. The times at which the signals are to be sent are agreed upon beforehand.

143. The Position of a Ship. — A mariner usually finds the latitude and longitude of his ship by observations of the sun made with a sextant, a little instrument easily held in the hand. A chronometer keeping some standard time, as that of Greenwich, is also necessary. In Fig. 96, let M represent the sun when on the meridian. The mariner measures its altitude, MS, with the

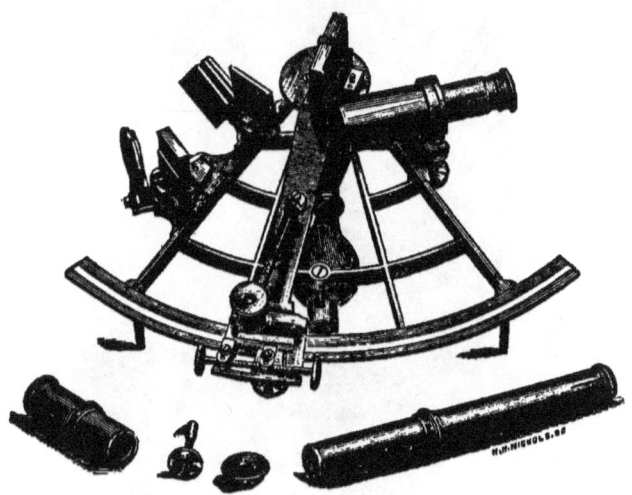

Fig. 99. — A Sextant.

sextant. From the almanac he finds PM, the distance of the sun from the pole. The sum of these gives PMS, which, subtracted from 180°, leaves PM, the latitude desired.

To find the longitude, the altitude of the sun is measured about the middle of the forenoon or afternoon, and the reading of the chronometer, keeping Greenwich time, is noted at the same time. Suppose that the measured altitude was 62° 15′ 20.″ By means of astronomical tables the mariner computes the time at which the sun had that altitude; it might have been 3 h. 16 m. 27 sec. If the Greenwich time, found from the chronometer,[1] was 4 h. 29 m. 48 sec., the ship was evidently in longitude 1 h. 13 m. 21 sec. west of Greenwich.

EXERCISES.

144. 1. Is the arctic circle on the earth a great circle or a small circle?

2. Consider the earth as a perfect sphere, and the equator as the fundamental circle; what is the name applied in geography to the secondaries?

3. Consider the earth as a perfect sphere. In estimating the longitudes of points from Greenwich, what point is taken as the fundamental point?

4. (*a*) When the sun is just rising, what is its altitude?

(*b*) When a star is in the zenith, what is its altitude?

5. (*a*) What is the azimuth of a point on the prime vertical, the point being west of the zenith?

(*b*) What is the azimuth of the north celestial pole?

(*c*) What is the azimuth of the east point of the horizon?

6. (*a*) Does the celestial meridian of any place pass through the nadir?

(*b*) Do the celestial poles lie on this meridian?

(*c*) Is there any point on the earth where the meridian coincides with the celestial equator?

(*d*) Does your celestial meridian cut the celestial equator?

(*e*) If so, can you point your finger toward a point of intersection?

(*f*) Where does the prime vertical cut the meridian?

(*g*) What position has the plane of the prime vertical with reference to that of the meridian?

7. (*a*) The declination of a star is $+20°$; what is its north polar distance?

---

[1] The reading of the chronometer face is not the true Greenwich time. Before leaving port the error of the chronometer (usually a few seconds) and the daily rate (§ 138) were found by astronomical observations. From these the error of the chronometer at any time during the voyage can be computed, and allowance made for it to get the true Greenwich time. While chronometers do not keep exactly the same rate from week to week, they run closely enough for the practical purposes of navigation.

(b) What is the north polar distance of a star whose declination is $-30°\ 43'$?

(c) What is the right ascension of the autumnal equinox?

(d) What is the sun's right ascension, when it is in the summer solstice?

(e) What is its right ascension when in the winter solstice?

(f) If the vernal equinox be on the meridian of Chicago, what is the right ascension of a star which is rising at that instant at the east point of the Chicago horizon?

(g) At the same instant as above a star is setting at the west point of the horizon; what is its right ascension?

8. (a) If a star having a right ascension of 18 hours is now on the meridian, what is the right ascension of a star which now has an east hour angle of 3 hours?

(b) When a star the right ascension of which is 8 hours is on the meridian, what is the right ascension of a star which has a west hour angle of 5 hours?

(c) May a number of different stars have the same right ascension?

(d) May a number of stars have the same declination?

(e) Is it possible for two stars to lie on the same hour circle, and have different right ascensions?

(f) If the right ascension of a fixed star now is 11 h. 28 m., what is it 3 hours hence?

9. (a) When a correct sidereal clock reads 17 h., the hour angle of a certain star is 5 h. west. What is the star's right ascension?

(b) The sidereal time being 17 h. 26 m., a star is found to have an east hour angle of 4 h.; what is the star's right ascension?

10. Reduce March 9, 7 A. M., civil time, to astronomical time.

11. The sun and a star are in the vernal equinox, and both are setting below the horizon of some place.

(a) A month afterwards, which will set the earlier?

(b) Which will rise the earlier?

(c) On July 20th, a certain star sets below the horizon of Boston at 8 P. M. A month afterwards, will it set at about the same time?

12. By use of the telegraph it was found that when a Washington clock read 9 h. 0 m. 0 sec., a St. Louis clock read 8 h. 7 m. 22.93 sec. The Washington clock was 26.37 sec. fast, and the St.

Louis clock was 15.92 sec. slow. What is the difference of longitude between the two places?

13. An astronomer noted the following readings of his sidereal clock when a certain star crossed the wires in the reticle of his meridian circle.

h.	m.	sec.
13	14	17.2
	14	30.6
	14	44.0
	14	57.4
	15	10.7

The right ascension of the star was 13 h. 14 m. 31.68 sec. If the meridian circle was in perfect adjustment, what was the clock error?

14. When Polaris is on the meridian above the pole, an observer measures its altitude, finding it to be 39° 46'. Twelve hours later its altitude is 37° 18'. What is the latitude of the place of observation?

15. (a) If the altitude of a star is 16°, what is its zenith distance?

(b) If the declination of a star is +34° 5', what is its north polar distance?

(c) The north polar distance of a star is 116° 35'. What is its declination?

16. A mariner measures the altitude of the sun at noon, getting 69° 47' 25" as his result. From the almanac he finds that the sun's declination at the time when the altitude was measured was −6° 37' 49". Find the latitude of the ship's position.

17. At midnight on July 25th, a chronometer was 38.92 sec. *slow*. Its daily rate was 0.84 sec. *gaining*. Assuming that it kept this rate, what was its error at noon of July 31st?

18. The captain of a vessel measures the altitude of the sun on the afternoon of May 16th; his chronometer (keeping Greenwich time) reads 4 h. 16 m. 29 sec. when the altitude is measured. By means of data given in the almanac, he computes that the local time when the sun had the measured altitude was 3 h. 27 m. 58 sec. What was the longitude of the ship at the time of the observation?

CHAPTER VII.

THE MOON AND ECLIPSES.

"In full-orbed glory yonder moon divine
Rolls through the dark blue depths."
SOUTHEY.

145. Distance, Diameter, Orbit, Nodes. — The moon, though the most conspicuous of all the heavenly bodies except the sun, is really quite small, being only 2,163 miles in diameter.

Its average distance from the earth's centre is 238,840 miles. As the earth journeys around the sun in an ellipse, so the moon travels around the earth in a similar orbit, the earth being at one of the foci of the ellipse. The orbit is nearly a circle, and is inclined to the plane of the ecliptic only 5°. The moon appears to us to describe a circle on the face of the sky every month, the circle being roughly coincident with the ecliptic. The moon's path intersects the ecliptic at two opposite points, called the moon's *nodes*.

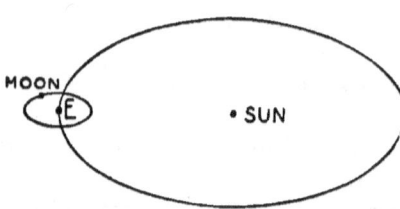

Fig. 100. — ORBITS OF THE EARTH AND MOON.

146. Periods, Sidereal and Synodic. — The *sidereal period* of the moon is the time required for making one revolution about the earth. In Fig. 101 the sun, the earth, and the moon are in line, in the positions S, E, and M. The earth and the moon pursue their appointed paths until they arrive at E' and M' respectively, the line E'M' being parallel to EM. The moon has now accomplished a complete revolution; the time required is nearly 27⅓ days, which is therefore the *sidereal period*. But the moon is not yet opposite the sun, as it was at the start. When it reaches M'', the earth being at E'', it is opposite the sun again, and a *synodic revolution* has been accomplished. The *synodic period* is over 29½ days.

147. Time of Crossing the Meridian. — Since the moon moves rapidly eastward among the stars, it does not cross the meridian of the observer at the same time every day, but crosses about 51 minutes later on the average each day than the preceding. The amount of daily retardation varies considerably from causes analogous to those which cause the sun to be an irregular timekeeper. (§ 126.)

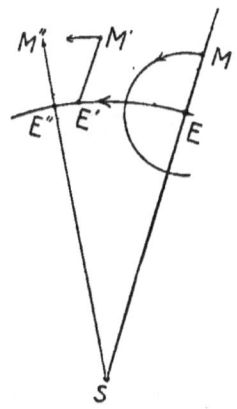

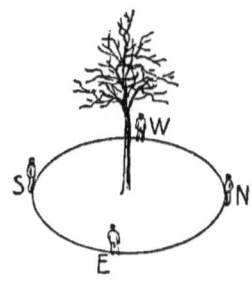

Fig. 101. — Sidereal and Synodic Periods.

Fig. 102. — Illustration of the Moon's Rotation.

148. Rotation. — The moon always presents the same face to us: an unthinking person might conclude from this that it did not rotate at all. Let a boy trace a circle on the ground around a tree, and station himself south of the tree and facing it; he then faces north. Let him walk around the circle, continually facing the tree. At S in Fig. 102, he faces north, at E west, at N south, and at W east. When he arrives at S again, he has turned completely around once.

149. Librations. — The moon rotates on its axis at a uniform rate, but since it does not move with uniform rapidity in its orbit, we sometimes see a short distance around one edge or the other. In Fig. 103, when the moon is at M, we see the portion ACB. When moving more swiftly than its average, it will describe 90° of its orbit and arrive at M' in a little less than one fourth of its sidereal period. So it will not have rotated one fourth of a complete turn, and an observer at the earth, though not able to see the point A, will look past B, as shown by the figure.

Furthermore, the moon does not stand quite upright on its orbit, that is, its axis is **not** perpendicular to the plane of its orbit. Hence, as shown in Fig. 104, we sometimes see past the north pole and sometimes past the south pole.

These apparent oscillations are called *librations*. There is a minute libration due to the fact that we are not at the earth's centre.

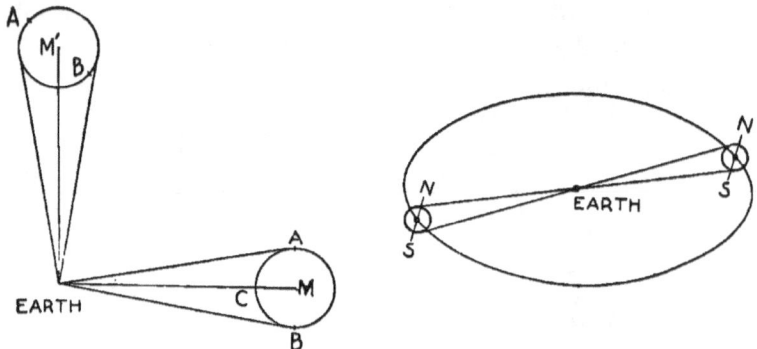

Fig. 103. — LIBRATION.   Fig. 104. — LIBRATION.

When the moon is rising, we can see farther over its upper edge than a man whose eye is at the earth's centre. Fifty-nine per cent of the moon's surface has been seen by astronomers.

150. Phases of the Moon. — The moon shines by reflecting the sunlight which strikes it. When the moon is between us and the sun, its illuminated side being toward the sun, we see the dark side. The moon is then said to be new. A week later, when it has moved from A to B (Fig. 105), half of the illuminated hemisphere is visible to us, and the moon is said to be at its first quarter. After the lapse of another week it is at C, opposite the sun, and the whole of the illuminated hemisphere can be seen by us; this phase is full moon. A week thereafter, when the moon has reached D, it is in its last quarter, half the bright hemisphere being visible. For a week before and after new moon, when but a small part of the moon looks bright to us, it is *crescent*. During the week preceding full moon, and also during the following week, when more than one half and less than the whole of the bright part of the moon is turned toward us, the moon is *gibbous*. The appearances of the moon are shown in Fig. 106.

151. Earth Shine. — When the moon is crescent, one easily sees the dark portion of it, as well as the brilliant crescent of light. The dark part is bounded on the side next to the sky by a narrow rim of silvery light, so that the whole looks not unlike a cake basket hung in the sky: it is popularly called " the old moon in the new moon's arms." Why is the dark part seen so easily? Some of the sunlight which falls upon the earth is reflected away, and, striking upon the side of the moon turned toward us, illuminates it sufficiently to render the dark part visible to us.

152. Occultations. — The moon in its monthly round passes between us and many of the stars, hiding them from view so that they are occulted (hidden) for a time. The occultation of bright stars

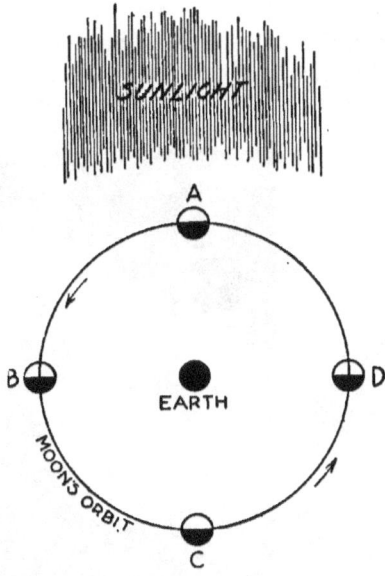

Fig. 105. — THE MOON ILLUMINATED.

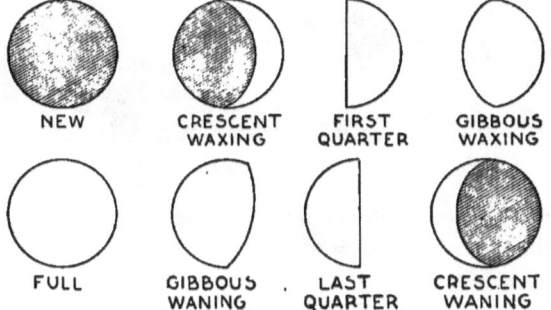

Fig. 106. — THE MOON'S PHASES.

can be observed with the naked eye. The fainter ones are blotted out by the moon's brilliancy as it approaches them. At the instant when the limb of the moon gets into line between the star and the observer's eye, the star vanishes as if annihilated. After an hour or less, the star reappears on the opposite side of the moon. Both the disappearance and the reappearance are instantaneous. Observations of occultations are sometimes made by mariners to find the

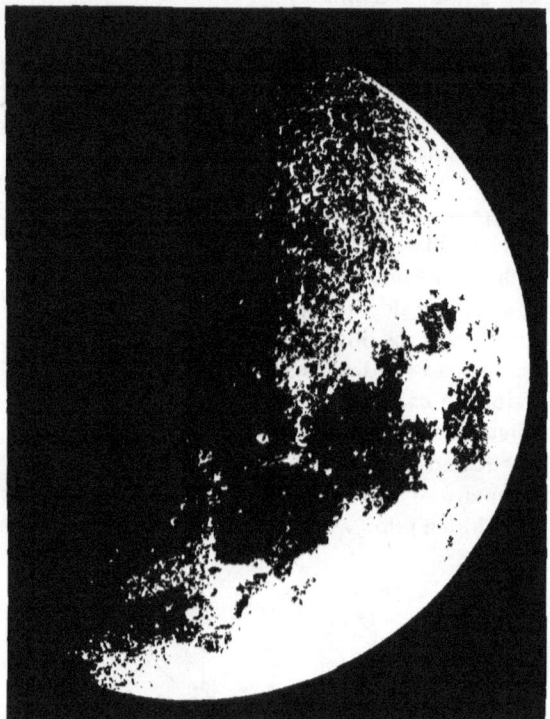

Fig. 107. — THE MOON: PHOTOGRAPHED AT THE LICK OBSERVATORY.

errors of their chronometers: from the data given in the Nautical Almanac the Greenwich time of the occurrence of an occultation of a given star, as seen at a given place, is computed. The chronometer reading is noted at the time of the star's disappearance; by comparing this reading with the computed time the error of the timepiece is found.

153. Appearance to the Naked Eye. — To the naked eye, the face of the full moon appears to be diversified with irregularly shaped dark spots. Most people see a strong resemblance to a human face. Many perceive a complete human figure, said among the French to be Judas Iscariot, transported thither as a punishment. Humboldt states that it is a popular belief among the people of Asia Minor that the moon is a mirror, which reflects back the image of the earth. When one examines the moon with an opera-glass, the dark spots are seen to be the smoother portions of the moon's surface. They are simply vast plains: on the maps they are designated as seas, being thought by the early lunar cartographers to be such.

154. Use of the Telescope. — It is well at first to put on a low magnifying power, so that the whole of the moon may be in the field of view at once. At the time of full moon the view is very much less satisfactory than at the first quarter (Fig. 107), and for three days thereafter. For at the time of full moon the shadows of the mountains on the moon are invisible to us, because they are cast directly behind them, and we lose the effect of contrast between the objects and their shadows. At the time of the first quarter, those mountains which are near the *terminator* (boundary between the illuminated and unilluminated portions of the moon) cast magnificent shadows; the rugged details of these mountainous forms are then very conspicuous in the telescope (Fig. 113). After viewing the entire lunar disk with a low power, higher powers may be tried with advantage on the more conspicuous objects. They bring out a wealth of detail, which wellnigh baffles delineation.

No telescope ever yet constructed can bear with advantage, even on the finest night, a power exceeding 3,000 diameters: such a power would bring the moon within 80 miles.

Objects as large as the largest buildings on the earth might be perceived, if they differed considerably in color from the background upon which they were seen.

155. Lunar Topography. — The features of the landscape may be divided into the following classes: plains, craters, mountain peaks, mountain ranges, rills, clefts, and rays. Some hundreds of these objects have received names: a few of the most prominent ones

114   DESCRIPTIVE ASTRONOMY.

are shown on the accompanying skeleton map (Fig. 108), in which the moon is represented as seen in an inverting telescope. The numbered craters have the following names: —

1. Clavius.	6. Cyrillus.	11. Gassendi.	16. Archimedes.
2. Schiller.	7. Theophilus.	12. Maskelyne.	17. Burg.
3. Schickard.	8. Arzachael.	13. Copernicus.	18. Aristotle.
4. Tycho.	9. Alphonsus.	14. Kepler.	19. Plato.
5. Catharina.	10. Ptolemy.	15. Eratosthenes.	

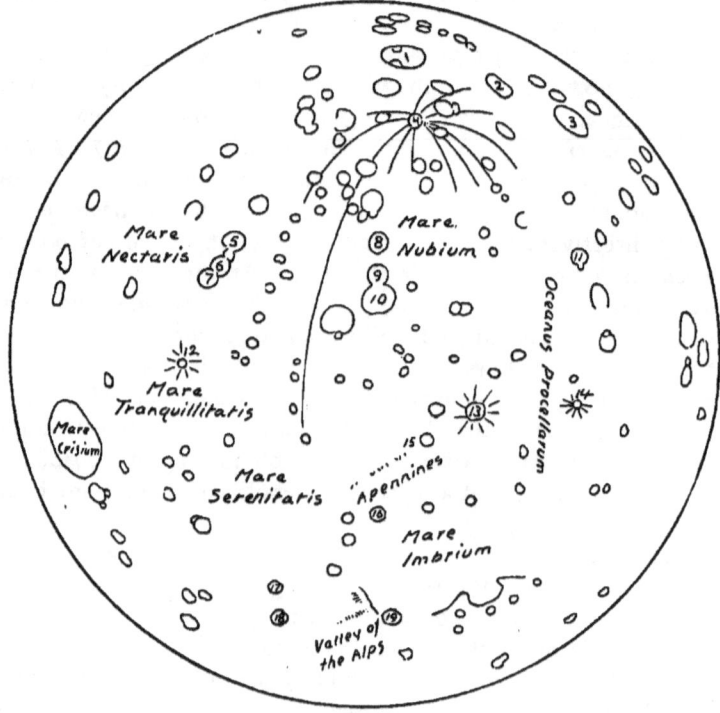

Fig. 108. — Skeleton Map of the Moon.

156. The Plains. — These are, as before remarked, darker than the rest of the surface, and smoother. With low powers they look much as if they were dry beds of ancient seas. Under a high power many minute pits are discovered besprinkling the plains;

the surface is found to be really quite rough and wrinkled. The boundaries of these "seas," as they are denominated on the map, are not always sharply defined; in some cases, the bounding "sea-wall" is nearly complete, and composed in part of precipitous cliffs, which exceed in grandeur any similar terrestrial formations.

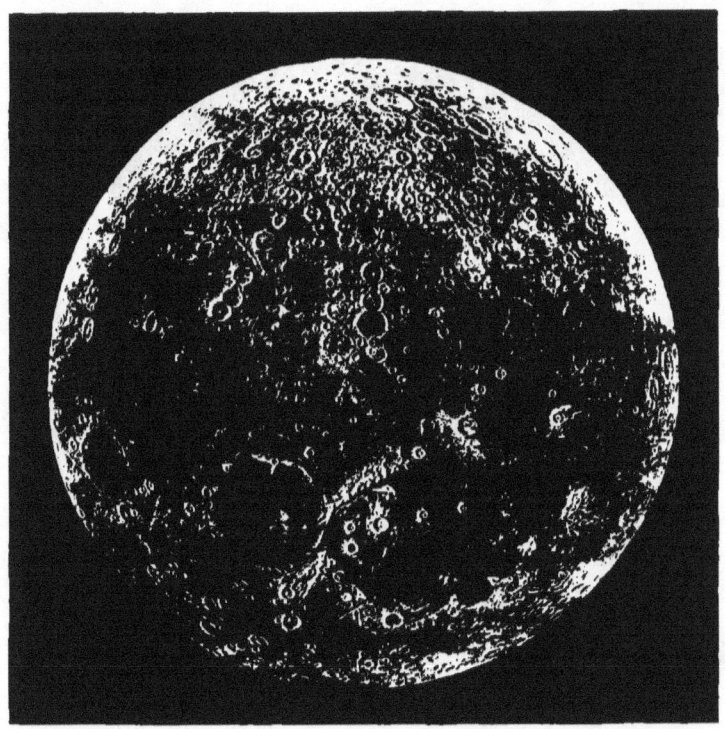

Fig. 109. — CONSPICUOUS CRATERS. (Nasmyth and Carpenter.)

157. Craters. — Even with an opera-glass one may see that the brighter portions of the moon's surface are thickly bestrewn with irregular ring-shaped mountains. Kepler[1] conjectured that these

---

[1] The great astronomer, 1571-1630, who discovered that the orbits of the planets are ellipses, and formulated certain famous laws concerning their motion.

were pits dug by the inhabitants of the moon to shelter themselves from the sun during the long lunar day.

Had he known that a large number of these pits are over fifty miles in diameter, and that the walls of some of them are three or four miles high, he would hardly have broached this theory. The craters present a wonderful diversity of size and aspect. Thou-

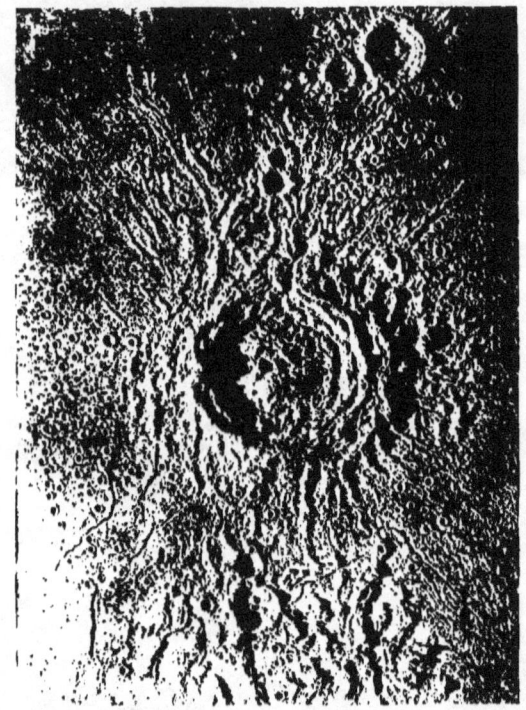

Fig. 110. — THE CRATER COPERNICUS. (Nasmyth and Carpenter.)

sands are so minute that in the most powerful telescope they look like mere pin-pricks, being half a mile or less in diameter. The largest ones are over one hundred miles across, and are perhaps more properly called walled plains, especially if the floor of the crater is quite smooth. In the centre of a crater a mountain or a small group of peaks is usually found.

The interiors of most of these craters are lower than the general surrounding level, but in some cases the interiors are elevated above the general surface. Some are isolated: others are crowded so thickly together that they overlap. Some walls are very precipitous; others are a series of magnificent terraces. The immensity of some of these formations is realized by looking at the cut of Copernicus (Fig. 110). The larger of the craterlets around it are as big as Vesuvius. In the figure, these, as well as the other features to be described, are easily distinguished.

Fig. 111. — COPERNICUS.

158. Nature and Cause of the Craters. — The craters are frequently referred to as the moon's volcanoes. It would be a mistake to infer from this that there are any signs of present volcanic activity on the moon. The entire appearance points to the theory that the moon was once a molten mass, and that by its cooling and solidification its various topographical features were formed.

Similar appearances are to be found upon the earth; Fig. 112 shows the marked similarity of the neighborhood of Vesuvius to a portion of the moon. On the cooling tap cinder from the furnaces for the production of iron there is formed a thin crust, which is soon broken open in spots by the pressure of the confined gases; the molten matter exudes through the holes and cracks, and frequently forms miniature volcanic cones. The central mountains in lunar craters were probably formed by the last sluggish oozings from the heated interior.

159. Mountains and Mountain Ranges. — Isolated mountain peaks are comparatively rare, though occasionally one can be found rising to a height of a mile or more out of a comparatively smooth landscape. There are a few mountain chains, the most prominent

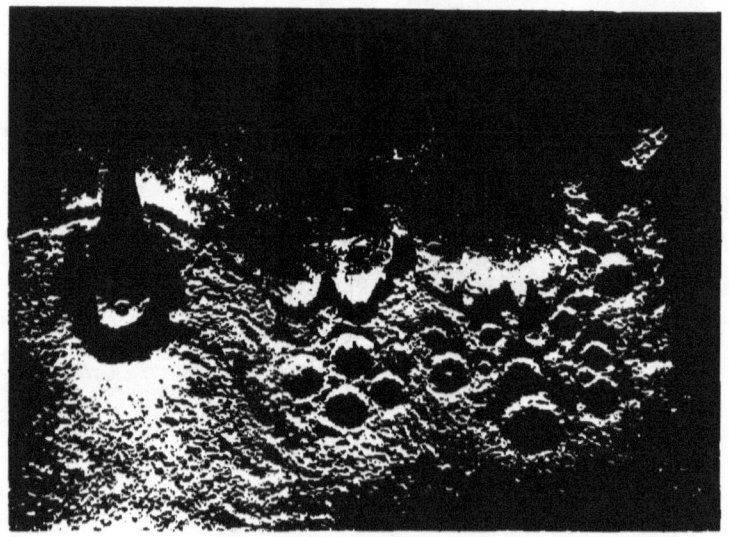

Fig. 112. — THE TERRESTRIAL CRATER VESUVIUS. (Nasmyth and Carpenter.)

of which is named the Apennines; it is 450 miles long, and bristles with peaks which rival the Andes in altitude, and cast magnificent shadows nearly 100 miles long athwart the neighboring plains. By measurement of these shadows the heights of many peaks have been determined. On one side, as shown in Fig. 113, they rise gradually from the plain, but on the other they are terminated by dizzy precipices, some of which are over three miles high.

160. Rills, Clefts, and Rays. — Rills are narrow, deep, and tortuous valleys, which look like the beds of dried up streams.

Clefts are narrow rifts of great depth. Two fine ones are shown in Fig. 113, starting from opposite sides of the largest crater: each is over 100 miles in length; near the centre it is a mile in width. They are thought to be not less than ten miles in depth, and must be appalling in grandeur to a lunar traveller.

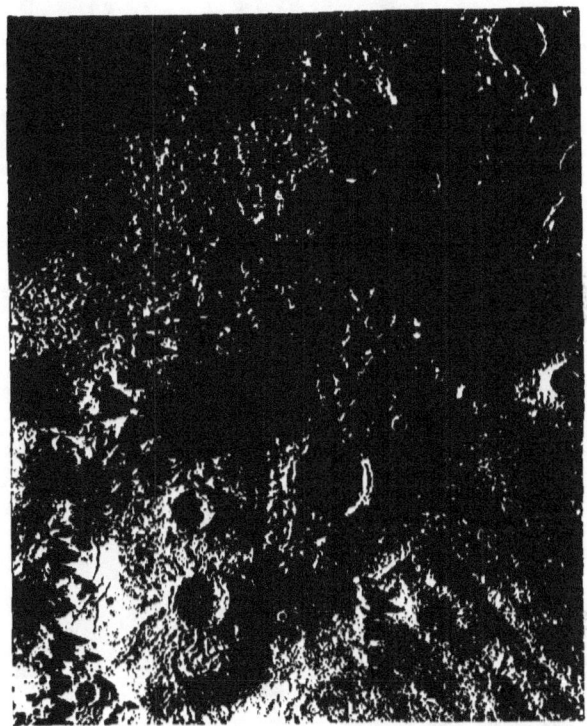

Fig. 113. — THE LUNAR APENNINES. (Nasmyth and Carpenter.)

Rays are streaks which diverge in all directions from some of the craters. They are best seen at the time of full moon. The finest system radiates from Tycho, which, with an opera-glass, looks as if it were a pole of the moon, the rays being meridians diverging from it. Copernicus has a smaller system, shown in Fig. 109. The rays are on the general surface, being neither elevated

120   DESCRIPTIVE ASTRONOMY.

above nor depressed below it; they go over crater walls and through valleys, just as if some one had painted them there with a gigantic brush after the landscape had assumed its present form. No satisfactory explanation of these has been given. Possibly

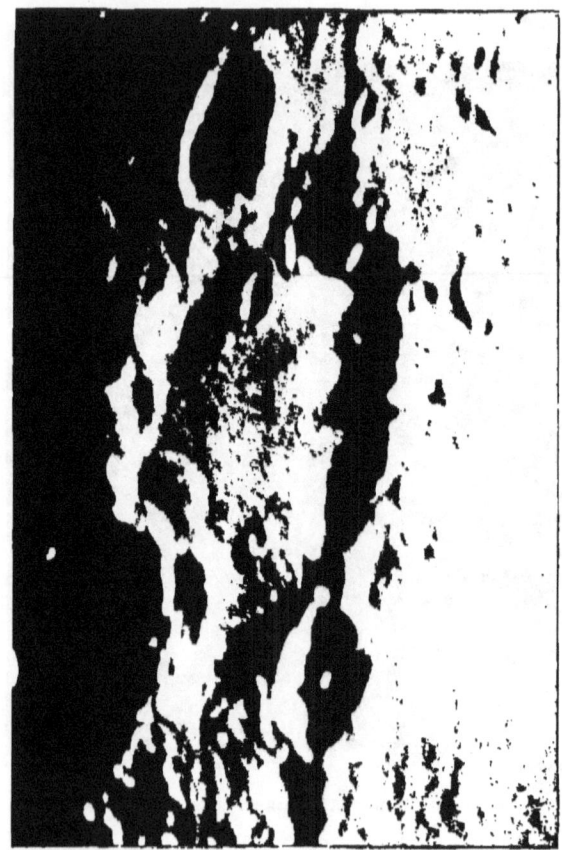

Fig. 114. — The Crater Vendelinus: Drawn from a Lick Photograph.

they are discolorations of the surface by vapors rising from cracks too narrow to be visible to us.

161. Changes. — There has been considerable discussion among astronomers as to whether any changes have ever been noted in the lunar topography. A given crater may change its aspect in an hour, because of the shifting of its shadow; such changes are most noticeable when the sun is just rising or setting at the crater (Fig. 114). For this reason, a careful examination, extending over several nights, is necessary to enable one to gain a correct idea of the details of the form of any crater or mountain. When we add to this the usual blurring caused by the unsteadiness of our atmosphere, and the minute errors which the most skilful draughtsmen are liable to make in their delineations, we can see how easy it is to imagine slight changes where none have really taken place. There is not the slightest evidence that any eruptive forces are at work. Possibly a very few land-slips have occurred. Lunar photography may after some years give us decisive results.

162. Atmosphere. — It has been demonstrated that the atmosphere, if it exists, is extremely rare, the pressure not exceeding a thousandth of that at the earth's surface. When a star is occulted, it ought, if there were a lunar atmosphere one tenth as dense as that of the earth, to suffer a change of brightness and color, when close to the moon's limb; further, as one sees the sun after it has really set, on account of refraction, so the time of the star's disappearance would be much retarded by the refraction of the lunar atmosphere, and its reappearance would be accelerated.

Twilight causes an illumination of the terrestrial landscape for some time after the sun has set. No *marked* illumination of this sort has been seen at any point on the moon.

The lunar spectrum is identical with the solar; this shows that the sun's rays when reflected from the moon suffer no noticeable absorption by its atmosphere.

163. Water. — What may be on the side of the moon which we never see, we cannot affirm, but there is no reason to think it different from the face presented to us. Any lake covering as much as a square mile, if not hidden from view by some obstruction, would have been discovered ere this.

On account of the coldness of the lunar days, as well as nights, it is not unlikely that water, if present, would exist only in a frozen state. There are no indications of either ice or snow.

164. The Water and Air Formerly. — If the moon was once, as is generally supposed, a portion of the earth, it must have carried some water and air with it when they separated, though the earth kept the lion's share, on account of its stronger power of attraction. What has become of the water we can only conjecture: great caverns may have been formed in the process of cooling, into which both the air and water have sunk. The water may have become chemically united with the molten rock in the process of crystallization. A rock when heated expels gases formerly absorbed; in cooling slowly it can absorb them again; perchance the lunar atmosphere was absorbed in this way. Still another theory is based on the exceedingly swift motion of the molecules of gases. The force of gravity at the moon's surface is but one sixth of that at the earth's, so that a rifle bullet there would "carry" 100 miles. Some have thought that the molecules of the lunar atmosphere may have escaped from this feeble attraction and gone off into space, never to be recovered; but this theory will not stand a critical examination.

165. Light and Heat reflected to the Earth. — Five sixths of the sunlight which falls upon the moon is absorbed, the rest being reflected away. The sun gives 600,000 times as much light as the full moon; yet the full moon in mid-heaven gives sufficient light to enable one to read this page. The measurement of the heat sent us by the moon is difficult, because its amount is "vanishingly small." If the full moon could shine upon us steadily for a year, it would give us as much heat as the sun does in three minutes.

166. Temperature at the Moon. — During the long lunar day the sun blazes upon the moon's plains with a fury unmitigated by a protecting atmosphere, and untempered by the presence of clouds; yet the plains are cold. The air of our own planet acts as a blanket to keep us warm. The solar rays pierce the atmosphere readily and find lodgment in the earth; but when the earth strives to radiate its heat back into space, the air checks the radiation. On lofty mountain tops, over which there is a much thinner air blanket than at their base, the rigors of eternal winter reign. The lunar atmosphere is entirely inadequate to check radiation, so that under direct sunshine the temperature of the moon's surface probably never rises above the freezing point of water. During the lunar night the temperature is believed to be no higher than 200° below zero on the Fahrenheit scale.

167. Life on the Moon. — Enough has been said to show that there is no such animal and vegetable life on the moon as on the earth. It is a land of death. The sky is a pall of black, studded with stars by day as well as by night. The rising sun, unheralded by the beautiful sky tints which accompany the dawn on earth, darts his garish beams athwart the desolate landscape, causing the lofty peaks to cast long shadows which vie with the sky in blackness. No bird song greets him; there is no rustle of a breeze, or plash of a brook, or murmur of an ocean. Should "lips quiver and tongues essay to speak," no sound from them would break the eternal silence. Dark pits innumerable yawn on every hand. The silvery rims of mighty craters encircle abysses of darkness. As the sun slowly rises in the sky, the fierce chill of the departing night is slowly mitigated; but no manlike being welcomes returning warmth.

The earth hangs continually in mid-heaven, waxing from crescent to full and waning again, swiftly spinning on its axis and bringing into view an ever shifting panorama of cloud and continent and ocean. No star forgets to shine; the weird glory of the solar corona and the fantastic forms of the protuberances can be seen in all their beauty by screening off the direct light of the sun. The Milky Way girdles the sky, bejewelled with thousands of glittering orbs. The eye is enchanted by the glories above, though the mind shrinks from contemplation of the desolation all about. After fourteen terrestrial days have elapsed, the long shadows stretch themselves eastward, the sun slowly sinks beneath the western horizon, and night with its terrible rigors of cold comes on apace. Such is a lunar day.

168. The Moon and the Weather. — Various fanciful notions concerning the moon's influence upon the weather are rife among ignorant persons. One hears of wet and dry moons; when the cusps of the new moon have a decided upward slant, fair weather is said to be presaged; when they do not slant upwards, foul weather is to be expected. Such ideas are arrant nonsense. The positions of the moon's cusps can be foretold for thousands of years; the weather, not for a single week. The connection of changes of the weather with changes of the moon's phases is likewise unfounded. Since the moon changes its phase every week, all weather changes must occur within four days of some change of lunar phase. We know of no ways in which the moon would affect the weather except by its heat, or by raising aerial tides, or by disturbances of the magnetic conditions.

Its heat is almost immeasurably small; the effect of aerial tides on the readings of the barometer is insignificant. Certain minute magnetic disturbances have been detected, which seem to be dependent upon the varying distance of the moon. The idea that the full moon clears away clouds probably has its foundation in the fact that the moon renders the *rifts* in a lightly clouded sky conspicuous, while they would otherwise escape notice.

169. The Moon's Worth to Man. — The most stupendous work done by the moon for man is the rise of the tides, of which it is the chief cause. The flood tide lifts ponderous ships over dangerous bars at the entrances of harbors. Merchantmen are carried from the mouth of the Thames up the river to the busy wharves of London on the bosom of the tide. The tides scour the mouths of rivers, carrying away the pestilence breeding matter which tends to accumulate there.

The enormous power of the tides may some day be utilized in driving dynamos to charge storage batteries, from which electricity can be taken when desired.

The moon also helps the navigator to guide his ship, as explained in § 152. In this capacity the moon has frequently been likened to the hand of a stupendous clock, whose dial is the starry vault.

In historical researches dates are frequently fixed by reference to eclipses, which inspired awe in the beholders, and were carefully recorded. The date of the beginning of the Christian era is determined by means of a lunar eclipse, which took place on the night of Herod's death. The moon's light is of use in various ways, which readily suggest themselves.

ECLIPSES.

170. How Caused: Shape of the Shadow. — An eclipse of the moon occurs when it is in the shadow of the earth; one of the sun is caused by the interposition of the moon between it and us. In order to understand them, we must study the shape of the shadow cast by the earth or moon.

THE MOON AND ECLIPSES. 125

In Fig. 115, S, E, and M represent the sun, earth, and moon, respectively. The heavily shaded portion CDV is called the *umbra* of the earth's shadow; it is of a conical shape. The lightly shaded portions, FCV and GDV, represent the *penumbra* of the shadow. An eye situated at X, between CF and CV, would see (neglecting the effect of refraction of the sun's rays, where they graze the earth at C) only a portion of the sun's disk. An object between CF and CV would not be as brilliantly illuminated as one at the left of CF, where light from every part of the sun's disk would strike it.

In Fig. 116, CHKD is the umbra of the moon's shadow; the penumbra occupies the space represented by FCH and KDG. A cross-section of the shadow of either the earth or the moon is shown in Fig. 117, the dark portion being the umbra, the lighter the penumbra.

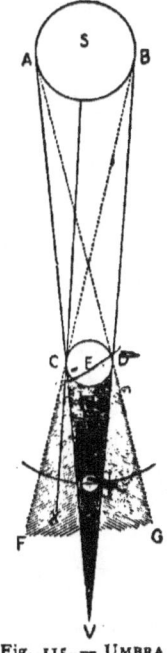

Fig. 115. — Umbra and Penumbra of the Earth's Shadow.

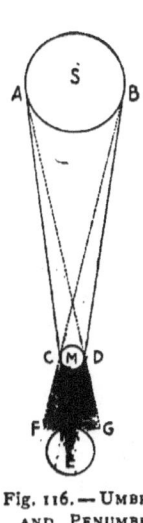

Fig. 116. — Umbra and Penumbra of the Moon's Shadow.

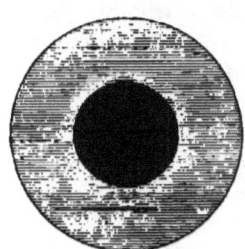

Fig. 117. — Cross-section of a Shadow.

171. Cause of a Lunar Eclipse. — Since the centres of the sun and earth lie in the plane of the ecliptic, the axis of the earth's shadow, a line drawn from E to V in Fig. 115, lies there also. If the moon moved exactly in the plane of the ecliptic, it would pass through the earth's shadow every month, and suffer eclipse. But as the moon is above or below the ecliptic, except when at its nodes (§ 145) it usually passes above or below the earth's shadow and escapes eclipse. On those occasions when it encounters the shadow, the eclipse is *total* if the entire moon passes into the umbra, and *partial* if only a portion of the moon is immersed in the umbra.

172. Phenomena of a Total Lunar Eclipse. — When the moon is in the penumbra of the earth's shadow, enough sunlight still strikes it to make it shine brightly; no one would surmise from its appearance that it was about to suffer eclipse. But as soon as it reaches the umbra, the portion of its limb in the dark shadow disappears from view, the moon having the appearance exhibited in Fig. 118. The dark notch grows until the entire moon is immersed in the umbra. But, strange to say, the whole moon usually becomes visible, shining with a dull copper-colored light. The explanation is not far to seek. Many of the sun's rays pass through the earth's atmosphere at C and D (Fig. 115), and, being refracted, pass into the umbra and light up the moon with the sunset tinge. Should the earth's atmosphere be charged with clouds where the sun's rays attempt to struggle through it, the sunlight will be stopped by the clouds, and the moon will be entirely invisible; this happens rarely. When the forward edge of the moon emerges from the umbra, totality is past; the eclipse ends when the entire moon has emerged from the umbra. Any phase of a lunar eclipse is visible from the whole of that hemisphere of the earth which is turned toward the moon.

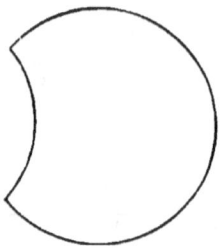

Fig. 118.—Beginning of a Total Lunar Eclipse.

173. Cause of a Solar Eclipse. — A solar eclipse is caused, as shown in Fig. 116, by the moon's passing between the earth and the sun, so as to obscure the sun either partially or wholly. Since the moon does not move in the plane of the ecliptic, it does not get within the conical space ABCD (Fig. 115), every month, but usually passes above or below it. But when any part of the moon enters this conical space, the sun is at least partially obscured at some point of the earth's surface.

174. The Moon's Shadow. — In Fig. 116, the moon's shadow, where it falls upon the earth, is quite narrow. On account of the variations of the earth's distance from the sun, and of the moon's distance from the earth, the moon's distance from the sun changes. The nearer it is to the sun, the shorter is its shadow (umbra): the farther away,

THE MOON AND ECLIPSES.

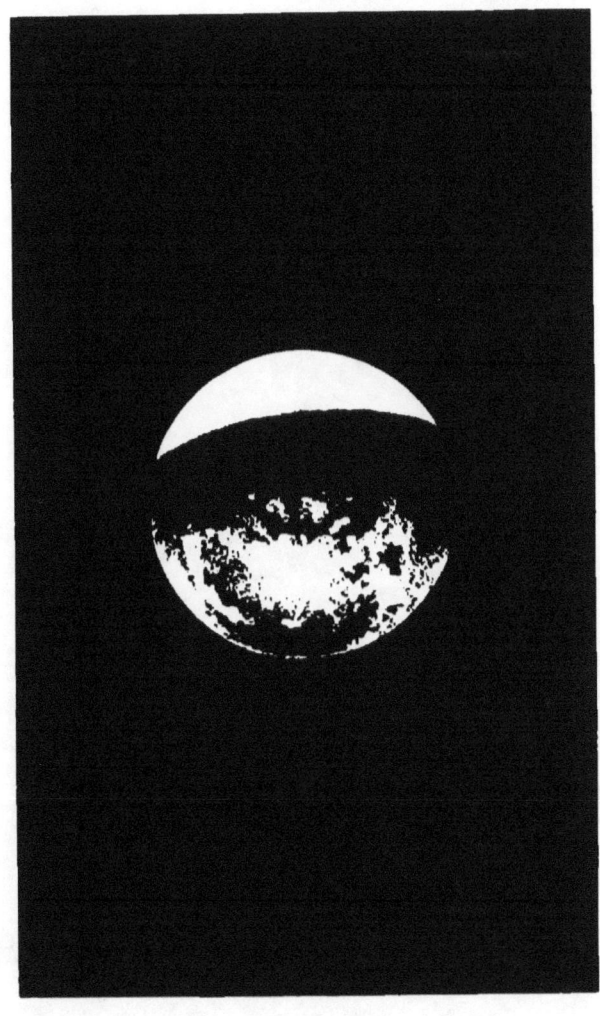

LUNAR ECLIPSE, January 28, 1888.

THE MOON AND ECLIPSES. 127

the longer the shadow. Usually the shadow is not quite long enough to reach the earth's surface. Under the most favorable circumstances, the diameter HK (Fig. 116) of the cross-section of the shadow at the earth's surface is 168 miles. The penumbra of the moon's shadow is shown by the light shading in Fig. 117. The moon hides a portion of the sun from an eye situated anywhere in the penumbra. The moon moves eastward, but as the earth turns in the same direction, the shadow does not skim over the continents as fast as it otherwise would. A projectile from a modern rifled cannon would keep up with it for a few seconds.

175. Varieties of Solar Eclipses. — A total solar eclipse occurs when the whole sun is hidden from view. This happens only when the observer is within the umbra of the moon's shadow. Since the diameter of the cross-section of the umbra at the earth

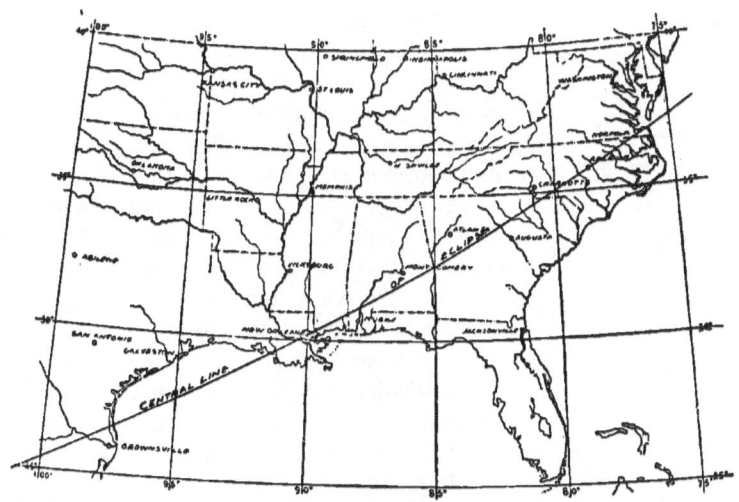

Fig. 120. — PATH OF THE CENTRAL LINE OF THE ECLIPSE OF MAY 27, 1900.

is always less than 170 miles, the path of the shadow on the earth's surface is long and narrow; a total eclipse is visible only to those who are in this path. Fig. 116 shows that the penumbra is much wider; the average diameter of its cross-section at the earth is 4,400 miles.

For any one situated within the penumbra there will be a partial eclipse. The nearer he is to the true shadow path, the more of the sun will be hidden. The next total solar eclipse visible in the United States occurs on May 27, 1900. The path of the shadow is shown in Fig. 120. When the umbra is not long enough to reach the earth, any one at R in Fig. 121, where the axis of the umbra prolonged cuts the earth's surface, can look past the moon's edge and see a part of the sun, which will then have the appearance shown in Fig. 122. Such an eclipse is called *annular*.

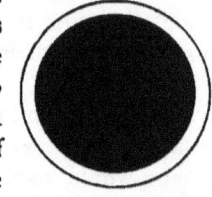

Fig. 122. — APPEARANCE OF THE SUN DURING AN ANNULAR ECLIPSE.

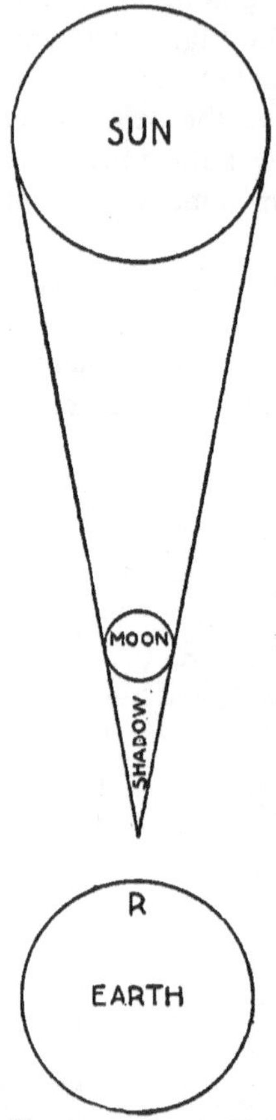

Fig. 121. — CAUSE OF AN ANNULAR ECLIPSE.

176. Phenomena of Partial and Annular Eclipses. — At the beginning of the eclipse, the moon appears to eat away the edge of the sun's disk, forming a notch similar to that shown in Fig. 118 for a lunar eclipse. The notch increases to its maximum size, and then diminishes. One may get a good idea of the appearance by taking two equal circles, one black, the other white, and passing the black one slowly over the face of the white one, leaving a greater or less portion of the white one exposed to view. To represent an annular eclipse, the black circle must be smaller than the white one.

With a telescope the lunar mountains are easily seen, projecting from the moon's limb where it eats into the sun.

177. Phenomena of Total Eclipses. — A total eclipse is perhaps the grandest of natural phenomena. It begins in the same way as a partial one; just before the sun is entirely covered, the landscape assumes an unearthly hue. Awe seizes the beholder: one sometimes sees the moon's shadow advancing through the air with terrifying swiftness, as if to smite him. In a few seconds it reaches him, and the last ray of sunlight is gone; the planets and bright stars appear. Around the black ball now hanging in the sky the pearly corona flashes out in all its weird beauty. At its base glow the prominences, like rubies set in pearl. Men's faces grow ghastly. The silence of death is upon the beholders. Soon there is a sudden flash of sunlight at the western limb of the moon: the corona and prominences fade apace.

The gloom is overpast, and silence gives place to exclamations of wonder and delight.

178. Observations During Totality. — Some of the more important of the observations made by astronomers are given below.

1. Photographs of the corona and prominences are taken.
2. The structure of the inner portions of the corona, which can be seen only during a total eclipse, is carefully studied with the telescope.
3. Spectroscopic observations are made on the corona, the protuberances, and the low-lying regions of the chromosphere.
4. Search is prosecuted for possible small planets near the sun: it is claimed that such objects were seen during the eclipse of July 29, 1878, by two American astronomers.[1] Diligent search has been made for these during more recent eclipses, but without success.
5. Drawings are made of the outer corona to determine its extent and boundaries.

179. Duration and Number of Eclipses. — An eclipse of the moon, if total, may last for four hours. During half this time, the *whole* of its disk will be in eclipse.

A total solar eclipse, from first to last contact, occupies about two hours. Totality may, on the rarest occasions, last nearly eight minutes. Its duration is ordinarily only two or three minutes. In some years there are no lunar eclipses: three may occur in a year, as will happen in 1898.

Every year there are at least two solar eclipses; there may be five.

The greatest number of eclipses that can occur in any year is seven, of which two are lunar.

NOTE. — The effects of a total solar eclipse on animals are interesting. Bees return to the hive. Chickens go to roost. Caged birds put their heads under their wings. Bats and owls fly out of their accustomed retreats. Dogs are terrified, and sometimes howl dismally. Horses have been known to lie down in the public highway and refuse to advance. Some oxen were once seen to range themselves in a circle, back to back, with horns outward, as if to resist an attack.

[1] Lewis Swift and James C. Watson.

EXERCISES.

180. 1. If the moon should cease to rotate on its axis, would its entire surface become visible to us?

2. When the moon is new, does it rise and set at about the same time that the sun does?

3. (*a*) When the moon is full, where is it to be looked for just after sunset?

(*b*) Where just before sunrise?

(*c*) Where at noon?

(*d*) Where at midnight?

4. (*a*) When the moon becomes a crescent, shortly after being new, does it set a little while before the sun, or after it?

(*b*) Does it rise before the sun, or after?

5. When the moon is at its first quarter, does the terminator (the straight edge) lie on the left hand side of the illuminated portion, or on the right hand side, as we look at it?

6. When the moon is at its first quarter, does it cross the meridian a few hours before the sun, or a few hours after?

7. When the moon is at its first quarter, and the sun is setting, do we look in the south for the moon, or in the east?

8. Does the full moon shine all night, if the sky is clear?

9. (*a*) When the moon is in its last quarter, in what direction (north, east, south, or west) is it to be seen at sunrise?

(*b*) In what direction at sunset?

10. On the ecliptic are four cardinal points; viz. the vernal equinox, the summer solstice, the autumnal equinox, and the winter solstice. (§§ 98, 99.)

(*a*) The sun being in the vernal equinox, if the moon were full, near what point of the ecliptic would it be?

(*b*) Where, if at first quarter?

(*c*) Where, if at last quarter?

11. If the moon on a given night be near either equinox, near what points of the horizon will it rise and set?

12. The moon on a given night is near the summer solstice.

(*a*) Will it, as seen from your home, rise in the northeast, or in the southeast?

(*b*) When crossing the meridian, will it be near the zenith, or low down near the southern horizon?

13. Is the moon visible an hour after sunrise, when it is at the last quarter?

14. If the moon be full about Christmas time, will it run high (that is cross the meridian near the zenith), or low?

[To answer this question first find, from the time of year, where the sun is in the ecliptic; then from the relative positions of the sun and moon determine what point of the ecliptic the moon is near.]

15. Why is not the dark part of the moon rendered plainly visible by earth shine at the first quarter, as well as when the moon is a narrow crescent?

16. A mariner computes that upon a certain date the moon will occult the bright star Aldebaran, the disappearance occurring at 8 h. 26 m. 47 sec., Greenwich mean time. By observing the occultation, he finds that his chronometer reads 8 h. 25 m. 58 sec. at the time of the star's disappearance. Is his chronometer fast or slow, and how mnch?

17. Can a lunar crater ever be filled with the shadow of its own wall, so that the bottom of the crater will be invisible to us?

18. Why are not the rays radiating from lunar craters overflows of lava?

19. How does the atmosphere prevent our seeing stars by day as well as we see them at night?

20. The lines AD and BV in Fig. 115 are tangent to the circle E. Are they tangent at exactly the same point?

21. If the moon were as large as the earth, would it ever suffer a total eclipse?

22. (*a*) At what kind (§ 175) of a solar eclipse does the moon look smaller than the sun?

(*b*) At what kind does it look larger?

23. If the earth were suddenly robbed of its atmosphere when the moon was visible during a total lunar eclipse, what change would there be in the moon's appearance?

24. In a daily paper, of wide circulation, the head lines of an article on a solar eclipse read thus: "The Moon Casts its Shadow on the Sun." Change that sentence so that it will express the truth.

25. When an observer at Chicago sees an annular eclipse, can an observer in some other city see the eclipse as total?

26. (*a*) When a solar eclipse is partial for one observer, may it be total for another at the same time?

(*b*) When a lunar eclipse is partial for one observer, may it be total as seen by another at the same time?

27. The total solar eclipse of January, 1889, was visible in both California and Nevada. Did an observer on the coast of California see it before or after one in Nevada saw it?

28. Does a total lunar eclipse end for an observer in Boston at the same instant as for one in Chicago?

29. What is the derivation of the word "annular"?

30. (*a*) Do lunar eclipses happen when the moon is new?

(*b*) Do solar eclipses happen when the moon is new?

CHAPTER VIII.

MOTIONS OF THE PLANETS.

> "'T is by the secret, strong attracting force,
> As with a chain indissoluble bound,
> The system rolls entire."
> — THOMSON.

181. Their Orbits. — The orbit of each planet is an ellipse (§ 96), one focus of which is in the sun. The planes of all the planetary orbits, excepting those of some of the asteroids (§ 224), are but little inclined to the ecliptic. If a dot were placed in the centre of this page, to represent the sun, and all the planetary orbits were accurately drawn around it, the deviation of any one of them from true circularity would not be perceived. The definitions of major axis, minor axis, perihelion, aphelion, and mean distance, given in § 96, apply to the orbit of any planet. The *radius vector* of a planet is a line drawn from the focus of its orbit to the planet's centre.

182. Motion in Orbit. — If one could station himself in space between the north star and the sun, and a billion miles from the latter, on looking back at the planets he would see that they were all moving about the sun in a direction opposite to that of the hands of a watch. This is an easterly motion. When a planet is at perihelion, it moves more swiftly than at any other point of its orbit. The planet nearest the sun moves more rapidly than any other.

183. Newton's Law of Gravitation. — This law, to which all bodies in the universe are supposed to be subject, may be stated in the following way. *The mutual attraction between any two particles is proportional to the product of their masses, and inversely proportional to the square of the distance between them.*

This law may be expressed as an algebraic equation: let m and m' be the masses of two bodies, d the distance between them, and k a number, the value of which depends on the units of mass and distance employed.

$$\text{Attraction} = k \frac{mm'}{d^2}.$$

To make this clearer, suppose that two lead balls a mile apart attracted each other with a force of an ounce. If one ball were suddenly made five times as massive, the resulting attraction would be five times as great as before. If at the same time the other were made three times as massive, the new attraction between the bodies would not be $5 + 3$, or 8 times the old attraction, but 5×3, or 15 times the old attraction. Again, suppose that the masses of the

Fig. 123. — Sir Isaac Newton.

balls remained the same as at first, but the distance between the balls was doubled, the new attraction would not be $\frac{1}{2}$ of the old, but the square of $\frac{1}{2}$, which is $\frac{1}{4}$, of the old.

The force of gravity binds each planet to the sun.

184. What keeps the Planets Moving? — Persons ignorant of the laws of mechanics frequently think that gravity alone cannot keep the planets moving, but that some other force is pushing them. But there is no such extra pushing force. One of the laws of mechanics is that a body once set in motion will continue to move

MOTIONS OF THE PLANETS. 135

in a straight line with a uniform velocity, unless acted on by some external force. The tendency to keep going if once set in motion, or to *remain at rest* if stopped, is known as inertia. So a planet needs no pushing force behind it: having in some way been set in motion, its tendency is to move in a straight line; but the gravitational pull of the sun compels it to describe a curve instead.

Fig. 124. — KEPLER.

185. Kepler's Laws. — Before the time of Kepler, who was born in 1571, the heavenly bodies were supposed to move in circles. He discovered three laws concerning the motions of the planets: —

I. The orbit of each planet is an ellipse, the sun being at one of its foci.

II. The radius vector of a planet describes equal areas in equal times.

III. The squares of the times of revolution of any two planets are to each other as the cubes of their mean distances from the sun.

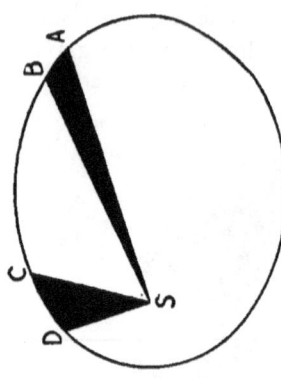

Fig. 125.—Equal Areas in Equal Times.

The second law is illustrated in Fig. 125. If a planet describes the arcs AB and CD in the same length of time, the area of SAB is equal to that of SDC.

Let t and t' denote the times of revolution of two planets, while a and a' are their mean distances. Then, by the third law, $t^2 : t'^2 :: a^3 : a'^3$.

The discovery of this law, known as the harmonic law, after seventeen years of arduous labor, caused Kepler the greatest exultation. He wrote concerning it: "The die is cast: the book is written, to be read either now or by posterity,— I care not which. It may well wait a century for a reader, as God has waited six thousand years for an observer."

186. Perturbations. — Gravitation being universal, it follows that the planets attract each other. These attractions cause disturbances of their elliptic motions. The computation of these perturbations has taxed the highest skill of mathematical astronomers; by a series of profound and elegant researches it has been proved that the stability of the planetary system is not endangered by them.

APPARENT MOTIONS.

187. Two Classes of Planets.— For convenience in discussing their apparent motions the planets are divided into two classes. The *inferior* planets are those the orbits of which lie within that of the earth: these are Mercury and Venus. The *superior* planets are those whose orbits are exterior to that of the earth: they are Mars, the asteroids, Jupiter, Saturn, Uranus, and Neptune.

188. Aspects. — One is aided in remembering the following explanations of the aspects of the planets by the thought that they all refer to the position of a planet with relation to the sun, as we, looking out from the earth, see the two bodies.

MOTIONS OF THE PLANETS.   137

Conjunction[1] occurs when a planet appears to be close to the sun. A superior planet is then beyond the sun. An inferior planet may be beyond the sun, in which case it is in *superior conjunction*, or it may be between the earth and the sun; in that case it is in *inferior conjunction*. Conjunction is indicated by the sign ☌.

Opposition occurs when the planet is in the opposite direction (from us) to that in which the sun lies. If the sun were near the

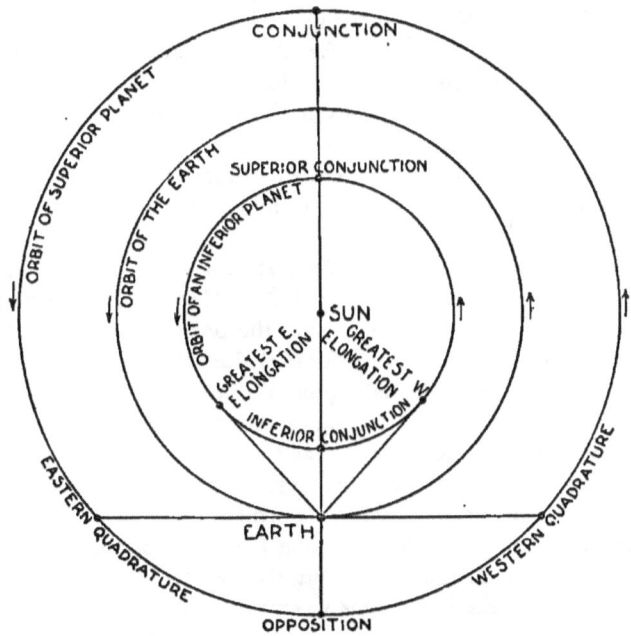

FIG. 126.—ASPECTS OF THE PLANETS.

east point of the horizon, a planet in opposition would be near the west point. Opposition is denoted by the sign ☍.

A planet's *elongation* from the sun is the angle formed at the earth by two lines drawn from it to the planet and the sun respect-

---

[1] There are different kinds of conjunction, opposition, etc., because the planets' orbits do not coincide with the ecliptic. Planets are at conjunction in longitude when their longitudes are the same: they are in conjunction in right ascension when their right ascensions are the same.

ively. The *greatest elongation* of an inferior planet is illustrated in Fig. 126.

A superior planet is in *quadrature* when its elongation is 90°. Quadrature is denoted by the sign □.

189. Apparent Movement of an Inferior Planet. — In Fig. 126 the orbit of Venus is drawn to illustrate that of an inferior planet. After being at inferior conjunction, Venus, moving in a direction opposite to the hands of a watch, goes to its greatest western elongation. If the earth stood still, Venus would arrive at its elongation in four weeks; but as the earth chases after it, the interval between inferior conjunction and greatest western elongation is lengthened to $2\frac{1}{3}$ months. The planet then passes on through superior conjunction and greatest eastern elongation to inferior conjunction again.

While it is travelling from inferior to superior conjunction, a man facing the sun will see the planet at the right (or west) of the sun. During the other half of its course it will be east of the sun.

190. Apparent Movement of a Superior Planet. — In Fig. 127 are represented the orbits of the earth and of Mars, P, P', and P'' being on the celestial sphere. E and M are the positions of the earth and Mars when the latter is at opposition. Mars then appears to be at the point P on the celestial sphere. Two weeks thereafter the earth has moved to E', and Mars, moving more slowly on account of its greater distance from the sun, has traversed the arc M M'. Mars then appears to be at P', which is west of P. So a superior planet, though really moving eastward in its orbit, appears when near opposition to move toward the west among the stars, because its motion is slower than that of the earth, and the two bodies are moving in nearly the same direction. This westward motion is said to be the *retrograde*.

Again, let Mars at M be in conjunction, the earth being at E'', and Mars appearing to us to be at P. In a few days the earth arrives at E''' and Mars at M', so that it appears to be at P'', having moved east from P. Had the earth remained at E'', Mars in moving from M to M' would have appeared to go east, but would not have reached P''.

Summing the matter up, we reach three conclusions: —

I. If the earth were stationary, the planet's easterly motion in its orbit would cause it to appear to move eastward among the stars.

MOTIONS OF THE PLANETS. 139

II. When the planet is near opposition, the more rapid motion of the earth causes its eastward motion to be apparently reversed, so that it retrogrades or moves westward among the stars.

III. When the planet is near conjunction, its apparent eastward motion among the stars is swifter than it would be, were the earth at rest.

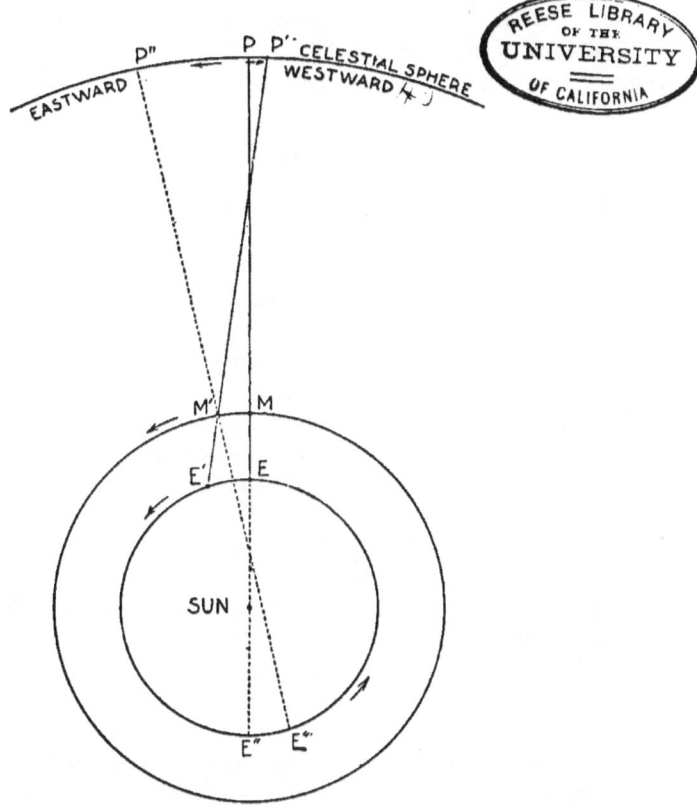

Fig. 127. — APPARENT MOVEMENT OF A SUPERIOR PLANET.

When changing its apparent eastward motion to a westward, and *vice versa*, the planet is said to be at a *stationary point*.

191. Evening and Morning Stars. — When a planet rises between midnight and the ensuing sunrise, it is called a morning star. When it is above the horizon at some instant between sunset and the following midnight, it is an evening star. Hence an evening star can be seen before midnight (if not too near the sun), and a morning star cannot.

192. Periods, Sidereal and Synodic. — The sidereal period of a planet is the time of a complete revolution around the sun. The synodic period is the time which elapses between two successive conjunctions of the planet with the sun. If the planet be an inferior one, the two conjunctions must be both inferior or both superior.

EXERCISES.

193. 1. (*a*) At what point of its orbit is a planet, when its radius vector has its greatest length?

(*b*) At what point when it is the shortest?

2. (*a*) Why does a planet move most swiftly when at its perihelion?

(*b*) Why does Mercury travel more miles in an hour than any other planet?

3. Two balls, a rod apart, attract each other with a force of one grain. If the mass of one ball be made ten times as great, while that of the other is halved, what will be the attraction between them, the distance remaining the same?

4. In exercise 3 what would have been the mutual attraction had the original balls been placed ten rods apart?

5. What would have been the mutual attraction had the original balls been placed one fourth of a rod apart?

6. What would have been the attraction, if each ball had been halved, and the distance had been halved also?

7. What would have been the attraction if the mass of one ball had been made three times as great, while that of the other was made ten times as great, and the distance between them shortened to one fifth of a rod?

8. If the gravitational pull between the earth and the sun were suddenly to cease, how would the former move?

9. How does Kepler's second law show that a planet when at aphelion must describe a shorter arc of its orbit in a day than when at perihelion?

MOTIONS OF THE PLANETS.

10. The mean distance of the earth from the sun being 93 millions of miles, while that of Jupiter is 483 millions, show by Kepler's third law that the period of Jupiter's revolution about the sun is nearly twelve years.

11. The mean distance of Neptune being thirty times that of the earth, show that its period is over 164 years.

12. The period of Uranus being eighty-four years, show that its mean distance from the sun is over nineteen times that of the earth.

13. Does a superior planet which is in conjunction set about sunrise?

14. Does a planet when in opposition rise about sunset?

15. (*a*) At about what time of day does an inferior planet, when in inferior conjunction, cross the meridian?

(*b*) At what time, when in superior conjunction?

16. What is the aspect of a superior planet which is on the meridian at midnight?

17. Why does a superior planet look brightest when at opposition?

18. Why are planets not easily observed when they are in conjunction?

19. When Mercury is at its greatest eastern elongation, being 28° from the sun, is it visible in the evening twilight?

20. If Mercury was seen going across the face of the sun, would it move from the sun's eastern limb towards its western, or *vice versa*?

21. If Venus is at its greatest eastern elongation, being 47° from the sun, does it rise before the sun?

22. When at its greatest western elongation, is Venus a morning star or an evening star, or both?

23. Just after an inferior planet passes its superior conjunction, is it a morning star or is it an evening star?

24. If Venus is at its eastern elongation, does it cross the upper branch of the meridian in the forenoon, or in the afternoon?

25. Could Jupiter and Venus ever appear to be close together?

26. At one of its oppositions Mars was near perihelion, while the earth was near aphelion. At another opposition Mars was near aphelion, while the earth was near perihelion. At which of the two oppositions could Mars be best seen by us?

27. When does a superior planet appear to have the smaller diameter, at opposition or at conjunction?

28. When does an inferior planet appear to have the smaller diameter, at inferior conjunction or at elongation?

29. Should an inferior planet, shining by reflecting the sun's light, show phases similar to those of the moon?

30. Draw a picture containing two concentric circles, one representing the orbit of the earth, the other that of a superior planet. Mark the positions of the sun, earth, and planet, when the planet is in conjunction with the sun. Determine whether the synodic period of the planet is longer than the sidereal.

31. Find, by making a drawing similar to that described in the preceding exercise, whether the sidereal period of an inferior planet is longer than the synodic.

CHAPTER IX.

MERCURY, VENUS, MARS, THE ASTEROIDS.

> "Now glowed the firmament
> With living sapphires: Hesperus, that led
> The starry host, rode brightest."
>
> MILTON.

194. Two Groups of Planets. — When the planets themselves are considered, instead of their orbits, they fall naturally into two divisions. Mercury, Venus, the earth, and Mars are all comparatively small bodies, are doubtless solid, and are quite dense. Each is sup-

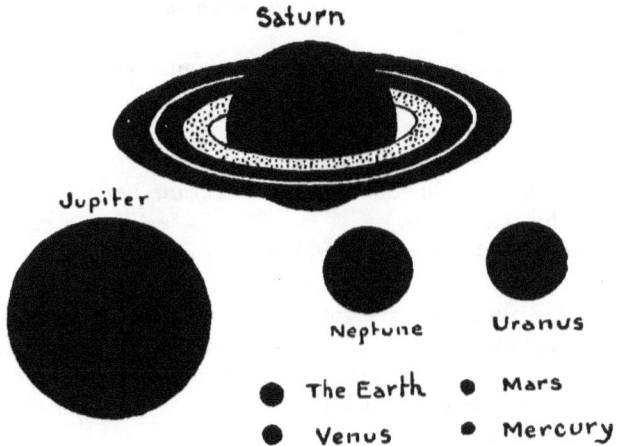

Fig. 128. — RELATIVE SIZES OF THE PLANETS.

posed to have an atmosphere of small mass compared with the mass of the body enveloped by it. Their equipment of moons is meagre. The relative sizes of the planets are shown in Figure 128.

Jupiter, Saturn, Uranus, and Neptune, in comparison with the other planets, are giants in size. But their densities are small, so that they have perhaps only little kernels of solid matter at their centres. Their atmospheres are very extensive and dense. They are liberally provided with satellites, except Neptune. Were he nearer, we might discover that he had a goodly retinue of them. The planets just mentioned, eight in all, are called the *major planets*. The *minor planets*, or asteroids, are quite insignificant in point of size. Very little is known of their physical constitution.

MERCURY, ☿.

195. Distance and Diameter.[1] — The mean distance of Mercury from the sun is 36,000,000 miles. The actual distance varies 7,500,000 miles each side of this value, the orbit being much more eccentric than that of any other of the large planets.

The diameter of Mercury is 3,000 miles.

196. Revolution and Rotation. — The sidereal period is 88 days, so that it performs a revolution in less than one fourth of the time required by the earth.

The time of its rotation upon its axis cannot be said to be certainly known. One astronomer, a century ago, thought he saw certain appearances on the planet due to the presence of high mountains; by observing them, he obtained a rotation period of about 24 hours. But his observations have not been confirmed by more powerful telescopes.

Schiaparelli, a distinguished Italian astronomer, who has made a special study of some very faint markings on Mercury since 1881, has concluded that Mercury rotates on its axis in the same time that it revolves about the sun. Thus, as our moon continually presents the same face to the earth, Mercury turns the same side to the sun. Schiaparelli announced his discovery to a friend in 1882 in the following lines: —

> "Cynthiae ad exemplum versus Cyllenius axe
>   Aeternum noctem sustinet, atque diem:
>   Altera perpetuo facies comburitur aestu,
>   Abdita pars tenebris altera Sole caret."

---

[1] The distance, diameter, sidereal period, and rotation time of each planet, should be thoroughly committed to memory.

197. Transits. — When Mercury is near inferior conjunction, it sometimes gets into line between the earth and the sun, so that it is seen by us as a small black circle crossing the solar disk. Thirteen transits occurred during the nineteenth century, the last one being on Nov. 10, 1894.

198. Appearance to the Naked Eye. — The planet keeps so close to the sun, that it is not readily seen with the naked eye. The times of its elongation are the best times to look for it: it can be well seen about a week before elongation, as well as a week after. The dates of elongation are given in the Nautical Almanac. The best conditions for seeing it in the evening occur at those eastern elongations which happen in March or April. It then appears like a star of exceptional brilliancy, near the western horizon, distinguishable in strong twilight, and conspicuous as soon as night sets in. Copernicus is said never to have seen it.

199. Telescopic Appearance. — The telescope shows that the planet has phases like the moon: it therefore shines by reflecting the light of the sun. When near inferior conjunction it is a narrow crescent, as is the moon when new. Its phase at superior conjunction is like that of the full moon. Favorable views of the planet are rare, since it must be observed either during the daytime, or at night when it is near the horizon. Faint dark markings are sometimes seen on its disk, but they are so indistinct that their nature can only be guessed at. They may be dark plains, like those on the moon, or possible lakes or seas.

200. Physical Condition. — There is spectroscopic evidence of the presence of water vapor; from this we conclude that both air and water are to be found on the planet. But it is probable that the atmosphere is not as dense as ours. The sun shines seven times as hotly as on the earth.

VENUS, ♀.

201. Morning and Evening Star. — Venus is the most brilliant of the planets, and when at its maximum brightness casts distinct shadows of objects at night, in the absence of the moon or bright artificial lights near at hand. It is then visible to the naked eye in full daylight. Because of its brightness it has received the distinctive appellations of the Evening Star and the Morning Star. The

Greeks called it Hesperus when it was an evening star, and Phosphorus when it was a morning star. Of late years many ignorant people, seeing it by day, have supposed it to be a reappearance of the Star of Bethlehem.

202. Distance and Diameter. — The mean distance of Venus from the sun is 67,000000 miles; its distance, when in different parts of its orbit, varies little, because its orbit is more nearly circular than that of any other planet. The planet's diameter is 7,700 miles: it is therefore nearly as large as the earth. When at inferior conjunction it is nearer to us than any other planet ever is.

203. Revolution and Rotation. — Venus accomplishes a revolution about the sun in 225 days. The time of its rotation is not now in much doubt. Until lately the only evidence (and that very insufficient) was that it revolved in 23 h. 21 m. But the recent researches of Schiaparelli, the keenness of whose vision is remarkable, render it probable that the time of rotation is 225 days, agreeing with the sidereal period. This result has been corroborated by two other Italian astronomers.

204. Transits. — Transits of Venus across the sun's face are much rarer than those of Mercury. The last one occurred on Dec. 6th, 1882, and the next one will not come until 2004. Another is due in 2012. These transits have a high degree of interest, because they have been used in finding the distance of the earth from the sun. Expensive scientific expeditions have been sent to various parts of the world, by the governments of the most progressive nations, to observe these transits.

Halley's [1] method of observation consists of observing the times of external and internal contact as seen from two stations widely different in latitude. As shown in Fig. 129, the planet as seen from these stations has different paths across the sun's disk. The distance and direction of one station from the other being known, and the lengths of the two paths being measured, it is possible by trigonometric methods, too difficult to be explained here, to find the sun's distance. The accuracy of the final result depends upon the precision with which the times of contact are noted.

Unfortunately, when the black circle of the planet's disk is internally tangent to the sun's limb at the beginning of the transit, it has

---

[1] Halley was an English Astronomer Royal in Newton's time.

the appearance shown in Fig. 130. As it moves away from the limb, it is, for a number of seconds, apparently attached to it by a black ligament, called the "black drop." The ligament stretches, contracts, and finally breaks. Thus it is very difficult to note the

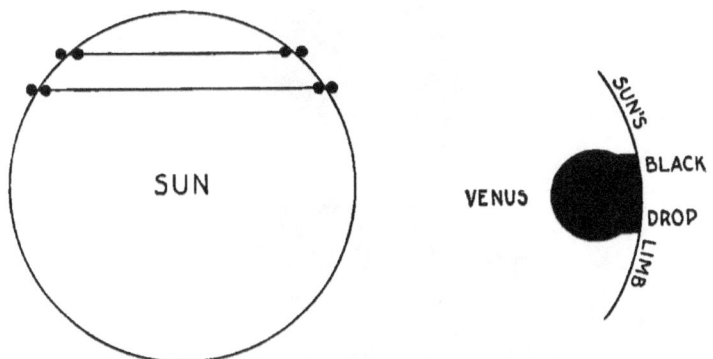

Fig. 129. — A Transit of Venus.   Fig. 130. — The Black Drop.

time of real internal contact. The action of the planet's atmosphere also vitiates the accuracy of the observation. A phenomenon similar to the black drop may be seen by placing the thumb and forefinger close together, and holding them six inches or less from the eye.

On account of these troubles astronomers now place more reliance upon other methods.

205. Phases and Maximum Brightness. — The phases of Venus are similar to those of Mercury and the moon. They are almost visible to the naked eye. A good spyglass brings out the crescent phase well. The time of greatest brightness does not occur when the planet looks like a full moon, for then it is farthest from us. It comes during the crescent phase, five weeks before, and the same time after, inferior conjunction.

The discovery of the phases of Venus was one of the first fruits of the invention of the telescope. Galileo[1] made the discovery and announced it in the following anagram: "Haec immatura a me jam frustra leguntur, o. y." This he afterwards transposed so that it read, "Cynthiae figuras aemulat mater amorum."

[1] Galileo Galilei (1564-1642), the famous Italian philosopher.

206. Telescopic Appearance. — The planet is of dazzling splendor, even in a small telescope; it looks almost as if made of quicksilver,

Fig. 131. — GALILEO.

and is surrounded by a marked purplish aureole caused by the lack of achromatism (§ 39) of the telescope.

On rare occasions ill defined spots of a leaden hue are seen on its surface. They may be continents or seas dimly descried. Certain very bright spots, said by some to be occasionally visible near the limb, have been thought to be due possibly to polar ice and snow.

207. Atmosphere. — When Venus is near inferior conjunction, being a very slender crescent, the horns or cusps of the crescent appear to be much prolonged, so that they really surround the dark disk of the planet. When about to enter upon a transit, a ring of light is seen surrounding the entire disk (Fig. 132). This is the sunlight shining through the planet's atmosphere, and being refracted by it to our eyes. The atmosphere has been shown to be

Fig. 132. — THE RING OF LIGHT.

denser than ours, and probably less than twice as dense. The vapor of water has been detected in it by spectroscopic observations.

208. Physical Condition. — The density of Venus being nearly equal to that of the earth, we conclude that it is a solid body. It probably owes its brilliancy to the fact that its sky is almost totally cloudy at all times. Any one looking at bright white masses of cumulus cloud in a summer sky will be convinced that such clouds reflect light much better than the general landscape does. The excessive cloudiness in turn, combined with the spectroscopic evidence of water vapor, indicates that water is abundant on the planet's face. There may not be a square foot of dry land to vary the monotony of a universal ocean.

MARS, ♂.

209. Distance and Diameter. — The mean distance of Mars from the sun is 141,500000 miles. Its orbit is, excepting Mercury's, the most eccentric of all the orbits of the major planets, so that the planet's distance varies 13,000000 miles each side of the average distance. Its diameter is 4,200 miles, which is not much more than half the earth's diameter.

210. Revolution and Rotation. — The sidereal period is 687 days, only 43 days short of two years. By comparison of drawings of the planet made soon after the invention of the telescope with those made during this century, the rotation time has been determined with great precision. It is 24 h. 37 m. 22.67 sec.

211. Appearance to the Naked Eye. — Mars, being a superior planet, is best seen at the time of opposition, when it is near the earth. At some oppositions it comes within 36,000000 miles of us, at others it is as much as 61,000000 miles away. This variation of distance is due to the eccentricity of the orbit. The favorable oppositions, which come when the planet is near its perihelion, occur about every fifteen years. The last was in August, 1892. At such times Mars is a brilliant object, shining with a fiery red light, and fairly rivalling Jupiter in splendor. It is then more than fifty times as bright as when faintest, at conjunction. When not near opposition, it might frequently be mistaken by an unpractised eye for one of the brightest of the fixed stars. Its motion among them would lead to its speedy identification. No other planet looks red, except when near the horizon.

212. Phases: Appearance in a Small Telescope. — When at opposition the planet's disk looks round, as seen with a small telescope, but at quadrature it is plainly gibbous. For at that time we are not in line between Mars and the sun, and so do not see all of its illuminated hemisphere. (See exercise 21 at the end of this chapter.) Besides the phase, an eye armed with a small telescope (three or four inches in aperture) sees at opposition that the surface is not all red, but bears certain darker markings, generally thought to be of an olive-green hue. At times a small white spot may be seen at one of the poles. The dark spots are supposed to be due to the presence of water; the white polar spot suggests snow.

213. The Polar Caps. — The caps are generally believed to be composed of snow and ice, not only because of their white appearance and their situation, but also because the northern one diminishes in size during summer time in Mars's northern hemisphere, and increases during the winter. The southern cap behaves in a similar fashion. During the opposition of 1892, the southern polar cap seemed to diminish with great rapidity. Its area was estimated to lose 1,500000 square miles in a month. First a dark spot was seen in the snow: this spot gradually enlarged, splitting the cap into two parts, each of which melted away at an astonishing rate. On several occasions white spots, apparently detached snowfields, were seen lying close to the main cap.

In 1894 a similar melting took place: in May hundreds of square miles of the polar cap disappeared daily. During the melting a dark band surrounded the cap, keeping at its edge continually, as would be expected if the snow and ice were turning into water. In October the cap had become so small that it was seen with the

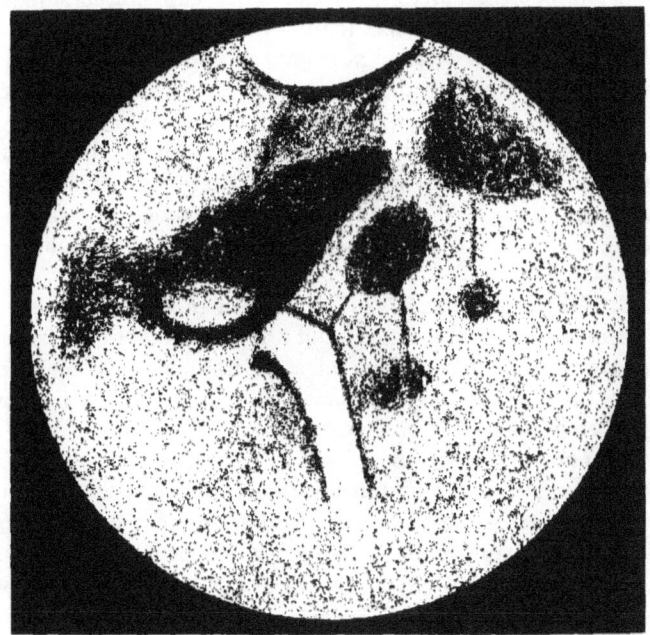

Fig. 133.—MARS: DRAWN BY BARNARD.

Lick telescope only; the remnant of it seemed to be almost hidden by some overhanging veil.

Fig. 133 shows the planet as it appeared to Dr. E. E. Barnard[1] with the Lick 36-inch telescope on August 19, 1892. The polar cap was then only one third as large in area as in June of the same year.

[1] Now of the Yerkes Observatory.

214. Seas. — The dark areas, if really seas, as generally supposed, are not as permanent in form as the oceans on the earth. The permanent water area has been estimated at about 500,000 square miles, which is only half as great as that of the Mediterranean Sea. When the polar cap melted in the summer of 1892, a portion of the region between it and one of the seas became dark, and the sea apparently increased in size. While we cannot be confident about the cause of such changes, it has been suggested that the water produced by the quick melting of the polar cap flowed across the land to a sea, increasing its size temporarily.

Though some of the dark portions of the planet's surface are probably bodies of water, there is reason to believe that much of the dusky area is not permanently covered with water. For canals (to be described later) have been seen in these "seas," and many different shades of color exist there: the same regions have different tints at different times. Sometimes a vast amount of detail is perceived, which would scarcely be found upon a water surface.[1]

215. Continents and Islands. — The reddish portion of the planet's disk is supposed to be dry land. But these hypothetical continents are not secure in their boundary lines. Disappearances of portions of them have been noted; they seem to be inundated by the waters of neighboring seas. Dr. S. P. Langley, in his work entitled "The New Astronomy," states that Lockyer Land is sometimes seen white, as if covered with ice; further, that Hall Island has this white appearance so frequently as to suggest the idea that some mountain or table-land on it rises into the region of perpetual snow. The changes on the surface of Mars during the opposition of 1892 were so noteworthy that Dr. E. E. Barnard was led to write as follows:

---

[1] Dr. Barnard describes some of his observations with the Lick telescope in 1894 as follows: —

"Under the best conditions these dark regions, which are always shown with smaller telescopes of nearly uniform shade, broke up into a vast amount of very fine details. I hardly know how to describe the appearance of these 'seas' under these conditions. To those, however, who have looked down upon a mountainous country from a considerable elevation, perhaps some conception of the appearance presented by these dark regions may be had. From what I know of the appearance of the country about Mount Hamilton, as seen from the observatory, I can imagine that, as viewed from a very great elevation, this region, broken by canyon and slope and ridge, would look just like the surface of these Martian 'seas.'"

"These striking changes are enough to make us pause and question whether what we see before us in the heavens is really another world like our own, with relatively fixed oceans and continents, or whether it is not a world like our own in its younger days, when continents were shifting and oceans changing, before the surface of the earth became firm and fixed by the process of cooling."

Some of the apparent changes in the forms of the continents have been ascribed to the spread of vegetation along their borders.

216. Clouds. — Transient spots, having the general aspect of cloud masses, have been observed. Sometimes they are small and of tolerably definite outline, but usually they are diffuse and of large extent. They have also appeared as long streaks projecting a trifle beyond the planet's limb. At times portions of the landscape have been so obscured as to give rise to the theory that the obscuration was caused by a passing cloud. But many details of the Martian landscape are usually seen so plainly that clouds must be considered as rarities. Their comparative absence would naturally follow from the small proportion of water surface.

217. Atmosphere. — Were the atmosphere dense, like that of Venus, we should never have discovered the mass of topographical detail now known. The rarity of Mars's atmosphere has been accounted for by the moderate size of the planet, and the weakness of the force of gravity at its surface. Could a rifle ball be shot upward with a velocity of 3.5 miles a second, it would, unless checked by atmospheric resistance, leave the planet never to return. The speed of molecules of hydrogen, in their incessant vibration, may considerably exceed this, so that free hydrogen is not to be looked for as a constituent of Mars's atmosphere. The best spectroscopic observations indicate that the atmosphere of Mars exerts no measurable absorptive effect upon the sunlight which strikes through it, and is reflected back to us. We are therefore ignorant of its composition, and can only say that, if it be similar to that of our air, its average density can scarcely be one fourth as great.

218. Description of the Canals. — In 1877 Schiaparelli discovered several of the markings which are commonly called "Schiaparelli's canals." A few had been seen previously. Many more have since been found by him and by others. The map of Mars made at the

Lowell observatory[1] in 1894, exhibits a bewildering network of canals, connecting small dark spots scattered over the surface. Not infrequently half a dozen canals radiate from a single spot, going straight to other spots. Most of the canals choose the shortest path from one spot to another: a few are curved. Some do not run from one small dark spot to another, but connect large dark areas, or go from a small spot to a large area, or occasionally connect two other canals. The small spots are less than 150 miles in diameter. The length of the canals ranges from a few hundred to 3,500 miles. Their average breadth is 30 miles. The most mysterious fact about them is that they become double at times, the two new canals being about 200 miles apart, and veritable twins. Schiaparelli thinks that the doubling may be periodical, and connected in some way with the planet's seasons.

219. Explanations of the Canals. — The canals have naturally been supposed to be water-ways. When a polar cap melts, the canals in the neighborhood become darker and wider, and remain dark until the snow stops melting. Then the width of the canals diminishes. These appearances have led Schiaparelli to the conclusion that the canals are natural furrows, through which the water is carried from the poles equatorward. Mr. Percival Lowell advocates the theory that the canals are strips of vegetation, which are watered by canals too small to be visible to us. A small spot at the junction of several canals is an oasis, according to this view. No satisfactory explanation of the doubling of the canals has been given. The majority of astronomers, while freely admitting the existence of the markings called canals, are inclined to be conservative with reference to any explanation of their nature. It has been aptly said that it is better not to know so much, than to know so many things that are not so.

220. Colors. — Orange and grayish green are the prevailing colors, outside of the polar caps. But various colors have been seen in different spots. The same spot has been of different hues at different times, though the utmost care was taken to avoid optical illusions. Light greens and bright greens have been seen often. At times places supposed to be bodies of water have exchanged

---

[1] A temporary observatory set up at Flagstaff, Arizona, by Mr. Percival Lowell, of Boston.

Fig. 134.—The Canals of Mars.

their ordinary color for dark blue. Gray and yellow tints are of common occurrence. Even so extraordinary a color as violet-lake was once perceived. Some of these colors may be explained as due to haziness or partial cloudiness. Perhaps some are due to the presence of vegetation.

221. Satellites. — Mars is attended by two moons, discovered by Prof. Hall [1] in August, 1877. Their names are Deimos and Phobos.[2] The distance of Deimos from the planet's centre is 14,600 miles; it completes a revolution about Mars in 30 h. 18 m.

Phobos is at a distance of but 5,800 miles and takes only 7 h. 39 m. for one revolution. The time of rotation of Mars being over 24 hours, Phobos by reason of its rapid motion rises in the west and sets in the east, as our moon would if its orbital motion were swift enough.

These moons are so minute that it is not possible to measure their diameters directly; but by measures of the amount of light that they give, Prof. Pickering [3] has concluded that the inner one is 7 miles in diameter, the outer one 5 or 6. Estimates made at the Lowell observatory give a diameter of 36 miles for Phobos and 10 miles for Deimos. Their discovery was as great a feat of telescopic vision as for a man in Boston to see a tennis ball at Philadelphia.

222. Habitability. — If we have simply to answer the question, "Would a man, as constituted at present, if transported to Mars, find it possible to exist there?" the most probable answer is, "No." While one must not be dogmatic, it may be said, with some assurance, that the man would gasp a few times and die. However, it is conceivable that manlike beings might find a home there. Plans for communication with the supposititious inhabitants of Mars by means of huge signals displayed in deserts or on table-lands, or by gigantic combinations of electric lights, are little better than phantasies of a disordered imagination. If some enter-

---

[1] Prof. Asaph Hall, formerly of the U. S. Naval Observatory, Washington, D. C.

[2] These names were given by Homer to the steeds which drew the chariot of the god of war. In one passage in the fifteenth book of the Iliad they are personified, and refer to the attendants of Mars. Bryant's translation is: —

"He spake, and summoned Fear and Flight to yoke
His steeds and put his glorious armor on."

[3] Edward C. Pickering, Director of the Harvard College Observatory.

prising and athletic individual on Mars should wave a flag as large as the State of New York, terrestrial astronomers might notice his greeting.

There have been curious anticipations of the discovery of the moons of Mars.[1]

Kepler, in a letter written after the discovery of four satellites of Jupiter by Galileo, said: "I am so far from disbelieving the existence of the four circumjovial planets, that I long for a telescope to anticipate you, if possible, in discovering two around Mars, as the proportion seems to require, six or eight around Saturn, and perhaps one each around Mercury and Venus."

Swift, in his satire, "The Travels of Mr. Lemuel Gulliver," puts the following language into the mouth of Gulliver, who had arrived among the inhabitants of Laputa, a flying island: —

"The knowledge I had in mathematics gave me great assistance in acquiring their phraseology, which depended much upon that science, and music: and in the latter I was not unskilled. Their ideas were perpetually conversant in lines and figures. If they would, for example, praise the beauty of a woman, or any other animal, they describe it by rhombs, circles, parallelograms, ellipses, and other geometrical terms, or by words of art drawn from music, needless here to repeat. . . . They spend the greatest part of their lives in observing the celestial bodies, which they do by the assistance of glasses far excelling ours in goodness. For although their largest telescopes do not exceed three feet, they magnify much more than those of a hundred with us, and show the stars with greater clearness. This advantage has enabled them to extend their discoveries much farther than our astronomers in Europe; for they have made a catalogue of ten thousand fixed stars, whereas the largest of ours do not contain above one third of that number. They have likewise discovered two lesser stars or satellites which revolve about Mars: whereof the innermost is distant from the centre of the primary planet exactly three of his diameters, and the outermost five; the former revolves in the space of ten hours, and the latter in twenty-one and a half; so that the squares of the periodical times are very nearly in the same proportion with the cubes of their distances from the centre of Mars; which evidently shows them to be governed by the same law of gravitation that influences the other heavenly bodies."

[1] The following interesting information is derived from Professor Hall's monograph on the satellites.

Voltaire represents, in one of his works, that Micromegas, an inhabitant of Sirius who visited our system, discovered that Mars had two moons, which made perpetual compensation for the lack of the brilliant sunlight which we enjoy.

THE ASTEROIDS, OR MINOR PLANETS.

223. Bode's Law. — In 1772 the astronomer Bode brought into prominence a relation between the distances from the sun of the then known planets. This relation had been discovered some years previously by Titius, but it is commonly called Bode's Law, and is found as follows. The series 0, 3, 6, 12, etc., in which each number except the first is double the preceding one, is written. To each term 4 is added.

0	3	6	12	24	48	96	192
4	7	10	16	28	52	100	196

The resulting numbers represent fairly the relative distances. Taking the earth's distance as ten, the real distances are given below.

Mercury . . . 3.9	Jupiter . . . 52.0
Venus . . . 7.2	Saturn . . . 95.4
Earth 10.0	Uranus . . . 191.8
Mars 15.2	

The number 28 in the scheme of Titius corresponded to no known planet. Astronomers generally became imbued with the notion that there was a planet to be discovered, which would fill the gap.

Neptune was then unknown: its distance does not conform to the law, being only 300.5.

224. Discovery of the First Minor Planet. — After Uranus was discovered in 1781, and its distance had been found to conform to the law of Titius, an association of astronomers was formed, to hunt for the missing planet between Mars and Jupiter. But the honor of the discovery was reserved for Piazzi, of Palermo, who was not a member of the association, but was engaged upon a star catalogue. It was his habit to observe the right ascension and declination of each star on several different nights, that he might determine its place accurately.

Upon the evening of the first day of the nineteenth century, he observed a list of stars, one of which was destined to bring him renown. On January 2d, 3d, and 4th he reobserved the same list, and upon comparing his observations, discovered that the thirteenth star on the list changed its position from night to night. Here at last was a planet, but was it the one sought? For six weeks he observed it upon every opportunity, and then he fell ill: when he recovered, the planet was so near to the sun that it could no longer be found.

225. Gauss computes the Orbit. — Here was a dilemma. The news reached Germany in the early spring, and Gauss, of Göttingen, then a rising young mathematician, set himself at the task of finding some method of computing its orbit. Finally he discovered the now classic method of computing a planet's orbit, when its right ascension and declination are known at three different dates. He applied the new method to Piazzi's observations, and predicted the future place of the planet; at last it was bound by the chains of mathematical analysis, more ethereal than a spider's web, but stronger than bronze. The association was already hard on the track of the wanderer, and when Gauss's results reached them, one of them speedily rediscovered it, on the last day of the year. Its distance from the sun was in fair agreement with the law of Titius, being 25.7 instead of 28. It received the name Ceres.

226. Further Discoveries. — In 1802, 1804, and 1807, Pallas, Juno, and Vesta were found. Astronomers were not again successful in the quest until 1845, when Astræa was brought to light. Soon afterward the pace of discovery quickened, and now the asteroid hunters find them with almost embarrassing rapidity. The family of these little strangers is so large, and increasing so rapidly, that the problem of taking care of them is becoming a very serious one. The orbit of each new one has to be computed, and its place in the sky (right ascension and declination) calculated from year to year, so that fresh observations can be taken, and a more accurate orbit figured out.

227. Methods of Search. — Almost all of these bodies are so small that they look like fixed stars, and can be detected only by their motion. An observer makes a chart of a certain region of the sky, containing all the stars visible there through his telescope. Then night after night he compares the heavens with his chart. If a star-like object not on the chart is seen, its position is carefully noted. In a few hours its motion will betray it, if it be a minor planet.

This process is quite laborious, and is now little used because photography has entered the field. A picture of a certain region of the sky is taken, the plate being exposed for a couple of hours. While the images of stars on the plate are circular, the image of the planetoid is a short streak, caused by its motion.

228. Orbits: Distances: Periods. — The orbits of the planetoids are more eccentric than those of the major planets. The orbit planes have greater inclinations to the ecliptic, the orbit of Pallas being inclined 35°. The mean distances vary from 198,000000 to 400,000000 miles, the periods from three years to nine.

The computations of the orbits, as well as of the annual *ephemerides*, giving the right ascension and declination of the minor planets, are made chiefly by German computers.

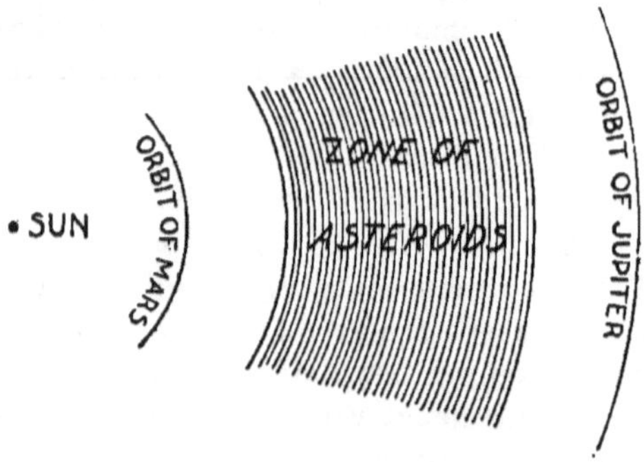

The *Berliner Jahrbuch*, issued from the Imperial Observatory at Kiel, Prussia, contains the results of their work.

Fig. 135.— The Zone of Asteroids.

The late Prof. Watson[1] left a fund to pay for the twenty-two which he discovered, intrusting it to the American National Academy of Sciences.

229. Designations. — Each asteroid has a number, which is usually printed thus, ⑯, the numbers being given in the order of discovery. Names are also given, chosen chiefly from those of female divinities in classical mythology. The number of these is about exhausted. Some of the unfortunate planetoids have been afflicted with such names as Xantippe, Vindobona, and Sophia, to say nothing of Walpurga and Chicago. The asteroid last mentioned

---

[1] James C. Watson, Director of the Observatory at Ann Arbor, Mich., and later of the Washburn Observatory at Madison, Wis., author of Watson's Theoretical Astronomy.

was named by the Astronomical Congress which met at Chicago during the World's Fair.

230. Number and Size.—The number is now (1896) over 400. Most of them are of quite insignificant dimensions. Vesta, the brightest one, is 250 miles in diameter. At opposition it is barely visible to a good eye. Ceres, the largest, is nearly 500 miles in diameter. The majority are less than fifty miles in diameter. Most of the faint ones now being discovered have diameters of only about ten miles. Compared with the earth they are as flour-dust to a football. Half a billion of them compacted together might equal the earth in bulk.

231. Atmosphere: Gravity.— The bodies are so small that they probably have very rare atmospheres. There are no reliable observations bearing on this point. On the assumption that they are as dense as the earth, the force of gravity at the surface of one of the small ones is about one thousandth part[1] of that which we daily contend with. A sharply batted base-ball would leave the planet; in a jumping match the spectators could eat lunch while waiting for the contestants to come back to terra firma.

232. Origin.— One view is that they have been formed from a larger body by a series of explosions. A single explosion would not account for them, for the fragments, after coursing about the sun would all return to the point where the explosion occurred. After the lapse of ages their orbits would be considerably modified by the attractions of the major planets, especially by that of Jupiter. But yet the theory of a single explosion is considered untenable by those mathematicians who have given particular attention to the matter. The present tendency of scientific opinion is to discard catastrophes, and to believe in an orderly evolution manifested throughout the universe. According to the nebular hypothesis, the material composing the minor planets was once collected in a ring surrounding the sun. The ring in condensing formed many planets instead of one: the cause of the disruption of the ring may have been the powerful attraction of Jupiter.

[1] The principles of mechanics show that for spheres of equal densities the force of gravity at their surfaces varies as their diameters. Thus, if two leaden spheres were respectively one foot and ten feet in diameter, a grain of sand lying on the surface of the latter would be attracted by it ten times as strongly as an equal grain on the surface of the former.

EXERCISES.

233. 1. If the axis of Mercury is perpendicular to the plane of its orbit, and the planet rotates on its axis at a uniform rate from west to east once in every revolution, are there alternations of day and night at a point on the surface directly between the centres of the sun and the planet?

2. In the case above, would the sun shine on more than half of Mercury's surface in 88 days, considering the eccentricity of its orbit?

3. On account of the relative sizes of the sun and Mercury, does the former, at each instant, illuminate more than a hemisphere of the latter's surface?

4. Why do Mercury and Venus look black during transit?

5. Mercury at times attains an elongation of 28° from the sun. If it is at eastern elongation about the last of March, its orbit being roughly coincident with the ecliptic, will it be above the celestial equator, or below? [In answering this, first fix in mind the position of the sun in the ecliptic.]

6. Should a planet, in order to be seen most advantageously from your home, be above or below the equator?

7. If Mercury be near its western elongation on April 1, will it be in a favorable position to be seen from your home?

8. If Mercury be near its eastern elongation when school opens in the fall, will it be in a favorable position for observation by you?

9. If you were searching for Mercury with the naked eye, would it be more convenient to have it at eastern or western elongation, considering only the time of night at which you would look for it?

10. When Venus is morning star, is it east of the sun, or west?

11. Draw two concentric circles of the proper relative sizes to represent the orbits of Venus and the earth. Locate the two planets upon them, so that Venus shall be at its greatest elongation. Then measure the angle of elongation with a protractor.

12. What phase has Venus when at elongation?

13. Is Venus gibbous between its superior conjunction and its greatest eastern elongation?

14. Is Venus gibbous between its greatest western elongation and superior conjunction?

15. Just before inferior conjunction do the cusps of the crescent Venus point toward the sun?

16. Find from the Nautical Almanac when Mercury and Venus next reach elongation.

17. If you have a telescope, make the following test of it and your eye. Make on white paper a drawing like Fig. 136. Look at it with the telescope, and estimate the width of the black drop as compared with the diameter of the black circle representing the planet. It is well to perform the experiment out of doors, with your back to the sun, so that the paper may be well illuminated.

Fig. 136.

18. Why is not a ring of light seen around Venus, when it is in transit?

19. The volumes of two spheres are to each other as the cubes of their diameters. The earth is how many times as large as Mars?

20. Assume that the diameter of the earth is 8,000 miles, and that of some asteroid is 10 miles. The earth is how many times as large as the asteroid?

21. Draw two concentric circles of the proper relative diameters to represent the orbits of the earth and Mars. (The representation will not be very accurate, because Mars's orbit is quite eccentric.) Mark a point on the inner circle for the earth, and another on the outer to represent the position of the centre of Mars, when in quadrature. Around this centre draw a little circle, to represent the planet itself, on an exaggerated scale. Shade one half of this little circle, so that it will represent the unilluminated hemisphere of Mars. How does the picture show that Mars, as seen from the earth, would be gibbous?

22. Does any planet, as seen from the sun, exhibit phases?

23. Deimos and Phobos move in the plane of Mars's equator. Could an observer at a pole of the planet see them?

24. Compute the area of the surface of Deimos, assuming it to be a sphere six miles in diameter.

25. Is Bode's Law anything more than a chance coincidence?

26. The first day of this century was January 1st in what year?

27. Why does the small size of an asteroid militate against its having a dense atmosphere?

CHAPTER X.

JUPITER, SATURN, URANUS, NEPTUNE.

> " Some displaying
> Enormous liquid plains, and some begirt
> With luminous belts, and floating moons, which took,
> Like them, the features of fair earth."
>
> BYRON.

234. The Outer Group. — We come now to the consideration of the outer group of planets, in comparison with which the planets before considered are but pygmies.

JUPITER, ♃.

235. Distance and Diameter. — The mean distance of Jupiter from the sun is 483,000000 miles; this is five and one fifth times the distance of the earth. Its mean diameter is 88,000 miles. The planets heretofore considered are nearly spherical, but Jupiter's disk as seen in a telescope is a marked oval, showing that the polar diameter of the planet is shorter than the equatorial.[1] Jupiter is larger than all the other planets put together, being 1,300 times as large as the earth.

236. Revolution and Rotation. — The sidereal period of this planet is nearly twelve (11.86) years. Despite its huge bulk, it rotates with amazing swiftness, in about 9 h. 55 m. The rotation period cannot be obtained with exactness, because, like the sun, different parts of the surface rotate in different times, those near the equator moving most rapidly. Even a particular feature of his surface does not have a uniform rotation time. The time for the great red spot (§ 240), for example, slowly increased from year to year during the period 1878–86, the total increase being seven seconds. Since 1886 there has been no change.

---

[1] The polar diameter is 84,300 miles and the equatorial 89,790 miles. The mean diameter is found by adding the polar diameter to twice the equatorial, and dividing the sum by 3.

237. Appearance to the Naked Eye. — To the naked eye, Jupiter, when near opposition, attains a greater brilliancy than any other planet, except Venus. At all times, except when too near conjunction, it is much brighter than any of the fixed stars. Its light is white, with the merest tinge of yellow. Except when near one of its stationary points, its planetary nature can be detected in less than a week by its motion among the stars.

Men of extremely acute vision, under the fairest of skies, have occasionally seen one of its satellites with the naked eye. One who suspects that he sees a satellite should move his head from side to side, and see if the suspected satellite moves also; if it does not, it may be a satellite or a fixed star.

238. Belts. — These are readily discerned with a small telescope. The surface seems banded by parallel belts, the most conspicuous ones being near the planet's equator. The belts are dark colored. In small instruments the dark belts appear of a grayish or brownish cast; but in larger ones a reddish hue is observed. At times they even appear pink. The belts are supposed to be rifts in the clouds, through which we look down deeper into his atmosphere than elsewhere. The light portions of the disk, as shown in Fig. 137, resemble masses of cumulus cloud. The appearance of the belts is sometimes reproduced in the terrestrial clouds lying below the summit of Mt. Hamilton, Cal., the home of the Lick observatory. The belts change their outlines somewhat from month to month.

239. Pickering's Theory of the Belts. — Prof. W. H. Pickering,[1] observing from a high Peruvian table-land, where the atmospheric conditions are very fine, says that the appearance of Jupiter is that of a uniform white mass of cloud, overlaid by a thin gauze veil of a brown material, not unlike our cirrus clouds in structure. This veil is more dense in some places than in others; the dense portions, by obscuring the white cloud beneath, cause the dark belts. The well known white spots are thought to be due to round or elliptical holes in the cirrus layer, through which we see the white surface below. He says: "In short, it appears that, were it not for this insignificant light gauzy veil of brown cloud, we should find the surface of Jupiter, like that of most of the other planets in the solar system, almost a perfect blank. This gauzy structure must float in

---

[1] Of the Harvard College Observatory.

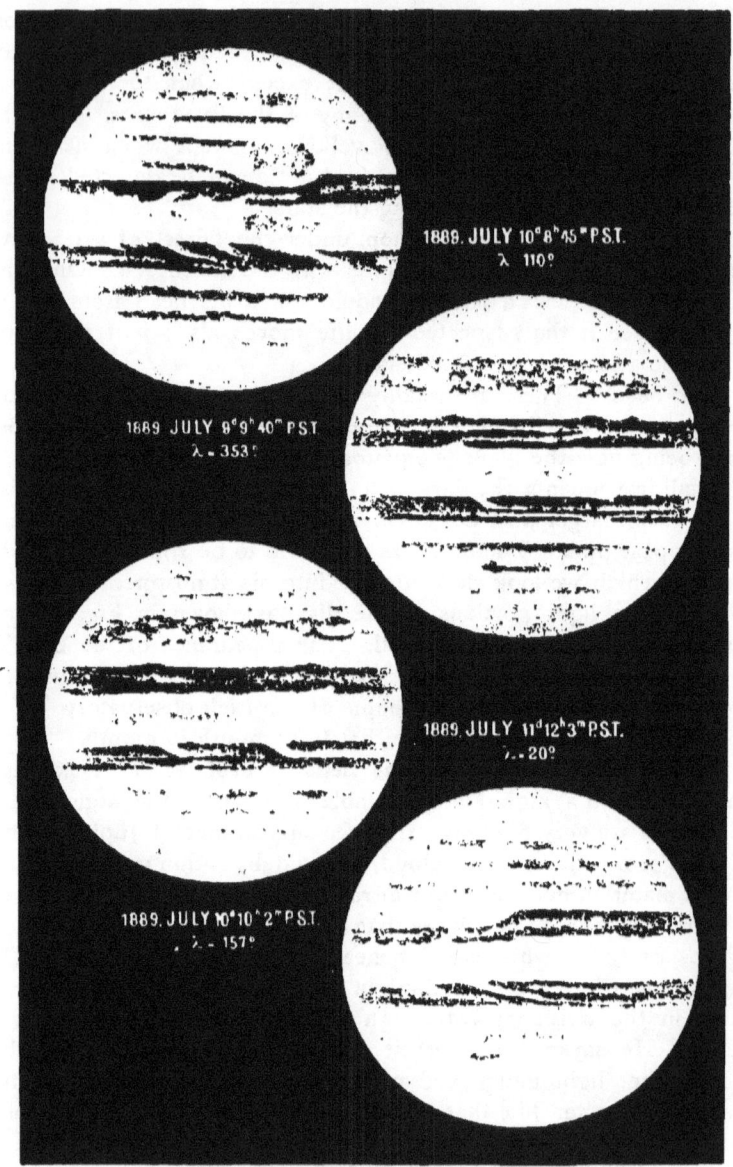

Fig. 137.—Jupiter, as seen with the Lick Telescope: Drawn by Keeler

a nearly transparent atmosphere, surrounding and rising above it; it is this atmosphere which causes the absorption, and which almost completely obscures the belts at the limb of the planet."

240. The Great Red Spot. — This was discovered in 1878; it is 30,000 miles long and 7,000 broad. It has had various degrees of brightness in different years, being almost invisible in 1883 and 1884, and again in 1892. It is no longer a conspicuous object, even in large telescopes. The spot is thought to be a rift in the clouds, similar in color to the belts, though usually more vivid. Its cause is a mere matter of conjecture. Perhaps it is due to some terrific ebullition in the depths of the planet, which causes heated vapors to arise and clear away the clouds which would otherwise be above it. Its remarkable persistency of form, and its movement (§ 236) are against this supposition.

241. Smaller Spots. — These have been seen frequently of late years, and are chiefly either white or black. They are usually round or elliptical; their average size is about that of our moon. Perhaps they are cloud masses which are above the general level, and therefore show more plainly. Their motions are independent, as is shown by the fact that the rotation time of the planet, determined by observations of one spot, does not generally agree with that found by employing some other spot.

242. Atmosphere: Spectrum. — All the evidence points to the conclusion that the atmosphere is very extensive. There is no reason to believe that any permanent markings have ever been seen on the planet, so deep and dense is the enveloping atmosphere.

The spectroscope gives no certain evidence concerning the composition of the atmosphere, the spectrum of Jupiter being almost identical with that of the sun. This shows that the light which gives the spectrum is merely reflected sunlight. If the light penetrated to any considerable depth it would suffer marked absorption, which would be manifested by bands in the spectrum. There is one large faint band in the spectrum, the origin of which is unknown.

243. Light and Heat. — If Jupiter were hot enough to give out light of its own, its moons would not suffer total eclipse when they passed into its shadow. But a body may be quite hot without being perceptibly luminous, as any disbeliever may discover by experimenting with a poker recently withdrawn from the fire. So cloudy is the planet, so great are the changes continually taking place on its surface, and so feeble is the action of the sun upon it on account of its great distance, that we are compelled to believe that the planet is hot. It may be nearly self-luminous, and has been called a semi-sun.

244. Physical Condition. — The average density of the planet is only a third greater than that of water. It is therefore chiefly, if not entirely, composed of matter in a fluid state; hot water may be one of its chief constituents. We are not to regard it as possessing a solid crust, like the earth, but rather as being a seething caldron, in which the hot fluids rise from the interior, become cooler, and sink back, in a ceaseless round of motion.

245. The Major Satellites. — These are four in number, and are designated in the Nautical Almanac by the Roman numerals I, II, III, and IV, according to their distances from the planet, I being

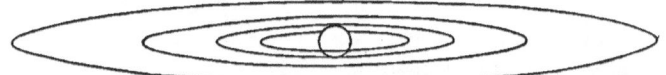

Fig. 138. — THE ORBITS OF THE MAJOR SATELLITES.

nearest, and IV the most remote. The smallest, II, is as large as the moon, and the largest, III, is nearly as big as Mars. They are all visible in a good opera-glass. Their orbits are nearly in the plane of the planet's equator.

246. Eclipses. — Jupiter casts so long and large a shadow away from the sun that all the satellites except the fourth suffer eclipse once during every revolution. The times of these eclipses are given in the Nautical Almanac, and they can be easily observed with a small telescope. For obvious reasons the satellite does not disappear instantaneously, but fades from sight gradually.

247. Occultations. — When a satellite, as seen from the earth, is behind Jupiter, it has suffered occultation. When it has been just disappearing behind the limb of Jupiter, or reappearing, many attempts have been made to see it shining through Jupiter's atmosphere, with the hope of measuring its refractive power. But most of the attempts (even with the Lick telescope) are acknowledged failures.

248. Transits. — A satellite, when passing between us and the planet, appears to cross its face and is in transit. The limb of Jupiter is darker than the centre of its disk: on this account a satellite is visible at the beginning or end of a transit as a bright spot on a dark background. When the satellite is projected upon some portion of the disk which has the same brightness and color, it becomes invisible. One occasionally appears dark, or even black at some time during transit: this may be because the background, on which it is projected at the time, is unusually bright. The shadows of the satellites also make transits: at times, a satellite and its shadow are seen journeying across Jupiter's face in company.

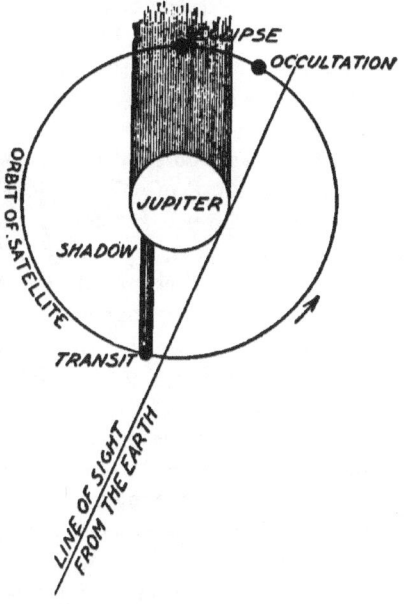

Fig. 139. — PHENOMENA OF THE SATELLITES.

249. Markings and Rotation. — Many observers have reported dark markings on the satellites. Some of the most authoritative recent work is that of Professors Schaeberle and Campbell[1] with

Fig. 140. — MARKINGS SEEN WITH THE LICK TELESCOPE.

the Lick telescope. Their drawings of the markings on satellite III, made with very high magnifying powers, lend strong support

---

[1] W. W. Campbell, astronomer at the Lick Observatory.

to the theory that it continually keeps the same face toward Jupiter. Their observations also show that satellite I is perceptibly elongated, and that its long axis points toward the planet's centre. These satellites therefore resemble the moon in that their times of revolution and rotation are coincident. Schaeberle and others have seen a bright polar cap on satellite III. Barnard discovered a white belt on satellite I, which causes it to appear double when crossing a white part of Jupiter.

250. Pickering's Observations of the Satellites. — In addition to studying the belts, Prof. W. H. Pickering has made careful observations of the satellites. He found the first satellite to be at times very plainly elliptical, the major axis exceeding the minor by ten per cent. For the time of rotation he has deduced a value of 13 h. 3 m., from a series of observations.

The rotation time of the second satellite was much more difficult to obtain, but a value of over 41 hours was settled upon.

The observations of the third and fourth satellites favor the theory that their times of rotation and revolution are coincident.

Prof. Pickering's results are in only partial agreement with those of other observers: the matter needs much further study.

251. The Fifth Satellite. — On Sept. 9, 1892, Dr. E. E. Barnard discovered a fifth satellite, with the Lick telescope. It is a tiny point of light, which can be observed with the most powerful telescopes only. Its distance from the centre of Jupiter is 112,000 miles and its time of revolution 11 h. 57 m. 22.56 sec. Its diameter is estimated as 100 miles. If it were a few thousand miles nearer to the planet, it would probably be torn in pieces by the attraction of the latter, which would be much more powerful upon the side of the satellite turned toward it at any time than on the opposite side.

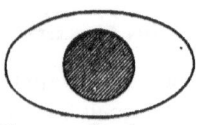

Fig. 141. — JUPITER AND THE ORBIT OF THE FIFTH SATELLITE.

252. Velocity of Light. — The fact that light does not travel from one point to another instantaneously was discovered in 1675 by Roemer, a Danish astronomer. The discovery was made by the discussion of observations of Jupiter's satellites. The eclipses recur at nearly equal intervals. By noting the times of the eclipses of satellite I, for example, during the period of one revolution of Jupiter about the sun, one can calculate with great accuracy the average interval of time between two successive eclipses: the satellite suffers some 2,500 eclipses during that period. When Jupiter is in opposition, let the time of an eclipse be noted: by means of the known interval between two successive eclipses, compute the day, hour, and minute when an eclipse will occur three months after opposition, at which time the earth will be farther from Jupiter. The eclipse will happen later than the predicted time. Predict another eclipse near the time of the planet's conjunction with the sun, when the earth is 186,000000 miles farther from Jupiter than at opposition. The eclipse will again be behindhand, and by a larger amount than before. Roemer sagaciously guessed that the eclipse which took place near the time of conjunction really happened on time, but that the light which brought the message to the observer took time to cross the extra distance of 186,000000 miles. In this he was right: the time required for light to cross the earth's orbit is close to 1,000 seconds.

SATURN, ♄.

253. Distance and Diameter. — The distance of this most enchanting of planets from the sun is 886,000000 miles. Its mean diameter is 74,000 miles.

254. Revolution and Rotation. — The sidereal period is 29½ years. The rotation time is hard to determine because so few small well defined spots have ever been seen on its surface. Prof. Asaph Hall has derived a value of 10 h. 14 m. 23.8 sec. from his observations of a white spot which appeared on the ball in December, 1876, and was visible for a month.

255. Appearance to the Naked Eye. — Because of its greater distance, Saturn is much fainter than Jupiter. It alone of the planets has a decided yellowish tint; it is generally as bright as a first magnitude star, and may be distinguished from a star by the fact that it does not twinkle. All planets have this peculiarity except when near the horizon. A person who is acquainted with the constellations may find it easily by looking up its right ascension and declination in the Nautical Almanac, and locating it on a star map.

256. Telescopic Appearance. — The first view of Saturn with a large telescope usually calls forth an exclamation of wonder and delight. For the globe is seen to be surrounded by a marvellous ring system, which is unique in the solar system, and, so far as we know, in the entire universe. A goodly retinue of satellites is also seen attending this majestic orb.

The ball is encircled by rather bright belts near the equator, and by fainter ones at higher latitudes. These belts are not subject to much change of appearance, except that due to imperfect seeing caused by the fluctuations of our own atmosphere. Serenity is natural for the oldest of the gods.

Fig. 142. — SATURN, AS SEEN WITH THE LICK TELESCOPE: DRAWN BY KEELER.

257. Discovery of the Rings. — In 1610 Galileo discovered that the planet appeared triform. This was due to the imperfection of his telescope.

He said that Saturn had two servants who aided him on his way. Great was his perplexity and chagrin to find that the attendants disappeared after a year or two. In a letter to a friend he said: —

"What is to be said concerning so strange a metamorphosis? Are the two lesser stars consumed after the manner of solar spots? Have they vanished, or suddenly fled? Has Saturn, perhaps, devoured his own children? Or were the appearances indeed illusion and fraud, with which the glasses have so long deceived me, as well as many others to whom I have shown them? . . . The shortness of the time, the unexpected nature of the event, the weakness of my understanding, have greatly confounded me."

Nevertheless, in the latter part of the letter he ventures to predict that the lost bodies will reappear; and he himself, as we learn from a later letter, saw them again as "ears," one on each side of the central ball. Forty odd years later, Huyghens, a Dutch astronomer, advanced the theory that Saturn had a ring, announcing it in the form "aaaaaaa ccccc d eccee g h iiiiiii llll mm nnnnnnnnn oooo pp q rr s ttttt uuuuu." These letters, properly arranged, form the Latin sentence, *Annulo cingitur, tenui, plano, nusquam cohaerente, ad eclipticam inclinato.* The translation is: "It is encircled by a thin flat ring, nowhere touching, inclined to the ecliptic."

258. Divisions and Dimensions of the Ring System. — The ring announced by Huyghens has been found with powerful telescopes to be composed of three, two of which are bright and the third dark. They are shown clearly in Fig. 142. The division between the outer ring and the middle one has been named Cassini's division, after the Italian astronomer who first noticed it, twenty years after Huyghens's announcement; it is about 2,200 miles in width. There is a finer division in the outer ring, known as the Encke division. Many others have been suspected. One has been found by Keeler[1] at the Lick Observatory.

The inner ring is much darker and fainter than the others; it is known as the dark or dusky ring. The extreme diameter of the ring system is 173,000 miles, and its breadth is about equal to the semidiameter of the ball. The rings are not of uniform thickness, as is shown when the edge of the system is turned toward us. The average thickness is not far from one hundred miles.

259. Disappearance of the Rings. — This phenomenon, which was so sore a trial to Galileo, is explained by Fig. 143. The plane of the rings coincides with that of the planet's equator, but is inclined 27° to the plane of the planet's orbit. Saturn keeps the successive positions of its rings parallel to each other in its journey around the sun. As the plane of the earth's equator passes through the sun in March and September, so the plane of Saturn's rings passes through the sun twice in one of its revolutions. Since the earth, as seen from Saturn, is close to the sun, the plane of the rings will pass through the earth within a few weeks of the same time. At such a time, the rings disappear because they are thin,

---

[1] James E. Keeler, Director of the Allegheny Observatory.

and edgewise to us. The disappearances happen at intervals of fifteen years: at times midway between them the rings are seen most favorably.

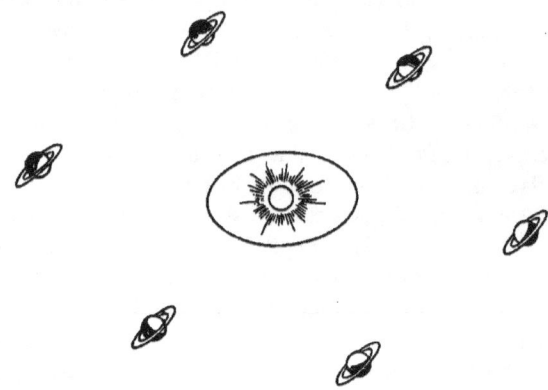

Fig. 143.—DIFFERENT POSITIONS OF THE RINGS.

260. The Dark Ring. — This ring is sometimes called the crape or gauze ring, because it is semi-transparent. Dr. Barnard, at the Lick telescope, on Nov. 1, 1889, observed an eclipse of one of the satellites. After emerging from the shadow of the ball it recovered its normal brightness, and soon plunged into the shadow of the dusky ring; it then became fainter and fainter, but did not disappear until it had passed through the shadow of the crape ring and into the shadow of the inner one of the two bright rings; then it disappeared entirely. This shows that sunlight sifts through the dark ring, and that the transparency of the latter decreases regularly from its inner edge to its outer, where it joins the inner bright ring.

261. Structure of the Rings. — The researches of mathematicians have demonstrated that neither ring can be an unbroken mass, either solid or liquid. In either case the ring would have been destroyed long ago by the attraction of the ball. The hypothesis now adopted is that it is composed of myriads of minute bodies, a congeries of closely packed moons, each of which has an orbit of its own. In the dark ring the bodies are less closely packed together than in the bright ones. At the outer edge of the dark ring they are thought to be more densely crowded than at its inner edge.

This hypothesis concerning the structure of the rings has been confirmed by observation. The separate particles are much too small to be seen separately, but their existence did not escape the spectroscope in the hands of Keeler in April, 1895. If the bright ring were solid, its outer edge would travel faster than the inner, just as a point on a tooth of a circular saw moves more swiftly than one nearer the centre. On the other hand, if the ring is made up of moonlets, those near its outer edge must move with less velocity than those near the inner. Professor Keeler's beautiful photographs of the spectrum of the bright ring showed that the outer and inner edges had respectively velocities of 10.1 and 12.4 miles per second. These values agree well with theoretical ones computed according to Kepler's Laws.

262. Stability of the System. — The Cassini division is supposed to be due to the attraction of the largest satellite, which has changed the orbits of the bodies which once occupied the division. The outer divisions were presumably caused in the same manner.

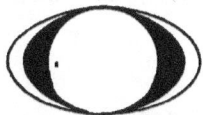

Fig. 144. — OLD DRAWING OF SATURN.

These minute bodies must be continually colliding with each other, so that some of them lose velocity, and are drawn into smaller orbits by the attraction of the ball. The appearance of the dark ring suggests that the ring system is being thus disintegrated. A comparison of the old drawing shown in Fig. 144 with Fig. 142 indicates that the space between the ball and the inner edge of the rings is now smaller than formerly. All these considerations have led to the hypothesis that Saturn is indeed "devouring his children."

However, no evidence of such a change is given by accurate measures of the dimensions of the ring made during the past one hundred years.

263. The Satellites. — These are eight in number. Japetus, the outermost, is at a distance of 2,212000 miles, and occupies seventy-nine days in a revolution. Mimas, the innermost, is only 30,000 miles beyond the outer edge of the ring system, and completes its circuit in less than a day. Titan, the largest, is nearly as big as Mercury. All move in the plane of the rings excepting Japetus, the orbit of which is inclined 10° to it. Japetus suffers remarkable and regular variations in brightness, which are explained by assuming that one hemisphere of it is much brighter than the other, and that it always presents the same face to the planet, as our moon does to the earth.

264. Physical Condition of the Planet. — The mean density of the ball is less than that of water, or even alcohol, closely agreeing with that of ether. The cloud shell surrounding the kernel of the planet is so deep that it hides beneath its placid exterior nearly all the commotions which are taking place. The central nucleus seems to possess heat sufficient to maintain this cloud mantle, but not sufficient to give rise to such activity as Jupiter manifests. The spectrum of the ball is that of the sunlight reflected from its surface, with the addition of some dark bands caused by the absorption of the sunlight by an unknown constituent of the planet's atmosphere. The spectrum of the rings contains no absorption bands.

URANUS, ⚴ OR ♅.

265. Discovery.[1] — William Herschel discovered Uranus in March, 1781. He was an organist at Bath, England,— a man of no mean musical attainments. In studying the mathematical theory of music, he had occasion to enlarge his knowledge of mathematics; from this he was led to optics, and became exceedingly interested in telescopes and astronomy. He resolved to make a reflecting telescope: supporting himself by his profession, he devoted his leisure to grinding and polishing specula and lenses. Rushing home from a concert, he would plunge at once into work on his mirrors, without even stopping to take off his lace ruffles. Mirror after mirror was constructed, put to use, and laid aside or sold, each giving place to a new one, more perfect, or of larger size. When engaged in putting the finishing touches on one of his great mirrors, he often sat at his work for hours, food being put into his mouth by his devoted sister Caroline, who sat by his side, and beguiled the time by reading "The Arabian Nights."

[1] This article is chiefly a condensation of material found in Ball's "Story of the Heavens."

URANUS.

Such unremitting enthusiasm and genius must find their reward. After half a dozen years of this assiduous toil, he succeeded in constructing a seven-inch reflector of exquisite optical perfection. He resolved to examine all the stars above a certain order of brightness. Now a fixed star is the merest point of light; the more perfect the telescope, the smaller is the image of the star.

Star after star passed in review before him. Finally, on the night of March 13, 1781, he perceived an object which looked like

Fig. 145.—SIR WILLIAM HERSCHEL.

a star, except that its disk was a trifle larger than that of a star of the same brightness. Many a time had this object been observed by other astronomers, but they had noticed no peculiarity in its appearance. Herschel soon found that it was in slow motion; he reasoned that it must be nearer than the fixed stars, and not dreaming that he had discovered a new major planet, the others having been known since the dawn of astronomical science, announced that he had found a comet. Astronomers at once set to work observing it. Computations of its orbit followed. Within a year the mathematicians had demonstrated that the orbit was nearly a circle, twice as large as the path of Saturn. The object was therefore a planet. Herschel proposed the name Georgium Sidus in honor of his sovereign; Laplace suggested the designation Herschel. The name finally adopted was proposed by Bode. This notable extension of the confines of the solar system was hailed with the greatest enthusiasm. King George knighted Herschel, and gave him £200 a year. The further career of Herschel, who finally constructed a reflector four feet in aperture and forty feet in focal length, stamps him as foremost among astronomical observers.

266. Distance and Diameter. — The distance of Uranus from the sun is 1,782,000000 miles. Its diameter is 32,000 miles, four times that of the earth.

267. Revolution and Rotation. — The sidereal period is eighty-four years. The time of rotation is unknown, because no sufficiently definite markings have ever been seen on its surface.

268. Appearance. — To the naked eye it appears as a small star just on the limit of visibility. It may be found by the use of the Nautical Almanac, which gives its right ascension and declination throughout the year.

In a large telescope it exhibits a greenish disk occasionally marked by faint belts. Granting, as mathematical theory demands, that the planes of the orbits of the satellites nearly coincide with that of the planet's equator, the belts are not parallel to the equator, an unexplained anomaly.

269. The Satellites. — Uranus is attended by four of these bodies, no one of which can be seen by an ordinary eye with a telescope less than eight inches in aperture. The diameter of the largest is probably five hundred miles. Their orbits lie in one plane, which, strange to say, is nearly perpendicular to the ecliptic. They also revolve backwards, that is from east to west, in their orbits, unlike any other satellites before considered.

270. Physical Condition. — Of this little is known. The spectrum of the planet exhibits some conspicuous bands, thought to be due to the absorption of a dense atmosphere. Sunlight at Uranus being only $\frac{1}{368}$ as intense as at the earth, the processes of cloud formation must be dependent chiefly on internal heat. Its mean density is less than that of bituminous coal.

NEPTUNE, ♆.

271. Discovery. — The discovery of Neptune is esteemed the most notable triumph of mathematical astronomy. It was no mere accident, nor was it brought about simply by a diligent search with the telescope. Forty years after the discovery of Uranus, Bouvard, a French astronomer, published tables of its motion, by means of which its place could be predicted for the future. But the planet refused to follow the path marked out for it; farther and farther it departed from the appointed course. In twenty years the discrepancy between theory and observation had become intolerable. To be sure, the difference could not yet be perceived by the naked eye, but the unfailing accuracy of the observations loudly proclaimed that there was some fault in the theory of the planet's motion. Was the law of gravitation partially inoperative at this enormous distance from the sun? Had a flaw been found at last in the marvellous researches of Newton? By no means. From many quarters came the suggestion that some unknown body was displacing Uranus by its powerful attraction. But could the position of the troublesome stranger be pointed out?

John Couch Adams, a tutor in the University of Cambridge, England, grappled with the problem. In October, 1845, he communicated to the Astronomer Royal of England the elements of the orbit of the suspected planet, together with a prediction of its place in the sky. But the Astronomer Royal[1] did not regard these investigations of a young and comparatively unknown man as entitled to much confidence. He however called the attention of a few of his friends to them, and wrote Adams asking some further information: no reply reached him. He therefore pigeon-holed the manuscript. One of the friends wrote to Lassell, who possessed a fine two-foot reflector which was mounted near Liverpool, begging him to search for the planet. But Lassell was suffering from a sprained ankle, and when he recovered, the letter was nowhere to be found, and the telescopic search was not made.

[1] Sir George Biddell Airy.

Meanwhile Leverrier, a brilliant French astronomer, likewise a young man, had employed his powers upon the same problem. On June 1, 1846, he sent a communication to the French Academy of Sciences giving the direction in which the planet was to be found.

Fig. 146.—John Couch Adams.

The English astronomers, finding that Leverrier's results agreed with those of Adams, awoke from their lethargy, and began to bestir themselves. Professor Challis, the astronomer of the University of Cambridge, commenced a search. Doubting the accuracy of the predictions, he began to map a large area of the sky, hoping by comparison of maps of the same region made on different nights to detect the planet by its change of position if it were really there.

Sir John Herschel (son of Sir William), in a public address, said concerning the unknown body: "We see it as Columbus saw America from the coast of Spain. Its movements have been felt, trembling along the far-reaching line of our analysis, with a certainty hardly inferior to that of ocular demonstration."

Three times Challis observed the planet, but did not look sharply enough to notice its disk, which was larger than that of the stars. While he was laboriously heaping up observations and neglecting to compare them, the prize of discovery slipped from his grasp. Leverrier had written to Galle, of Berlin, where some excellent star charts were being made, asking him to direct his telescope to a certain point on the ecliptic, and saying that he would find within a degree of that point a new planet, as bright as a star of the ninth magnitude (§ 1) and having a perceptible disk. Galle did as he was bidden, and found the planet within half an hour, on Sept. 23, 1846. Success is to the confident.

272. Distance and Diameter. — The mean distance of Neptune from the sun is 2,792,000000 miles. It is therefore a billion miles farther than Uranus, and thirty times as far as the earth. The diameter is 35,000 miles.

273. Revolution and Rotation. — The sidereal period is nearly 165 years. The time of rotation is unknown, because no well defined spots have ever been seen on the surface.

274. Appearance. — Neptune is too faint to be visible to the naked eye. A good opera-glass will show it. It may be found by using the Nautical Almanac and a star map, as formerly explained (§ 255). In a large telescope its greenish disk is readily perceived, but no marks have been seen upon it.

275. Satellite. — There is one satellite, a very faint object, supposed to be of the size of our moon. The plane of its orbit is inclined 35° to the ecliptic, and the satellite, like those of Uranus, moves backwards from east to west.

276. Physical Condition. — The spectrum is similar to that of Uranus, showing faintly the same absorption bands, which are presumably due to a dense atmosphere. The sunlight is only $\frac{1}{900}$ as intense as at the earth; perhaps no cheering ray of sunlight penetrates the clouds in which the planet is entirely enveloped. The density of Neptune is a little less than that of Uranus. The two planets are almost identical in size and general make up.

277. Planets beyond Neptune. — Such planets have been suspected on various insufficient grounds; they have been hunted for with large telescopes, both visually and by means of photography, which brings to light stars too faint to be seen with the most powerful telescopes. No success has yet attended these efforts. The 24-inch Bruce photographic telescope,[1] if used for long exposure photographs in the vicinity of the ecliptic, would reveal hosts of new asteroids, and might bring to notice ultra-Neptunian planets.

EXERCISES.

278. 1. Why is Jupiter's disk elliptical?

2. The volumes of spheres are to each other as the cubes of their radii or diameters. Verify the statement that Jupiter is 1,300 times as large as the earth.

3. What reasons are there for thinking that Jupiter has no solid crust?

4. Though Jupiter is 1,300 times as large as the earth, its density is only 0.24 as great. Its mass is therefore how many times that of the earth?

5. Ought Jupiter to appear gibbous, when at quadrature, like Mars?

6. Why do Jupiter's belts, if they are due to the absence of clouds, look darker than the cloudy portions?

7. If the interior of Jupiter were so hot as to shine through his atmosphere, would the spectrum be continuous, or crossed by dark lines?

8. Can one of Jupiter's satellites be in occultation and also in eclipse at the same time?

---

[1] By far the most powerful telescopic camera in existence, — the property of Harvard College Observatory.

JUPITER, SATURN, URANUS, NEPTUNE. 183

9. (*a*) If one of Jupiter's satellites were in transit, and were almost exactly between us and its own shadow, would Jupiter be near opposition or near quadrature?

(*b*) Might it be near conjunction?

10. (*a*) Why is an eclipse of one of Jupiter's satellites not instantaneous?

(*b*) Is an occultation instantaneous?

11. If Jupiter's atmosphere were sufficiently transparent to let the light of a satellite through when it was disappearing in occultation, would the time of disappearance be delayed?

12. Would the refractive power of Jupiter's atmosphere delay the time at which a satellite entered upon a transit over his disk?

13. Our moon, when eclipsed, is usually visible. Why are not eclipsed satellites of Jupiter similarly visible?

14. Suppose that the shadow of one of Jupiter's satellites, when moving across its disk, fell upon some portion that was decidedly brighter than the average, would the shadow look darker in consequence, or lighter?

15. A person on Jupiter, in the shadow of one of its satellites, would see an eclipse of what?

16. If satellite I was once, or is now, a fluid mass, why is it elongated?

17. If satellite I was once fluid, and rotated more swiftly than now, what force has checked its velocity of rotation?

18. If satellites III and IV were fluid, being of the same size and composition, why should III be more elongated than IV?

19. What is the velocity of light, in miles per second, on the assumption that light takes just 1,000 seconds to cross the earth's orbit?

20. If Jupiter's fifth satellite has the same albedo as satellite IV, that is, reflects sunlight just as well, state two reasons why it is difficult to see.

21. The volume of Saturn is how many times that of the earth, if its diameter is nine times as great?

22. The earth's diameter being taken as unity, the diameters of the other planets are roughly as follows: Mercury $\frac{1}{3}$, Venus 1, Mars $\frac{1}{2}$, Jupiter 11, Saturn 9, Uranus 4, Neptune $4\frac{1}{2}$. Show that

the volume of Jupiter is greater than that of all the other major planets together.

23. Assuming the approximate data in the preceding exercise, find whether the surface of Jupiter is as great as the combined surfaces of the other major planets.

24. Could we ever see an occultation of Mars by Jupiter?

25. Why did Galileo's two attendants of Saturn disappear?

26. What appearance in Fig. 142 shows that the dark ring of Saturn is transparent?

27. Is the shadow of the ball of Saturn, as cast upon the rings, visible in Fig. 142?

28. Is the shadow of the bright rings of Saturn, cast upon the ball, visible in Fig. 142?

29. Does the plane of Saturn's rings, when extended indefinitely, ever pass between the earth and the sun?

30. Does the sun ever illuminate both sides of Saturn's rings at the same time?

31. Is one side of Saturn's rings perpetually unilluminated by the sun?

32. If the plane of the rings ever passed between the sun and the earth, could we then see the bright side of the rings?

33. Suppose that the ball of Saturn was a perfect sphere of uniform density throughout; also that the ring system was a solid sheet of matter, truly circular, uniform in both thickness and density, and concentric with the ball; suppose further that one of the satellites attracting the ring pulled it to one side, so that it was no longer concentric with the ball, would the attraction of the ball pull it farther until it struck the surface of the ball?

34. Would a great difference in brightness between the outer edge of Saturn's dusky ring and the inner edge of the bright ring next to it militate against the theory advanced in § 262, that Saturn is "devouring his children"?

35. What does the absence of absorption bands from the spectrum of the rings indicate concerning their atmosphere?

36. Why is the direction east to west called backwards in § 269?

37. How can the statement in § 276, that sunlight at Neptune is only $\frac{1}{900}$ as intense as at the earth, be figured out from the

statement in § 272, that Neptune's distance is thirty times that of the earth?

38. Ought Neptune to look very gibbous when at quadrature?

39. When Neptune is at opposition, show that the light by which we see it left the sun 8 h. 11 m. 40 sec. before it reached us. Assume that light takes five hundred seconds to come from the sun to the earth, and that Neptune's distance from the sun is thirty times ours.

40. Sunlight at Neptune would be how many times as intense as our moonlight? (§ 165.)

41. (*a*) Does Neptune disturb the motion of Mercury at all?
(*b*) Does Mercury disturb that of Neptune?

CHAPTER XI.

COMETS AND METEORS.

"Stranger of heaven, I bid thee hail!
Shred from the pall of glory riven,
That flashest in celestial gale,
Broad pennon of the King of Heaven!"
                                        HOGG.

279. Comets in General. — The word "comet" is derived from a Greek word, which means the long-haired one; the designation evidently came from the resemblance of the tail to dishevelled tresses. These bodies are very different in behavior from the staid and trusty planets. They usually come unheralded, change their form and brightness from night to night, display all their antics in a few weeks or months, and are off again, perchance to whisk about some other world in like gay fashion.

280. Discovery. — In the early ages only those comets were discovered which were bright enough to be conspicuous to the naked eye. But of late years a comet does not often become visible to the naked eye before one of the comet-hunters[1] has detected it with his telescope.

These observers usually employ small telescopes equipped with low powers, so that the field of view may be large. Hour after hour they scan the face of the sky, hunting for nebulous-looking

---

[1] The following extract about Messier, a comet-hunter of the eighteenth century, is taken from Langley's New Astronomy; it is given there as a translation from Delambre's History of Astronomy: "He has passed his life in nosing out the tracks of comets. He is a very worthy man, with the simplicity of a baby. Some years ago he lost his wife, and his attention to her prevented him from discovering a comet he was on the search for, and which Montaigne of Limoges got away from him. He was in despair. When he was condoled with on the loss he had met, he replied, with his head full of the comet, 'Oh dear! to think that when I had discovered twelve, this Montaigne should have got my thirteenth!' And his eyes filled with tears, till, remembering what it was he ought to be weeping for, he moaned, 'Oh my poor wife!' but went on crying for his comet."

objects. Faint comets ordinarily look so much like nebulæ that they cannot be distinguished from them, except by their motion. A comet-hunter, finding such an object, looks at his catalogue of nebulæ to see if it is given there. If not, it may be a comet, and he watches it until he has found out whether it is in motion; if in motion, he announces it as a comet.

Photography has now scored its first success in this field. Dr. Barnard was the first to discover a comet by photography.[1] Special photographic lenses are employed which enable the astronomer to photograph on one plate a large region of the sky. One drawback to this method is that the exposure times are necessarily long, since a faint object does not impress itself on the plate quickly.

281. Number: Designation. — During the past three thousand years there have been recorded about seven hundred of these bodies. Before the invention of the telescope the rate of discovery was slow, because only a few comets are conspicuous objects to the naked eye. At present about half a dozen are found annually, the majority of them being merely telescopic, i. e. too faint to be seen without a telescope.

There may be thousands of comets which never come near enough to the earth to be discovered. It has been estimated that millions of them never come nearer to the sun than Neptune does. Kepler thought comets to be as numerous in the heavens as fishes in the ocean.

Comets especially noteworthy receive special names. The great comet of 1858 received the name of Donati's comet, Donati being its discoverer. Encke's comet was named for him, because he made some striking researches concerning its movements. The wonderful comet found by Finlay, at the Cape of Good Hope, in the fall of 1882, was so majestic that no man's name has been attached to it. It is known as "The Great Comet of 1882."

Other designations are used for the convenience of astronomers. Comet *a* 1892 denotes the first comet discovered in that year: Comet *f* would be the sixth comet. Roman numerals are also

---

[1] So faint was the photographic impression that, when another keen-sighted astronomer was asked to find the comet on the plate, he was unable to do so, though he succeeded in seeing it after it was pointed out to him.

used to denote the order of arrival at perihelion. Comet 1889 V. was the fifth in that year to arrive at its perihelion.

282. Brightness and Visibility. — Comets vary greatly in brightness, some being so faint that only a powerful telescope reveals them, others being so brilliant that they can be seen in full daylight though close to the sun. The brightness continually changes as the distances of the comet from the earth and sun change. But there are also irregular fluctuations of brightness.

There is rarely a week through the year when some comet is not in sight. Some of them are seen only a few weeks before they become too faint to be observed longer. But the large telescopes scattered throughout the world now enable astronomers to follow comets for a much longer time than before. One comet was seen with the Lick telescope over two years after its discovery.

283. Parts of a Comet. — Three parts of a comet are usually mentioned, — the coma, or head, the nucleus, and the tail.

The coma is the cloudlike form, which is the distinguishing mark of a comet. Faint comets are frequently all coma, no tail or nucleus being visible.

The nucleus is a starlike or planetary point in the coma, the most condensed portion of the comet. It is likewise the most brilliant part, and usually contains most of the comet's mass.

The tail is the train of tenuous matter which, streaming from the head, is the chief glory, to the naked eye, of a large comet.

284. Forms of Orbits. — If a right triangle be revolved about one of its perpendicular sides as an axis, it will generate a cone. The base of the cone will be a circle (Fig. 147). A section CD of the cone, made by a plane parallel to the base, is a circle. If the cutting plane is inclined to the base by a less angle than VAB, the section EM is an ellipse. When the cutting plane FGH is parallel to VA, the section is a parabola. A plane IKL, which is more nearly parallel to the axis VO than FGH was, cuts an hyperbola out of the conical surface. The circle and ellipse are closed curves, but the parabola and hyperbola are not.

The three curves are delineated in Fig. 148. The branches of a parabola become more nearly parallel to each other the farther they extend. The branches of an hyperbola continually diverge. A comet which travels in an ellipse will return to our vision at

COMETS AND METEORS.   189

regular periods, unless it undergoes some powerful disturbance, which alters its path. A parabolic or hyperbolic comet never returns.

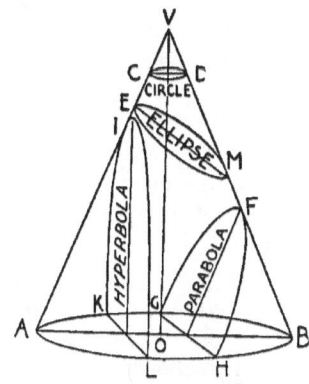

Fig. 147. — CONIC SECTIONS.

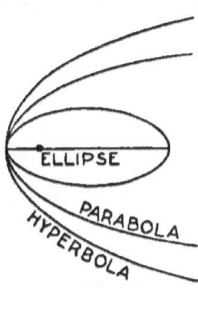

Fig. 148. — VARIETIES OF ORBITS.

285. Significance of these Forms. — Suppose that a small body is at a very great distance from the sun, and both bodies are motionless. The body will begin to fall toward the sun, its path being a straight line directed toward the sun's centre. Another small body, likewise at a distance practically infinite, has a slight motion of its own, but is not moving *directly toward* the sun; urged on by the sun's imperious attraction, its velocity will continually increase; however, as it is not going directly toward the sun, it will not strike it, but as it goes past the pull of the sun will cause its path to be violently curved; whirling around the sun, it will return toward the infinite depths of space from which it came; its orbit is a *parabola*. A body which has originally a very considerable velocity of its own will come down to the sun in an hyperbolic orbit, and then retreat, never again to visit us.

A body moving in a parabola may have its velocity checked, as it approaches the sun, by the attraction of some planet: its orbit will thus be changed to an ellipse. Were the movement of the body accelerated by the planet's action, the orbit would become an hyperbola.

286. Groups of Comets. — A comparison of the orbits of comets shows that there are certain groups of them, pursuing nearly the same paths. The Great Comet of 1882 belonged to one of these groups, the orbits of those of 1668, 1843, 1880, and 1887 being very similar to its orbit. Since each of these four comets approaches very close to the sun's surface, when at perihelion, a startling theory was promulgated in 1882 that these were one and the same, the periodic time being continually lessened by passing through the sun's atmosphere, and that the comet would plunge into the sun in a few months. It is needless to say that this anticipation was not verified. Tisserand[1] has recently shown that comet groups may be caused by the disruption of the nucleus of a single comet, in consequence of the heat or tidal action of the sun. The fragments would thereafter pursue very similar orbits, the chief difference being in the periodic times. A comet moving in an ellipse is called a *periodic* comet, because it returns at regular intervals.

287. Planetary Families of Comets. — Fig. 149 shows the orbits of a number of recent periodic comets. Inspection shows that the aphelion of each orbit lies near the orbit of Jupiter. This fact suggests that Jupiter is the planet which retarded these comets as they were sweeping down towards the sun from interstellar space, and transformed their orbits into ellipses.

Jupiter, having a much more powerful attractive force than any other planet, is credited with a larger family of comets, about twenty individuals in all. Neptune, the outpost of the solar system, has succeeded in capturing half a dozen.

It should be borne in mind that a planet's influence does not always work in favor of a comet's capture. The planet may be so placed with reference to the comet as to accelerate its motion.

288. Successive Changes in Orbits: Exact Parabolas. — A comet which approaches near a planet and suffers a change of orbit may come near it again after a few years and suffer another change. An ellipse may be changed into another ellipse, in which the comet revolves in a longer or shorter period than formerly. A number of such instances are known. Comet 1889 V. (see § 292) was in 1884 revolving in an ellipse having a period of about thirty years. In 1886 it came so near to Jupiter that it was

---

[1] Late Director of the Paris Observatory.

for a short time almost dominated by that planet, and described an hyperbola about it; when it finally escaped from Jupiter, and yielded to the power of the sun again, its period was only seven years. In 1921 Jupiter will modify its orbit seriously again, probably enlarging it greatly. The ellipse may become a parabola or even an hyperbola. When this is said, it must be remembered

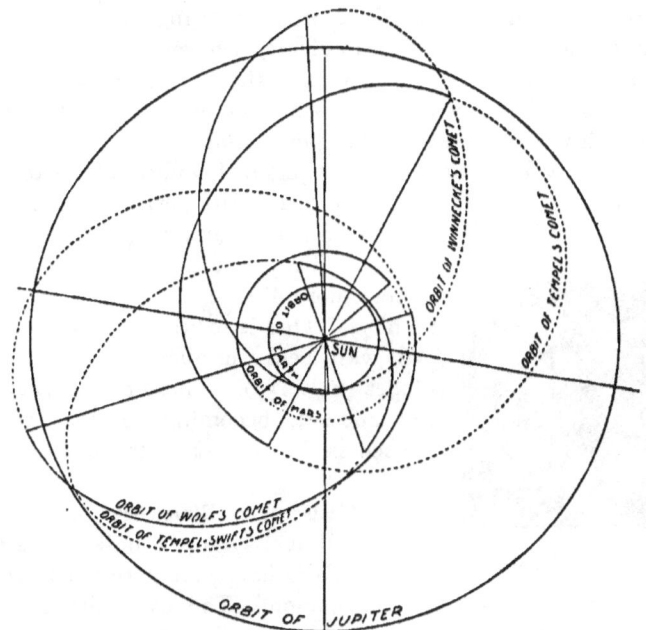

Fig. 149.—Orbits of some Comets of Jupiter's Family.

that an orbit is called a parabola when its form approaches that curve so nearly that our observations detect no appreciable deviation from it. The chances are that no orbit is an *exact* parabola, for if a comet were moving at any instant in a parabolic orbit, the slightest attraction from any body (it must suffer many such pulls) would change the orbit into an ellipse of very long period, or an hyperbola. The orbits of most comets are *sensibly* parabolic.

289. Changes of Appearance. — When a telescopic comet is first seen, it appears, as has been said, like a filmy cloud on the bosom of the sky. The coma usually looks more condensed toward the centre. As it approaches the sun, it grows brighter, and the nucleus, if it has any, comes into view, like a blurred star shining through a mass of foggy light.

As it is warmed by the sun signs of activity become manifest. The tail gradually forms, increasing in size and splendor as the comet comes nearer the sun. The nucleus seems to be in ebullition, throwing off masses of vapor, or ejecting jets. After perihelion passage the nucleus gradually becomes fainter, the jets feebler, the head larger, and the tail shorter, until the comet has reached its former low estate, having laid aside the gay trappings with which it was ornamented at perihelion.

290. Jets and Envelopes. — The jets or fountains of matter which spurt out from the nucleus as the body nears perihelion are emitted from the sunward side of the nucleus, and are directed toward the sun. They rise higher and higher and become more diffuse, until they are lost in the head. One is exhibited in Fig. 150.

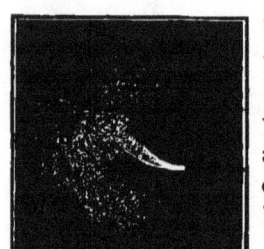

Fig. 150. — A Jet.

A well behaved nucleus throws off envelopes (Fig. 157). These rise sunward, one after another, becoming fainter and more diffused as they approach the outside of the head.

291. Tails: their Dimensions and Varieties. — The tail is by far the bulkiest part of a comet. Tails long enough to reach from the earth to the sun are not uncommon. The extremity of such a tail is millions of miles in thickness. The tail of the comet of 1843 was estimated to be 581,000000 miles long at one time. A tail a tenth as long as this is reckoned highly respectable. Some tails are narrow and straight, like prodigious spines. The forms of others are like half-opened fans. A comet occasionally has several tails, pointing in widely different directions.

292. Companion Comets. — Comet 1889 V. (Brooks) was very remarkable on account of the group of companions which attended it. There were four of these comrades, moving along a little in advance of the main comet.

Two of the companions were excessively faint, and finally disappeared. The two brighter ones were perfect miniatures of the main comet, having tiny nuclei and shapely tails. But their beauty was evanescent. For a while they receded from the principal comet. In three weeks the nearer companion ceased to recede; it then enlarged, became very diffuse, and disappeared completely, as if blotted out of existence. The farther com-

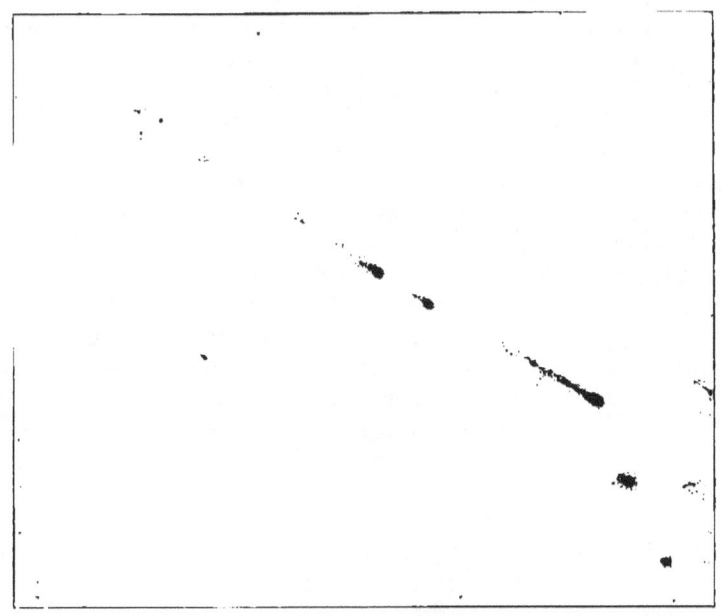

Fig. 151.—COMPANIONS OF BROOKS'S COMET.

panion continued to recede, until it had become (a month after discovery) brighter than the main comet. In a month more it began to come back and shed its tail; its head swelled and became diffuse and faint, so that it appeared to be in a sorry plight. The companions may have been caused by a disruption of the parent mass by the attraction of Jupiter in 1886. At that time the comet was within the system of Jupiter's satellites for over two days and a half, and may have been struck by one of them; it may even have grazed the planet's surface. Companion comets are not very common.

293. Constitution of the Head and of the Nucleus. — The most plausible theory is that the head is composed of a mixture of solid and gaseous matter. The presence of gas is shown by the spectrum. The connection known to exist between certain comets and meteors (§ 332) renders it wellnigh certain that solid bodies are scattered throughout the head. That portions of the solid matter become liquid temporarily, when a comet like that of 1882 dashes through the sun's corona, is almost inevitable.

The size of the solid bodies is largely a matter of conjecture. Some think that they are like grains of sand; others liken them to paving-stones and brick-bats. The nucleus is supposed to be the densest portion of this swarm of meteoric bodies. The nuclei of some large comets may be small solid bodies of great density.

294. Evolution of the Tail. — Comets' tails point away from the sun, except in a few rare and anomalous instances. The material carried up by the jets and envelopes seems to be repelled by the sun, and driven away from it, despite its gravitational pull. The nature of the repulsive force is unknown, but it is generally thought to be electrical. Many experiments described in works on physics show that electrical attractions and repulsions, acting upon light bodies which have a large surface in comparison with their mass, frequently overcome the force of gravity. A body, on the other hand, which has a small surface, but considerable weight, obeys the force of gravity. So the lightest portions of a comet's head might be driven away by an electrical repulsion originating in the sun, while the heavier portions, being but slightly affected by this repulsion, obeyed the law of gravitation. There is evidence that the nucleus, as well as the sun, repels the finely divided matter. Photographs of Rordame's comet, taken in 1893,[1] showed that certain condensations in its tail were receding from the nucleus at the rate of fifty miles a second.

Fig. 152. — Development of a Tail.

---

[1] By Prof. W. J. Hussey, at the Lick Observatory.

295. Types of Tails. — A Russian astronomer, Bredichin, has made an elaborate investigation of the forms of comets' tails, and has divided them into three types.

Tails of Type I. are nearly straight, and point almost directly away from the sun. They are thought to be composed of hydrogen.

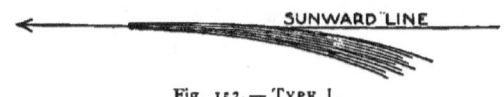

Fig. 153.— Type I.

Type II. consists of the gently curving trains which are most common. These trains are probably composed of compounds of hydrogen and carbon, known to chemists as hydro-carbons: marsh gas and olefiant gas are two of these.

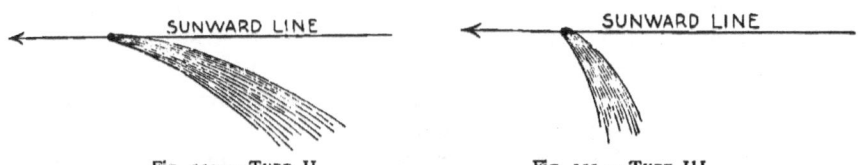

Fig. 154.— Type II. Fig. 155.— Type III.

Type III. is not common; it includes short tails of great curvature. The axes of such tails are far from pointing away from the sun. Hence they are composed of heavy materials, such as iron vapor.

296. Mass and Density. — The masses of comets must be very small compared with those of the major planets; otherwise the earth and other planets would have been disturbed appreciably by comets which have come near to them. No such perturbation has ever been manifest. The combined mass of 100,000 bodies, each as massive as one of the greatest comets, would not equal that of the earth. Since they are of prodigious size, their mean density must be exceedingly small. Sir John Herschel watched a comet as it passed in front of a cluster of very minute stars; the lustre of the stars was not perceptibly dimmed. Even when a star is nearly behind the nucleus of a large comet, its light is scarcely dimmed. But careful observations of stars which were shining through hundreds of thousands of miles of cometary matter have shown that their light was refracted a trifle by the gases of the comet. While the mean density of a comet is low, the density of the particles of solid matter which make up most of its mass is probably comparable with that of the materials composing the earth's crust. Were the particles closely packed, the mean density would be largely increased. The tail of a comet is so tenuous that it may be appropriately likened to "such stuff as dreams are made of."

297. Light and Spectra. — The brightness of a comet generally varies according to the changes of its distance from the earth and the sun. But there are frequent anomalous variations of brilliancy which would not take place were the light merely reflected sunlight. The spectrum of a comet is ordinarily a combination of two spectra: one is a faint continuous spectrum due to reflected sunlight; the other is a spectrum of bright bands, like that produced by the flame of a Bunsen burner. It is due to glowing hydrocarbon gases. Comets which go near the sun, so as to be especially excited by its influence, exhibit spectra in which the lines due to sodium and iron are plainly visible.

There is a rapidly accumulating weight of evidence in favor of the theory that a comet derives its light, except that portion which is merely reflected sunlight, almost wholly from electrical discharges between its particles. The electrical action is stimulated by the sun, being more intense the nearer the comet is to it.

298. Fate of Comets. — The tail of a comet is not to be regarded as the same to-day that it was yesterday. When one of those comets which dash through the corona goes from one side of the sun to the opposite side in a few hours, the tail, though millions of miles in length, appears also to be swung around, like a gigantic scimetar brandished athwart the sky. No known force could cause the tail to swing around with such prodigious velocity. We therefore conclude that the tail resembles the cloud of smoke puffed out from the smoke-stack of a locomotive. Fresh material is driven off from the head each second, to form the tail. As the smoke of a locomotive does not return to it again, so the particles driven off from the comet in such profusion at its perihelion passage are lost in space.

Thus at each perihelion passage a periodic comet loses a portion of its mass. It must therefore in the course of ages be much reduced in mass and brightness. Sir Isaac Newton expressed the opinion that it was the fate of comets *diffundi tandem et spargi per coelos universos*, — "to be finally diffused and scattered through the celestial spaces."

Comets which are not periodic, and which therefore do not visit the sun every few years, may in their infinite journeyings encounter other suns, swing about them in unwonted splendor, and continue their wanderings till they are captured for some sun by the aid of one of its planets, and are then gradually shorn of their beauty.

299. Superstitions.[1] — Milton says, in the second book of Paradise Lost: —

> "On the other side,
> Incensed with indignation, Satan stood
> Unterrified; and like a comet burned,
> That fires the length of Ophiuchus huge
> In the arctic sky, and from his horrid hair
> Shakes pestilence and war."

Such superstitions have been rife from early times. Josephus mentions, among the prodigies which foretold the destruction of Jerusalem, a comet with a tail like the blade of a sword, which hung over the city a year.

The Roman Emperor Vespasian, when nearing his end, heard some of his courtiers conversing in a low tone about a comet then visible. But he treated the matter lightly, saying, "This hairy star does not concern me; it menaces rather the king of the Parthians, for he is hairy and I am bald."

Throughout the Middle Ages comets seem to have been regarded as especially presaging the death of kings.

The comet afterward known as Halley's appeared in April, 1066, when William the Conqueror was about to invade England. "Nova stella, novus rex," was the proverb of the time. A monk, apostrophizing the comet, said: "Here art thou, source of the tears of many mothers. Long have I seen thee; but now thou appearest to me more terrible, for thou menacest my country with complete ruin."

---

[1] See the English edition of Guillemin's "World of Comets."

The comet of 1528 must have struck terror to the hearts of the beholders. Ambrose Paré, one of the most learned men of that time, writes of it as follows: —

"This comet was so horrible, so frightful, and it produced such great terror in the vulgar, that some died of fear and others fell sick. It appeared to be of excessive length and was of the color of blood. At the summit of

Fig. 156. — COMET OF 1528.

it was seen the figure of a bent arm, holding in its hand a great sword, as if about to strike. At the end of the point there were three stars. On both sides of the rays of this comet were seen a great number of axes, knives, blood-colored swords, among which were a great number of hideous human faces, with beards and bristling hair."

Through the instrumentality of modern science the terror formerly inspired by great comets has largely given place to a lively delight in watching their beautiful forms and wonderful changes.

300. Collisions. — Comets are still feared by many people, on the ground that they may collide with the earth and arrest its motion, so that it will begin to fall toward the sun, or that they may produce such intense heat by the impact that, in the words of Prospero, —

> "The great globe itself,
> Yea, all which it inherit, shall dissolve,
> And, like this insubstantial pageant faded,
> Leave not a rack behind."

From what we have already learned concerning the masses of comets, it is plain that there is no ground for apprehension that the earth's orbit would be much changed by collision with even the largest of them. Computations of the orbit of the magnificent comet of 1861 (Fig. 157) showed that the earth probably passed through its tail on a certain night. The result was no more serious than if our planet had been smitten by the club of a phantom. If the earth encountered the head of an ordinary comet, the meteoric masses of which it is presumably composed might be dissipated into vapor when they struck the atmosphere.

Should these particles prove to be metallic masses as large as the fist, able to plough through the atmosphere, and to make a fiery rain upon the earth's surface, the bombardment would be memorable.

While there are no very definite data to reason from, it is believed that an encounter with the nucleus of one of the largest comets is not to be desired.

So vast are the celestial spaces in comparison with the bodies by which they are peopled, that the chance that the earth will strike a good-sized comet some time during the next 100,000 years is exceedingly slight.

Most astronomers would be delighted with the prospect that the earth was going to blaze a pathway through some ordinary comet. They would also be pleased to watch some large comet dashing headlong into the sun. Professor Young thinks that the heat evolved by the collision would be chiefly liberated below the

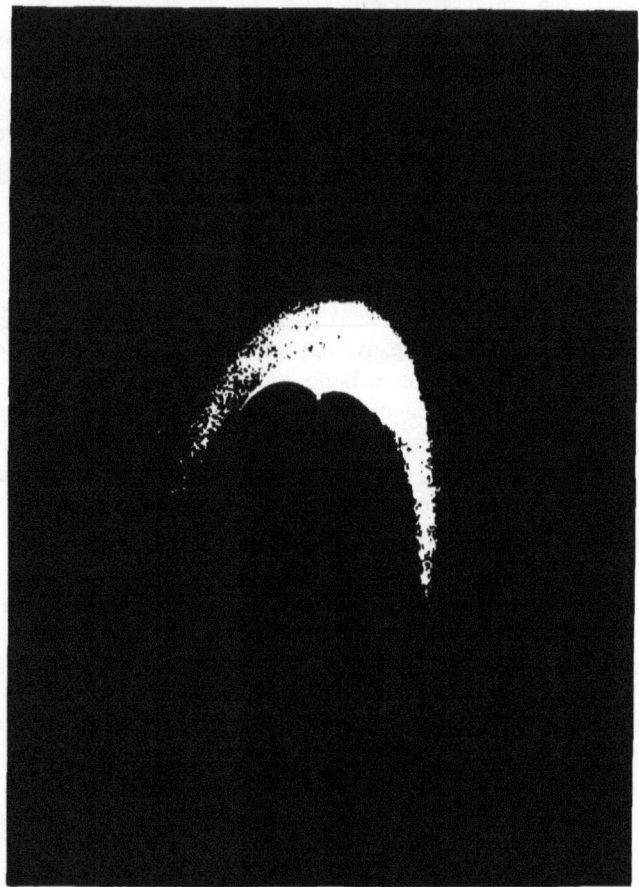

Fig. 157. — Comet of 1861.

solar surface, and would simply add a trifle to the sun's store of energy.

In November, 1892, when it was supposed that Biela's comet was about to strike the earth, there was considerable fright. The following despatch from Atlanta, Georgia, was printed in a daily paper.

"The fear which took possession of many citizens has not yet abated. The general expectation hereabouts was that the comet would be heard from on Saturday night. As one result, the confessionals of the two Catholic churches here were crowded yesterday evening. As the night advanced there were many who insisted that they could detect a change in the atmosphere. The air, they said, was stifling. It was wonderful to see how many persons gathered from different sections of the city around the newspaper offices with substantially the same statement. As a consequence, many families of the better class kept watch all night, in order that if the worst came they might be awake to meet it. The orgies around the colored churches would be laughable, were it not for the seriousness with which the worshippers take the matter. To-night (Saturday) they are all full, and sermons suited to the terrible occasion are being delivered."

REMARKABLE COMETS.

301. Halley's Comet. — Halley, who was a contemporary of Newton, having learned that, according to the recently propounded theory of gravitation, comets might move in elliptic orbits, and thus be visible at several returns, computed the orbits of two dozen comets. On comparing the computations he observed that the orbits of the comets of 1531, 1607, and 1682 were strikingly similar; he reasoned from this that these three were one and the same body, revolving about the sun in about seventy-five years. He predicted its return about 1758; knowing that he would be in his grave before that time, he expressed a modest hope that, if the comet should return then, "posterity would not refuse to acknowledge that this was discovered by an Englishman." In 1757 astronomers began to watch for it. For weary months the quest was vain. Clairaut, a French mathematician, showed by an elaborate investigation, which challenged the admiration of the world, that the comet would be retarded 618 days by the attraction of Jupiter and Saturn, and would arrive at perihelion in the middle of April, 1759. He said that this might be a month in error. The comet was first seen on Christmas night, 1758, and arrived at perihelion on March 13, a month before the time set. Thus the Newtonian principle of gravitation received a striking verification.

This comet was seen many times before Halley's day. Its earliest recorded appearance is supposed to be that of B. C. 11. It is expected again in 1910 or 1911.

302. Encke's Comet. — This comet is insignificant in appearance, rarely exhibiting a sharply defined nucleus, and sporting the scantiest of tails. It was discovered in 1786, and thirty-two years afterwards was found to be revolving in a period of only three years and a quarter, the shortest known period. It is specially interesting because its motion suffers much at the hands of Mercury, and is also accelerated in a strange way. Encke's laborious computations showed that its periodic time was shortened nearly three hours at each revolution. More recent observations and discussions show a reduction of the acceleration to one half its former value. The acceleration was at one time considered a triumphant proof of the existence in space of a resisting medium, the luminiferous ether. Such a medium, by retarding the comet's motion, would cause it to drop toward the sun, and revolve in a smaller orbit, in which it would move with greater speed. But the recent diminution of the acceleration does not bear out this theory. The comet's disturbance may be due to collisions with small bodies coming across its path, or to its own feeble activities in the line of throwing off envelopes or jets.

Its perturbations by Mercury afford a means of determining the mass of that planet.

303. Biela's Comet. — This was discovered by Biela, an Austrian, in 1826; its periodic time was computed to be 6¾ years. It was due again in 1832, and then gave rise to the first comet scare of this century. For calculation showed that it came close to the earth's orbit, and ignorant people became much alarmed at the prospect of a collision. Though it came near the earth's orbit, the earth itself was at no time nearer to it than 15,000000 miles. In December, 1845, it was found to be elongated, and ten days afterward it split into two comets, one of them being much smaller than the other. Both became brighter and developed well defined nuclei and tails. The smaller one grew in brightness until it surpassed the other for a time. Their distance apart became 157,000 miles, and they were lost to view in April, 1846.

In 1852 the twins were seen again; the distance between them had increased to a million and a half miles; sometimes one was the brighter, sometimes the other. They faded from sight again, and have never been seen since, though they were in a very favorable position in 1872. Comet Holmes, which appeared in November, 1892, was at first thought to be the long lost Biela, but the computation of its orbit showed that this was not the case.

304. The Great Comet of 1882. — This was discovered early in September by observers in the southern hemisphere. On September 17, the observers at the Cape of Good Hope saw this astonishingly brilliant body move swiftly up to the limb of the sun,

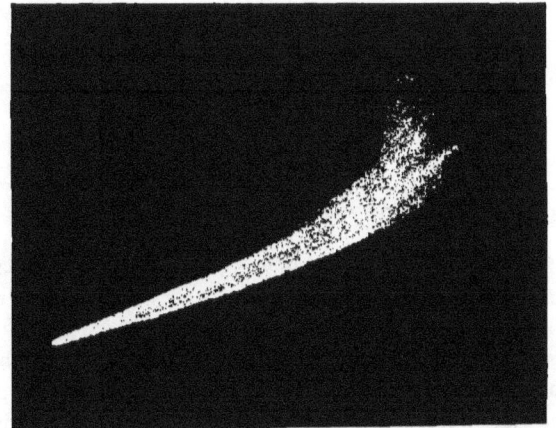

Fig. 158. — THE GREAT COMET OF 1882.

and then vanish completely as it swept over its broad disk. On the following day it was seen close to the sun by observers all over the world. It was only necessary to screen off the sun's light by holding up the hand at arm's length in order to see the comet. In less than a week the nucleus, formerly round, became oval, and by the end of a month two centres of condensation were seen. During the next three months the nucleus became divided into four or five condensations, ranged in a line and connected by a hazy mass of light.

Meanwhile a magnificent train, 100,000000 miles in length, had been developed. More than half a dozen companion comets were seen, all evanescent. The fiery object seemed to be strewing its path with filmy débris, thrown off by some unknown force. Possibly they were fragments driven off by the intense repulsive action of the sun, as the comet dashed through the corona. When at perihelion, it was less than 300,000 miles from the sun's surface.

There was a faint but prodigious sheath of cometary matter which enveloped most of the comet, and projected millions of miles

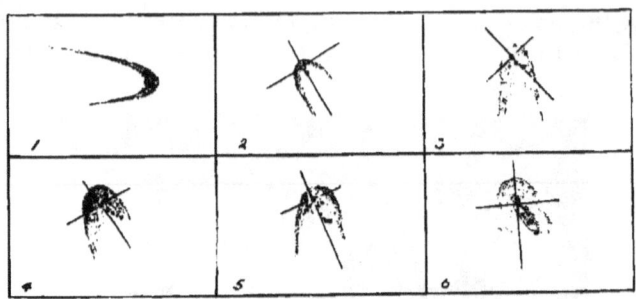

Fig. 159. — NUCLEUS OF THE GREAT COMET OF 1882, AT DIFFERENT TIMES.

in front of the head. The orbit was not appreciably changed by any resistance due to the coronal matter. The periodic time is 772 years.

Besides the hydro-carbons ordinarily found in comets, there were in this body sodium and iron; some of the numerous bright lines in the spectrum were probably due to calcium and manganese.

305. Swift's[1] **Bright Comet of 1892.** — This is mentioned on account of the marvellous changes observed in its tail. On April 4 it was 20° long, straight and slender; in the telescope it was seen to consist of two branches, between which scarcely any cometary matter was visible. The next morning a new tail had formed between the other two, and each tail was composed of several lying close together. At least a dozen could be counted. After the lapse of another day, one of the original three tails had vanished, and the other two were blended.

Then one of these grew bright, and the other faded away; the bright one had a sharp bend in it, as if turned aside by some

---

[1] Lewis Swift, of Echo Mountain, California.

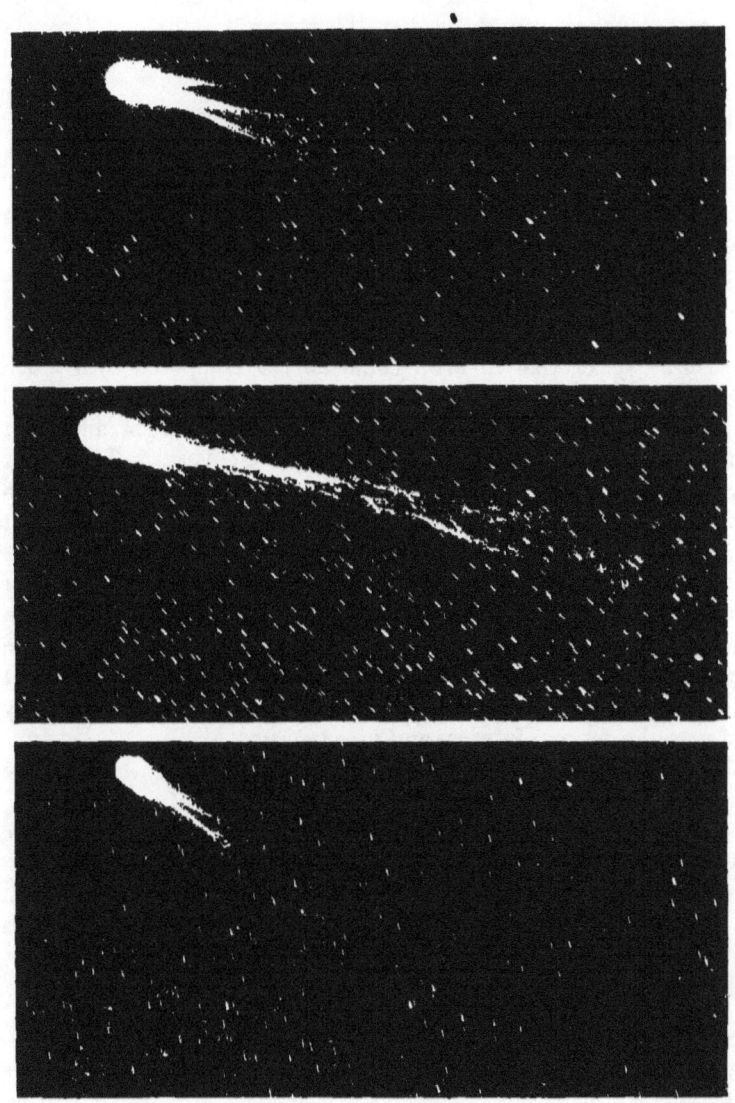

Fig. 160.—Swift's Comet: Photographed by Barnard.

obstacle. Near the point of deflection were two dark spots in the brightest part of the tail. Finally the tail split up into six branches. All these changes and some others took place in five days.

306. Comet Holmes. — This was discovered on Nov. 6, 1892, by Mr. Holmes, an English amateur astronomer. Its position in the sky was near that in which Biela's comet might appear, and the latter (if still in existence) was due. Therefore the comet was supposed by some to be Biela's, and preliminary computations led to the interesting result that the comet was likely to collide with the earth. On this account a wide-spread popular interest was awakened (§ 303). The comet changed its position in the sky so little, for several weeks, that its orbit could not be computed with much accuracy at first. It was finally found to be moving in a small ellipse, which is more nearly circular than the orbit of any other known comet; the period is less than seven years. The orbit resembles that of an asteroid. The comet, which was at first visible to the naked eye, grew faint and diffuse in a few weeks. But in the middle of January, 1893, it suffered a strange transformation, changing into a starlike object surrounded by a small circular nebulosity. On January 16, Dr. Barnard saw the nucleus brighten considerably while he was observing it. During the next week the nucleus suffered marked changes of brightness, being very plain at times, and almost invisible at others. The surrounding nebulosity soon grew larger and fainter, and faded away.

307. Comet c 1893 (Brooks). — This comet was discovered on the morning of Oct. 17, 1893, by William R. Brooks, of Geneva, N.Y. At first it had a short tail issuing from the northern side of the head, in addition to the main tail, which was straight and of a graceful form. But a photograph taken by Dr. E. E. Barnard on the morning of October 21 (October 20 by astronomical time) showed remarkable changes in the tail, which Dr. Barnard thus describes.[1]

"It presented the comet's tail as no comet's tail was ever seen before. The graceful symmetry was destroyed; the tail was shattered. It was bent, distorted, and deflected, while the larger part of it was broken up

---

[1] Popular Astronomy, December, 1893.

into knots and masses of nebulosity, the whole appearance giving the idea of a torch flickering and streaming irregularly in the wind. The short northern tail was swept entirely away, and the comet itself was much brighter.

"The very appearance at once suggested an explanation, which is probably the true one. If the comet's tail, in its flight through space, had suddenly encountered a resisting medium which had passed through the tail near the middle, we should have precisely the appearance presented by the comet. It is not necessary that the medium should be a solid body; if it possessed only the feeblest of ethereal lightness it would deflect, distort, and shatter the tail. What makes this explanation all the more probable is that the disturbance was produced from the side of the tail that was advancing through space."

Fig. 161.—Brooks's Comet: Photographed by Barnard.

The appearance may also be explained by variations in the amount and in the direction of motion of matter driven off from the comet's head.

METEORS.

308. The Two Classes. — Meteors are divided into two classes, meteorites and shooting stars. Meteorites are the bright bodies which from time to time dash through the air, like balls of fire, and fall to the ground. There are various other names for them, the most common one being aerolites. Brilliant meteoric objects which do not fall to the earth are ordinarily designated only by the general term "meteor." Shooting stars, on the other hand, are less conspicuous bodies, which can be seen on any clear dark night, darting across the sky; they usually attract no especial attention by their brightness, and never fall to the earth.

309. Past Appearances of Meteorites. — Falls of meteorites are recorded before the present era. Though there are many records of the falling of stones from the sky, they were at the close of the last century regarded by most scientific men as old wives' fables.

There is one at Mecca, which is adored by the faithful Mussulman. An Emperor in the Middle Ages was said to have a sword which was fashioned from one of these celestial visitors. In April, 1889, copper earrings plated with meteoric iron were found in an Indian mound in Ohio. During the last decade of the eighteenth century, several falls of meteorites occurred, which were so reliably substantiated that scientific men began to inquire into the matter earnestly.

In 1803 such a shower fell at L'Aigle in Normandy, that the French Academy sent one of their number to inquire into the matter. So exhaustive was his investigation, and so convincing his report, that the most sceptical were forced to admit that stones fell from the sky. The story of one of the best authenticated as well as most remarkable of meteorites is told in the next section.

310. The Ensisheim Meteorite. — This meteorite fell on Nov. 7, 1492, at Ensisheim, in Alsace, and an account of it, together with the stone itself, was put in the church at that place. The account states that on the day in question, some minutes before noon, there was a loud noise, like the rumbling of thunder, and a stone weighing 280 lbs. was seen by a child to dash into a ploughed field and bury itself about three feet in the earth. Some small pieces of it were taken for examination, but the parent mass was suspended in the choir of the church. There it remained until it was ruthlessly taken away during the French Revolution. It has since been restored to the town hall of the village.

311. A Detonating Meteor. — On Dec. 21, 1876, a superb fireball appeared over the State of Kansas, and moved thence eastward south of Chicago across Indiana, over Lake Erie, to Lake Ontario, where it disappeared. When nearly 200 miles from Bloomington, Indiana, the meteor burst, and the inhabitants of that city saw a magnificent array of fireballs sweeping through the evening sky. After the excitement aroused by the marvellous spectacle was over, there came a tremendous crash, like the heaviest reverberations of thunder. The concussion which accompanied it led some to think that a light earthquake had shaken the town. How terrific must a detonation have been, which was so startling nearly 200 miles away, after the sound waves had been on their journey a quarter of an hour!

312. Kiowa County (Kansas) Meteorites. — In March, 1890, the attention of scientific men was called to several strange pieces of iron, which had been ploughed up from time to time in Brenham township, Kiowa County, Kansas. They had been put to various uses, such as holding down the cover of a rain barrel, and keeping the roof of a stable from blowing away, and helping to stop a fence hole through which hogs escaped from their feeding ground. One had risen to the dignity of ornamenting the sidewalk in front of a real estate office.

A cowboy and a woman were the only people in the vicinity who seemed to realize the value of these articles. The cowboy, being unable to carry his off, buried them, and died shortly afterward. The woman sent for a college professor, and disposed of hers for enough to pay off the mortgage on her farm.

The meteorites were found scattered over an oval area about a mile long. The largest mass, called by the farmers the "moon meteorite," weighed 466 pounds. The total weight of the twenty odd pieces found was about a ton.

313. A Meteorite in Flight. — A flying meteorite is an object of dazzling splendor, when seen by night. It is generally followed by a luminous train, which may remain for some minutes. A noise like the roar of artillery is heard, with occasional crashes like those caused by the explosion of shells, which signalize the breaking of the main body.

When the meteorite is many miles away, one may see a flash of light without hearing the accompanying detonation. In a very few seconds all is over, save that there is a bright irregular streak of light on the sky, marking the meteor's path. A recent meteorite is reported as having the distinct shape of a banana, and as turning end for end as it flew, scattering sparks along its pathway: it glowed like a piece of red-hot iron, though the sun was half an hour above the horizon.

The meteor's velocity is so effectually checked by the resistance

210   DESCRIPTIVE ASTRONOMY.

of the air, that it finally comes to earth like a spent cannon ball or a shower of grape.

314. Path and Velocity. — Meteorites move in orbits about the sun: ninety per cent of those orbits which have been computed are elliptical. These bodies generally become inflamed at a height of eighty miles or more above the earth's surface, despite the rarity of the air at that elevation. The path is occasionally hundreds of miles

Fig. 162. — METEOR SEEN AT BASSEIN, BURMAH.
(From Winchell's "World Life," by permission.)

in length. The velocity of a meteorite with reference to the earth depends upon the relative directions of their motions. When the collision occurs "head on" the relative velocity exceeds forty miles a second. When the meteor catches up with the earth, both being in motion in the same direction, the relative velocity sinks below ten miles a second. The velocity with which the meteor reaches the ground is often considerably less than that of a cannon ball, as is shown by the slight depth to which it penetrates. Notwithstanding this comparatively low velocity, a meteorite is no insignificant missile. There are a few records of the destruction of buildings by them. The Chinese, not to be outdone by Western nations, have a record of one which came to earth 2,500 years ago, destroying several chariots and killing ten men.

Though the meteorite which flew into fragments over Madrid on Feb. 10, 1896, was about fifteen miles above the city, the concussion caused strong vibrations of partitions of houses, and extensive damage to windows.

315. Cause of Light and Heat. — When the motion of a cannon ball is arrested by striking an armor plate, the ball and the plate are heated, so that the armor plate becomes viscous at the point of striking, and flows like tar. The energy possessed by the ball because of the swiftness of its motion is transformed into heat when the motion is arrested. By the same principle a nail is heated, when struck repeatedly by a hammer. The energy in the moving hammer is changed into heat. As the speed of a rifle ball is checked when it is fired into water, the speed of a meteorite, which may be one hundred times as great as that of the rifle ball, suffers disastrous diminution even in the upper regions of the atmosphere, and is almost destroyed before the body reaches the ground. The energy lost by the meteor, as its speed diminishes, reappears in heat. The air is heated enormously; the quantity of heat developed, if it were all spent on the meteorite, would liquefy it, were it of iron. The meteor shines, because its surface is intensely hot: most of the light which we see undoubtedly comes from the incandescent gases surrounding the meteor. The train left behind remains luminous for so long a time that its light cannot be accounted for by heat alone: it may possibly be due to phosphorescence.

316. Effect of the Heat. — If a candle were thrown through the flames of a large bonfire, some of its surface would be melted off, but the interior of the candle might not be heated perceptibly. In like manner, a meteor when dashing through the heated air is affected as if it were passing through a sea of burning gas raging with uncontrollable fury. The outside of the meteor is fused at once, and wiped off to form the train. As the exterior is very hot, the meteorite is liable to crack, and strew its path with its own débris. Sometimes the heating causes a terrific explosion, or a series of explosions, which reduce the meteor to small fragments. So rapid is the entire process that the heat at times does not penetrate to the interior of the mass. While most pieces of freshly fallen meteorites are too hot to handle, some are cold. A portion of one which fell in India was found, about half an hour afterward, embedded in moist earth, and coated with ice.

The intensity of the heat to which a meteor is exposed may be illustrated by the case of a fireball which was observed in England in 1869. The luminous fiery envelope was more than four miles in diameter, and the entire meteor was vaporized in five seconds, while travelling 170 miles. There remained a cloud of glowing vapor about fifty miles long and four miles broad, which was visible for fifty minutes.

317. Meteoric Stones. — Most of the meteoric masses which fall to the earth are of a stony nature. When found they are glazed over with a thin crust formed by the fusion of the exterior during the flight. When a meteorite bursts just before falling, the freshly broken surfaces are not thus incrusted, and the pieces have in some cases been fitted together again. The surface is usually indented with numerous pits caused by the fusion of parts of the meteoric mass. The structure of some of these objects is like that of certain volcanic rocks, which are formed of irregular masses of various materials held together by a cement. In half a dozen meteorites compounds of carbon have been found, which are like those resulting from the decay of vegetable life; but no forms of vegetation such as we frequently find in terrestrial sandstones have been discovered.

318. Meteoric Iron: Intermediate Forms. — A small percentage of meteorites are composed of iron, which is alloyed with nickel in all yet analyzed. Only about a dozen of these have actually been seen to fall. The others have been found lying on or near the surface, in places where there is no other iron in the vicinity. A few of these masses weighed several tons.

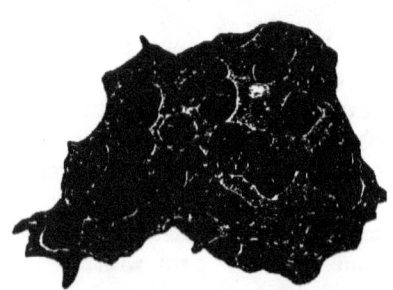

Fig. 163. — A Meteorite.
(From "Science," by permission.)

There are forms intermediate between meteoric iron and stone. In some of these there is a honeycombed mass of iron, the cavities in which are filled with various minerals. In others bits of iron are found scattered through a stony mass.

319. Elements found in Meteorites. — More than a third of the known chemical elements are found in meteorites; no new element has been discovered in them, but some new compounds have been found. Most of the elements are common ones, such as sulphur, phosphorus, copper, tin, aluminum, calcium, etc. There are, as

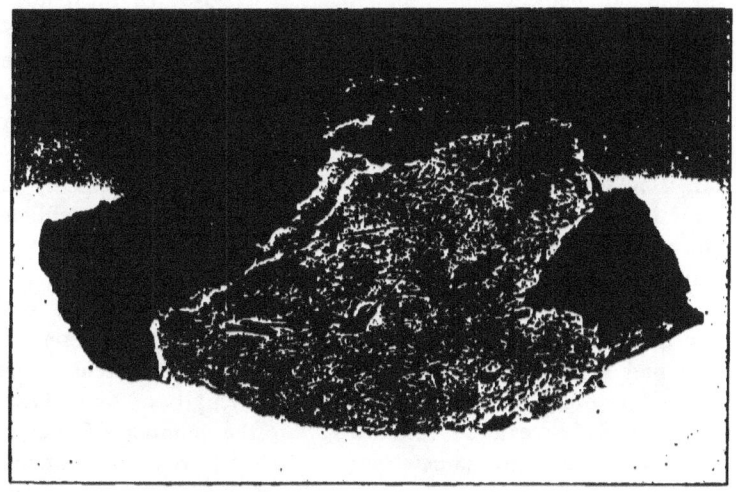

Fig. 164. — THE CANYON DIABLO METEORITE.

yet, no traces of gold or silver. Small black diamonds, and also minute white ones, have been found in cavities of meteoric iron, which came from the Canyon Diablo, in Arizona, where about three hundred fragments of meteoric iron were discovered in 1891: the largest piece, weighing 1,015 pounds, was on exhibition at the World's Fair in Chicago. Dust from the diamonds was employed in the Tiffany pavilion at the Fair, to polish other diamonds: the success of the experiment proved conclusively that the hard black grains from the meteorite were genuine diamonds.

320. Origin. — The Austrian mineralogist, Tschermak, after a careful study of the structure of meteorites, reached the conclusion that they had a volcanic origin. The volcanoes of the moon are now extinct. No terrestrial one has sufficient power to eject a missile with a velocity of six miles a second, which would be necessary to carry it away from the earth's attraction, if the earth had no atmosphere, and to render it obedient to the sun. But when these bodies or other planets were young, their volcanoes may have possessed the necessary energy. The sun, as we have mentioned (§ 77), has been seen to eject masses of heated vapor with such a velocity that they would not fall back again. Such masses, exposed to the cold of space, would be condensed into solid bodies, like the meteorites. It has been the general belief among astronomers that meteorites originated like the large heavenly bodies, from the condensation of nebulous matter scattered throughout the universe. But Tschermak's theory is considered worthy of careful examination.

321. How to Observe a Meteorite. — The observations necessary for determining a meteor's path can be easily made by any intelligent person who gets a fair view of it. Two things are to be observed, the time and the direction of movement.

At night one familiar with the constellations may note its path among the stars, and the time at which it disappears. By repeating "Mary had a little lamb," etc., beginning when the meteor is first seen and stopping at its disappearance, the length of time during which it is visible can be estimated; for the number of seconds required to repeat the same snatch of rhyme is easily obtained afterwards by rehearsing it, watch in hand. In the daytime, the position of the body when first and last seen can be noted with reference to surrounding objects. The altitude and azimuth (§ 121) of the object at each of these times can be measured later with a surveyor's transit, placed at the point where the observer stood.[1]

SHOOTING STARS.

322. Numbers. — One can scarcely look at the face of the sky for fifteen minutes on a clear moonless night without seeing at least one of these objects dart harmlessly across the sky, and disappear in silence, leaving no trace behind. It has been estimated that if ob-

---

[1] A careful report of such observations, however rude they may seem to the observer, would be welcomed by any astronomical periodical. Such communications may be sent to the "Astronomical Journal," Cambridge, Mass., or to "Popular Astronomy," Northfield, Minn.

servers were uniformly distributed over the earth, in such a way as to command a view of all the shooting stars entering the atmosphere, ten or fifteen million of them would be found to strike the earth during a day.

They are twice as frequent at 6 A.M. as at 6 P.M. For in the morning we are in front of the earth, as it moves in its orbit, while in the evening we are in the rear, as shown in Fig. 165. At A the sun is rising: at B it is setting. The meteors are supposed to be coming from all directions.

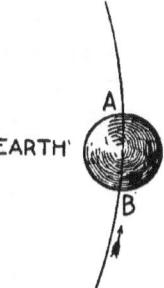

Fig. 165.— RELATIVE FREQUENCY OF METEORS IN THE MORNING AND EVENING.

323. Paths and Velocity. — A shooting star which is coming directly toward the observer has no visible path. It is simply an evanescent bright spot on the sky. Those which shoot to one side of him usually have paths several degrees in length. The paths of some meteors exhibit abrupt changes of curvature: the meteors appear to glance, as a skipping stone does on the water.

By means of observations taken by men stationed several miles from each other, shooting stars have been found to be on the average seventy-five miles above us when they are ignited, and fifty miles when they disappear. While glowing they travel forty or fifty miles at rates of from ten to fifty miles per second. Like the meteorites, they have orbits about the sun. A few double meteors have been seen moving side by side, some of them being connected by a ligament of light. They were telescopic.

324. Masses and Constituents. — Since these bodies perish when they have encountered the extremely rare atmosphere which exists at heights of from fifty to seventy-five miles, they must be insignificant in mass. Most of those which compose a shower are believed to be less than a grain in weight. One as brilliant as Jupiter or Venus at their best, may weigh 50 or 100 grains. These rather insecure estimates are based upon measurements of their light, combined with those of their velocity. The spectroscope shows that sodium and magnesium are constituents of shooting stars.

Some years since, the Swedish naturalist Nordenskiold melted a quantity of snow taken from polar regions, and discovered in the water minute particles which proved to be compounds of iron: they were hailed as the débris of shooting stars.

But the great eruption of Krakatoa in 1883 taught us that fine volcanic ashes may be carried in the air for thousands of miles before they finally settle to the earth. The particles found by Nordenskiold may therefore be the products of volcanic eruptions.

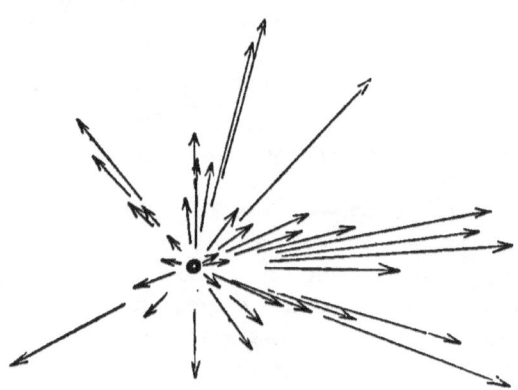

Fig. 166. — THE RADIANT.

325. Radiant. — When a shower of shooting stars comes, the apparent paths of the bodies when produced backward meet at a spot on the sky, which is called the radiant point, or simply the radiant. One who looks upward during a gentle fall of snow will observe the same phenomenon with reference to the paths of the snowflakes.

The paths prolonged backward seem to converge toward the zenith. But the snowflakes are descending in parallel paths, and the convergence is explained as an effect of perspective. Hence we infer that the shooting stars are coming in parallel paths. As the hours of the night wear away, the radiant remains in the same place among the stars: from this we conclude that the meteors come from the same direction, so that there must be a stream of them, pouring a bootless fusillade in upon the earth.

Meteoric showers are frequently named from the constellation in which the radiant lies. The Leonids, Perseids, and Andromedes come from the constellations Leo, Perseus, and Andromeda, respectively.

326. The August Shower. — The August meteors are popularly known as the "Tears of St. Lawrence." They are most numerous about August 10, when an observer may see one every minute, the radiant being in the constellation Perseus. Perseids are visible in greater or less numbers during the latter half of July and the first three weeks of August (Fig. 167). This shows that the meteoric stream is very broad, for the earth moves about 60,000000 miles while passing through it.

The meteors are distributed rather uniformly along the orbit, though there are occasional gaps. In August, 1892, the shower did not come. The orbit is an ellipse extending beyond the orbit of Neptune, and the period of revolution is over 100 years.

327. The November Leonids: Appearance: Velocity: Orbit. — Every year about November 13 there is a shower of meteors emanating from the constellation Leo. In most years they are rather insignificant, but once in 33 years the magnificence of the display is appalling. When the encounter takes place, the meteors come in a direction nearly opposite to that in which the earth is moving. The velocity of the meteors is 26 miles a second, and that of the earth 18 miles a second, so that the missiles pelt the earth as furiously as if they were going 44 miles a second, and the earth were at rest. They have a brilliant bluish light, and leave vivid trails.

This meteoric system is not diffused around its orbit, like the August meteors, but is largely condensed in a single shoal about 2,000,000000 miles long. Their orbit is a long ellipse, the perihelion of which is near the path of Uranus. The periodic time is $33\frac{1}{3}$ years.

328. The November Leonids: Past Showers. — The earliest recorded appearance of this shower was in 902 A. D. On the very

218   DESCRIPTIVE ASTRONOMY.

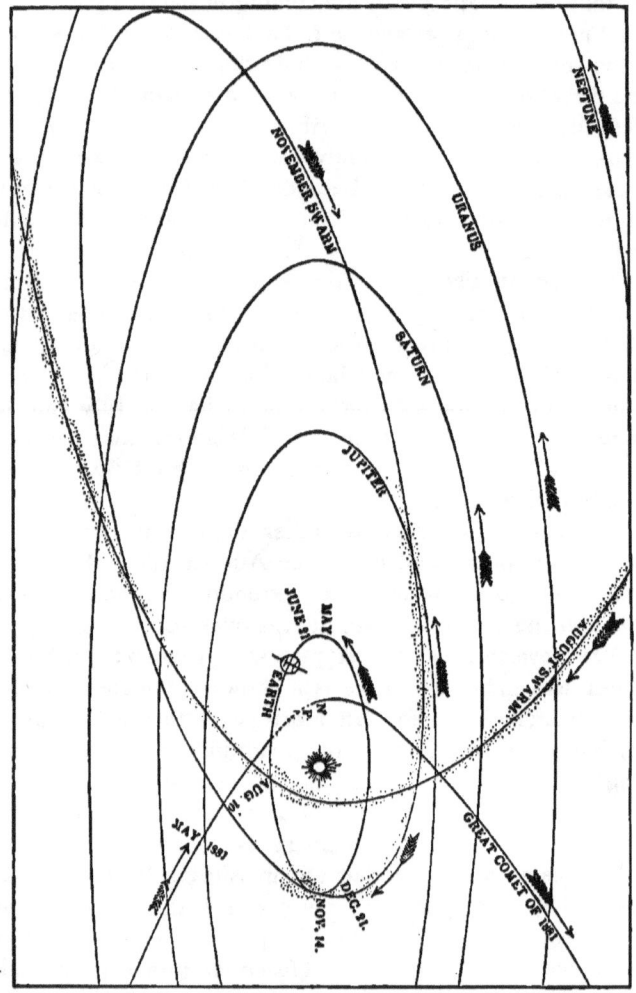

Fig. 167.—The Orbit of the August Shower.
(From Winchell's "World Life," by permission.)

night when a Moorish tyrant died, "by the judgment of God," there were seen, "as it were lances, an infinite number of stars, which scattered themselves like rain to right and left." That year was called the "Year of the Stars." On the night of Nov. 12, 1833, the display was probably the most magnificent on record. The falling stars were as thick as flakes in a snowstorm; there were many fireballs brighter than Venus; one is said to have looked larger than the full moon. The utmost terror was inspired in the ignorant. A South Carolina planter wrote: —

"I was suddenly awakened by the most distressing cries that ever fell on my ears. Shrieks of horror and cries for mercy I could hear from most of the negroes of the three plantations, amounting in all to about six or eight hundred. While earnestly listening for the cause I heard a faint voice near the door calling my name. I arose, and, taking my sword, stood at the door. At this moment I heard the same voice still beseeching me to arise, and saying, 'The world is on fire!' I then opened the door, and it is difficult to say which excited me the most, — the awfulness of the scene, or the distressed cries of the negroes. Upwards of one hundred lay prostrate on the ground, — some speechless, and some with the bitterest cries, with their hands raised, imploring God to save the world and them. The scene was truly awful; for never did rain fall much thicker than the meteors fell to the earth: east, west, north, and south, it was the same."

In 1866 there was another wonderful display, on the night of November 13. The next great shower is expected in 1899; the meteoric shoal is so long, that there may be a fair shower in 1898.

329. History of the Leonids. — Fig. 168 illustrates the supposed introduction of the Leonids into our system. Their probable history is as follows. Prior to the second century of our era they were coming toward the solar system in a tolerably compact swarm moving in a parabolic orbit. Neptune, the first picket, was successfully passed. But Uranus came along opportunely, and in A. D. 126 gave them so powerful a tug that their orbit was changed to the ellipse shown in the figure, and they found themselves subject to the sun. The attraction of Uranus also distorted the shoal, and caused its various components to move in *slightly* different orbits: the separate meteors were made to move with slightly different velocities, so that the shoal became elongated. Time and time again the earth dashed through it. Furthermore, the attractions of Jupiter and Saturn kept shifting its orbit, until it now occupies the position shown by the dotted lines in the figure. Looking ahead, we may prophesy that the shoal will, in the course of ages, become distributed around the orbit, as are the August meteors.

330. The Bielids. — This meteoric shower comes in the latter part of November each year. It overtakes the earth, striking it with a

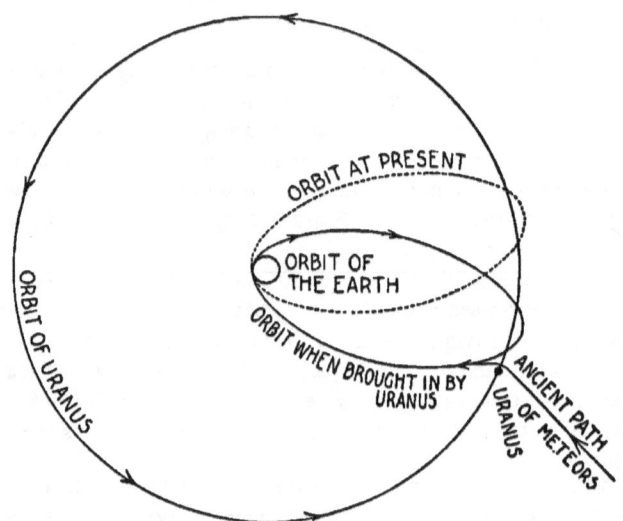

Fig. 168. — Capture of the Leonids.

relative velocity of only 12 miles a second. The radiant point is in Andromeda. Brilliant displays were seen in 1872 and 1885. In 1892 the meteors were expected on November 27, but arrived on November 23. The early arrival was afterwards discovered to be an effect of Jupiter's attraction upon the meteoric stream. Comparison with old records shows that the shower, though somewhat irregular in the date of its appearance, comes gradually earlier and earlier, gaining a fortnight in a century. The swarm derives great interest from its supposed connection with Biela's comet (§ 303). The comet seems to be lost, but a meteoric shower more pronounced than the average comes when the comet is due. Some writers speak of these meteors as fragments of Biela's comet. In the shower of 1892 several could be seen every minute by a single observer. Another fine display is expected in 1898.

331. Meteoric and Cometic Orbits. — As soon as the orbits of the great meteoric swarms were computed, it was perceived that they were similar to those of certain comets. The August meteor swarm moves in an orbit which is identical with that of the bright comet of 1862.

The meteors which cause the great 33 year November shower follow hot on the trail of Tempel's comet (1866, I.).

Several other similar coincidences are now known.

332. Relation between Comets and Meteors. — The Bielids are considered by many to be portions of Biela's comet.

The bright comet of 1862 seems to be simply a condensed portion of the August meteoric swarm.

Tempel's comet and the 33 year shower may both be parts of the original mass brought into our system by the attraction of Uranus.

The general opinion is that shoals of meteoric matter accompanying comets are the products of the disintegration of the cometary masses.

333. How to Observe a Meteoric Shower.[1] — In order to calculate the orbit of a shower it is necessary to know the position of the radiant point. A careful map of the stars visible to the naked eye in the vicinity of the radiant is first prepared. This may be done easily by putting a piece of tracing paper or tracing cloth over a good star map. On tracing cloth the stars may be well marked by small dots of ink. The completed map should be securely fastened to a smooth board. A watch of the sky for a few minutes during the shower will enable one to locate the radiant point fairly. With eyes directed toward this spot, the observer notes the apparent path of some meteor; he then traces it upon the map, marking as accurately as possible the beginning and end of the path. A stick held in the hand, and placed parallel to the meteor's path, will be of decided assistance. Those meteors having short paths are best suited for fixing the position of the radiant. When the observations are finished, the paths marked on the map should be prolonged backward till they intersect: they will not all intersect at the same point. After studying the map, the observer should mark the spot which

---

[1] See articles by W. F. Denning in "Popular Astronomy" for October, November, and December, 1893.

he deems to be the true position of the radiant, and find its right ascension and declination.

Another person, or several others, may make repeated counts of the number of meteors visible in ten minutes, noting the time when each set of observations was begun.

Still other observers may note the paths of brilliant ones, and interesting phenomena concerning them, such as their brightness, color and length of train. Successful observations should be published as recommended in the note to § 321.

The apparent paths of the brighter meteors can now be determined with more accuracy by photography, than by visual observations.

THE ZODIACAL LIGHT.

334. In the early spring one may see, when twilight has faded away, a faint hazy beam of light projecting up from the horizon in the west. It lies in the ecliptic, and can be traced 90° or more from the sun without much difficulty.

In autumn it can be well seen in the morning before sunrise. It is said to have been observed to follow the ecliptic clear around the sky. There are many theories as to its cause: the most widely accepted is that it is due to a countless host of meteoric bodies revolving about the sun, and constituting a huge figure resembling in shape a double convex lens.

The *Gegenschein*, or Zodiacal Counterglow, lies opposite the sun, and is a very faint round appearance, a trifle brighter than the adjoining portions of the zodiacal light. Observations of it are exceedingly difficult.[1]

EXERCISES.

335. 1. May Comet *a* 1907 be also Comet 1907 II.?

2. Why are jets spurted out from the nucleus of a comet on the side next to the sun rather than on the other side?

3. Why are comets' tails when composed of a heavy material (Type III.) more sharply curved than when composed of a light material (Type I.)?

---

[1] See Dr. Barnard's interesting and important observations, published in No. 308 of the "Astronomical Journal."

4. If a comet were a compact sphere 80 miles in diameter, the average density of which equalled that of the earth, its mass would be what fractional part of the earth's mass, the earth's diameter being called 8,000 miles?

5. A circular shield in front of the earth, to protect it in case of collision with a comet, would have an area of about 50,000000 square miles if it were 8,000 miles in diameter. Verify this statement. Suppose that 1,000,000000 masses of the size of a man's fist uniformly distributed throughout the comet pelted the shield during such a collision. Is it likely that a particular house located on the front of the shield would be struck?

6. If the nucleus of a comet spurts out a jet toward the sun, does that action tend to drive the nucleus away from the sun?

7. If a meteorite *overtake* the earth, is it less liable to be shattered in the air than if it *meet* the earth?

8. What evidence is there that a meteorite, before it strikes the atmosphere, is a cold body?

9. On some clear moonless night observe a meteor, estimating its time of flight, and the direction in which it moved. Note its color and the length of its train (in degrees), remembering that the distance between "The Pointers" in the Great Dipper is five degrees.

10. Do meteors gradually increase the size of the earth?

11. Do those meteors which meet the earth, and thus resist its motion, tend to lengthen or shorten the year? (§ 302.)

12. The sun must be struck by meteors, as well as the earth. Do meteors tend to increase the attraction between the sun and the earth?

13. If the attraction between the sun and the earth be thus increased, does the increase operate to shorten the year?

14. Would a decrease of the distance between the sun and the earth operate to shorten the year?

15. Judging by the effect of meteors on the temperature of the earth, do you think that the sun's heat can be accounted for by their impact?

Fig. 169.— Stars Visible to the Naked Eye.

CHAPTER XII.

THE FIXED STARS.

"What involution! what extent! what swarms
Of worlds, that laugh at earth! immensely great!
Immensely distant from each other's spheres!"
                                                        YOUNG.

336. Number Visible. — The stars visible to the naked eye are by no means countless. Over 2,000 of them can be seen at one time, under favorable circumstances. Were it possible to see the entire celestial sphere as well as one sees the portion of it near the zenith, more than 6,000 stars could be enumerated. There are multitudes of stars just below the limit of naked-eye vision which a spy-glass brings out without difficulty (Fig. 169). It will show twenty stars for every one seen without its aid. The forty-inch Yerkes telescope (Fig. 170) of the University of Chicago may be capable of revealing 1,000 times as many stars as a lady's opera-glass. As faint stars are much more numerous than bright ones, only a few hundred stars can be seen without a telescope when the full moon dominates the heavens.

337. Scintillation. — Comparison of stars near the zenith with those at a greater distance from it shows that stars twinkle the more, the nearer they are to the horizon. Since the light coming from those near the horizon passes through a greater thickness of air than that from those at higher altitudes, it is more violently disturbed. The strata of air through which it passes have many degrees of density, so that the light is refracted hither and thither on its way to the eye. The image of a star in a telescope is made to boil or dance. The irregular refraction of the light also causes a phenomenon described in works on physics as "interference." In consequence of this there are continual changes of color; the flashes of many colors which emanate from Sirius, the brightest of the fixed stars, when it is near the horizon in the early evening in midwinter, are very beautiful. An electric arc light scintillates when seen at a distance of several blocks. Scintillation is generally most marked on windy or frosty nights. When the stars twinkle violently, telescopic observations are usually of little value. A little haze uniformly suffused through the atmosphere reduces scintillation

Fig. 170. — THE YERKES TELESCOPE AT THE WORLD'S FAIR, 1893.

to a minimum: on a slightly hazy night the stellar images seen in a telescope are in general small and neat, and bear magnifying well.

THE FIXED STARS.   227

The planets, having much broader disks than the fixed stars, twinkle very little; when one point of their disks is temporarily darkened by interference, another may become brighter, so that the total quantity of light from all points of the disk remains about the same.

Fig. 171. — A Portion of the Milky Way.

338. The Milky Way. — The Milky Way, or Galaxy, is the broad bright stream of stars which encircles the heavens, and exhibits a fine contrast with the blackness of the sky at times when the moon is not visible. The Galaxy is not of uniform brightness; in places there are striking dark spots, many of which look like vast abysses: one in the constellation of the Centaur is called the Coal Sack: in Cygnus there is another starless space, smaller than the Coal Sack. The portion of the Milky Way seen south of the zenith in middle north latitudes in midsummer is divided into two streams, lying side by side. The sheen of the Galaxy is due to the fact that it is composed of millions of closely packed faint stars. In the brighter portions of it, hundreds of stars can be seen in the field of view of an opera-glass. Photographs taken with large lenses and long exposures show that there is a marvellous complexity of structure; there are sprays of stars, and vast cloud-like appearances,[1] which are crossed by dark lanes and bestrewn with dark spots.

339. Tree-like Structures. — Many solar prominences have tree-like forms: one is astonished to find such forms in the Milky Way, but photography gives indubitable evidence of their existence. Some of these are dark, and others are bright. Fig. 172 represents a dark plant-like structure near Alpha Cygni, which appears on a photograph taken by Dr. Wolf[2] with an exposure time of eleven hours. It has been conjectured that these forms are due to colossal uprushes into a resisting medium. But the dimensions of these mysterious objects are so enormous that this explanation seems inadequate. The matter is still further complicated by the fact that many of the dark structures are bordered by lines of stars.

Fig. 172. — Plant-like Structure.

340. The Constellations. — In the early ages men grouped the brighter stars fantastically, and gave names to the groups. The Latin forms of these names are now employed. Some of the most commonly known constellations visible in the United States are Cassiopeia (the Lady in the Chair), Cygnus (the Swan), Leo (the Lion), Lyra (the Lyre), Orion, and Ursa Major (the Great Bear). Most of the constellations are named after mythological personages, or after animals. Ptolemy, who died A. D. 170, revised the scheme

---

[1] Dr. Barnard first photographed these.
[2] Dr. Max Wolf, of Heidelberg, one of the foremost of celestial photographers.

of constellations known to the ancients and transmitted to us forty-eight of them. More modern astronomers have added a large number of other constellations to fill in the spaces not covered by the old ones. Nineteen of these are now generally recognized.

341. Names of Individual Stars. — Many of the brighter stars have received proper names, drawn from the Latin, Greek, and Arabic languages. Such are Sirius, Polaris, Rigel, Aldebaran, and Vega. Practical astronomers use only a few of them. Such names as Skat, Rotanev, Muphrid, and Zavijava are sinking into deserved oblivion.

Naked-eye stars are most commonly designated by letters or numbers prefixed to the genitive case of the Latin name of a constellation. The general plan is to call the brightest star in a given constellation by the Greek letter Alpha, the next brightest being Beta, and so on through the alphabet. Thus Alpha Lyræ is the brightest star in Lyra. After the Greek alphabet (§ 405) is exhausted, the Roman is used. Thus we have such names as Delta Herculis and f Herculis. The system of Greek and Roman letters does not follow the order of brightness accurately. There is a system of numbering which is independent of the other two, the stars of a constellation being numbered according to the order in which they cross the meridian. For instance 1 Orionis crosses before 2 Orionis. A star may have both a letter and a number, the former being preferred: Eta Aurigæ is the same star as 10 Aurigæ.

For telescopic stars the names are taken from catalogues. Lalande 19,486 is the 19,486th star in Lalande's catalogue of stars (§ 344).

342. Orders of Brightness. — Stars visible without telescopic aid are divided into six orders of brightness, called *magnitudes* (§ 1). Stars of the sixth magnitude are just perceptible by an ordinary eye: two thousand of them are visible in the United States. A few of them may be seen within the bowl of the Great Dipper. Those of the fifth magnitude are plain to persons who are not short-sighted. The uppermost of the three distinct stars in the sword-handle of Orion is of the fifth magnitude. There are twenty stars of the first magnitude, fourteen of which lie between the north pole and 35° of south declination (§ 122), and can be seen from any point in the United States. Polaris is of the second magnitude. An average star of the first magnitude is one hundred times as bright as one of the sixth magnitude.

343. Magnitudes of Telescopic Stars: Ratio of Magnitude. — The system of magnitudes outlined in the preceding section is extended to telescopic stars. Of late years a uniform ratio of brightness between stars of successive magnitudes has been adopted by astronomers; it is called the "light ratio." A star of a given magnitude is $\sqrt[5]{100}$ times as bright as a star of the next lower magnitude: $\sqrt[5]{100} = 2.5$ nearly. A star of the third magnitude is 2.5 times as bright as one of the fourth. The forty-inch telescope mentioned in § 336 should reveal stars of the seventeenth magnitude. Stars even fainter than this can be photographed. The brightness of a star the magnitude of which is between two integral magnitudes is expressed by the aid of decimals. Thus a star of the 6.4 magnitude is fainter than one of the sixth, and brighter than one of the seventh magnitude.

344. Star Catalogues. — An observer with a meridian circle and a clock can determine the right ascensions and declinations of a large number of stars, as explained in Chapter VI. These, when arranged in the order of their right ascensions, constitute a star catalogue. The names of the stars and their magnitudes are also given. A small catalogue is given each year in the Nautical Almanac. Each of the star places given in this catalogue depends upon hundreds of observations.

345. Photographic Star Charts. — Stars whose right ascension and declination have been found can be charted, but the work is very laborious. Charts are made much more expeditiously by the use of photographic plates. A number of observatories, scattered throughout the world, are now (1896) engaged in securing photographs of the entire sky; the plates will exhibit millions of stars which have never been catalogued.

Prof. E. C. Pickering has planned a similar campaign with the Bruce photographic telescope. This instrument should do such work with much greater rapidity than others hitherto constructed. Its objective is a quadruple lens, two feet in aperture.

346. Distribution. — The stars visible to the naked eye are distributed over the face of the sky with tolerable uniformity. This is shown in Fig. 169. When telescopic stars are taken into consideration the case is very different. These are massed in great profusion in and near the Milky Way. The farther one goes from the Galaxy, the fewer the stars become. This fact was established by the observations of the Herschels, father and son, who pointed a large telescope equipped with a certain magnifying power to a few thousand different places in the sky, and counted the number of stars visible in the field of view each time. In the Galaxy, 122 stars, on the average, were visible at one time in the field of view; $15°$ from the Galaxy, only thirty were similarly brought into view; at a distance of $30°$, only eighteen were seen; at $45°$, ten were counted; $90°$ away, the average number sank to four. There is here a resemblance to the distribution of vegetation on the earth: it is most luxuriant at the equator, and diminishes as one goes toward the poles.

347. Clusters. — The unassisted eye reveals several coarse clusters, of which the best known is the Pleiades, in the constellation Taurus. The Hyades in the same constellation, Præsepe in Cancer, and the cluster in the sword-handle of Perseus are plain to the naked eye, and will well reward the trouble of looking at them with an opera-glass. In some telescopic clusters, the stars crowd upon one another so closely that the telescope cannot separate them; near the centre of the well known cluster in Hercules star crowds upon star in a blaze of glory (Fig. 173). When looking at one of the closely packed clusters with a large telescope, one is apt to get the impression that he is gazing across measureless vistas of space at a remote system of stars, which appear faint and crowded together on account of their stupendous distance. But such is not the case. The best evidence at command renders it practically certain that their distances from us are no greater than those of more scattered stars. Though the stars in a given cluster are supposed to be near enough to one another to be subject to considerable mutual attraction, no motion due to such a force has yet been detected. Their motions will probably be recorded on the photographic plates in due time.

Ranyard[1] held that there is evidence that collisions are taking place between the stars, as a result of their mutual attraction. If two such bodies collided, the rapid evolution of heat at their point of contact would expand the contiguous gases so violently

---

[1] The late Mr. A. C. Ranyard, who was editor of "Knowledge," London, Eng.

that the effect of an explosion would be produced, and the stars might rebound like caroming billiard balls, while the gases heated at the point of impact would diffuse themselves in the surrounding space. To this he attributed the radiated appearance of the outlying stars, which are frequently arranged in streams, as if ejected from the central mass. The stars in a stream are often connected by a band of nebulous matter. Photography has revealed the fact that nebulosity is associated with very many star clusters.

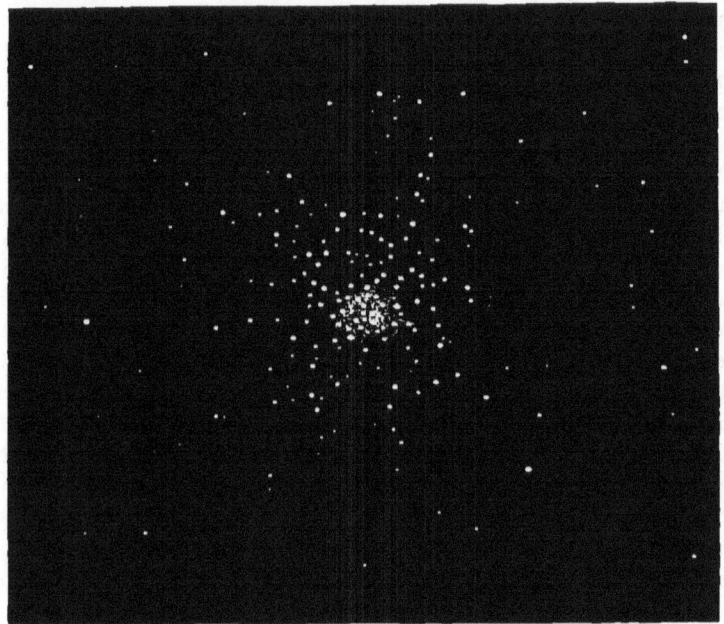

Fig. 173. — THE GREAT CLUSTER IN HERCULES.

348. Dimensions and Nature of the Stars. — The larger the magnifying power employed, the larger does a near object, like the moon or a major planet, appear. The diameters of these bodies have been measured. But with the fixed stars the case is entirely different. The larger and more perfect the telescope, the smaller the disk of a star, under the best atmospheric conditions. The visible disk is a spurious one, the cause of which is explained in works on optics.

The diameter of the sun, as seen from the nearest fixed star, is equivalent to that of a small marble a thousand miles from the observer. Though the diameters of stars subtend so small a visual angle as to defy direct measurement, yet the spectroscope has given us a little knowledge concerning them. The star Algol (§ 379) has been shown to be over a million miles in diameter: it has an

Fig. 174. — The Cluster Omega Centauri: Photographed by Dr. Gill, at the Cape of Good Hope.

invisible companion of nearly the same size as the sun. Arcturus, Capella, and Vega are believed to be much larger than our sun: the diameter of Arcturus may be a hundred times that of the sun. The second magnitude star in the crook of the handle of the Great Dipper (Zeta Ursæ Majoris) is forty times as massive as the sun. The spectroscope has also shown that the stars are self-luminous bodies, similar to the sun.

349. Distances. — The distances of the stars are inconceivably great, though easily expressed in figures. Alpha Centauri is nearer than any other star the distance of which has yet been measured. Its distance from us is 275,000 times the distance of the earth from the sun; light consumes over four years in traversing this distance. Sirius, the Dog Star, is twice as far away. Most of the stars are at distances so stupendous as to defy measurement. It is considered probable that the vast majority of the stars are so far away that their light occupies over a century in coming to us. The light which reaches our eyes from many a one of them, may have been on the journey for thousands of years. Less than one hundred stars have been found to lie within measurable distances.

In estimating such stupendous distances it is convenient to employ as a unit the "light-year," that is, the distance over which light would travel in a year. A locomotive with driving-wheels 60 miles in diameter, which were revolving 1,000 times a second, would traverse the distance in a few days less than a year.

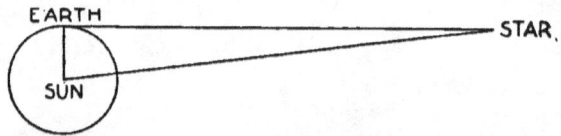

Fig. 175. — STELLAR PARALLAX.

350. Stellar Parallax. — The annual parallax of a star is the apparent semidiameter of the earth's orbit as seen from the star. This angle, formed at the star by the two lines shown in Fig. 175, is very small. In the case of Alpha Centauri, our nearest neighbor, the parallax is only as great as the apparent diameter of a sphere one foot through, located fifty miles from the observer.

Fig. 176. — METHOD OF OBSERVING STELLAR PARALLAX.

The method most employed for determining parallax is illustrated in Fig. 176. Usually some stars much fainter than the star the

THE FIXED STARS. 235

parallax of which is sought can be seen in the same telescopic field of view with it. It is reasonable to suppose that these are much further away. When the earth is at E the star A will appear to be situated at the point X among the fainter stars. Six months later, when the earth is at E', 186,000000 miles from its former position, the star A will appear to be located at Y. This apparent shift of position, when accurately measured, gives an astronomer the means of computing the star's parallax. The explanation of the methods of observation and calculation by which the parallax is found lies beyond the scope of this book. The parallax being known, it is a simple matter to find out how far away the star is. For the semi-diameter of the earth's orbit is 93,000000 miles, and the parallax is the angle at the star in Fig. 175. The problem then is to find how far from the star a line 93,000000 miles long must be, in order to subtend a visual angle equal to the star's parallax. Its solution is given in the next section.

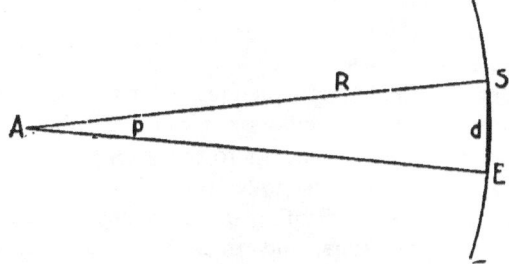

Fig. 177. — RELATION OF PARALLAX TO DISTANCE.

351. Solution of the Problem. — In Fig. 177 let the star be at A, the sun at S, and the earth at E. Then the angle SAE is the star's parallax; this angle is so minute that the arc SE is practically of the same length as its chord, and we may use d to designate either of them. Represent the distance AS by R, and let p equal the number of seconds in SAE. The circumference of the circle of which SE is an arc is $2\pi R$. There are 360°, or 1,296000", in the circumference; hence the length of an arc of 1" is $\frac{2\pi R}{1,296000}$, which equals $\frac{R}{206265}$. The length of an arc of p seconds equals p times this expression.

Hence $d = \frac{pR}{206265}$, whence $R = \frac{206265}{p} d$.

According to this formula, if any star had a parallax as large as five seconds, its distance from the sun would be $\frac{206265}{5}$, or 41,253 times the earth's distance from the sun.

352. Colors. — Most of the stars are white: there are many of a yellowish or reddish tinge. A few are of very pronounced colors: Sirius is white; Vega has a bluish tinge; Arcturus is reddish. A few faint stars are deep red. Those which are close to brighter ones are usually bluish or greenish.

It was once thought that the color gave a clue to the temperature of a star, the white stars being much hotter than the red ones, just as white-hot iron is at a higher temperature than red-hot. But this theory is now abandoned: the colors are probably dependent on the materials which enter into the composition of the star, as well as its temperature. The references to the color of Sirius by ancient writers render it highly probable that it was red at the beginning of the Christian era.

353. Spectra. — Secchi, an Italian astronomer, divided stellar spectra into four arbitrary classes, or types.[1]

Type I. The dark lines due to hydrogen are very pronounced; other lines are few and inconspicuous. This type embraces the majority of the stars; their colors are white or bluish. They are called Sirian stars, as Sirius belongs to the group.

Type II. The spectrum resembles that of the sun, being crossed by numerous dark lines, indicating the presence of various metals. These are called solar stars, and their colors are mostly yellow. Our nearest neighbors among the stars have recently been shown to belong to this type.

Type III. In spectra of this type, shaded bands are seen, each of which is darkest at the edge nearest the violet end of the spectrum, and shades off toward the red end. The color of these stars is orange or red.

Type IV. As in Type III. we have here a banded spectrum, but the bands are darkest at the edge nearest the red end of the spectrum, and shade off toward the violet end. These stars are faint, red, and few in number.

To these a fifth class is now added, embracing the so called "Wolf-Rayet" stars, which have bright line spectra. More than fifty of these are known.

---

[1] Some of these spectra are shown in the frontispiece.

354. Discussion of Stars of Different Spectral Types. — Two thirds of the Sirian stars are situated in the Milky Way, while the solar stars are about evenly divided between galactic and non-galactic regions. Each square mile of the surface of a Sirian star is brighter than an equal area of a solar star, but solar stars are on the average much more massive than Sirians, and give a greater quantity of light.

The Wolf-Rayet or "bright-line" stars lie in or near the Milky Way: these stars are of special interest, because they apparently form a connecting link between the nebulæ (§ 388) and other stars. Bright lines are not uncommonly found in the spectrum of the sun itself, and are thought to be due to masses of vapor hotter than the underlying photosphere.

The stars in Orion (with the notable exception of Betelgeuse) have a special variety of spectrum, scarcely found outside of that constellation. This indicates that these stars have a similar structure; probably they are "chips off the same block."

"In general, it may be stated that, with a few exceptions, all the stars may be arranged in a sequence, beginning with the planetary nebulæ (§ 385), passing through the bright-line stars to the Orion stars, thence to the first type stars, and by insensible changes to the second and third type stars. The evidence that the same plan governs the constitution of all parts of the visible universe is thus conclusive." [1]

Different spectra doubtless indicate, in many cases, different stages of evolution, but many more observations must be made before any far reaching theory can be suitably fortified.

355. Light and Heat. — The amount of light received from some of the stars has been compared with that given us by the sun. Though Sirius far outshines any other fixed star, being nearly six times as bright as Vega, 7,000,000000 stars like it would be required to furnish daylight; 9,000000,000000 stars of the sixth magnitude would be necessary for the same purpose.

Professor Young estimates that the full moon gives sixty times as much light as the entire starry sphere; and that ninety-five per cent of the latter comes from stars invisible to the naked eye.

---

[1] Prof. E. C. Pickering, in "Astronomy and Astrophysics" for October, 1893.

No trustworthy measures of the heat reaching the earth from any particular star have been made. It is too small to affect the most delicate thermometric appliances.

356. Bird's-eye View of the Stellar System. — The following conclusions have been reached by a study of the star gauges made by the Herschels, assuming that the faint stars are, as a class, more distant than the bright ones. Though subject to considerable uncertainty, they are generally given in works on descriptive astronomy.

(*a*) Most of the stars are not arranged in the form of a sphere, but in that of a thin disk; the shape of the disk is about that of a silver dollar.

(*b*) Only a small proportion of the stars lie on one side or the other of the disk, but the majority of the nebulæ find their homes there; i. e. outside of the disk.

(*c*) Within the disk are the stars embraced in the Milky Way, which contains most of the Sirian stars.

(*d*) The stars are not evenly distributed throughout the disk. The fainter ones are grouped in clusters and streams, as a nation is divided into families. Many of the brighter stars are thus grouped, but each " family " consists of fewer individuals than in the case of the faint ones.

(*e*) The sun lies near the centre of the disk.

357. Kapteyn's Investigations. — Prof. J. C. Kapteyn, a Dutch astronomer, has made the most exhaustive discussion of the form of the sidereal universe. The most interesting of his conclusions may be summed up under three heads.

(*a*) The nearer stars are chiefly of the solar spectral class, and are scattered about the sun on all sides, independently of the position of the Milky Way. They form with the sun a scattered cluster.

(*b*) Those stars the distances of which from us are immeasurably great, whether Sirian or solar, are more numerous the nearer they lie to the plane of the Milky Way.

(*c*) Of the stars of any given brightness (say sixth magnitude), those which lie in or near the Milky Way are, on the whole, more remote from us than those which lie in other parts of the heavens.

The stellar universe thus bears a rude resemblance to the planet Saturn, consisting of a central ball of stars, surrounded at a great distance by an apparently ring-shaped collection of stars. Professor

Kapteyn likens it to the nebula in Andromeda (§ 389), the central nucleus of which corresponds to the solar cluster, while the outlying whorls are miniatures of the Galaxy.

358. Proper Motions. — Though the stars are called "fixed," they are far from being so. They are moving with various degrees of rapidity in all conceivable directions; but on account of their prodigious distances from the earth, their positions with reference to one another change by minute amounts only, from year to year. Proper motion is this apparent shifting of a star's position on the celestial sphere.

The proper motion is not the star's real motion in space. If the earth were at rest, and a star were coming directly toward it or going directly away from it, the star would appear to be fixed on the celestial sphere, and would have no proper motion. The largest proper motion yet discovered is that of the star Groombridge 1830, which has been graphically termed the "runaway star." In 270 years it moves over a space equal to the apparent diameter of the moon. The bright stars have, *on the average*, larger proper motion than the faint ones. This is probably due to the fact that their average distance from us is less than that of the faint stars. Arcturus has apparently moved over a space equal to one fifth of the distance between the Pointers in the Great Bear, during the Christian era.

It has been shown, by combining a mass of observations on numerous stars, that the average proper motion of a first magnitude star is six times that of one of the sixth magnitude. Stars having a large proper motion are at less distances from us, on the whole, than those of small proper motion.

359. Proper Motion Groups. — While proper motions have all sorts of directions, there are many groups of stars the components of which move in the same direction. The stars in the Great Dipper, with the exception of the one at each end of the figure, belong to such a group. By spectroscopic observations (§ 360) it has been found that these five stars are all retreating from us to greater depths of interstellar space. They are separated from one another by distances inconceivably vast. Yet there seems to be some common bond, and the laws of motion of this stupendous system may forever elude the keenest search of man.

The Pleiades constitute a similar system. Of the four hundred stars catalogued in this cluster, only a few refuse to conform to a common proper motion possessed by the others. These *outré* stars are probably between us and the cluster proper, or beyond it. The other stars all agree in having the same spectra.

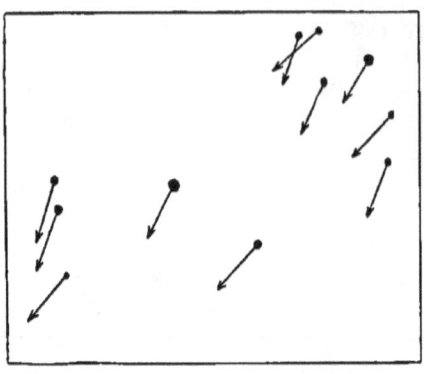

Fig. 178.— Proper Motions of the Pleiades.

360. Motions in the Line of Sight. — Every star is constantly sending forth luminous vibrations of various wave lengths. If the star be approaching, the number of waves which reach us in any given time is increased, and their wave length is shortened. Hence, when a star is coming toward us, its light is rendered more refrangible, and all of the lines in its spectrum are shifted toward the violet end of the spectrum. By comparing the position of the hydrogen lines, for example, in the spectrum of the star, with the spectrum of hydrogen obtained in the laboratory (§ 73), the shifting of the lines can be measured. The velocity of approach or recession of the star can then be computed, due allowance being made for the earth's motion.

The majority of the stars yet observed in this way exhibit velocities of less than thirty miles a second. The best modern results in this line of work are not subject to errors exceeding a mile a second.

361. The Sun's Path. — A man is in a boat on a small lake surrounded by a forest. The boat is drifting, he knows not whither. He watches the trees carefully, and finally perceives that the trees at his right appear to be spreading apart and growing taller. Those on the left seem to be crowding more closely together. He can detect no change in the relative situations of the trees ahead of him, or those behind him. He at once decides that his boat is drifting toward the right.

In this manner astronomers have discovered the direction in which the sun with its attendant planets is drifting. While the proper motions of the stars are in all directions, when we combine large numbers of them in a single discussion, a prevailing common drift comes out clearly. The stars in the constellations Lyra and Hercules are slowly separating from one another. Those in the opposite part of the sky are crowding together. The proper motions are so small that it is not possible to fix the point toward which we are moving with much precision. Spectroscopic observations of the velocities of stars make the sun's velocity only from 8 to 12 miles a second.

362. The Central Sun. — There is a persistent idea that there is a central sun. One theory, which has obtained a wide currency, is that Alcyone, the brightest of the Pleiades, is the central sun. This theory arose fifty years ago from a study of the proper motions of the Pleiades. In the light of our present knowledge concerning proper motions, the theory is considered untenable.

The hypothesis that the sun is sweeping around a gigantic curve is a reasonable one; but no deviation from a straight line has yet been detected in its motion. Even if the centre of its motion be found, it by no means follows that all the other bodies in the universe move about that centre.

363. The System of the Stars. — Evidences of order and obedience to law are so numerous in the entire domain of physical science, that the human mind instinctively seeks for some law or set of laws, in accordance with which all the stars pursue their journeyings.

The only law now known, which the motions of the heavenly bodies follow, is that of gravitation. But while there are many systems more or less similar to the solar system among the stars, each is so far from its neighbors that it experiences very little attraction from them. They exist in great variety, from the largest and most complicated clusters, down to simple double stars; their connection with one another is only a matter of conjecture. It seems very probable that there is no central sun, or even central point, about which the universe moves in orderly fashion.

The solar system is a fairly well regulated family. The stellar system seems to be made up of families and tribes which are largely independent; while each family or tribe exercises some influence upon the neighboring ones, it apparently attends pretty strictly to its own affairs.

DOUBLE AND MULTIPLE STARS.

364. Appearance to the Naked Eye. — By surveying the heavens for a few minutes one may find several places where two stars lie in close proximity to each other. Theta Tauri, in the head of the Bull, and Alpha Capricorni, are good examples. But neither of these is ordinarily classed as a double star, for the components of each pair are too far apart. The stars which make up a real " double " are so close together that a telescope is required to separate them.

365. Appearance through a Telescope. — Fig. 179 exhibits some of the double stars, when seen under a high magnifying power. When

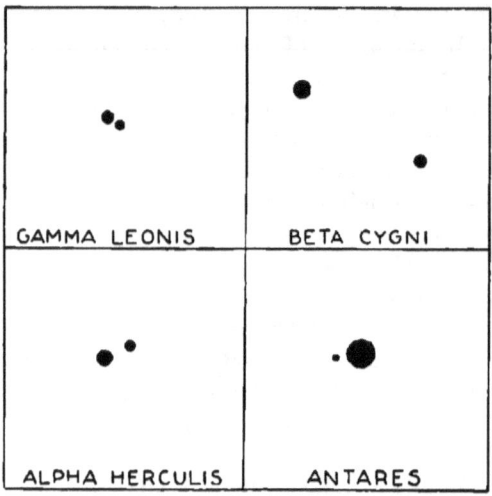

Fig. 179. — DOUBLE STARS.

the two stars are of the same brightness they are also of the same color. When they differ considerably in brightness the smaller star is apt to have a bluish cast. Beta Cygni, in the foot of the Cross, is one of the finest of those colored doubles which can be seen with a small telescope. The large star is reddish yellow, the small one greenish blue. The colors may be seen beautifully, by putting the stars out of focus. The two stars are often so close to each other that even a very powerful telescope shows them bunched together in an oblong mass of light. At times the blaze of a bright star quite overpowers the feeble light of its faint companion.

366. Numbers and Nomenclature. — The number of doubles thus far catalogued is over 10,000. New ones are being discovered continually, but not at a rapid rate, since there are few stars above the eighth magnitude which have not been scrutinized carefully with large instruments. Doubles, the principal stars of which are no brighter than the ninth magnitude, are rarely catalogued.

Each double retains its ordinary name, such as Sirius, Gamma Virginis, 61 Cygni, etc., and acquires an additional one taken from the name of the discoverer. Thus h 1064 is one of Sir John Herschel's discoveries: β 462 was found by Prof. S. W. Burnham of Chicago, the greatest living double-star astronomer.

367. Optical Double Stars. — An optical double star is one the components of which seem to be near each other, but are not; one of the stars lies far beyond the other. Optical pairs form but a very small percentage of doubles. They are detected by the absence of such motion as would ensue were the stars so near together that their mutual attraction caused relative motion.

368. Physical Double Stars. — The stars forming a physical double are subject to the sway of their own mutual attraction. Observations of them reveal the fact that they move in elliptical orbits. This leads to the belief that gravity is the force which controls their motions. A force acting according to some other law might produce elliptical motion, as is proved in works on mechanics. But since the spectroscope shows that the stars are composed of much the same materials as the sun, it is reasonable to suppose that their attractions for one another follow the same law which holds good in the solar system. Gravitation may therefore be considered as universal.

Physical double stars are usually termed *binaries*. Many of the periods of revolution are hundreds of years in length; a few are less than a year. Some of the orbits are several times as large as that of Neptune. Others are smaller than that of Mercury.

369. Spectroscopic Binaries. — When the components of a binary are so close together that the most powerful telescopes fail to separate them, or to give any indication that the star is double, the spectroscope in a few instances has revealed the duplicity. The star

Mizar at the crook of the handle of the Great Dipper is a case in point. A small telescope easily resolves this into two stars. Prof. E. C. Pickering, in 1889, found by his photographs of this double, that the spectrum of the brighter component exhibited strange anomalies. At regular intervals of a few weeks the dark lines in the spectrum were doubled. The explanation of this depends upon the principle (§ 360) that when a star is approaching us the lines of its spectrum are shifted toward the violet, and when it is receding the lines are shifted toward the red. When two bright stars, close together and composed of the same substances so that they give the same spectra, are revolving about their common centre of gravity in an orbit the plane of which is nearly edgewise to us, one star will be approaching when the other is receding. Were the stars at rest, their spectra would coincide in position. But when, on account of their motion, the lines in one spectrum are shifted in one direction, and those in the other in the opposite direction, the lines which formerly coincided will appear side by side.

Fig. 180. — A Spectroscopic Binary.

When the stars are at A and B in Fig. 180, they are neither approaching the earth nor receding from it so far as their orbital motion is concerned.

The two close stars in Mizar complete a revolution in one hundred and four days,[1] in an orbit of the same size as that of Mars.

Spica, in Virgo, is a yet more wonderful double. The components are only about 6,000000 miles apart, and complete a revolution in four days.

370. Sirius. — Certain minute movements of Sirius on the face of the sky, hither and thither, were for a long time a source of perplexity to astronomers. Fifty years ago the illustrious German astronomer, Bessel, announced that the observations of Sirius indicated that it was describing a tiny ellipse. He also advanced the theory that the motion was caused by the proximity of a companion. Less

[1] Possibly in just half that time.

THE FIXED STARS. 245

than ten years thereafter, two other German astronomers declared, as the result of an elaborate investigation, that the period of orbital revolution of Sirius and his unseen satellite was fifty years; they also pointed out the direction in which the companion lay from the larger star, and the direction of its motion. Eight years later, when the Clarks were testing an $18\frac{1}{2}$-inch object-glass, they turned it upon Sirius. The keen eye of Alvan Clark, Jr. quickly detected a faint star in the blaze of light surrounding the large star. It was soon found to be moving in the way predicted. The mass of the system is six times that of the sun. The faint star, which gives less than $\frac{1}{10000}$ as much light as the main star, may contain one third of the mass of the system.

371. Planetary Systems. — As the sun is the ruler of a planetary system, many of the stars may be centres about which troops of planets roll and shine. Such planets, in order to be discovered by us, must be much more brilliant in comparison with their suns than are those of the solar system. Jupiter himself, if searched for from Alpha Centauri with the most powerful telescope ever constructed by man, would elude the most searching scrutiny. Professor Young has computed that a refracting telescope ten feet in aperture would be needed. Such companions, if not too near their primaries, may in the future impress themselves on photographic plates of great sensitiveness.

372. Multiple Stars. — Epsilon Lyræ is a fine specimen of a multiple star. It is one of the two fourth magnitude stars near Vega

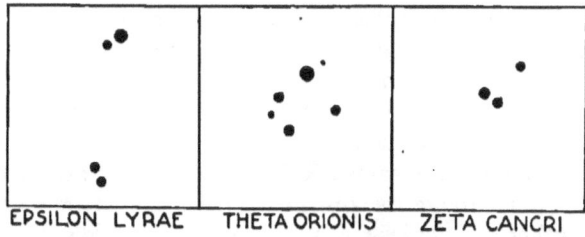

Fig. 181. — MULTIPLE STARS.

which form with it an equilateral triangle. To a good eye the star appears oblong; a keen eye separates it into two. An opera-glass shows them finely. A telescope three inches or more in aperture reveals each star as a double. We have, therefore, a quadruple star. Each pair is a binary: it is probable that the two pairs revolve about their common centre of gravity, completing a single revolution in many thousands of years.

Theta Orionis is composed of six stars. It is located in the sword-handle of Orion, and is involved in the great nebula of Orion (§ 390). There is good evidence that these stars have been formed by the condensation of a portion of the nebula.

Zeta Cancri is visually a triple star, two being close together, the other farther away. The close pair is a binary, and the third star apparently revolves about the binary, but with singular irregularities of motion. The irregularities are thought by some astronomers to be due to a fourth star near by, but invisible. The system is in that case composed of two binaries, which revolve about their common centre of gravity.

VARIABLE STARS.

373. Definition: Number: Names. — Variable stars are those the brightness of which has been observed to change. Those that repeat the same series of changes over and over are known as *periodic*, the period being the time required for the star to pass through one complete cycle of change. Some naked eye stars become too faint to be seen with a telescope four inches in aperture. New variables are discovered from time to time, and the number now (1896) well authenticated is 400. This number does not include those variables which were discovered in 1895,[1] in certain globular star clusters; nearly 100 variables were noted in a single cluster. When such stars already have names (§ 341) other than mere numbers in some star catalogue, no new name is added to denote variability. But when the stars are faint, so that they have not received such names, the first such variable discovered in the constellation Andromeda, for instance, is named R Andromedæ. The second would be S, and so on through the alphabet. After the letter Z has been reached, further discoveries receive the designations RR, RS, etc.

374. Classes. — These are classified in five groups.

Class I. embraces *temporary stars*, which suddenly experience an enormous increase in brightness, and then fade away gradually.

[1] By Prof. S. I. Bailey, at Arequipa, Peru.

Class II. includes periodic stars which suffer great variations of light in not less than several months.

In Class III. are found stars which exhibit slight irregular fluctuations of brightness.

For Class IV. are taken those stars of short periods, the light of which varies smoothly and regularly.

Class V. is devoted to those periodic stars which suffer a remarkable diminution of light for a few hours, every few days. They behave as if temporarily partially eclipsed.

Fig. 182. — TYCHO BRAHE.

375. Temporary Stars. — One evening, in November, 1572, when Tycho Brahe was taking his usual walk, he perceived in the constellation of Cassiopeia a new star, brighter than Sirius, and comparable with Venus at her best. Doubting the evidence of his eyes, he called the attention of several others to the splendid object.

For some days the star could be discerned in full daylight, and at night shone through light clouds which obscured all other stars. In December it began to wane; at the end of that month it had become fainter than Jupiter. Finally, in March, 1574, it disappeared from view. There were no telescopes then to watch it further. Its color changed from white to yellow and red successively, and returned to white before it faded from vision.

Tycho determined its place, but his observations are so rude, from lack of telescopic aid, that it is impossible to tell whether the star was any one of half a dozen now visible in the vicinity.

Fig. 183.— TYCHO'S STAR IN CASSIOPEIA.

Nova Aurigæ (§ 381) belongs to this class of stars.

376. Mira.— Class II. is fitly represented by Mira, which is Omicron Ceti. The period of this star is eleven months. Most of the time it is invisible to the unassisted eye, but once during its period it rises to its maximum brightness, which varies from the second to the fifth magnitude, remains there about a week, and then sinks more slowly back. The rise and fall together consume about one hundred days. During the remainder of its period it is of about the ninth magnitude, and can therefore always be seen with a good field-glass. It is visible to the naked eye about six weeks, when near its maximum.

377. Class III.— To this belong Alpha Orionis and Alpha Cassiopeiæ. Alpha Orionis is the bright reddish star in the shoulder of Orion. The amount of fluctuation is small, and no period or regularity of fluctuation has been found.

378. Beta Lyræ.— This star is a good example of Class IV. It is of the fourth magnitude, and varies half a magnitude on each side of this. The period is nearly thirteen days; during this time the star first reaches a maximum of the 3.4 magnitude, then sinks to the 3.9 magnitude, next rises again to the 3.4 magnitude, and finally sinks to the 4.5 magnitude. These changes are thought to be due in some way to the action of one or more companions, revolving about the main star.

379. Algol.— Beta Persei was called by the Arabians Algol, which means the Demon Star; they had therefore undoubtedly noticed the variation of its light. Its mean period has been very accurately determined, and is given by Chandler as 2 d. 20 h. 48 m. 55 sec. During most of the time it is of the second magnitude. Its variation occupies ten hours, the magnitude falling to the fourth, remaining there for twenty minutes, and rising again to the normal amount.

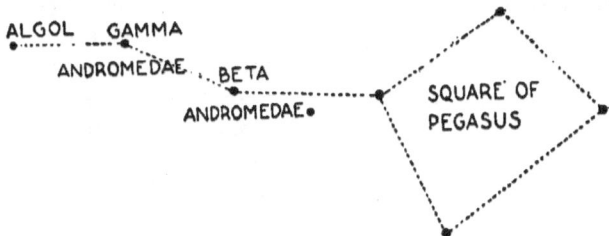

Fig. 184. — How to find Algol.

The cause of this sudden diminution of light has long been suspected to be the presence of a dark star revolving about Algol and partially eclipsing it at each revolution. The truth of this has recently been rendered nearly certain by spectroscopic observations (§ 360) which show that Algol alternately approaches us and recedes, just as if it were one component of a binary system. The following approximate data concerning this binary have been derived: —

Diameter of the principal star,	1,000,000 miles.
Diameter of the dark companion,	800,000 "
Distance between their centres,	3,000,000 "
Velocity of the companion,	55 miles per second.
Mass of the principal star,	$\frac{4}{9}$ of the sun's mass.
Mass of the companion,	$\frac{2}{9}$ of the sun's mass.

There are certain small inequalities in the period of variability which Chandler explains by the theory that the binary already mentioned is involved in an orbital revolution with a heavy faint star, in a period of about 130 years. The size of this new orbit is about equal to that of the orbit of Uranus. It is possible that there are other bodies in the system. Algol belongs to Class V.

380. Y Cygni. — This star is one of the most interesting of variables: it belongs to the Algol type. Twice in every three days it has a minimum, at which the light is one half of the maximum amount. This fluctuation is explained by the supposition that the star is a close double, the two components being equal in size and brightness, and revolving in a plane which is turned edgewise to us. Twice in each revolution about their common centre of gravity one star eclipses the other: the period of revolution is thus 72 hours. If we consider several successive minima, calling them first, second, third, etc., we find that the time from the first to the third is 72 hours, as is also the interval between the second and fourth, but the interval from the first to the second is not 36 hours as would be expected. The interval between the first and second minima may be 32 hours, for instance: then 40 hours would elapse between the second and third, and the interval between the third and fourth

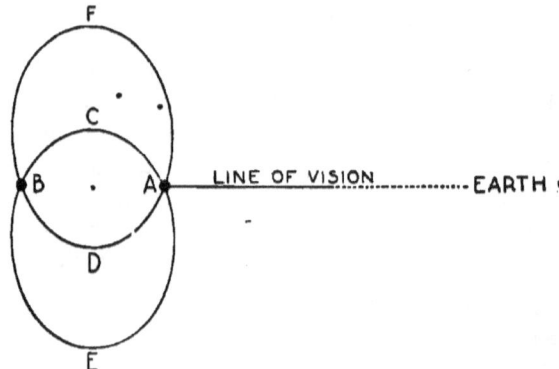

Fig. 185. — Y Cygni.

would be 32 hours again. This irregularity is accounted for by the assumption that the stars revolve in ellipses which lie "broadside" to our line of vision, as shown in Fig. 185. When the stars are at A and B respectively, there is an eclipse or minimum. Between the first and second minima the stars are describing the short parts (ACB and BDA) of their orbits. Between the second and third minima the long portions, BEA and AFB, are described.

This simple explanation does not wholly account for the observed irregularities in the times of the eclipses. In 1886 each period was 36 hours, while in 1891 the successive intervals were respectively 31 hours and 43 hours. This anomaly can be explained upon the hypothesis that the ellipses are shifting their position with reference to our line of sight, the disturbance being due to the attraction of some neighboring unseen body.

381. Nova Aurigæ. — Nova Aurigæ was discovered in the latter part of January, 1892, by Dr. Thomas D. Anderson of Edinburgh, an amateur astronomer, who was in the habit of observing with a hand telescope magnifying only ten diameters. It was of the fifth magnitude. Soon astronomers all over the world were observing the spectrum and changes of brightness of this new star. The question at once arose whether it had previously been a telescopic star, and when it first displayed itself. Fortunately photographs of the region of sky in which it lay were at hand. On Dec. 10, 1891, six weeks before its visual discovery, it had impressed itself on one of the photographic plates exposed at the Harvard College Observatory. A photograph taken in Europe on December 8 showed no trace of the star. The photographic evidence shows that it was somewhat brighter in the latter part of December, 1891, than a month later, when the attention of astronomers was called to it.

The spectrum was found to be of bewildering complexity; there were fine bright lines and broad dark ones; some of the lines were shifted in one direction, and others in the opposite, as if there were two bodies moving in widely different directions. In a few weeks it began to decline in brightness rapidly. On April 24 it was only of the sixteenth magnitude, and two days later it was hardly perceptible with the Lick telescope.

The complexity of its spectrum led to the greatest variety of theories as to the cause of the outburst. By some it was attributed to the near approach of two bodies moving with immense speed; their proximity caused great mutual disturbances of a tidal nature, leading to the production of enormous eruptions similar to solar prominences, though on a vastly greater scale.

Another hypothesis was, that some unknown heavenly body, speeding along its far distant path, came into collision with a cloud of cosmical matter, similar to the meteoric aggregations encountered by the earth, but much denser. Photography has revealed the presence of such clouds (§ 338) in the Milky Way, and the Nova, like most temporary stars, was situated in the Galaxy.

But another strange chapter is to be added to the history of this remarkable object. In August it was found to have brightened up, having attained the tenth magnitude. It then appeared like a small star surrounded by a nebulous atmosphere, and its spectrum was that of a planetary nebula (§ 385). It still (1896) retains this appearance. It is not improbable that this wonderful object is at so stupendous a distance that all these changes occurred before the astronomers who have observed them were born.

The amount of light given out, when the Nova was at its best, may have been many times greater than that radiated by the sun.

382. Causes of Variability. — There have been many theories upon this topic. The variability of stars of the Algol type is well explained by the hypothesis of eclipses by unseen bodies revolving about the variables.

The behavior of many variables can be explained by the hypothesis that they have spots, like the sun's, though much larger, and that these spots have their times of maximum and minimum frequency, as do the solar spots. If a star had one or more large companions revolving about it, their attractions might cause considerable tidal disturbances, which would give rise to variability.

The sudden appearance of temporary stars may be explained by terrific outbursts of heated vapors, analogous to the solar prominences. Lockyer has advanced the theory, that the variables are not single masses, but are rather compact swarms of meteoric bodies, attended by satellite swarms revolving in very eccentric orbits. The satellite swarms are supposed, when nearest the main swarm once in every revolution, to collide with its outlying meteors, thus producing a temporary increase of light.

Much research must yet be made before the complex phenomena exhibited by variable stars can receive any adequate explanation.

383. How to Observe Variables. — The observations of the variations of these stars in brightness often do not require the use of any telescope larger than an opera-glass. When a star is near its maximum or minimum, it is compared with adjoining stars of nearly the same brightness: it is noted as being equal in brightness to some particular one of its neighbors, or a trifle brighter or fainter than others, at a given time. The object of the observations is to determine the time of maximum or minimum brightness.

The approximate times are given in various publications,[1] for the observer's guidance. Most of the observations made in this country on these interesting objects are by amateur astronomers.

EXERCISES.

384. 1. With an opera-glass or spy-glass look at some portion of the sky, which appears to the naked eye to be barren of stars, and count the number in the field of view.

2. On a night when the moon is not shining, direct an opera-glass or spy-glass toward some bright spot in the Milky Way, and find out whether the light from that particular locality is due to a number of faint stars, or to a few brighter ones.

3. On a night when the moon is not shining, find a dark spot in the Milky Way, and make a drawing showing its location among the stars.

4. Observe five of the brightest stars visible at any given hour, and write down the name of each, together with its color.

5. Estimate the color of Zeta Ursæ Majoris (Mizar), and of the minute star (Alcor) close by it.

6. What is the origin of the name Groombridge 1830? (§ 341.)

7. Count the stars visible to the naked eye inside the bowl of the Great Dipper, when the moon is not shining, and the Dipper is not low down.

8. The light of a sixth magnitude star is equivalent to the combined light of how many of the eighth magnitude?

9. If a cluster were spherical in form, and the stars distributed uniformly through it, would it appear to be more condensed near the centre than at the edge?

10. The intensity of light varies inversely as the square of the distance; that is, if two equal lights are at distances of one mile and three miles from the eye, the farther one would not look one third as bright, but one ninth as bright. If a given star were placed at half its present distance from us, it would look how many times as bright as before?

---

[1] The times of minima of variables of the Algol type are given in "Popular Astronomy," every month. For methods of observation, see articles by Mr. J. A. Parkhurst in "Popular Astronomy" for December, 1893, and January, 1894.

254   DESCRIPTIVE ASTRONOMY.

11. The semidiameter of the earth's orbit being 93,000000 miles, how far off is a star which has an annual parallax of one tenth of a second of arc?

12. Show that the time required for light to come to us from a star having a parallax of one hundredth of a second of arc is over three hundred years.

13. Do Sirian stars have atmospheres of large absorptive power?

14. Do the spectra of solar stars indicate that they are probably more dense than Sirian stars or less dense?

15. Do the spectra of the Wolf-Rayet stars show that they are surrounded by extensive atmospheres, which absorb the rays coming from within? (§ 73.)

16. Show that the sun, if removed to the distance of Sirius, would appear to be less than one fortieth as bright as the latter.

17. If the stellar system were in the form of a sphere, throughout which the stars were distributed uniformly, and we were at its centre, would the stars appear to be uniformly distributed over the face of the sky?

18. Does the fact that there are many more stars visible when we look toward the Galaxy than when we look in other directions indicate that the stellar universe is shaped somewhat like a thin cheese? (In answering this question, assume that the stars are distributed with some uniformity through the space which they occupy.)

19. Might the appearance of the Galaxy be accounted for on the supposition that it is an irregular ring of closely packed stars surrounding us?

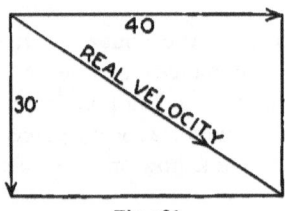

Fig. 186.

20. Spectroscopic observations show that a star is approaching us at the rate of thirty miles a second, and visual observations show that it is apparently moving perpendicular to the line of sight with a velocity of forty miles a second; according to the principles of mechanics its real velocity is represented by the diagonal of the rectangle in Fig. 186. Prove that the real velocity is fifty miles a second.

21. If the earth and a certain star are moving, at a given time, with the same velocity in the same direction, will the lines of the star's spectrum be shifted from their normal place?

22. Give some reasons why the stars differ in brightness.

23. Examine Theta Tauri with the naked eye; if you cannot see it double, your vision is defective.

24. If the orbit of a certain binary were a perfect circle, and a line drawn from the observer's eye to either of the stars were oblique to the plane of the circle, would the orbit appear to us to be a circle or an ellipse?

25. If the plane of the orbit of a binary passed through an observer's eye, would one of the stars ever occult the other, if they were equal?

26. If one star of a binary is more massive than the other, to which one will their common centre of gravity lie the nearer?

27. If one component of a binary is much brighter than the other, does it follow that it is more massive?

28. If the earth were fixed, and the plane of the orbit of a binary were perpendicular to a line drawn to the star from the observer's eye, would the spectroscope enable us to determine the velocity of either star?

29. As binaries revolve, do the components sometimes appear closer together than at others?

30. If the plane of the orbit of a binary passed through the observer's eye, how would the star appear in a telescope, when one body was between us and the other?

31. What does the name Y Cygni signify?

32. What is the signification of the designation Nova?

33. If the outburst of a temporary star be due to the collision of some star with a meteor-like cloud of comparatively small bodies, why does it gradually fade away?

34. Upon the collision theory how can the reappearance of Nova Aurigæ in August, 1892, be explained?

35. Suppose Mira to be a dense cluster of meteoric bodies, about which another cluster is revolving, in a very elliptical orbit. Could the variability of Mira be accounted for by the hypothesis of a periodic collision between Mira and its companion?

36. Could the fact that Mira, when brightest, may be anywhere

from the second to the fifth magnitude, be explained by the collision theory advanced in the preceding exercise?

37. If Y Cygni is a binary consisting of two stars of equal size and brightness, will its minima occur when one of the stars is behind the other?

38. If the ellipses in Fig. 185 lay "endwise" to the earth, so that our line of vision went through the points E and F, would each interval between successive minima of Y Cygni be 36 hours?

39. If the ellipses in Fig. 185 did not lie either exactly "broadside" or "endwise" to our line of vision, would the time intervals between successive minima of Y Cygni be equal?

40. Is there any reason not mentioned in § 380 why one of the stars would traverse the arc BDA of Fig. 185 more quickly than the arc AFB?

CHAPTER XIII.

THE NEBULÆ.

> "This world was once a fluid haze of light,
> Till towards the centre set the starry tides,
> And eddied into suns, that wheeling cast
> The planets."
>
> TENNYSON.

385. Various Forms. — Nebulæ are cloud-like objects of a bewildering variety of forms. They are to be carefully distinguished from clusters, which are aggregations of stars. A true nebula does not consist of separate stars. Many clusters, however, have nebulous matter associated with them, and many nebulæ contain stars within their borders. A large nebula is in general of an irregular shape. In it are to be seen many spots brighter, and presumably more condensed, than the rest of the nebula: there are also found dark spots, rifts, and streams of various shapes. The cuts of the nebulæ of Orion and Andromeda (Figs. 189 and 190) illustrate these peculiarities.

Spiral nebulæ, of which there are several, exhibit convolutions like those of the hair-spring of a watch; the appearance resembles that of a Catherine wheel.

Annular nebulæ are ring-shaped objects, darker in the centre than at the edge.

Planetary nebulæ have small round disks of approximately uniform brightness throughout. They are usually brightest in the centre.

A nebulous star has a strong central condensation, surrounded by a nebulous envelope. It is frequently difficult to decide whether an object should be called a planetary nebula or a nebulous star.

Double and variable nebulæ are known: no orbital revolution has been detected in the double nebulæ: no law of variation is known for the variable ones.

386. Number, Distance, and Grouping. — The number of known nebulæ is about eight thousand. New ones are continually being discovered, especially by photography, but most of the discoveries are exceedingly faint and uninteresting.

No nebula has yet revealed any parallax (§ 350). Yet the many and intimate associations of nebulæ with stars lead to the belief that they are at the same distances.

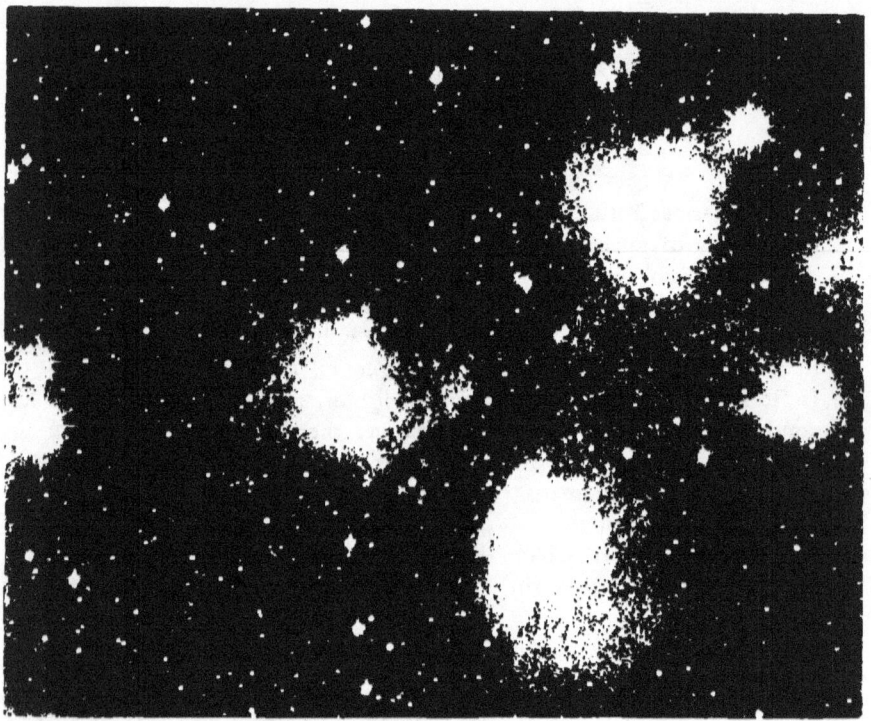

Fig. 187. — The Pleiades: Photographed by Roberts.[1]

In the Pleiades, photography has revealed the presence of a mass of nebulous matter surrounding four of the bright stars, and connected with another by a faint ray. The brightest star, and some smaller ones near it, are involved in a similar nebula. Other faint stars in the vicinity are connected by wisps of nebulous matter emanating from the vicinity of one of the bright stars.

[1] An English amateur astronomer.

The multiple star Theta Orionis (§ 372) lies in a dark space in the Great Nebula of Orion, the four brighter stars looking like eggs in a bird's nest. The appearance suggests that the stars are condensations formed from the surrounding nebulous matter. Furthermore, certain lines in the spectrum of Theta Orionis are matched by corresponding ones in the spectrum of the nebula.

While the stars are crowded together in the vicinity of the Milky Way, the majority of the nebulæ lie outside of it. Their law of distribution over the sky is opposite to that of the stars (§ 346). They are most numerous where the stars are least numerous, and *vice versa*.

387. Sizes: Changes of Appearance. — Nebulæ vary greatly in size. Some are so small as to look like stars in a small telescope. Others are the most gigantic objects ever revealed to the eye of man. The Great Nebula in Orion, as recently photographed, covers a large part of the entire constellation.

There are serious discrepancies between old drawings of some of the nebulæ and recent delineations of them. Drawings of so faint objects, made with telescopes of different sizes and under widely different circumstances, would naturally fail to agree. While many of the apparent changes are due to such causes, there remains a small residuum of cases which cannot be explained reasonably, except on the hypothesis that real changes in the nebulæ have taken place. The "Trifid" Nebula shown in Fig. 188 is an illustration in point. A star, which was located in one of the dark lanes at the opening of the nineteenth century, is now involved in the nebulous matter. The star has not changed its position with respect to the neighboring stars: therefore the nebula must have changed. Such is the result of an investigation made by Professor Holden, Director of the Lick Observatory.

388. Spectra. — About half of the nebulæ give spectra containing bright lines; thus showing (§ 73) that they may be composed of glowing gas under low pressure. Four of these lines are generally seen without difficulty with the powerful spectroscopes now employed. Two of them demonstrate the presence of glowing hydrogen. The origin of the other two is unknown. Besides these characteristic nebular lines, several others have been seen; by some of these, helium and sodium are fairly recognized. The Great Nebula in Orion is the finest specimen of this class.

Most of those nebulæ which do not exhibit bright-line spectra give continuous spectra (§ 73) simply. They may be composed of gaseous matter under high pressure, or of glowing liquid matter, or

Fig. 188. — THE TRIFID NEBULA.

of a mixture of both. The Nebula in Andromeda belongs to this class: it is plentifully besprinkled with stars. Incandescent solid matter, unenveloped by a gas, would give a continuous spectrum.

We have no proof, however, that matter exists in that form anywhere in the universe. A few nebulæ give both continuous and bright-line spectra.

Fig. 189. — THE NEBULA IN ANDROMEDA: PHOTOGRAPHED BY ROBERTS.

389. The Nebula in Andromeda. — This nebula is plainly visible to the naked eye, and has often been mistaken for a comet. It has a tolerably regular elliptical outline, and a strong central condensation.

Fig. 189 gives the impression that it is surrounded by rings like those of Saturn, or that it is a gigantic spiral. The appearance of this nebula is very interesting in its relation to the nebular hypothesis (§ 394), that all stars and planets were formed by the condensation of nebulous matter. According to this theory, the two condensations outside of the main elliptical portion may be planets

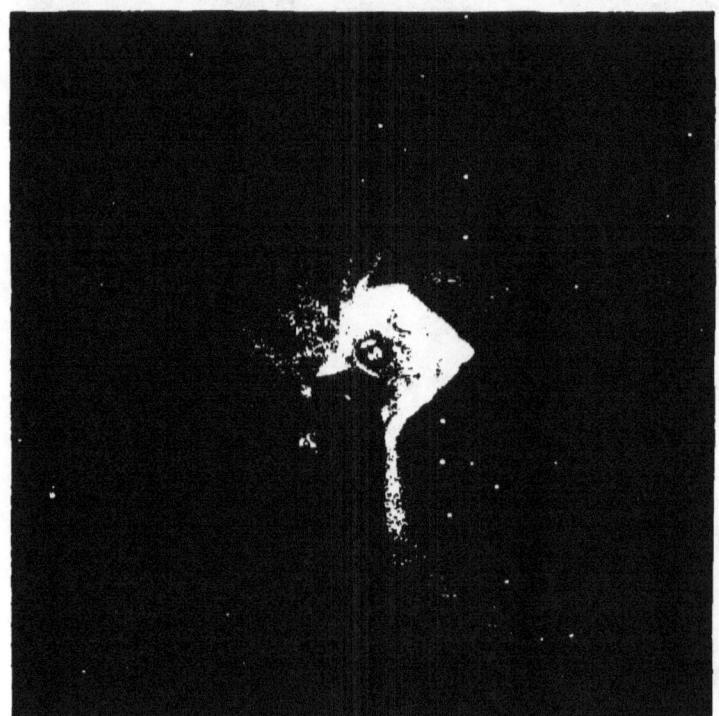

Fig. 190. — The Nebula in Orion: Drawn by Bond at the Harvard College Observatory.

in the process of formation. In August, 1885, a new star appeared close to the nucleus of the nebula; at first it was bright enough to be seen with an opera-glass, but it faded away to invisibility in a few months. Its spectrum was almost the same as that of the nebula; hence the star was probably in the nebula. It exhibited no sensible parallax.

390. The Great Nebula of Orion. — In the sword-handle of Orion are three stars in a line, easily seen with the naked eye. The central one of these appears hazy: it is the multiple star Theta Orionis, shown in Fig. 190, near the centre of the nebula. This star is commonly known as the Trapezium, because the four brighter stars in it form that geometrical figure. The spectrum of one of these stars has been photographed, and exhibits bright lines corresponding to lines in the spectrum of the nebula. This indicates that the star is a sphere of nebulous matter, not yet condensed as much as stars ordinarily are. The brightest portion of the nebula is in the immediate vicinity of the multiple star. Thence it branches off in wonderful forms, which contrast beautifully, in their delicate tracery, with the blackness of the adjacent regions. Photography reveals a vast extension of the nebulosity which the most powerful telescopes fail to show.

Keeler has determined spectroscopically that the nebula is retreating from us at the rate of nearly eleven miles per second.

If the moon be absent, the nebula, even in a small telescope, must call forth the admiration of the beholder. It is the finest object of its class in the heavens.

391. Other Notable Nebulæ. — The Dumb-bell Nebula in Vulpecula (between Lyra and Delphinus) appears in a small telescope to be composed of two oval masses in contact.

The Ring Nebula in Lyra is situated a third of the way from Beta to Gamma Lyræ. It is the only one of its kind which can be seen with a small telescope, and is shown in Fig. 191, as seen in a 15-inch telescope.

Of Spiral Nebulæ, one of the most remarkable is the one in Canes Venatici, shown in Fig. 192. It is three degrees from the star in the end of the tail of the Great Bear. The appearance is as if a slow rotation were taking place.

The Trifid Nebula is situated in Sagittarius: it is distinguished by the curious triple-pronged dark area, which gives it the appearance of being cracked open. This is the nebula previously mentioned, which affords distinct evidence of change. It is shown in Fig. 188.

392. Real Form of Spiral Nebulæ. — While these nebulæ exhibit to the eye, more or less perfectly, the appearance described in § 385,

264   DESCRIPTIVE ASTRONOMY.

this may not be their real form, since we see simply their projections on the sky. In 1888 Professor Holden discovered, at the Lick Observatory, that one of the planetary nebulæ had a spiral filament

Fig. 191.— The Ring Nebula in Lyra: Drawn by Bond at the Harvard College Observatory.

within it. This led him to a study of the best extant drawings of the spiral nebulæ. He found that their various forms can be explained on the assumption that the filaments which give the spiral appearance are really of the form of a corkscrew. He bent a wire

THE NEBULÆ.   265

into this shape, and was able, by holding it in different positions, to represent the shapes of the various spirals shown in the drawings.

393. The Magellanic Clouds. — The Magellanic Clouds, or Nubeculæ, are situated in the southern celestial hemisphere, and are not visible in middle north latitudes. They are two cloudy masses of

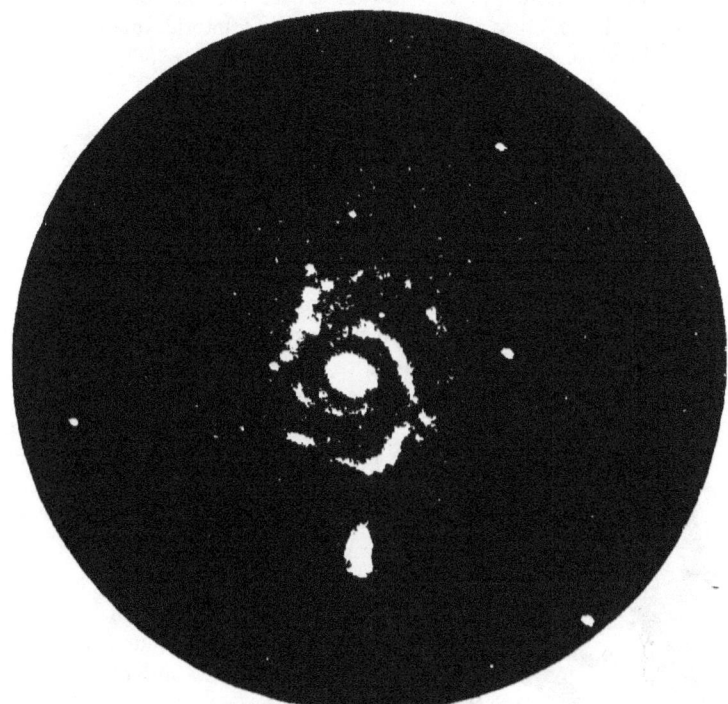

Fig. 192. — THE SPIRAL NEBULA IN CANES VENATICI:
PHOTOGRAPHED BY ROBERTS.

light, the larger one of which has an area about equal to that of the bowl of the Great Dipper; the smaller one is only one fourth as large. Both are plainly visible to the naked eye, and resemble portions of the Milky Way. They exhibit a marvellous structure in a telescope: nebulæ, both regular and irregular in form, and star clusters of all degrees of condensation, are mingled promiscuously. The larger cloud contains about three hundred of these objects.

THE NEBULAR HYPOTHESIS.

394. General Statement. — The celebrated Nebular Hypothesis is an attempt to account for the present form of the solar system by a process of orderly evolution. Its name indicates that it presupposes the existence of a nebulous mass, the parent of the well ordered worlds which we now behold. The chaotic mass of world stuff may be described, in Milton's words, as

> "A dark,
> Illimitable ocean, without bound,
> Without dimension, where length, breadth, and height,
> And time and place, are lost; where eldest Night
> And Chaos, ancestors of Nature, hold
> Eternal anarchy, amidst the noise
> Of endless wars, and by confusion stand."

Various writers suggested, and partially worked out, the nebular hypothesis, but the first to give it an extensive mathematical development was Laplace. We proceed to state his theory, and its modifications, setting forth afterwards the facts which give color to it.

Fig. 193. — LAPLACE.

395. Laplace's Theory. — According to this theory the original nebula was a mass of intensely heated gas, which had by reason of the mutual attractions of its particles assumed a globular form, and had acquired a motion of rotation. As its heat was radiated away, the nebula contracted, and rotated more swiftly; the mass became flattened at the poles, and when the "centrifugal force" at the equator balanced the force of gravity there, a ring of equatorial matter was abandoned. The spheroid left within the ring rotated still more rapidly until another ring was left behind, etc. The matter in each ring gradually condensed into a planet, which in turn rotated and abandoned rings, which usually condensed into satellites: in the case of Saturn some of the rings failed to break up into satellites of goodly size.

396. Changes in the Theory. — As facts and laws unknown in Laplace's day have been discovered, various modifications of the original theory have been proposed. It is no longer necessary to suppose that the parent nebula was originally at a high temperature: it is regarded as more probable that it was a cold cloud of finely divided matter, which became heated in the process of contraction.

Since some parts of the parent mass were probably denser than others, it is not likely that *rings* were usually abandoned, but rather that balls of matter were left behind. When the material at the equator was unusually homogeneous, a ring similar to Saturn's might be formed.

Laplace supposed that the outermost planet was formed first, but it is now believed that several of the planets may have been liberated at about the same time.

Faye, a French astronomer, has shown that the inner planets may have been formed before the outer ones.

The retrograde motions of the satellites of Neptune and Uranus contradict Laplace's supposition that the rings from which they were formed rotated as if solid, before they broke up to form the satellites. But if it is admitted that different portions of the ring were of different degrees of density, and that the inner edge rotated more swiftly than the outer, mathematicians find no difficulty in accounting for the retrograde motions of the satellites.[1]

According to Laplace's theory alone the inner satellite of Mars should not complete a revolution in less time than that planet requires to rotate on its axis. This anomaly has been explained in a marvellous manner as a result of the tides which the sun causes on Mars.[2]

397. The Evolution of Double Stars. — Laplace's theory of the abandonment of rings, which gradually condensed into satellites, answers very well for the solar system, but fails for the double stars. In the solar system we have a number of comparatively small planets re-

---

[1] See Young's General Astronomy, Art. 914.
[2] An elucidation of this matter in a popular way is found in Ball's Story of the Heavens, Chapter XXVII.

volving about a central body, which is 750 times as massive as all its planetary attendants put together. But the two bodies composing a double star are more nearly equal to each other. If the original nebula were quite homogeneous, rings might be formed as supposed by Laplace. But as there were probably great differences in density in different parts of the parent nebula, the densest portions would attract to themselves the surrounding matter. Under such conditions it is probable that the rotating and contracting nebula would separate into two or more portions.

Dr. See[1] has specially emphasized the fact that, while the ring formation is ideally possible, the nebula would be more likely to separate into two globular masses. Many double nebulæ are known, which seem to substantiate this theory of "fission." Probably such a double nebula will condense into a double star after thousands or millions of years have elapsed.

398. Testimony of the Nebulæ. — We have seen that the nebulæ are aggregations of tenuous matter, ranging from the vast filmy irregular nebulæ to the neat round compact planetary nebulæ. Between these two extremes there seems to be every gradation of size and brightness.

The great nebula of Andromeda and those which are distinctly spiral give the impression that they may be rotating. The globular bright spots found in some of the larger nebulæ look as if they were condensations of the surrounding matter.

Planetary nebulæ usually have a brightening at the centre, and nebulous stars seem to be approaching the end of the process of transformation into stars.

The nuclei of planetary nebulæ and stars like those in the Trapezium of Orion (Theta Orionis) exhibit spectra similar to those of the nebulæ in which they are involved. Immediately around the stars of the Trapezium there is a dark place, as if the matter once there had been used up to form the stars.

399. Testimony from the Stars. — The wonderful associations of nebulæ and stars, such as are found in the Pleiades and in Orion, point to a close connection. Some of these stars have wisps of nebulous matter clinging to them, as photography has shown. Others,

---

[1] Dr. T. J. J. See, Professor in the University of Chicago, who has worked out an elaborate theory of the evolution of double stars.

though giving the ordinary spectra of stars (§ 353), have quite an extensive nebulosity connected with them. The Wolf-Rayet stars give bright line spectra, and one class of the nebulæ does. One naturally concludes that we have different stages of a process of condensation, which will finally lead to the production of such highly finished orbs as Sirius, or the sun.

400. Testimony of the Earth and Moon. — The deeper we go into the crust of the earth, the warmer we find it. Volcanoes give abundant evidence of the presence of intensely heated matter in the interior of the earth. The granite which we prize so highly owes its toughness to its having passed through primeval fires. Statuary marble is but common limestone which has been metamorphosed by heat. Mountain chains are thought to have been formed by the wrinkling of the earth's crust, as it contracted in the process of cooling. The earth and the sun are composed of the same substances in large part. Were the former heated to incandescence it would give essentially the same spectrum as the latter.

The moon bears the marks of its igneous origin, written in large characters over its face. The following extract is taken from Nasmyth and Carpenter's book on the Moon:—

"We trust that we, on our part, have shown that the study of the moon may be a benefit not merely to the astronomer, but to the geologist, for we behold in it a mighty 'medal of creation,' doubtless formed of the same material and struck with the same die that moulded our earth; but while the dust of countless ages and the action of powerful disintegrating and denuding elements have eroded and obliterated the earthly impression, the superscriptions on the lunar surface have remained with their pristine clearness unsullied, every vestige sharp and bright as when it left the Almighty Maker's hands."

401. Testimony from the Planetary Systems. — We note the following harmonies in the motions and densities of the planets.

I. They all revolve eastward about the sun, in orbits nearly circular, which lie approximately in the same plane.

II. They rotate eastward on their axes (except probably Uranus and Neptune), the planes of their equators being but little inclined to those of their orbits (except probably that of Uranus).

III. The satellites revolve in the same direction in which the planets rotate, their orbit planes being nearly coincident with the equators of their respective planets.

IV. The four inner major planets are small bodies of great density; they rotate slowly, as far as is known. The four outer major planets are great bodies of small density; they rotate swiftly, as far as is known.

402. Testimony of the Sun. — The accepted theory of the source of the tremendous quantity of heat continually radiated by the sun is the contraction theory (§ 86). If the sun be now contracting it must have been larger 1,000 years ago than to-day. Reasoning backward, we find it highly probable that at one time the diameter of the sun equalled that of the orbit of Mercury. But we may go yet farther back in imagination and see the sun as a tenuous nebulous mass, the confines of which lie beyond the orbit of the farthest planet.

403. Is the Testimony Sufficient? — The human mind is irresistibly attracted toward a grand and far-reaching theory, which explains a variety of observed results by a single process of development. With a limitless duration of time and an infinite extent of space at its disposal, it leaps over the most stupendous chasms in knowledge as nimbly as a mountain goat leaps from rock to rock, scaling the precipitous heights of its native wilds.

The limitations of our knowledge are so great that the Nebular Hypothesis must probably remain a mere theory, as long as man inhabits the earth; Bacon has said that the subtlety of nature transcends in many ways the subtlety of the intellect and senses of man. Yet the theory explains many facts of observation so simply and so reasonably, that the speculations of men will probably be guided by its broad lines for centuries to come.

So inadequate is the sum total of our present knowledge of the processes of celestial evolution that we are led to cry out with Job: "Lo, these are parts of His ways: but how little a portion is heard of Him? but the thunder of His power who can understand?"

404. The Future of the Visible Universe. — As the sun is continually radiating its heat away, with boundless prodigality, it is reasonable to suppose that the stars, which are but distant suns, are doing likewise. We know of no way in which this expenditure is to be repaid. We can look forward to the time when the sun will become a cold cinder, feeling its way by the starlight through the darkness of infinite space. But will there be starlight then? Many of the stars are larger and hotter than the sun, and, though much diminished in radiance, will yet be able to shed a kindly though feeble light upon his pathway. But the time will come when even the brightest and hottest, having radiated its heat away, will roll a cold corse among its dead compeers. Such is the gloomy teaching of our philosophy.

Once there lived a race of ephemerans, whose dwelling place was upon a thermometer. The span of life of one of them was but a second. Being of a scientific turn of mind they made records of the readings of the instrument. After observations had been made for ten generations they promulgated the theory that the mercury was rising one hundredth of a degree every second. After the lapse of ten generations more the theory was confirmed, and was then called a law. When one hundred generations had passed away, the law was considered so firmly established, that no reasonable ephemeran could doubt it. It was the one grand and inexorable law of nature: one might question everything else, but never this. During the next ten generations they executed a laborious triangulation, determining the distance over which the mercury must still travel before it reached the top of the thermometer, and burst the glass tube. Then it was an easy matter to calculate that the utter ruin of their beautiful dwelling place could not be delayed beyond the ten-thousandth generation.

Great was the humiliation of their scientists, but still greater the joy of the ephemerans at large, when it was found, after the lapse of two thousand generations, that the mercury was actually going the other way. Even the scientists were constrained to admit that there were more things in heaven and earth than were dreamed of in their philosophy.

CHAPTER XIV.

THE CONSTELLATIONS IN DETAIL.

"Sit, Jessica. Look how the floor of heaven
Is thick inlaid with patines of bright gold:
There's not the smallest orb which thou behold'st
But in his motion like an angel sings,
Still quiring to the young-eyed cherubins."

SHAKESPEARE.

405. The Greek Alphabet. — Since very many of the stars are named by means of Greek letters, the Greek alphabet is subjoined. In pronouncing the names of the letters ē should be given like *ay* in *bay*: ī is pronounced like *ee*.

α	Alpha.	ν	Nu.
β	Bēta.	ξ	Xī (Ksee).
γ	Gamma.	ο	Omicron.
δ	Delta.	π	Pī.
ε	Epsilon.	ρ	Rho.
ζ	Zēta.	σ	Sigma.
η	Ēta.	τ	Tau.
θ	Thēta.	υ	Upsilon.
ι	Iō′ta.	φ	Phī.
κ	Kappa.	χ	Chī.
λ	Lambda.	ψ	Psī.
μ	Mu.	ω	Omĕ′ga.

406. Use of the Data in this Chapter. — Before making use of the data in this chapter, the student should be familiar with §§ 1 and 8–12.

Under each constellation the directions for finding its principal stars are first given. These directions presuppose an acquaintance with Ursa Major, Ursa Minor, and Cassiopeia (§ 10). They should be used in conjunction with the maps.

When attention has been called to the configuration of the principal stars of the constellation, the chief objects of interest in it are mentioned. The numbers in [ ] refer to the lists at the end of the chapter. For the mythological history of the constellations, the reader is referred to a classical dictionary.

At the end of the chapter the right ascensions and declinations of interesting telescopic objects are given, together with simple directions for finding them by means of a telescope equatorially mounted, and provided with graduated circles.

407. Andromeda, the Chained Lady. [Map I.] — Andromeda may be easily learned after Cassiopeia. A line drawn from Polaris to β Cassiopeiæ, and prolonged an equal distance, strikes a, which is the head of Andromeda: it is also one corner of the square of Pegasus. A line drawn from Polaris to ϵ Cassiopeiæ, and prolonged nearly the same distance beyond, ends very near γ, which is in one foot of the figure. The row of stars from a to γ bounds the left side of Andromeda, so that her body lies between this row and Cassiopeia. Her outstretched arms run from λ to η.

The great nebula [83] which is plainly visible to the naked eye is in line with β and μ, μ being half way between the other two.

It has been described in § 389. In a small telescope it is simply a bright oval mass, none of the wonderful details of its structure being perceptible.

γ [6] is a fine double, the larger star being orange and the smaller sea-green: the small star is a very close double; γ is therefore really a triple star. The small star is of the sixth magnitude, and $11''$ distant.

408. Aquarius, the Water Bearer. [Map V.] — A line drawn from β Pegasi to a of the same constellation, and prolonged as far again, terminates just east of a group of fourth magnitude stars having the form of a Y. This is the jar from which Aquarius pours a never exhausted stream of water which meanders southward into the mouth of the Southern Fish.

The remainder of this dull-looking constellation lies south of the jar, and extends to quite a distance east and west of it. Thirty degrees south and a little east of the Y is the first magnitude star Fomalhaut, in the Southern Fish. Between the two lies a portion of Aquarius which has been likened to the contour of South America. It is formed by the stars θ, λ, τ, δ, c^2, and ι. The stream from the water jar to the Southern Fish is marked by pretty groups of stars, and is indicated on the map by a dotted line. The stars a, β, ν, ϵ, and 3, in the western portion of the constellation, form a rude short-handled dipper.

ζ [81], the central star of the Y is a fine binary, the components being nearly equal; they are $3''$ apart now.

A little over a degree west of ν lies a small bright planetary nebula [136], with a stellar nucleus: it is of a greenish blue cast.

Almost directly north of β, at a distance of $5°$, lies an exceedingly compact globular cluster [138] of faint stars.

409. Aquila, the Eagle. [Map V.] — Altair, the brightest star, is easily found by means of β and γ, which lie on either side of it; the three stars lie athwart the Milky Way, there being no other very bright stars in the immediate vicinity. The triangle formed by γ, θ, and λ embraces most of the bright stars of the constellation, which bears no resemblance to an eagle.

A degree and a half northeast of γ lies the sixth magnitude star π [69], which is a close double, a test for the power of a three- or four-inch telescope, on a fine night; the components are nearly equal, and only $1''.5$ apart.

Three degrees east and a trifle south of 12 Aquilæ lies a fan-shaped cluster [131] of telescopic stars. η varies between the fourth and fifth magnitudes in a period of seven days and a fraction.

410. Argo Navis, the Ship. [Map III.] — Only a portion of this huge constellation is visible in the United States. The rest is too far south. The few bright stars visible to us lie east and south of Canis Major, and can be identified by the use of the map, after that constellation is known.

A line from Sirius to γ Canis Majoris, when prolonged nearly twice as far, terminates just north of a diffuse cluster [102] of stars, some of which are visible to the naked eye.

A little over a degree east of the preceding and $20'$ south of it is a circular telescopic cluster [103] $30'$ in diameter. A degree west of [102] lies a red star [150] of the sixth magnitude.

411. Aries, the Ram. [Map II.] — A line from Polaris through ϵ Cassiopeiæ to γ Andromedæ, when prolonged a distance equal to that between the latter stars, pierces the triangle composed of a, β, and γ Arietis, which is the distinguishing mark of the constellation. The triangle is in the Ram's head. His body lies to the eastward, and bears no resemblance to the configuration of the stars.

γ [4] is a fine double star, the components of which are nearly equal; the distance between them is 9″.

412. Auriga, the Charioteer. [Map I.] — Capella, the brightest star, is of the first magnitude, and forms a rude square with Polaris, ε Cassiopeiæ, and o Ursæ Majoris, the star in the nose of the Great Bear. It is one of the brightest stars in the sky, and shines with a pure white light. β, θ, ι, and β Tauri form with it an irregular five-sided figure, which is readily discerned. δ is in the head of the Charioteer: ι and β Tauri mark his feet. He carries in his arms a kid marked by the stars ε, ζ, and η.

14 Aurigæ [14] is a triple star having a seventh magnitude companion at a distance of 14″ and one of the eleventh magnitude at a distance of 13″.

Inside of the triangle formed by λ, ι, and χ are a number of star clusters most of which lie near the line between λ and χ. Half way between λ and ι is a rich field of stars [90] fainter than the seventh magnitude. A line from β to a point midway between θ and ν, prolonged as far again, strikes a beautiful cluster [96] of small stars: the whole field seems strewn with gold dust. These stars are so closely associated that one must believe them to be really near together, and not merely in the same line of vision. This combination of stars of very different degrees of brightness is an evidence that a faint star is not necessarily at a great distance from us. A line from ι to θ, prolonged half its length, ends near a deep red star [149] of the sixth magnitude.

413. Boötes, the Bear Keeper. [Maps I. and IV.] — A line from δ Ursæ Majoris to η of the same constellation, prolonged an equal distance, strikes a very small triangle composed of the fourth magnitude stars θ, ι, and κ, which are in the uplifted hand of Boötes. They lie midway between Polaris and Arcturus, the most brilliant star in Boötes, and one of the brightest in the heavens: it has a pronounced ruddy hue. It is at the lower end of an immense kite-shaped figure formed by β, δ, ε, a, ρ, and γ. β is in the head of Boötes; γ and δ are in his shoulders; ρ and ε form his belt. In his right foot is the triangle ζ, o, π; in his left foot is another triangle, η, τ, υ. Arcturus is in his sword.

ϵ [41] is a fine slow binary: the companion is of the sixth magnitude, and $3''$ away. The large star is yellow, the small one blue.

ξ [42] is a fine binary, having a period of about 130 years. The companion is now less than $4''$ distant, of the seventh magnitude, and purple. The distance is diminishing.

ι [39] is $5°$ east and $2°$ north of η Ursæ Majoris, and has a companion of the eighth magnitude, $38''$ away.

π [40] is $6°$ east and $3°$ south of Arcturus, and has a companion of the sixth magnitude, $6''$ distant.

414. Camelopardus, the Camelopard. [Map I.] — The stars in this constellation are faint. The head of the creature consists of four fifth magnitude stars situated one fifth of the way from Polaris to the bowl of the Great Dipper. His fore feet are almost on the head of Auriga, while his hind feet are in position to give Perseus a kick in the stomach. If he were not such a weakling, he might give trouble.

There is a rich, though coarse cluster [89] two thirds of the way from a Persei to δ Aurigæ. It is close to the fifth magnitude star 7 Camelopardi.

415. Cancer, the Crab. [Maps III. and I.] — The principal start form an inverted Y, as shown on Map III. A line drawn from Polaris to h Ursæ Majoris, a fifth magnitude star in the head of the Great Bear, and prolonged $1\frac{1}{2}$ times its own length, strikes ι, the uppermost star in the Λ.

ζ [27] is found by alignment with Castor and Pollux. It is a fine multiple star, and has been described in § 372. The two stars forming the bright one are in rather rapid motion, sixty years sufficing for a revolution. The visible companion of this binary is $5''$ distant. The large star looks oblong with a high power on a three- or four-inch telescope.

Between γ and δ lies the cluster [104] Præsepe, the Beehive, which is visible to the naked eye on a moonless night. A good-sized opera-glass shows it better than a larger telescope.

416. Canes Venatici, the Hunting Dogs. [Map I.] — This constellation is not especially noteworthy. Its brightest star, a or 12, is called Cor Caroli (the Heart of Charles II. of England), and is found by prolonging a line from Polaris to ϵ Ursæ Majoris half its length.

Cor Caroli [36] has a sixth magnitude companion 20″ distant.

2 [33] is an orange star of the fifth magnitude, having a blue companion of the ninth magnitude, 11″ distant.

There is a bright globular cluster [114] containing upwards of 1,000 stars, lying nearly midway between Cor Caroli and α Boötis (Arcturus), but a little nearer the latter: it is close to a star of the sixth magnitude.

The Great Spiral Nebula [113] (§ 391) lies about one fourth of the way from η Ursæ Majoris to Cor Caroli. It is called the Whirlpool Nebula, but in small telescopes it looks simply like a faint double nebula. The entire constellation is plentifully besprinkled with faint nebulæ.

417. Canis Major, the Great Dog. [Map III.] — This constellation is best learned after Orion. The line of the three stars in Orion's belt prolonged eastward passes near Sirius, which is α in this constellation, and by far the brightest fixed star in the heavens. The triangle δ, ε, η is in the haunches of the animal, and Sirius is in his head: β is the extremity of one uplifted fore paw. The animal sits upright, in the attitude of begging his master Orion for permission to put his teeth into the Hare, which is under Orion's feet.

Sirius is a very interesting double star (§ 370), but is much too difficult for a small telescope, the faint companion being in the blaze of light surrounding the bright star. The period of revolution is about fifty years.

μ [24] has a ninth magnitude companion at a distance of less than 4″.

A superb cluster [100] visible to the naked eye lies about one third of the way from Sirius to ε. There is a ruddy star near the centre: many of the brighter stars are arranged in curves.

418. Canis Minor, the Little Dog. [Map III.] — It is well to learn Gemini before Canis Minor. A line from Polaris to β Geminorum (Pollux), prolonged one third as far again, reaches Procyon, a first magnitude star, which is α Canis Minoris. The only other conspicuous star is β, which is 4° northwest of Procyon.

Procyon is of interest because of its irregular proper motion, supposed to be caused by the presence of close companions, which have often been searched for by the largest telescopes, but without success. In the same field with Procyon is a star of the seventh magnitude which is a close double. The components are only $1''.5$ apart, but the star can be elongated by a good four-inch glass.

419. Capricornus, the Goat. [Map V.] — It is well to know Cygnus before attempting to learn Capricornus. A line from Polaris to γ Cygni (where the arm of the cross is fixed to the upright piece), prolonged an equal distance, reaches the naked-eye double a, below which is β at a distance of $2°.5$. δ and γ form another such pair of stars, and ψ and ω a third. The constellation is chiefly embraced in the triangle formed by these three pairs. a and β are in the head of the animal, while ψ and ω are in his knees; the rest of the Goat may be supplied to suit the fancy.

ρ [73] and π [72] are pretty doubles, each having a companion of the ninth magnitude, less than $4''$ away. A good night is needed for their observation with a four-inch glass.

420. Cassiopeia, the Lady in the Chair. [Map I.] — This brilliant constellation is quickly found by using Map I. according to the directions in § 10. The stars ϵ, δ, γ, a, β, and κ form a rude broken-backed chair. The Lady, however, refuses to sit in it, preferring to sit on empty space. The stars β, a, γ, and κ form her body; δ is in her knee, and ι in her foot; ζ is in her head; her arms are uplifted, possibly in prayer to the gods to spare her lovely daughter Andromeda, who has been chained to a rock, as prey for a sea monster.

η [1] is a splendid binary, having a purple companion of the eighth magnitude, $5''$ distant. It is less than half the way from a to γ. The period of revolution is 200 years: the combined mass of the two stars is thought to be from five to ten times that of the sun. Near κ appeared Tycho's new star described in § 375.

As the Milky Way runs through Cassiopeia, there are many beautiful fields which can be best seen with a low power.

Near β, between ρ and σ, is a large cloud of minute stars [142] discovered by Caroline Herschel, the sister of Sir William Herschel.

Between π and o in the uplifted left hand of the Lady is a magnificent region.

One degree east and a little north of δ is a beautiful field [84]. A line from δ to a, prolonged $1\frac{1}{4}$ times its former length, ends near

R, a vivid red star which varies from the fifth to the twelfth magnitude in a period of 433 days.

421. Centaurus, the Centaur. [Maps III. and IV.] — Centaurus, even when most favorably situated, is too near the southern horizon for satisfactory observation in the United States, except in Florida and Southern Texas. It is of especial interest, because it contains our nearest neighbor among the stars, a Centauri.

422. Cepheus. [Map I.] — This constellation lies between Cassiopeia and Draco. Cepheus is the husband of Cassiopeia, who, with her daughter Andromeda, nearly monopolizes the brilliancy of the family. The five brightest stars are a, β, γ, ι, and ζ, which form a figure composed of a rude square surmounted by a triangle which is nearly isosceles. a forms with Polaris and γ Cassiopeiæ an isosceles triangle which is nearly equilateral. Near ζ are δ and ϵ: the three are in the head of the figure.

β [77] is a double star, the companion being blue, of the eighth magnitude, and 14" distant.

δ [82] has a companion of the seventh magnitude, 41" distant: the primary is yellow, the companion blue: the main star is a noted variable, having a period of $5\frac{1}{3}$ days.

ζ [80] has a blue seventh magnitude companion, 6" distant.

423. Cetus, the Whale. [Maps II. and V.] — A line from Polaris to δ Cassiopeiæ, prolonged so that the prolongation is $2\frac{1}{3}$ times the original length of the line, reaches the centre of this huge and ungainly constellation, which can be best learned by following the dotted lines given on the map. The monster has about the shape of a walrus. The most noticeable portion of the constellation is an irregular pentagon, rudely kite-shaped, formed from the third magnitude stars β, η, θ^1, ζ, and τ. The pentagon formed by a, γ, ξ^2, μ, and λ marks the head.

Nearly half way from γ to ζ lies o (Mira) [143], the wonderful variable described in § 376. It is visible to the naked eye only six weeks in the year.

γ [8] is not a very difficult double for a four-inch glass. A star of the seventh magnitude nestles close to the larger star: the distance is $2".5$.

a [144] is a fine orange-colored star, having a blue neighbor in the same low-power field.

424. Columba, the Dove. [Map II.] — The full name is Columba Noachi or Noah's Dove. The asterism lies south of Lepus, and is too low down in the south to be seen well. A line drawn from β Orionis (Rigel) to β Leporis, and prolonged as far again, terminates near a and β, the two brightest stars.

425. Coma Berenices, the Hair of Berenice. [Map I.] — This constellation consists of faint stars; most of those visible to the naked eye are of the fifth and sixth magnitudes. They are well crowded together. A line from Polaris to δ Ursæ Majoris, when prolonged an equal distance, terminates near the most crowded part of the asterism. It is a fine sight in a small opera-glass.

A little over one third of the way from η Boötis (near Arcturus) to β Leonis is the fifth magnitude star 42; 50' northeast of this is a condensed mass of minute stars [112], which cannot be well seen with a telescope of less than four inches aperture.

426. Corona Borealis, the Northern Crown. [Map I.] — Corona lies a little south of a line from a Boötis (Arcturus) to a Lyræ (Vega), at about one third the distance from the former to the latter. Seven of its principal stars form a figure so similar to a crown that it is instantly recognized.

ζ [44] has a bluish green companion of the sixth magnitude 6" distant.

A degree south of ϵ is a ninth magnitude star called T Coronæ [155]. It suddenly blazed up in May, 1866, and equalled a in brightness; it then slowly declined, and after a month reached its former low estate, which it has held ever since.

427. Corvus, the Crow. [Map IV.] — A line from Polaris to δ Ursæ Majoris, prolonged until it is $3\frac{1}{2}$ times its former length, strikes a small but conspicuous quadrilateral, 15° west and 10° south of a Virginis (Spica). a is in the Crow's bill; the Crow stands upon and pecks at Hydra.

δ [34] is accompanied by a purple star of the eighth magnitude, at a distance of 24".

428. Crater, the Cup. [Map III.] — Crater adjoins Corvus on the west, and stands upon Hydra. The stars η, ζ, γ, δ, ϵ, and θ form the bowl of a crooked goblet, in the base of which are a and β. The goblet leans as if to discharge its contents upon its neighbor, the Crow.

Just east of a and in the same field of view with a very low power is R [152], a notable red star of the eighth magnitude. Sir William Herschel described it as "scarlet, almost blood-colored; a most intense and curious color."

429. Cygnus, the Swan. [Map I.] — Cygnus is readily discovered by following the directions for using Map I. given in § 10. It lies in the Milky Way, just east of Lyra, and is quickly recognized by the cross, the upright piece of which is composed of a, γ, η, χ, and β, and has the same trend as the Milky Way. The cross arm consists of the stars δ, γ, and ϵ.

β is in the Swan's head, and a in its tail. The cross piece of the cross, extended, forms the wings of the bird.

β [66] has a blue seventh magnitude companion at a distance of 34″. It is the finest colored double for a small telescope in the northern sky; the colors are beautifully seen by putting the telescope slightly out of focus.

μ [78] is a much closer double, the fifth magnitude companion being only 4″ distant. A third star of the seventh magnitude is over 200″ distant.

17 [68] lies in a beautiful field, and has a ninth magnitude companion 26″ distant.

61 [76], which is in one corner of a parallelogram formed by a, γ, ϵ, and itself, is a pretty double when seen with a low power: the components are nearly equal. This star is celebrated as the first one the distance of which from us was measured. It is about 550,000 times as far off as the sun.

There are fine fields in many places, especially within a few degrees of a (Deneb). One of the best is a little north of the middle of a line from a and δ, near o. In the northeast corner of the constellation, about half way between ρ and π^1, is a large cluster [139] in a rich vicinity.

430. Delphinus, the Dolphin. [Map V.] — A line from Polaris to a Cygni, when prolonged until it is two thirds longer than before, strikes a small diamond, composed of three stars of the fourth magnitude and one of the third. These, with a fifth of the fourth magnitude, which lies southwest of them, form a narrow wedge, called Job's Coffin. This is the principal portion of Delphinus.

γ [74] is a golden yellow star having a greenish blue companion of the sixth magnitude, at a distance of 11″.

431. Draco, the Dragon. [Map I.] — The head of the Dragon consists of a bright quadrilateral formed of β, γ, ξ, and ν, which is so situated as to form an equilateral triangle with Cassiopeia and the bowl of the Great Dipper, Polaris being inside of the triangle. It also forms a much smaller right triangle with a Lyræ (Vega) and a Cygni, the right angle being at Vega.

From the head the constellation winds in magnificent convolutions, shown by the dotted line on the map, around between the two Bears. λ, the last bright star in the tail, is two thirds of the way from Polaris to the centre of the bowl of the Great Dipper.

About half way between ζ Ursæ Majoris (Mizar) and γ Ursæ Minoris (one of the two brighter stars in the Little Dipper) lies a, which is distinguished as having been the pole star four or five thousand years ago. About half way between δ and ζ lies the pole of the ecliptic, which is near a bright planetary nebula [125], 35″ in diameter. Unlike most such objects, it can be seen very well with a four-inch glass.

μ [52] is a neat double, the two stars being nearly equal in brightness, and less than 3″ apart. A planetary nebula has been mentioned above.

432. Equuleus, the Little Horse. [Map V.] — a lies 7° west and nearly 5° south of ϵ Pegasi, which is in the nose of the animal. It contains only five stars above the sixth magnitude.

ϵ [75] has a companion of the seventh magnitude at a distance of 11″: the main star is a close rapid binary, which now looks elongated in a four-inch telescope, armed with a high power.

433. Eridanus, the River. [Map II.] — Three degrees north and two west of β Orionis lies β Eridani, which may be considered as the source of the river. Thence it flows west, following the sinuous line on the map, till it reaches the star π Ceti, where it laves the paws of Cetus; then it drops south about 5°, thence east, southeast, and southwest in succession, till it is lost beneath our horizon.

32 [11], which has a right ascension of 3 h. 49 m. and a south declination of 3° 15′, is a fifth magnitude star having a companion of the seventh magnitude 7″ distant. The primary has been called topaz-yellow, and the companion sea-green.

434. Gemini, the Twins. [Maps I. and II.] — A line drawn from the bowl of the Little Dipper to the head of the Great Bear, and prolonged an equal distance, terminates near the two bright stars a and β (Castor and Pollux). Pollux is the brighter of the two. These two are in the heads of the twins, who stand side by side. The chief stars can be traced by the dotted lines on Maps I. and II. The entire figure is much like an end view of an upright piano. a and β are at the top, μ, γ, and ξ at the bottom, while λ and ζ are at the key-board. The summer solstice is close to the fifth magnitude star 1, which is a little west and north of η and μ.

Castor [26] is a magnificent double, the components differing one magnitude in brightness, and being nearly 6" apart. It is a binary, the period of which is thought to be about 1,000 years.

δ [25] has an eighth magnitude companion at a distance of 7".

Four degrees west and two north of μ (at the base of the back of the piano) is a cluster [97], visible to the naked eye as a faint cloud on the sky. It is 20' in diameter and consists of stars from the ninth magnitude down to the faintest points of light.

435. Hercules. [Maps I. and IV.] — Directly east of Corona lies the belt of Hercules, composed of the stars ϵ and ζ; β and δ are in the shoulders; η and π are in the thighs; a marks the head. The limbs and arms are traced by the dotted lines on the maps. The whole forms a fair picture of a giant, with his head toward the equator.

a [54] is a fine double, having an emerald companion of the sixth magnitude 5" away: it is also variable.

ρ [57] is a binary, having a greenish companion of the fifth magnitude at a distance of 4": it is near π in one thigh.

δ [55] in one shoulder has an eighth magnitude companion, which has, if one compares the estimates of different observers, nearly all the colors of the rainbow, and is at a distance of 19".

The finest globular cluster [118] in the northern hemisphere, pictured in Fig. 173, is one third of the way from η to ζ, and is just visible to the naked eye. The stars are so thickly crowded near the centre, that a small telescope shows them simply as a nebulous mass.

About one third the way from ι, in one foot, to η, in the opposite thigh, is a very condensed cluster [121], which is fine, but inferior in interest to the preceding.

436. Hydra, the Snake. [Maps II. and III.] — A line from Polaris through the middle of the triangle which forms the head of the Great Bear, carried on through Cancer, meets the head of Hydra, which is just beyond Cancer; the head is a good representation of that of a hissing snake. Thence it may be traced in a south and east direction by following the dotted line on the map. A line from Polaris through h at the vertex of the obtuse angle of the triangle in the Great Bear's head, passing in front of the Sickle in Leo (through κ Leonis) meets a, which is also called Cor Hydræ. The distance from a to κ Leonis is one half the distance of the latter from Polaris. One is helped in tracing the eastern end of the constellation by the recognition of Corvus, which stands upon it.

ϵ [28], the northernmost star in the head, has a blue companion of the eighth magnitude at a distance of $3''.5$.

At a right ascension of 10 h. 20 m., 2° south of μ, is a bright planetary nebula [108], which appears as large as Jupiter when the latter is at opposition.

437. Lacerta, the Lizard. [Map I.] — Lacerta lies between Cygnus and Andromeda. The middle point of a line connecting a Cygni with a Andromedæ lies a little south of the centre of the constellation.

Two and a half degrees west of 7, which is the brightest star in the constellation, lies a fair cluster [141]. The constellation furnishes some fine fields, when viewed with a low power.

438. Leo, the Lion. [Map III.] — A line from Polaris to the middle point of a line connecting a Ursæ Majoris and h of the same constellation, when prolonged to nearly three times its original length, passes through a conspicuous figure known as The Sickle, and terminates at a (Regulus), in the end of the handle of the Sickle. At the east of this figure is a conspicuous right-angled triangle which lies in a line drawn from Polaris through the bowl of the Great Dipper. The Sickle constitutes the head and the fore part of the body of the crouching lion. The large triangle is in his haunches. Regulus is sometimes called The Lion's Heart.

γ [30] is a golden yellow star, having a companion of the fourth magnitude, at a distance of $3''.5$. It is one of the finest binaries in the northern sky: its period is about 400 years.

ι [32], the nearest bright star south of the west end of the right triangle, has a bluish companion of the seventh magnitude, less than $3''$ away.

A little over half the way from a to ξ is the crimson variable R [151], which ranges between the fifth and tenth magnitudes; the period is 312 days.

439. Leo Minor, the Little Lion. [Map I.] — Adjoining the Sickle, in a line from it to the bowl of the Great Dipper, lies Leo Minor, a shapeless constellation containing a few naked-eye stars, three of which are as bright as the fourth magnitude.

440. Lepus, the Hare. [Map II.] — Lepus crouches under Orion's feet, and does not particularly resemble a hare.

γ [21] is a triple star; the larger companion is of the seventh magnitude, and is 93" distant; the small companion is 45" from the other one, and is visible with a three-inch glass.

45 [19] is a seventh magnitude star $1\frac{1}{2}°$ east of a; it has four companions visible with a small telescope, at distances varying from 60" to 126". There are four other companions to be seen with larger telescopes.

A line from a to μ, prolonged two thirds of its length, ends close to the crimson star R [147], which varies from the sixth to the ninth magnitude; the period is 438 days.

441. Libra, the Scales. [Map IV.] — Libra is best learned after Virgo and Scorpio, between which it lies. a lies a little more than half way from a Virginis (Spica) to β Scorpii. The chief configuration is a quadrilateral formed by a, β, γ, and ι.

a looks elongated to a keen eye; an opera-glass shows that it has a fifth magnitude companion.

δ [153] is a variable, situated $4°.5$ west and $1°$ north of β. Its period is $2\frac{1}{3}$ days, and it varies from the fifth to the sixth magnitude. The change in brightness consumes 12 hours.

β [154] is a pale green star.

442. Lupus, the Wolf. [Map IV.] — Lupus lies south of Libra, and even when best seen is too near the southern horizon for observers in middle north latitudes.

443. Lynx, the Lynx. [Map I.] — The Lynx occupies a dull region between Ursa Major on one side, and Auriga and Gemini on the other. The leading stars form an irregular line, traced on the map.

38 [29] in the southeastern corner of the constellation, has a lilac companion of the seventh magnitude, 3" distant. The pair 38 and

40 form an equilateral triangle with two pairs in the feet of the Great Bear.

5 [148] is a fiery red star of the sixth magnitude, in a fine group.

444. Lyra, the Harp. [Map I.] — The leader of this constellation (Vega) is one of the brightest of the first magnitude stars. To the naked eye its color is pale sapphire. It is easily identified by means of the two fourth magnitude stars, ϵ and ζ, which form with it an equilateral triangle, each side of which is nearly 2° in length. The constellation lies between Hercules and Cygnus. The equilateral triangle is perched on one corner of a rhomboid, ζ being common to both figures.

a (Vega) [60] has a blue companion of the tenth magnitude, 48" distant.

β [63] is a multiple star, having three companions of about the eighth magnitude, at distances of 46", 66", and 86", respectively. It is also one of the noted variables. See § 378.

ϵ [61] is one of the equilateral triangle, and appears elongated to the average eye: a sharp eye splits it into two stars. An opera-glass separates them widely, and a small telescope shows each star as a double. The distance between the components of one pair is 3"; the other pair is a little closer.

ζ [62] has a fifth magnitude companion, 44" distant.

8° east of Vega are the two stars η [65] and θ. The former has a blue companion of the ninth magnitude, 28" distant. δ, one of the stars of the rhomboid, is double in an opera-glass, and is situated in a fine field.

Beautiful fields lie between ϵ and R, which is 5° northeast of it. The only annular nebula [132] which small telescopes reveal lies one third of the way from β to γ. It has been described in § 391.

445. Monoceros, the Unicorn. [Maps III. and II.] — This constellation contains only four stars as bright as the fourth magnitude. It lies east of Orion, and stretches itself in the Milky Way between Canis Major and Canis Minor.

8 [22] lies in the northwestern part of the constellation, at a right ascension of 6 h. 19 m. A line from λ Orionis (in his head) to a Orionis, prolonged $1\frac{1}{3}$ times its own length, stops just south of 8. It is a golden yellow star with a lilac companion of the seventh magnitude, 13" distant: it is in a splendid field.

11 [23], which lies in the southwestern part of the constellation, has a double companion of the sixth magnitude, 7″ distant. The components of the companion are 2″.3 apart. It is a star of the fourth magnitude, about three eighths of the way from Sirius to a Orionis (Betelgueuse), a little east of a direct line.

2° east of 8, and 1° south of the middle point of the line joining γ Orionis (Bellatrix) with a Canis Minoris (Procyon) is a cluster [99] visible to the naked eye, and very pleasing with a low power. Some of the faintest stars are arranged in straight lines.

A line from Sirius to θ Canis Majoris, when prolonged three fourths of its length, reaches a brilliant coarse cluster [101], in a "superb" neighborhood.

There is a fine field one fifth of the way from 11 to 8; the fifth magnitude star 10 is in it.

446. Ophiuchus, the Serpent Bearer. [Map IV.] — Ophiuchus lies between Hercules and Scorpio. The two portions of Serpens lie respectively at the east and west sides of this constellation. Ophiuchus is represented as standing on the Scorpion and grasping the Serpent with both hands.

A line from Polaris to β Draconis (in the Dragon's head), prolonged an equal distance, ends near a, which is in the head of Ophiuchus and near a Herculis. β and γ mark his right shoulder, ι and κ the left; ν and τ are in his right hand, δ and ε in his left. His right knee contains η and his left ζ. The right foot is at θ, the left at ρ.

The parallelogram (nearly) formed by ζ and λ Ophiuchi with a and μ Serpentis is shown by the dotted lines on the map, and is noteworthy to the eye: one diagonal of it contains five bright stars.

λ [51] is a binary, having a period of about 230 years. The companion is of the sixth magnitude, and is now (1896) 1″.7 distant.

36 [53], a fifth magnitude star in the southernmost part of the constellation, 11° east of a Scorpii (Antares), has a sixth magnitude companion at a distance of 5″.

70 [58], 4°.5 east of γ, is a fine binary, completing a revolution in less than a century: the seventh magnitude companion is reddish. The distance is now (1896) 2″.

ρ [49], in the left foot, has an eighth magnitude companion at a distance of 4″.

A cluster [120] 3′ in diameter lies 9°.5 due east of a Scorpii

(Antares), nearly in line with 36. There are a number of other clusters in the vicinity.

3° south and 1° west of ζ lies a cluster [117] 5' in diameter.

One third of the way from ε to β lies a cluster [119] 8' in diameter, in the centre of which the stars are very closely crowded. A line from σ to β prolonged 2½ times its former length strikes a large coarse cluster [128].

447. Orion. [Map II.] — Orion is the finest constellation in the heavens, and strikes the eye at once: it is best seen in the early evening in midwinter. The mighty hunter stands in the attitude of smiting Taurus. His belt is formed of three second magnitude stars, δ, ε, and ζ; it is about 3° in length, and has been called the Ell and Yard. Below it dangles the sword, composed of three, or to good eyes four, stars in line. The shoulders are marked respectively by α (Betelgueuse) and γ (Bellatrix). In the head is a small isosceles right triangle. The left foot is marked by β (Rigel), a bluish white star of the first magnitude: κ occupies the right knee. The right arm and club, with which he is to smite Taurus full in the face, are indicated by the dotted lines going upward from α. The left arm with which he holds up the skin of the Nemæan lion, is similarly outlined by a dotted line.

β [15] has a ninth magnitude companion at a distance of 10″. It is not hard to see with a four-inch glass, under good atmospheric conditions, and is itself a very close double.

ζ [20] is a triple, having a sixth magnitude companion 2″.6 distant, and one of the ninth magnitude 57″ away.

ι [17], the southernmost star in the sword, has an eighth magnitude companion at a distance of 12″, and one of the tenth magnitude 49″ distant.

λ [16], in the head, has a companion of the sixth magnitude, 4″ distant.

σ [18] is a triple star, having a seventh magnitude companion at a distance of 42″, and one of the eighth magnitude 12″ distant: near by is a small triangle of three eighth magnitude stars.

1° south of ν, in the right hand, is a cluster [98] of 30 stars of the ninth magnitude or fainter.

A brilliant field [95] lies 1° north of θ, containing quite a number of stars of the sixth and seventh magnitudes.

In the sword is the multiple star θ, surrounded by the Great Nebula [94], the finest object of its kind in the sky. See § 390. In a four-inch telescope the central portion, around the Trapezium, can be well seen, in the absence of the moon.

448. Pegasus, the Winged Horse. [Maps V. and I.] — The chief configuration of this constellation is a large rude square which is in the body of the horse. A hook-shaped figure starting from one corner of the square makes the neck and head of the animal. One corner of the square is found by drawing a line from Polaris to β Cassiopeiæ, and prolonging it an equal distance. The star thus found is really a Andromedæ, but has at times been called δ Pegasi. The neck starts from the opposite corner of the square, and embraces the stars ξ and ζ; the head starts at θ, and ϵ is in the nose.

κ [79], which is 16° due north of ϵ, has a companion of the eleventh magnitude 12'' distant. The main star is a very close double.

A line from θ to ϵ, prolonged two thirds of its length, reaches a condensed globular star cluster [137], 3' or 4' in diameter.

Midway between ϵ and θ is a bright group [140].

449. Perseus. [Map I.] — Perseus lies between Auriga and Andromeda. a, its chief star, lies on a line from β Andromedæ to γ Andromedæ, prolonged $1\frac{1}{2}$ times its own length. The most striking configuration is the trapezoid of which a is one vertex, from which springs a curved line of stars shown by the dotted line on the map. 9° south of ι (which is in one corner of the trapezoid) lies β (Algol), the wonderful variable described in § 379. Near Algol are a few stars which form the head of Medusa, the Gorgon which Perseus slew. 10° southeast of Algol lie a few scattered stars which complete the constellation: there is no resemblance to the figure of a man.

ϵ [12] has a lilac companion of the eighth magnitude, at a distance of 8''.

ζ [10] has three companions of the ninth, tenth, and tenth magnitudes, respectively, at distances of 13'', 90'', and 122''.

η [9] has an eighth magnitude companion at a distance of 28''.

Just south of the middle point of a line from δ Cassiopeiæ to γ Persei is a large hazy spot, visible to the naked eye even in strong moonlight. It is a double cluster [85], the finest object of its class in the northern hemisphere. The lowest power should be used in viewing it.

1° north of a point five eighths of the way from γ Andromedæ to β Persei (Algol) is one of the finest of low-power fields.

450. Pisces, the Fishes. [Maps V., II., and I.] — One of the Fishes, which is marked by a six-sided polygon, is located just south of the square of Pegasus. The star ι in this figure forms nearly an isosceles right triangle with the two stars α and γ, which form the southern side of the square. Thence a ribbon, represented on the map by a row of stars connected by a dotted line, extends eastward to α, just east of the head of Cetus, thence northward to the other Fish, which is an insignificant and chiefly imaginary creature, the mouth of which is near β Andromedæ. Though none of the stars are especially bright, they are in a dull region, and so are easily traced.

A line drawn from Polaris through β Cassiopeiæ to α Andromedæ (in one corner of the square of Pegasus), and prolonged nearly one half of its former length, terminates close by the vernal equinox, east of the hexagon which marks the southern one of the two Fishes.

α [5] has a companion of the fourth magnitude, distant 3″.

ζ [2], 12° east and 5° north of α, has an eighth magnitude companion 23″ away.

451. Piscis Australis, the Southern Fish. [Map V.] — Prolong the line of the western edge of the square of Pegasus southward, until the prolongation is four times the length of the original line, and α (Fomalhaut) will be reached: it is of the first magnitude. The other stars of the constellation are then found readily. The constellation is too far south for good telescopic views.

452. Sagitta, the Arrow. [Map V.] — This constellation is just north of Aquila and south of Vulpecula. It is a fair representation of an arrow, the butt of which is marked by the pretty pair α and β, which lie midway between β Cygni and α Aquilæ (Altair). The point of the arrow is at η.

ζ [70] has a companion of the ninth magnitude 9″ distant. The large star is a very close double.

θ [71] has two companions, one of the ninth magnitude at a distance of 11″, and one of the eighth, 70″ distant. The colors of the three stars are called pale topaz, gray, and pearly yellow.

About a degree south of β lies a double [67] composed of a ruby star of the ninth magnitude, and a blue star of the tenth magnitude, 20″ distant.

Midway between γ and δ is a faint but very condensed cluster [133].

η lies in a beautiful low-power field [135], in which are a number of doubles.

453. Sagittarius, the Archer. [Maps V. and IV.] — The conspicuous part of this constellation looks like a bent bow, with the point of the arrow just west of its centre, and the butt $2\frac{1}{2}$ times as far east, in one corner of a bright quadrilateral. Sagittarius is a Centaur; the two southern stars of the quadrilateral are in his body. The naked-eye double, β, far to the south, not on the map, marks one of his front hoofs.

A line from Polaris through Vega, prolonged $1\frac{1}{4}$ times its former length, strikes the quadrilateral. The winter solstice lies $2\frac{1}{3}°$ south and 2° west of μ, and is 1° north of the naked-eye cluster [124].

μ [59], in the northwest part of the constellation, has two companions of the ninth and tenth magnitudes, at respective distances of 40″ and 45″.

Midway between μ and σ is a cluster [130], 8′ in diameter, surrounded by five stars irregularly placed. It shows well with a four-inch glass.

A line from σ to λ prolonged three fourths of its length terminates just south of a splendid portion [124] of the Milky Way, which well repays examination by its richness.

3° north of μ and 1° east is an offshoot [126] of the Milky Way, which shows a fine field with a low power. 2° north of μ and 5° east is a brilliant region [129] visible to the naked eye.

4° north and $1\frac{1}{2}°$ east of μ is a very rich field [127].

A line from σ to μ prolonged three eighths of its length terminates at a good low-power field [122] containing about 100 stars from the ninth magnitude down.

The line from σ to λ prolonged an equal distance stops just south of a pair of fifth magnitude stars: close by the northern one is the Trifid Nebula [123] described in § 391. A large telescope is required to see it well.

454. Scorpio, the Scorpion. [Map IV.] — A line from Polaris to β Herculis, prolonged two thirds of its former length, strikes α (Antares), a star of the first magnitude. The downward curve from α is easily followed by the eye. At the west of Antares the stars β, δ, and π form a fine curve, like the blade of a scythe, one of the handles of which is at α.

a [50] is an elegant double, having a seventh magnitude companion less than 4" distant.

β [46] has a fifth magnitude companion, 13" distant.

ν [47], near β, has a seventh magnitude companion 40" distant: each is a close double.

ξ [45] has a companion of the seventh magnitude, 7" away. The large star is also double, and may be seen elongated with a four-inch telescope without difficulty.

σ [48] has a plum-colored companion of the ninth magnitude, 20" distant.

The most condensed mass of stars [116] in the heavens is situated half way between a and β: it lies in a beautiful field, and looks like a comet through a small telescope.

455. Sculptor, the Sculptor. [Maps II. and V.] — This constellation lies south of β Ceti and east of a Piscis Australis (Fomalhaut). It is an insignificant group.

456. Scutum, the Shield. [Map V.] — Scutum is sometimes called Clypeus Sobieskii, the Shield of Sobieski; it is small and inconspicuous, but lies in the thick of the Milky Way: a line from Polaris to a Lyræ (Vega), when prolonged nine tenths of its former length, ends in Scutum, near the brightest star. There are many faint doubles and rich fields.

457. Serpens, the Serpent. [Map IV.] — The head of the Serpent is a triangular figure just south of Corona, between Hercules and Boötes. Thence the Serpent's body extends southward through the conspicuous parallelogram described in § 446, across Ophiuchus, east and northeast, following the dotted line on the map, till it terminates at θ, nearly three fourths of the way from β Ophiuchi to δ Aquilæ.

δ [43], near the head, has a companion of the fifth magnitude, 3".6 distant.

θ [64] has a companion of nearly the same magnitude, 22" distant.

Close by the star 5, which forms a nearly equilateral triangle with ϵ and μ in the quadrilateral, is a rich and condensed cluster [115].

458. Sextans, the Sextant. [Map III.] — Sextans is an insignificant group lying south of the Sickle. A line from η Leonis to Regulus, prolonged $2\frac{1}{2}$ times its former length, nearly strikes 15, the brightest star in the constellation.

Half a degree north of the middle point of a line joining 8 and 22, in the southwest corner of the constellation, is a narrow nebula [107] 5' long, having a bright nucleus.

459. Taurus, the Bull. [Map II.] — The face of the Bull is marked by a V-shaped figure containing the red first magnitude star a (Aldebaran), which is nearly pointed at by the belt of Orion. Sirius is as far from the belt on one side as Aldebaran is on the other. The horns of the animal are very long, their tips being at β and ζ. The well known cluster of the Pleiades is in his fore shoulder. Though the latter half of his body is missing, he makes a brave feint of charging upon Orion. The V is known as the Hyades: one of its stars, θ, is a naked-eye double.

a [13] has a tenth magnitude companion at a distance of 113″.

The Crab Nebula [92] lies 1° northwest of ζ. Through a small telescope it is a simple oval.

460. Triangulum, the Triangle. [Map I.] — The three bright stars of this constellation form a right triangle, immediately north of the triangle in the head of Aries.

6, or ι [7], nearly south of β, at a distance of 5°, is a "topaz-yellow" star of the fifth magnitude, and has a bluish companion of the seventh magnitude, 3″.5 distant.

461. Ursa Major, the Great Bear. [Map I.] — After the Great Dipper has been learned, the rest of the constellation can be made out by the help of the dotted lines on the map. The stars h, v, and o form the head: ι and κ mark one of the fore feet: λ and μ are in one of the hind feet, ν and ζ in the other. The stars in the Great Dipper have the following names from a to η: Dubhe, Merak, Phecda, Megrez, Alioth, Mizar, and Benetnasch. The small star near Mizar is called Alcor.

ζ [38] (Mizar) has a companion of the fifth magnitude, 14″ distant.

ξ [31] is a rather close and rapid binary, having a period of only 61 years; the companion is of the fifth magnitude.

10° north of v and $1\frac{1}{2}$° nearly east of the fifth magnitude star d is a double nebula [105, 106], one component of which is fairly bright: they are half a degree apart.

A line from a to γ, prolonged three fourths of its own length, strikes a large oval nebula [110].

462. Ursa Minor, the Little Bear. [Map I.] — Polaris is the brightest star, and is in the end of the tail. The stars β, γ, ζ, and η are in the Bear's body, and form the bowl of the Little Dipper. The length of the tail may be ascribed to adaptation to environment.

a (Polaris) [3] has a companion of the ninth magnitude, 19″ distant.

463. Virgo, the Virgin. [Maps IV. and III.] — The head of the Virgin is 5° south of β Leonis (Denebola). Thence the body stretches east and south to Libra. The lines on the map show its general contour. The right arm is graciously extended to take in ϵ, and the left hand is given to a (Spica), a star of the first magnitude.

The autumnal equinox lies 1° south of the middle point of a line connecting β and η.

γ [35] is a fine binary having a period of 185 years: the components are equal in magnitude, and are now (1896) 5″ apart.

6° north and 4° west of Spica is the triple star θ [37]; its companions are of the ninth and tenth magnitudes, at distances of 7″ and 65″ respectively.

In the wonderful nebulous region of Virgo, bounded by the stars β, η, γ, δ, ϵ, and β Leonis, the sky is crowded with nebulæ, most of which are too faint for small telescopes. One of the brighter ones [111] is west of ϵ and δ, forming with them an equilateral triangle.

464. Vulpecula, the Fox. [Map I.] — Vulpecula contains one star of the fourth magnitude, which is $3\frac{1}{2}°$ south of β Cygni in the foot of the Cross. The rest of the stars are fainter, and most of them lie east of the fourth magnitude star, being bounded by Delphinus and Sagitta on the south, Cygnus on the north, and Pegasus on the east.

$3\frac{1}{2}°$ due north from γ Sagittæ, nearly in line with 6 Vulpeculæ (the brightest star) and γ Delphini, the Dumb-bell Nebula [134] is located: a description of it has been given in § 391.

USE OF A STAR FINDER OR OF AN EQUATORIAL.

465. Graduation of the Circles. — In §§ 8–12, directions have been given for finding many objects of telescopic interest by the aid of the maps. It is often more convenient to find them by means of a star finder (Fig. 194), or of a telescope equatorially mounted

THE CONSTELLATIONS IN DETAIL. 295

and provided with an hour circle and a declination circle (Fig. 195). Such circles can be affixed to almost any telescope mounting which

Fig. 194. — THE STAR FINDER.

is destitute of them by a bright boy of a mechanical turn of mind. Two opposite points of the hour circle (the lower one in Fig. 194) may be marked 0 h. and 12 h. respectively. Each half of the circle would then read 0, 1, 2, 3, . . . 12 h. The circle may then be subdivided into five minute spaces. It is well to mark two opposite points of the declination circle (the upper one in Fig. 194) 0°, and to run the graduations each side of 0° up to 90°. Each whole degree should be indicated. The cut of the star finder[1] shows that it is like an English equatorial (§ 44), a stick taking the place of the telescope.

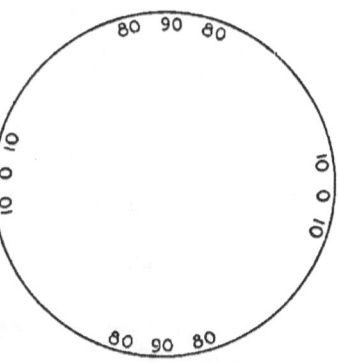

Fig. 195. — THE DECLINATION CIRCLE.

When the stick or telescope lies in the plane of the meridian, and is perpendicular to the polar axis, the pointer on each circle

[1] A detailed description of this instrument, together with Prof. Wm. A. Rogers's method of tracing the constellations by its aid, is given in the "Sidereal Messenger" (published by W. W. Payne, Northfield, Minn.) for April, 1889.

should be opposite the zero of the circle. Both circles of the star finder are fast to the polar axis. Any object in the lists at the end of this chapter may be found by the star finder, or an equatorial telescope, if the sidereal time is known, as will be explained in the following sections.

466. The Sidereal Time at any Instant. — The Nautical Almanac gives data and rules for finding with precision the sidereal time at any instant, when the mean time is known. The time may be obtained with sufficient accuracy for present purposes by means of the following table and its accompanying explanations.

SIDEREAL TIME AT MEAN NOON.

Jan.	1,	18 h. 44 m.	July	1,	6 h. 38 m.
"	16,	19 h. 43 m.	"	16,	7 h. 37 m.
Feb.	1,	20 h. 47 m.	Aug.	1,	8 h. 40 m.
"	16,	21 h. 46 m.	"	16,	9 h. 39 m.
March	1,	22 h. 37 m.	Sept.	1,	10 h. 42 m.
"	16,	23 h. 36 m.	"	16,	11 h. 42 m.
April	1,	0 h. 39 m.	Oct.	1,	12 h. 41 m.
"	16,	1 h. 38 m.	"	16,	13 h. 40 m.
May	1,	2 h. 37 m.	Nov.	1,	14 h. 43 m.
"	16,	3 h. 37 m.	"	16,	15 h. 42 m.
June	1,	4 h. 40 m.	Dec.	1,	16 h. 41 m.
"	16,	5 h. 39 m.	"	16,	17 h. 40 m.

For any date not given in the table, subtract the last preceding tabular date from the given date, multiply the difference by 4 m., and add the product to the time given opposite the tabular date used.

If the sidereal time at mean noon is required for March 27, the last preceding tabular date is March 16; the difference between the dates is 11 days: 11×4 m. $= 44$ m., which added to 23 h. 36 m. (the time given opposite March 16) gives 24 h. 20 m. As 24 h. is identical with 0 h., we call the answer 0 h. 20 m. This then is the reading of a sidereal clock at noon on March 27.

To find the sidereal time at 9 h. 23 m. P. M., we reason that, if the sidereal time at noon was 0 h. 20 m., and 9 h. 23 m. have elapsed since then, the sidereal time will be found by adding 9 h. 23 m. to 0 h. 20 m., giving 9 h. 43 m. for the time sought.[1]

To find the sidereal time at 7 h. 42 m. P. M., on December 21, we reason as follows. At noon of December 16 it was 17 h. 40 m.; December 21 is five days thereafter: 5 × 4 m. = 20 m., which added to 17 h. 40 m. gives 18 h. 0 m. as the sidereal time at noon of December 21. Since 7 h. 42 m. have elapsed since noon, we add 7 h. 42 m. to 18 h. 0 m., obtaining 25 h. 42 m., which is equivalent to 1 h. 42 m.

To find the sidereal time at 3 h. 10 m. A. M., October 24, we first notice that the last preceding noon was October 23. The sidereal time at noon of October 23 was 13 h. 40 m. + 7 × 4 m., which equals 14 h. 8 m. The interval of time between noon of October 23 and 3 h. 10 m. A. M. of October 24 was 15 h. 10 m., which added to 14 h. 8 m. gives 29 h. 18 m. Since this sum is over 24 h. we subtract that from it, and get 5 h. 18 m. for the time sought.

467. The Hour Angle of a Star at any Instant. We can find this if we know the right ascension of the star, and the sidereal time at the instant at which the hour angle is desired. Suppose that it is required to find the hour angle of α Geminorum at 8 h. 15 m. P. M., on February 12. From the table in § 466 we find that the sidereal time at noon on February 12 was 21 h. 31 m. Then at 8 h. 15 m. it would be 5 h. 46 m., as explained in the preceding section. The right ascension of α Geminorum is 7 h. 28 m., as given in the list of double stars at the end of this chapter. From the discussion in § 131, we see that the hour angle of a star at any instant is the difference between its right ascension and the sidereal time at that instant. The difference between 5 h. 46 m. and 7 h. 28 m. is 1 h. 42 m., which is the east hour angle of the star. If the sidereal time had been 10 h. 41 m., the hour angle of the star would have been 3 h. 13 m., and the star would have been west of the meridian, as explained in § 131.

Astronomers use the following rule for computing the hour angle of a star at any instant.

---

[1] This reasoning is not strictly correct, because sidereal hours are not quite of the same length as mean hours. As a sidereal clock goes faster than a mean time clock, it will tick off more than 9 h. while a mean time clock is measuring 9 h.

Subtract the star's right ascension from the sidereal time at the instant. If the remainder is positive, the star is west of the meridian; if negative, the star is east of the meridian.

Thus, if the star's right ascension is 11 h. 41 m., and the sidereal time 8 h. 50 m., the subtraction gives —2 h. 51 m., and the star has an east hour angle of 2 h. 51 m. Had the sidereal time been 13 h. 5 m., the subtraction would have given +1 h. 21 m., which would have been the west hour angle of the star.

468. Practical Directions. — In order to find an object with an equatorial, or star finder, it will be advantageous to give heed to the following detailed directions, which are based upon the articles immediately preceding: —

I. Look up the right ascension and declination of the object sought.

II. Turn the telescope about the declination axis until the reading of the declination circle equals the declination of the object.

III. Compute the sidereal time: also the hour angle of the object.

IV. Turn the instrument about the polar axis, not disturbing the reading of the declination circle, until the reading of the hour circle corresponds to the hour angle just computed.

V. An eyepiece of low power should be on the telescope. If the object is not in the field of view, move the instrument to and fro a little around the polar axis.

469. Lists of Telescopic Objects. — The following telescopic objects have been selected because they can be seen with small telescopes. Everything in the list will yield to a four-inch telescope: a three-inch will show most of them. The right ascensions and declinations are given for the year 1900.

APPENDIX I.

470. NAMES OF STARS.

The following list contains the proper names of some of the prominent stars, together with their corresponding designations in the Greek letter nomenclature.

A-cher'-nar . . . . α Eridani	Dĕ'-neb . . . . α Cygni
Al-bī'-re-o . . . . β Cygni	De-neb'-o-la . . . . β Leonis
Al-cȳ'-o-ne . . . . η Tauri	Dub'-he . . . . . . α Ursæ Majoris
Al-deb'-a-ran . . . . α Tauri	E'-nif . . . . ε Pegasi
Al'-ge-nib . . . . γ Pegasi	Fomalhaut (Fō'-mal-ō) α Piscis Australis
Al'-ge-nib (sometimes) . . . α Persei	Gem'-ma . . . . α Coronæ
Al'-gol . . . . β Persei	Ham'-al . . . . α Arietis
Al'-i-oth . . . . ε Ursæ Majoris	Kō'-chab . . . . . β Ursæ Minoris
Al'-kaid . . . . η Ursæ Majoris	Mar'-kab . . . . α Pegasi
Al'-phard . . . . α Hydræ	Mē'-grez . . . . . δ Ursæ Majoris
Al-phec'-ca . . . . . . α Coronæ Bor.	Mī'-ra . . . . o Ceti
Al'-phe-ratz . . . . . α Andromedæ	Mī'-rach . . . . β Andromedæ
Al'-tair . . . . α Aquilæ	Mī'-zar . . . . . . ζ Ursæ Majoris
Ant-ār'-es (ēz) . . . . . . α Scorpii	Phec'-da . . . . . γ Ursæ Majoris
Arc-tū'-rus . . . . α Boötis	Po-lā'-ris . . . . . α Ursæ Minoris
Ar'-i-ded . . . . α Cygni	Pol'-lux . . . . β Geminorum
Bel'-la-trix . . . . γ Orionis	Prō'-cy-on . . . . . α Canis Minoris
Be-net'-nasch . . . . η Ursæ Majoris	Ras'-al-hag'-ue . . . . . α Ophiuchi
Betelgueuse (Bĕ'-tel-jūz) . . . α Orionis	Reg'-u-lus . . . . α Leonis
Ca-pel-la . . . . α Aurigæ	Rigel (Rī'-ghel) . . . . . β Orionis
Caph . . . . β Cassiopeiæ	Scheat . . . . β Pegasi
Cas'-tor . . . . α Geminorum	Sir'-i-us . . . . . . α Canis Majoris
Cor Car'-o-li . . . . . α Can. Ven.	Spī'-ca . . . . α Virginis
Cor Hȳ'-dræ . . . . α Hydræ	Thū'-ban . . . . α Draconis
Cor Le-ō'-nis . . . . α Leonis	Vē'-ga . . . . α Lyræ
Cor Ser-pen'-tis . . . . . α Serpentis	

APPENDIX II.

471. ASTRONOMICAL CONSTANTS.

	d.	h.	m.	s.
Sidereal Year	365	6	9	8.97
Tropical Year	365	5	48	45.51
Sidereal Month	27	7	43	11.54
Synodic Month	29	12	44	2.68

	h.	m.	s.
Sidereal Day	23	56	4.090 of mean solar time.
Mean Solar Day	24	3	56.556 of sidereal time.

Obliquity of the Ecliptic . . . . 23° 27′ 8″.0
Constant of Precession . . . . 50″.264
Constant of Aberration . . . . 20″.492

The lengths of the year, the obliquity of the ecliptic, and the constant of precession are given for the year 1900. The lengths of the year and of the month are given in mean solar time.

APPENDIX III.

472. PLANETARY DATA.

Planet.	Mean Distance, the Earth's being Unity.	Mean Distance, Millions of Miles.	Sidereal Period.	Eccentricity of Orbit.	Inclination of the Orbit to the Ecliptic.
Mercury	0.387099	36.0	d. 87.969	0.2056	° ′ 7 0
Venus	0.723332	67.2	224.701	0.0068	3 24
The Earth	1.000000	92.9	365.256	0.0168	0 0
Mars	1.523691	141.5	686.980	0.0933	1 51
Jupiter	5.202800	483.3	yrs. 11.86	0.0483	1 19
Saturn	9.538861	886.1	29.46	0.0561	2 30
Uranus	19.18329	1782.1	84.02	0.0463	0 46
Neptune	30.05508	2792.0	164.78	0.0090	1 47

Planet.	Mean Diameter in Miles.	Mass, the Sun's being Unity.	Density, the Earth's being Unity.	Time of Rotation.	Inclination of Equator to Orbit.	Superficial Gravity, the Earth's being Unity.
Mercury	3,030	$\frac{1}{2,668,700}$	2.21	88 days	0° (?)	0.85
Venus	7,700	$\frac{1}{425,000}$	0.86	225 days	0° (?)	0.83
The Earth	7,918	$\frac{1}{331,100}$	1.00	h. m. s. 23 56 4.09	23° 27′	1.00
Mars	4,230	$\frac{1}{3,104,700}$	0.72	24 37 22.67	24° 50′	0.38
Jupiter	88,000	$\frac{1}{1045}$	0.24	9 55	3° 5′	2.65
Saturn	73,000	$\frac{1}{3486}$	0.13	10 14 24	26° 49′	1.18
Uranus	31,900	$\frac{1}{22765}$	0.22	Unknown	Unknown	0.91
Neptune	34,800	$\frac{1}{19149}$	0.20	Unknown	Unknown	0.88

Primary.	Satellite.	Distance in Miles.	Sidereal Period.				Inclination of Orbit to Ecliptic.			Approximate Diameter in Miles.	Discovery.
			d.	h.	m.	sec.	°	′	″		
The Earth	Moon	238,840	27	7	43	11.5	5	8	40	2,163	
Mars	Deimos	5,830	0	7	39	13.9	26	17	12	7	Hall, 1877
	Phobos	14,550	1	6	17	54.4	25	47	12	5	" "
Jupiter	Nova	112,000	0	11	57	23	.	.	.	100	Barnard, 1892
	I, Io	262,000	1	18	27	33.5	2	8	3	2,500	Galileo, 1610
	II, Europa	417,000	3	13	13	42.1	1	38	57	2,000	" "
	III, Ganymede	665,000	7	3	42	33.4	1	59	53	3,600	" "
	IV, Callisto	1,169,000	16	16	32	11.2	1	57	0	3,300	" "
Saturn	Mimas	117,000	0	22	37	5.7	28	10	10	600	W. Herschel, 1789
	Enceladus	157,000	1	8	53	6.9	28	10	10	800	" "
	Tethys	183,000	1	21	18	25.7	28	10	10	1,100	Cassini, 1684
	Dione	235,000	2	17	41	9.4	28	10	10	1,200	" 1672
	Rhea	328,000	4	12	25	11.9	28	10	10	1,500	" "
	Titan	759,000	15	22	41	24.7	27	38	49	2,700	Huyghens, 1655
	Hyperion	934,000	21	6	39	27.0	27	4	48	500	Bond, 1848
	Japetus	2,212,000	79	7	56	39.7	18	31	30	2,000	Cassini, 1671
Uranus	Ariel	120,000	2	12	29	21.1	97	51		500	Lassell, 1851
	Umbriel	167,000	4	3	27	37.2	97	51		400	" "
	Titania	271,000	8	16	56	29.5	97	51		1,000	W. Herschel, 1787
	Oberon	363,000	13	11	7	6.4	97	51		800	" "
Neptune	Unnamed	221,000	5	21	2	38.5	145	12		2,000	Lassell, 1846

APPENDIX IV.

473. LANDMARKS IN THE HISTORY OF ASTRONOMY.

The data to be given under this heading may serve to outline, though in a rude and imperfect way, the historical development of the science of astronomy. Many suggestions for essays to be written by the students may be derived from it.

Herodotus declared (with his customary accuracy!) that the Egyptians had made astronomical observations for more than 11,000 years, and had seen the ecliptic perpendicular to the equator. Though these statements are manifestly untrue, they indicate that the Egyptians cultivated astronomy from a remote antiquity. Diodorus states that they were able to calculate eclipses. Their year consisted of 365 days: religious ceremonies were regulated by the phases of the moon. As their writings are lost, the real extent of their knowledge is largely a matter of conjecture. The gigantic Pyramid of Cheops, set square with the points of the compass, silently testifies to astronomical knowledge on the part of its unknown builders.

The Chaldeans lived in and about Babylon. Porphyry states that Callisthenes transmitted to Aristotle a series of Babylonian observations reaching back to 2200 B.C. But Ptolemy, who made use of the Chaldean observations, quotes none prior to 720 B.C. They learned to predict eclipses by means of their discovery of the eighteen-year cycle, called the Saros: similar series of eclipses recur in successive cycles.

The Hindoos seem to have possessed an extensive knowledge of astronomy in olden times. But the dates of their ancient writings are very uncertain. Some believe that their knowledge was derived from the Greeks, while others assign to it a much higher antiquity. There are references in their writings to a conjunction of the planets which took place 5,000 years ago. It is supposed that their knowledge of it was not obtained by observation, but by calculating backwards. Modern tables show that the conjunction was far from exact.

The Chinese refer the beginning of their astronomical observations to a date about 3000 B.C. Over 5,700 years ago the Emperor Fou-Hi is reputed to have been a diligent student of astronomy. About 2600 B.C. Hoang-Ti, likewise an emperor, is said to have built an observatory, and to have established a mathematical tribunal for the purposes of correcting the calendar and predicting eclipses. It is stated that a solar eclipse, which occurred some 4,000 years ago, was of more than usual interest to Hi and Ho, two imperial astronomers, who failed to predict it, and so lost their heads through heedlessness. It seems probable that the records after 720 B. C. are authentic. They embrace accounts of eclipses and of remarkable comets.

B. C. **640–546**. Thales, the chief of the Seven Sages, flourished. He was the founder of the Greek school of astronomy; he taught that the moon receives its light from the sun, while the stars are self-luminous; he believed that the earth was a sphere.

B. C. **611–547**. Anaximander, of Miletus, was the immediate successor of Thales in the school of Ionian philosophers. He was distinguished for his wide knowledge of astronomy and geography, and is thought to have introduced the sun dial into Greece.

B. C. **569–470**. Pythagoras, of Samos, is reputed to have taught his disciples that the earth was not the centre of the universe, but that there was a central fire about which the sun, moon, earth, planets, and stars revolved.

B. C. **520–460**. Parmenides, who lived about this time, wrote a poem on Nature, fragments of which have come down to us. He is said to have taught that the earth was a sphere, and that Lucifer, the morning star, was the same body as Hesperus, the evening star.

B. C. **500–428**. Anaxagoras, of Clazomenæ, an intimate friend of Pericles, was another philosopher of the Ionian school, who explained eclipses correctly.

B. C. **469–399**. Socrates used his influence against the study of astronomy, except for the practical purposes of surveying and determination of time. This was, however, a mere incident in his teaching, which was chiefly directed to moral ends.

B. C. **460**. Diogenes, of Apollonia, asserted that the oblique position of the earth's axis with reference to the plane of its orbit was a cause of the changes of the seasons.

B. C. **433**. Meton, an Athenian, discovered the "Metonic Cycle," which is still used in finding the time of Easter. The cycle embraces 235 synodic months, which are almost exactly equal to 19 years of $365\frac{1}{4}$ days each. This cycle is also of use in predicting eclipses.

B. C. **366**. Eudoxus is said by Pliny to have introduced into Greece the common year of $365\frac{1}{4}$ days.

B. C. **340**. Autolycus, of Æolis, wrote two astronomical works, the oldest extant specimens of astronomical writing.

B. C. **330**. Pytheas, a noted Greek navigator, pointed out the fact that there was a connection between the tides and the moon.

B. C. **287–212**. Archimedes made great strides in pure and applied mathematics : he attempted to measure the sun's diameter. A planetarium which he constructed was celebrated in its day.

B. C. 280. Aristarchus, of Samos, flourished. He was the first to maintain that the earth revolved about the sun : he also devised a correct method of determining the relative distances of the sun and moon from the earth.

B. C. 276–196. Eratosthenes, of Cyrene, determined the obliquity of the ecliptic, and was the first to attempt to measure the magnitude of the earth by a correct method.

B. C. 190–120. Hipparchus, of Nicæa in Bithynia, did the memorable work which has given him the appellation of the Father of Astronomy. He was the first to use right ascensions and declinations, and made the earliest catalogue of stars. The solution of plane and spherical triangles by principles closely akin to those now employed in trigonometry, was first accomplished by him. He devised the method of locating places on the earth by latitude and longitude, discovered the precession of the equinoxes, calculated eclipses, divided the day into periods of twelve hours each, and determined the periods of the planets.

A. D. 100–170. Ptolemy, the Alexandrian astronomer, produced a number of astronomical and geographical works, the most celebrated of which is now known as the Almagest, a name given by the Arabians. The theory of the celestial motions which he advocated is known as the Ptolemaic theory, and enthralled astronomers for 1,400 years. It placed the earth, a motionless sphere, in the centre of the universe, which revolved about it.

A. D. 415. The modest and beautiful Hypatia, daughter of Theon, an Alexandrian philosopher, was murdered. She was the first woman known to have been profoundly versed in mathematics.

A. D. 877–929. Albategnius, an Arabian astronomer, made his observations : he was the most accomplished astronomer from the days of Hipparchus to those of Tycho Brahe. He made a star catalogue, and obtained more exact values of the annual precession and of the obliquity of the ecliptic than had been known previously.

A. D. 1214–1294. Roger Bacon laid the foundations of the modern experimental method in science, afterwards elaborated by Francis Bacon: he was a conspicuous champion of intellectual liberty. His researches in optics, if pursued a little further, might have led him to the invention of the telescope.

A. D. 1288. The first important public clock in England was erected : the pendulum was not yet applied to timepieces.

A. D. 1436–1476. John Müller, of Königsberg, better known as Regiomontanus, brought trigonometry to a high degree of advancement, wrote several valuable works, calculated the places of the planets for many years to come, and improved the imperfect clocks then in use.

A. D. 1543. The great work of Copernicus, entitled *De Revolutionibus Orbium Celestium*, was published. This work set forth the theory that the sun was the centre of the solar system. The theory gained acceptance only after a sturdy battle with the adherents of the Ptolemaic system, which had been generally believed for fourteen centuries.

A. D. 1576. Tycho Brahe, a Dane, begins the construction of the splendid observatory called Uraniburg, erected upon an island in the Baltic Sea through the munificence of Frederick, the king of Denmark. The instruments which he employed were much more accurate than any others that had ever been constructed. The study of his observations of the planets led Kepler to the discovery of his famous laws.

A. D. 1583. Galileo, of Pisa, noticed that the vibrations of a pendulum were isochronous (performed in equal times). This he discovered by observing the oscillations of a great bronze lamp suspended from the ceiling of the cathedral in his native town.

A. D. 1596. Fabricius discovered the variability of Mira.

A. D. 1600. Giordano Bruno, who had unsparingly exposed many of the absurdities of the Aristotelian system of natural philosophy, had pointedly ridiculed it, and had propagated heretical notions, (as, for instance, that the stars were suns,) was burned at Rome.

A. D. 1608. Hans Lippershey, of Middleburg in Holland, invented the refracting telescope.

A. D. 1609. Kepler published his "Treatise on the Motion of the Planet Mars," in which his first and second laws of planetary motion were enunciated. Galileo made a telescope having a concave lens for the eyepiece: opera-glasses have such eyepieces.

A. D. 1610. Galileo announced that his telescope had revealed moons accompanying Jupiter, mountains on the moon, the phases of Venus, etc.

A. D. 1613. Galileo published his discovery of spots on the sun: by observations of them he detected its rotation.

A. D. 1614. Napier, a Scotchman, published his *Mirifici Logarithmorum Canonis Descriptio*. Though he is the inventor of logarithms, those commonly employed in calculation are due to his friend Briggs.

A. D. 1618. Kepler discovered his third law of planetary motion.

A. D. 1631. The first recorded transit of Mercury was observed by Gassendi, one of the most eminent of Galileo's disciples.

A. D. 1638. Gascoigne invented and used the filar micrometer. The present precision of observations of the places of the celestial bodies is largely due to the use of this instrument.

A. D. 1639. A transit of Venus was observed for the first time: Horrocks and Crabtree were the observers.

A. D. **1655**. Huyghens discovered that the mysterious appendage of Saturn was a ring.

A. D. **1656**. Huyghens made the first pendulum clock, thus giving to astronomers the priceless boon of an accurate instrument for measuring time.

A. D. **1663**. James Gregory, a Scotch professor, invented the form of the reflecting telescope which bears his name (the Gregorian form).

A. D. **1675**. Römer, a Dane, the inventor of the transit instrument, announced that light occupied time in traversing the celestial spaces, and determined its velocity roughly.

A. D. **1687**. Newton published the *Principia*, universally conceded to be the masterpiece of the world's scientific thought.

A. D. **1705**. Halley predicted that the Great Comet of 1682 would return in 1759.

A. D. **1727**. Bradley, an English astronomer, discovered the aberration of light.

A. D. **1731**. Halley invented the sextant, which has proved invaluable to mariners.

A. D. **1758**. Dollond, an English optician, invented the form of achromatic object-glass now generally used.

A. D. **1765**. Harrison, an English watchmaker, finally obtained a portion of the reward offered by Parliament for improvement in watches for the benefit of navigation. His chronometer ran very well, but was much larger than the chronometers of to-day. He was the inventor of the "gridiron" pendulum.

A. D. **1781**. Sir William Herschel discovered the planet Uranus.

A. D. **1795**. Rehabilitation of the French Academy of Sciences, as a branch of the Institute. The latter part of the eighteenth century and the early years of the nineteenth were distinguished by many profound and elegant mathematical researches concerning the movements of the bodies composing the solar system; special attention was paid to the perturbations due to their mutual attractions. Foremost among the investigators were Laplace and Lagrange, the most eminent of French mathematicians.

A. D. **1801**. Piazzi, of Palermo, discovered Ceres, the first minor planet.

A. D. **1803**. Sir William Herschel published his discovery that certain double stars have a motion of revolution about their common centre of gravity.

A. D. **1840**. The moon was first photographed by Dr. J. W. Draper, of New York.

A. D. **1846**. The planet Neptune was discovered: this is esteemed the greatest triumph of mathematical analysis.

A. D. **1859.** Spectrum analysis, which has lately yielded marvellous results, entered the service of astronomy.

A. D. **1867.** The orbit of the November meteor showers was proved to be practically identical with that of Tempel's comet.

A. D. **1868.** The sun's prominences were observed by Janssen and Lockyer by means of the spectroscope, in full sunshine: they had hitherto been seen only during total solar eclipses.

A. D. **1877.** The satellites of Mars were discovered by Professor Asaph Hall, with the twenty-six inch telescope of the United States Naval Observatory, at Washington.

A. D. **1887.** An International Photographic Congress, meeting at Paris, decided upon a plan for photographing the entire heavens.

A. D. **1892.** The fifth satellite of Jupiter was discovered by Barnard.

A. D. **1895.** Saturn's rings were spectroscopically proved by Keeler to be composed of small bodies. Helium was found to be widely disseminated throughout the universe.

APPENDIX V.

474. TOPICS FOR ESSAYS.

The following subjects are suggested for essays. The topics cover a wide range, and are of various degrees of difficulty.

1. The Astronomy of the Chinese.
2. The Astronomy of the Chaldeans.
3. Astronomy among the Ancient Hindoos.
4. The Ancient Greek Astronomy (especially the work of Thales, Pythagoras, and Hipparchus).
5. The Astronomical Work of Ptolemy (explaining particularly the system of cycles and epicycles embraced in the Ptolemaic theory).
6. The Debt of Astronomy to the Arabians.
7. The Origin of the Constellations.
8. Ancient Ideas of the Nature and Movements of the Heavenly Bodies.
9. Ancient Ideas of the Shape, Support, and Motion of the Earth.
10. The Reckoning of Time among Ancient Nations.
11. Astrology.
12. Astronomical References in the Bible.
13. Copernicus.
14. Tycho Brahe.
15. Kepler.
16. Galileo.
17. Newton.
18. Laplace.
19. The Herschels (William, Caroline, and John).
20. Growth of Knowledge of the Planetary Motions (especially the relation between the advances made by Copernicus, Tycho, Kepler, and Newton).
21. Invention and Development of the Refracting Telescope.
22. Invention and Development of the Reflecting Telescope.
23. Astronomical Spectroscopy.
24. Astronomical Photography.
25. The Nebular Hypothesis.
26. Habitability of other Worlds.
27. Does Astronomical Research tend to produce Scepticism?
28. The Characteristics of an Ideal Astronomer.
29. Geodesy, or the Measurement of the Earth's Form and Dimensions.

30. The Work of the United States Coast Survey.
31. The System of Standard Time in the United States, and its Advantages.
32. Methods of Measuring the Velocity of Light.
33. The Decay of the Universe.
34. The Magnitude of the Forces at work in the Sun.
35. Pending Problems in Astronomy.
36. The Making of a Modern Object-glass.
37. The Stability of the Solar System.
38. The Great Telescopes of the World.
39. The Evolution of the Moon from the Earth.
40. Electricity as a Handmaid of Astronomy.
41. Personal Equation.
42. An Ideal Site for an Observatory.
43. Usefulness of Astronomy.
44. The Mental Training to be derived from the Study of Astronomy.
45. Foucault's Pendulum Experiment.
46. History of Clocks and Watches.
47. Progress of Astronomy during the Nineteenth Century.
48. The Moon and the Weather.
49. The Tides.
50. The Sun as a Source of Terrestrial Energy.

APPENDIX VI.

475. QUERIES FOR USE IN REVIEWS AND EXAMINATIONS.

THE following questions are intended to embrace the most important topics treated in Chapters I. to XIV.

1. Name the principal classes of celestial objects.
2. What is the celestial sphere, as defined by mathematical astronomers?
3. Define the celestial poles, the celestial equator, the zenith, the nadir, and the plane of the horizon.
4. Explain the chief difference between reflecting and refracting telescopes.
5. Explain the function of the object-glass, and of the eyepiece of a telescope.
6. Give the meanings of the terms reflection, refraction, and dispersion of light.
7. Explain how a telescope is made to follow any star by means of an equatorial mounting.
8. Give some hints as to the method of using a small telescope.
9. State the distance, diameter, and rotation time of the sun.
10. Describe the appearance of a sun spot, and tell of the periodicity and cause of these strange objects.
11. Describe the photosphere, chromosphere, prominences, and corona.
12. Describe the construction of a spectroscope.
13. Give the laws of spectrum analysis.
14. Give some illustrations of the distance, light, and heat of the sun.
15. Explain the "contraction theory" of the maintenance of the sun's heat.
16. Explain how the earth's diameter is found.
17. Why does not the plumb-line always point toward the earth's centre?
18. Tell how to draw an ellipse: define foci, major axis, minor axis, perihelion, and aphelion.
19. Define ecliptic, equinoxes, and solstices.
20. Explain why the days are long in summer, and short in winter, in middle latitudes.
21. Why is the sun continuously above the horizon, at the north pole, for six successive months?
22. Explain the two principal causes of the changes of the seasons.
23. Give the cause of the precession of the equinoxes, and draw a diagram showing the movement of the north celestial pole due to precession.

24. Show how the aberration of light affects the direction in which a telescope points.

25. State the cause of refraction, and its effect on the apparent place of a star.

26. Define the sidereal year and the tropical year, and show why one is longer than the other.

27. State the principle according to which leap years are determined in the Gregorian calendar.

28. Give accurate definitions of the plane of the meridian of any place, and of the latitude and longitude of the place.

29. Define celestial meridian (of any point on the earth), prime vertical, altitude, and azimuth.

30. Define hour circle, right ascension, declination, north polar distance, and hour angle.

31. What is meant by the horizontal parallax of a celestial object?

32. What is the difference between a mean solar day and an apparent solar day?

33. State the causes of the unequal lengths of apparent solar days.

34. What is the distinction between a civil day and an astronomical day?

35. Explain the relation between sidereal time and right ascension.

36. Describe a meridian circle.

37. Tell how to find the error of a clock by observing stars with a meridian circle.

38. Prove that the altitude of the pole equals the latitude of the place of observation.

39. Give the demonstration for finding the latitude of a place by observing altitudes of the pole star.

40. How is the longitude between two cities found by aid of the telegraph?

41. How is the position of a ship found at sea?

42. What is meant by the sidereal and synodic periods of the moon?

43. State the causes of the libration of the moon.

44. Describe and explain the phases of the moon.

45. Describe the general characteristics of the lunar surface.

46. State some reasons for believing that the lunar atmosphere is extremely rare.

47. Give an explanation of the disappearance of the air and water which the moon may have possessed in the past.

48. Explain the cause of the coldness of the lunar surface.

49. State a few superstitions about the moon, and tell of its real worth to man.

50. Draw a diagram and make plain the meanings of the umbra and penumbra of the shadow of the earth or of the moon.

51. Describe the successive appearances of the moon during a total lunar eclipse.

52. Give the reasons why solar eclipses are sometimes partial, sometimes total, and sometimes annular.

QUERIES FOR USE IN REVIEWS AND EXAMINATIONS. 317

53. Describe the phenomena of a total solar eclipse.
54. What observations are made by astronomers at the time of a total solar eclipse?
55. State Newton's law of gravitation.
56. State Kepler's laws of planetary motion.
57. Define superior and inferior planets.
58. Define the conjunction, opposition, elongation, and quadrature of a planet.
59. Explain why a superior planet retrogrades.
60. State the diameters, distances (from the sun), times of revolution, and times of rotation, of Mercury, Venus, the Earth, and Mars.
61. Tell of the telescopic appearance and physical condition of Mercury.
62. Tell of the telescopic appearance and physical condition of Venus.
63. Describe a transit of Venus, and tell the special use that astronomers have made of such transits.
64. Tell about the polar caps, seas, continents, clouds, and atmosphere of Mars.
65. Describe the canals and satellites of Mars.
66. State and comment on Bode's law.
67. Recount the circumstances of the discovery of the first minor planet, and the computation of its orbit.
68. Describe the present methods of discovering and keeping track of the asteroids.
69. Give theories of the origin of the asteroids.
70. State the diameters, distances (from the sun), times of revolution, and times of rotation, of Jupiter, Saturn, Uranus, and Neptune.
71. Describe the telescopic appearance of Jupiter.
72. Tell of the atmosphere, light, heat, and physical condition of Jupiter.
73. Describe the satellites of Jupiter: also explain their eclipses, occultations, and transits.
74. Show how the velocity of light was discovered by observations of Jupiter's moons.
75. Describe the telescopic appearance of Saturn.
76. Narrate the history of the discovery of Saturn's rings, and describe their changes of appearance.
77. Discuss the structure and stability of Saturn's ring system.
78. Tell about Saturn's satellites, and the physical condition of the planet.
79. Narrate the history of the discovery of Uranus.
80. Tell of the telescopic appearance, the satellites, and the physical condition of Uranus.
81. Tell the history of the discovery of Neptune.
82. Tell of the telescopic appearance, the satellite, and the physical condition of Neptune.
83. Describe the present methods of searching for comets.
84. Tell how comets are designated.
85. Name and describe the parts of a comet.

DESCRIPTIVE ASTRONOMY.

86. Name the forms of the orbits of comets and state the significance of these forms.
87. Tell about groups and planet's families of comets.
88. Describe the changes in the appearance of a comet as it approaches the sun.
89. State the supposed constitution of the head and nucleus of a comet.
90. Describe the evolution of a comet's tail, and the three types of tails.
91. What causes give to comets their brightness?
92. Why have comets been dreaded, and what occasion is there for dread?
93. Narrate the histories of three remarkable comets.
94. Describe the two classes of meteors.
95. Give an account of some noted meteorite.
96. Explain carefully the effect of the swift rush of a meteorite through the air.
97. What are meteorites composed of?
98. State the theories of the origin of meteorites.
99. Tell how to observe the path of a meteorite.
100. Explain why more shooting stars are seen in the early morning than in the evening.
101. Tell about the velocities and masses of shooting stars.
102. Define and explain the radiant of a meteoric shower.
103. Describe a great meteoric shower.
104. Give the supposed history of the Leonids.
105. Tell the interesting facts about the Bielids.
106. State the relation between comets and meteors.
107. Describe the zodiacal light, and give a theory of its cause.
108. Tell about the number of fixed stars visible with different means, and explain their scintillation.
109. Describe the appearance of the Milky Way.
110. Give the history of the naming of the constellations now recognized.
111. State the methods of naming individual stars.
112. How is the brightness of a star denoted?
113. How are the stars distributed in the heavens?
114. Tell about star clusters.
115. What are the stars, and how large are they?
116. Define the parallax of a fixed star.
117. Explain how the distances of the fixed stars are found.
118. State the supposed causes of the various colors of stars.
119. Describe the types of stellar spectra.
120. Give the theories as to the form of the visible stellar universe.
121. What is meant by the "proper motions" of the stars?
122. How are the velocities of stars in the line of sight found?
123. How has the direction of the sun's motion in space been determined?
124. What evidence is there bearing on the question whether the stellar universe is an orderly system?

125. What is the method of naming double stars?
126. State the distinction between physical and optical doubles.
127. How does the spectroscope show that some stars are binaries, when simple visual observations with a telescope would never reveal the fact?
128. Tell the story of the discovery of the companion of Sirius.
129. Describe two multiple stars.
130. Define a variable star, and a periodic variable.
131. State the five classes of variable stars.
132. Give an account of Tycho's temporary star.
133. Describe the variations of Algol, and their cause.
134. Tell the story of Nova Aurigæ.
135. How are variables observed by astronomers?
136. State the supposed causes of stellar variability.
137. Tell the different forms of nebulæ.
138. What is the law of distribution of the nebulæ over the face of the sky?
139. What kinds of spectra do nebulæ give?
140. Describe the great nebula in Orion, or that in Andromeda.
141. What are the Magellanic Clouds?
142. What is Professor Holden's theory of the real form of spiral nebulæ?
143. State the nebular hypothesis according to Laplace.
144. What modifications of Laplace's theory have been made?
145. Give the testimony of the nebulæ and of the stars to the truth of the nebular hypothesis.
146. State the testimony to the truth of the nebular hypothesis given by the motions of the planets.
147. What is the testimony of astronomy as to the future of the visible universe?
148. Tell how to find the northern constellations on any evening by the aid of Map I.
149. Tell how to find the southern constellations on any evening by the aid of Maps II. to V.
150. Give some hints useful for learning and fixing in mind the constellations.

APPENDIX VII.

476. LIST OF REFERENCE BOOKS.

The following list of books upon Descriptive Astronomy is given to aid in the formation of a reference library. With such a wealth of good material to choose from, one ought not to go far astray. A generous selection of such books would be found very helpful.

Ball. Atlas of Astronomy. D. Appleton & Co., Publishers. $4.00.

There are 72 plates, 34 of which are devoted to star maps, on which all stars down to the sixth magnitude inclusive are shown with great distinctness. The very complete index map of the moon occupies several plates. Directions are given for locating the planets among the stars, up to 1902. The list of select telescopic objects contains exceptionally full descriptions of them. Many unique features commend the Atlas strongly to students and amateur observers.

Ball. Great Astronomers. Isbister & Co., Publishers. pp. 372. 7s. 6d.

In this sketchy book are pen pictures of 18 astronomers from Ptolemy onward. There is much chatty information, together with numerous illustrations of these famous men and their observatories.

Ball. In Starry Realms. J. B. Lippincott Co., Importers. pp. 364. $2.50.

A series of finely written essays on interesting matters pertaining to the heavenly bodies. They are suited for supplementary reading in connection with any text-book on elementary astronomy. There are two non-astronomical chapters, one devoted to the eruption of Krakatoa in August, 1883, and the other to the relation of Darwinism to various sciences.

Ball. In the High Heavens. J. B. Lippincott Co., Publishers. pp. 383. $2.50.

A readable book on various astronomical topics of interest.

Ball. Starland. Ginn & Co., Publishers. pp. 376. $1.00.

A charming book for boys and girls, and for "children of a larger growth," who have a desire to refresh their knowledge of astronomy. Gladstone read it with pleasure.

Ball. The Story of the Heavens. Cassell & Co., Publishers. pp. 536. $5.00.

A popular astronomy, written in a delightful style: the chapter on the tides is especially noteworthy: it explains in a simple manner Prof. G. H. Darwin's theory of tidal evolution, as illustrated in the case of the moon and the earth.

BLAKE. Astronomical Myths. Macmillan & Co., Publishers. pp. 431. $2.00.

This is based on Flammarion's "History of the Heavens." It treats of the beginnings of astronomy, and of the many theories held in ancient and mediæval times concerning the structure of the heavens and of the earth.

BOEDDICKER. The Milky Way. Longmans, Green & Co., Publishers. $10.00.

Dr. Boeddicker has prepared four plates of the Milky Way, each 18 × 23 inches, showing that wonderful aggregation of suns, as it appears to the keen eye of a painstaking observer. The Via Lactea is delineated from the north pole to 10° of south declination. The exceeding complexity of its structure is a revelation to one who has never made a careful study of it.

BREWSTER. The Martyrs of Science. Chatto and Windus, Publishers. pp. 248. $1.80.

Brief and interesting biographies of Galileo, Tycho, and Kepler, by Sir David Brewster.

CHAMBERS. Handbook of Descriptive and Practical Astronomy. Fourth Edition. The Clarendon Press, Oxford, Publishers. 3 vols. pp. 1618. $14.00.

A miniature encyclopædia in its field; valuable to amateur astronomers; a good reference book for teachers and advanced scholars.

CHAMBERS. Pictorial Astronomy for General Readers. Whittaker & Co., Publishers. pp. 268. $1.25.

The descriptive matter is good, but some of the cuts are atrociously executed. There are lists of the most interesting celestial objects suitable for observation with a three-inch telescope.

CLERKE. History of Astronomy during the Nineteenth Century. Adam and Charles Black, Publishers. Third Edition, revised and enlarged. pp. 500. $4.00.

An excellent work, written in an interesting style. Those teachers and older scholars who take special interest in astronomy will find its perusal delightful and helpful.

CLERKE. The Herschels and Modern Astronomy. Macmillan & Co., Publishers. pp. 224. $1.25.

A delightful account of the lives and scientific activities of Sir William Herschel, his devoted sister Caroline, and his son Sir John. The ardent purposes and high ideals of the subjects of the sketch are well set forth.

CLERKE. The System of the Stars. Longmans, Green & Co., Publishers. pp. 440. $7.00.

This is the most exhaustive work on the fixed stars in the English language: it is a useful book of reference. Sidereal astronomy is making rapid strides, which are well described; stress is laid upon the latest theories of the construction of the sidereal universe.

COLAS. Celestial Planisphere. Poole Bros., Publishers. $3.00.

This is one of the best of planispheres. It consists of a movable disk, 19 inches in diameter, attached by a pivot to a heavy rectangular piece of cardboard which measures $18\frac{3}{4} \times 23$ inches. Nearly all stars visible to the naked eye, down to 50° of south declination, and the chief nebulæ, are depicted on it. It can, like all planispheres, be adjusted and held in such a way as to show the face of the sky at any moment; the time when any star rises, sets, or culminates on a given day, can be ascertained from it. It is accompanied by a celestial handbook of 110 pages, in which, after a few pages of definitions, detailed descriptions of the constellations are given; the principal objects of interest in each are mentioned. The price of the handbook is $2.00.

COLAS. The Moon, a Map. Poole Bros., Publishers.

The map is 20 inches in diameter, and is printed in colors: an index pamphlet of 24 pages by Prof. W. W. Payne accompanies it. Extremely satisfactory.

DENNING. Telescopic Work for Starlight Evenings. Taylor and Francis, Publishers. pp. 361. $2.00.

The first three chapters are devoted to the telescope: the methods of testing and handling it are explained. The relative merits of refractors and reflectors are set forth. The remaining chapters are filled with descriptive matter about the heavenly bodies. Meteors and meteoric observations are treated quite fully, the author being a specialist in that line of work.

DREYER. Tycho Brahe, a Picture of Scientific Life and Work in the Sixteenth Century. Adam and Charles Black, Publishers. pp. 405. $3.50.

A thoroughly reliable and readable account of the life and scientific surroundings of one of the greatest of astronomers.

ELGER. The Moon. George Philip and Son, Publishers. pp. 173. 5s.

This work is devoted to a description of the craters, seas, etc., on the lunar landscape, and contains excellent maps. The best medium-priced lunar handbook.

FROST. Astronomical Spectroscopy. Translated from the German of Dr. J. Scheiner, and revised with the author's sanction. Ginn & Co., Publishers. pp. 450. $5.00.

The most practical methods of spectroscopic observations are set forth in detail, and the knowledge thus far gained by means of astronomical spectroscopy is admirably stated. The book is fairly entitled to be called indispensable to workers along spectroscopic lines. Teachers will find it useful as a work of reference.

GORE. Flammarion's Popular Astronomy. Chatto and Windus, Publishers. pp. 679. 16 shillings.

This is a translation from the French, the original having reached a sale of over 100,000 copies. The book is finely illustrated, and very popular in style.

GORE, J. E. The Scenery of the Heavens. Roper and Drowley, Publishers. pp. 320. $4.00.

This work contains a general account of the heavenly bodies, together with lists and descriptions of the most interesting double stars, nebulæ, and variable stars.

GORE, J. E. The Visible Universe. Macmillan & Co., Publishers. pp. 340. $3.75.

This work deals with the different theories of solar and stellar evolution, the ether, the constitution of matter, and the theories of the shape of the visible universe, large space being given to the last subject. The elegance of the illustrations befits the excellence of the text.

GORE, J. H. Geodesy. Houghton, Mifflin & Co., Publishers. pp. 218. $1.25.

The author has given an historical sketch of the various important attempts to measure the magnitude and determine the form of the earth, from the earliest times.

KIRKWOOD. The Asteroids. J. B. Lippincott Co., Publishers. pp. 60. $0.50.

In addition to general descriptive matter, the author makes a special study of the distribution of the orbits of asteroids, giving reasons for the gaps which are found in them.

KLEIN. Star Atlas. E. & J. B. Young & Co., Publishers. pp. 72, aside from maps and plates. $2.00.

The maps are twelve in number, each measuring 12 × 9 inches: they contain all stars, from the sixth magnitude upward, between the north pole and 30° of south declination. There is a 60-page list of interesting telescopic objects, with a good description of each one. This is probably the best low-priced atlas in the English language.

LANGLEY. The New Astronomy. Houghton, Mifflin & Co., Publishers. pp. 260. $5.00.

The term "new astronomy" is used chiefly with reference to spectroscopic and photographic work. The book is very finely illustrated: the author's style is so elegant that the reader's attention is closely held throughout. It would be hard to find an astronomical work more attractively written, or better illustrated.

LOCKYER. The Dawn of Astronomy. Macmillan & Co., Publishers. pp. 432. $5.00.

This work contains a study of the mythology and temple worship of the ancient Egyptians, with special reference to their astronomical bearings. The book is elaborately illustrated, and is suitable for reference, rather than for general reading.

LOCKYER. The Meteoritic Hypothesis. Macmillan & Co., Publishers. pp. 560. $5.25.

The sub-title is " A Statement of the Results of a Spectroscopic Inquiry into the Origin of Cosmical Systems." The book sets forth the theory that all celestial bodies are composed of meteors, more or less thickly crowded together, and gives in detail the observations and experiments on which the theory is based. The illustrations are fine: some portions of the text are of interest to non-astronomical readers.

LOWELL. Mars. Houghton, Mifflin & Co., Publishers. pp. 217. $2.50.

A popular account of Mars, with special reference to the question of the existence of intelligent beings on its surface: elegantly illustrated by full page plates.

MITCHEL. Ormsby Macknight Mitchel, Astronomer and General. Houghton, Mifflin & Co., Publishers. pp. 392. $2.00.

An admirable biography of a remarkable man, who built the Cincinnati Observatory, raising the necessary funds by a popular subscription. Most of the subscriptions came from tradesmen and mechanics: many were payable in commodities or labor.

NASMYTH AND CARPENTER. The Moon. Scribner and Welford. pp. 213. $9.00.

During more than thirty years the authors studied the moon's surface with powerful telescopes; they made careful drawings, and then constructed accurate models of the lunar craters; these were photographed. The book contains 25 very fine plates.

NEWCOMB. Popular Astronomy. School Edition. Harper and Brothers, Publishers. pp. 578. $1.30.

An excellent presentation of the subject, written by one of the ablest of astronomers.

PARKER. Familiar Talks on Astronomy. A. C. McClurg & Co., Publishers. pp. 264. $1.00.

These are such talks as a teacher might give to a class in elementary astronomy, in addition to the regular class work. The last four chapters are about time and nautical astronomy, viewed from the standpoint of a practical navigator.

PROCTOR. Half Hours with the Stars. G. P. Putnam's Sons, Publishers. pp. 38. $2.00.

The book is in quarto form, and contains twelve large maps, showing the aspect of the heavens throughout the year. The text is devoted to explaining how to find the star groups. Very few stars fainter than the fourth magnitude are shown. The work is admirably adapted to the needs of a beginner, who wishes to become familiar with the constellations.

PROCTOR AND RANYARD. Old and New Astronomy. Longmans, Green & Co., Publishers. pp. 824. $12.00.

This volume is published in the form of a quarto. Mr. Proctor considered it as, in a sense, the summing up of his numerous writings on astronomy. It was not completed at the time of his death, and Mr. Ranyard supplied the portion lacking. The work is a fitting crown to Mr. Proctor's long service in popularizing astronomy. Mr. Ranyard's careful editing and supplementary writing add much to its value.

SERVISS. Astronomy with an Opera-glass. D. Appleton & Co., Publishers. pp. 154. $1.50.

Maps of the constellations are given, and directions for finding them: prominent celestial objects are described; the author gives directions for choosing a good opera-glass, and shows that many pleasurable views of the heavenly bodies may be obtained by its aid.

THORNTON. Advanced Physiography. Longmans, Green & Co., Publishers. pp. 338. $1.40.

One of the very best works on this subject: it is largely an elementary astronomy, but about one fourth of the book is devoted to atmospheric and oceanic motions, magnetism, and the secular cooling of the earth.

WEBB. Celestial Objects for Common Telescopes. Fifth Edition, revised and greatly enlarged by T. E. Espin. 2 vols. Longmans, Green & Co., Publishers. $3.50.

This is the most complete and authoritative book, in its field, in our language. Volume I. tells how to use a telescope for visual, photographic, and spectroscopic work, and contains chapters on the sun, moon, planets, comets, and meteors. Volume II. gives lists and full descriptions of the principal stars, clusters, and nebulæ visible to us.

WINCHELL. World-Life, or Comparative Geology. S. C. Griggs & Co., Publishers. pp. 642. $2.50.

The work is written from the standpoint of a geologist, and is chiefly devoted to an elaborate account of the formation of the different planets, in accordance with the principles of the nebular hypothesis. There are also chapters on Planetary Decay, The Habitability of Other Worlds, and The Evolution of Cosmogonic Doctrine.

YOUNG. The Sun. D. Appleton & Co., Publishers. pp. 363. $2.00.

The best work on this subject, in English: suitable for reference and for collateral reading. The author is one of the most distinguished students of the sun.

YOUNG. General Astronomy. Ginn & Co., Publishers. pp. 551. $2.50.

A text-book for advanced collegiate students, replete with accurate information: easily the first of its kind.

INDEX.

All numerical references are to Sections.

Abbe, Professor, 39.
Aberration of light, 116.
Achromatic Object-glass, 39.
Achromatism, almost perfect, 39.
Adams, J. C., computes orbit of Neptune, 271.
Aerolite. (*See* **Meteorites.**)
Age of the sun, 87.
Algol, diameter of, 348; variations of, 379; position, 449.
Alpha Centauri, 349, 350.
Alphabet of the Greek language, 405.
Altitude defined, 121.
Anderson, Thos. D., discovers Nova Aurigæ, 381.
Andromeda, nebula in, 389, 398, 407; constellation, 407.
Andromedes, 330.
Annular eclipses, 175, 176; nebulæ, 385.
Aphelion, explained, 96.
Apparent Motion, of the stars daily, 13; of the celestial sphere, 17; of the sun, 125.
Aquarius, 408.
Aquila, 409.
Argo Navis, 410.
Aries, a sign of the zodiac, 100; the sun enters, 112; non-coincidence of sign and constellation, 112; the constellation, 411.
Aspects of the planets, 188.
Asteroids, discovery, 224–227; orbits, distances, periods, 228; designations, 229; number and sizes, 230; atmosphere and surface gravity, 231; origin, 232.
Astræa discovered, 226.
Astronomical Constants, 471.
Astronomy, landmarks in the history of, 473.
Atmosphere of the moon, 162 and 164; of the planets (*see* each planet).
Attraction of gravitation, 183, 368.
Auriga, 412.
Azimuth, defined, 121.

Bailey, S. I., discovers variables in clusters, 373.
Ball, Sir Robert, accounts for the rarity of the atmosphere of Mars, 217.
Barnard, E. E., drawing of Mars, 213; observes changes on Mars, 215; observes Jupiter's moons, 249; discovers the fifth satellite of Jupiter, 251; observes a moon of Saturn in the shadow of the dark ring, 260; discovers a comet by photography, 280; photographs Brooks's comet, 307; observes the Gegenschein, 324, note; first photographed the star clouds of the Milky Way, 338.
Berliner Jahrbuch, 228.
Beta Lyræ, 378.
Bethlehem, star of, 201.
Biela discovers a comet, 303.
Bielids, 330.
Binary Stars, 368; spectroscopic, 369.
Black Drop, 204.
Bode's Law, 223.
Books for reference, 476.
Boötes, 413.
Brashear, J. A., optician, 39.
Bredichin, investigates the forms of comets' tails, 295.
Brooks, Wm. R., discovers comet c 1893, 307.
Bruce photographic telescope, 277, 345.
Burnham, S. W., 366.

Cæsar, Julius, his calendar, 114.
Calendar, the Julian, 114; the Gregorian, 115.
Camelopardus, 414.
Campbell, W. W., observes Jupiter's moons with the Lick telescope, 249; also observes Nova Aurigæ, 381.
Canals of Mars, 218, 219.
Cancer, 415.
Canes Venatici, 416.
Canis Major, 417.
Canis Minor, 418.
Capricornus, 419.
Capture of comets, 287.
Carrington, observation of the sun, 60.
Cassini discovers the main division of Saturn's rings, 258.
Cassiopeia, 11, 406, 420.
Catalogues of stars, 344.
Celestial Sphere, defined, 15, 16; daily motion of, 17.
Centaurus, 421.
Cepheus, 422.
Ceres discovered, 224, 225.
Cetus, 423.

Chandler, S. C., catalogue of variables, 373; period of Algol, 379; variation of latitude, 95.
Changes on the moon, 161.
Chinese record of a meteor, 314.
Chromosphere, described, 76.
Chronograph, 139, 140.
Chronometer, used on shipboard, 143.
Civil Day, 129.
Clairaut, investigates the orbit of Halley's comet, 301.
Clark, Alvan, 39; his son, Alvan G., discovers the companion of Sirius, 370.
Classification, of the planets, 187; of stellar spectra, 353; of variable stars, 374.
Clocks, 135; their errors determined, 138.
Clusters of stars, 347; list of, 469.
Colored stars, list of, 469.
Columba, 424.
Coma of a comet, 283; first appearance of, 289.
Coma Berenices, 425.
Comet, of 1861, 5, 300; of 1843, 291; 1889 V (Brooks), 292; Halley's, 299, 301; of 1528, 299; Biela's, 300, 303, 306, 330, 332; Encke's, 302; Holmes's, 303, 306; of 1882, 304; Swift's, of 1892, 305; c 1893 (Brooks), 307; Tempel's, 332.
Comets, derivation, 5; in general, 279; discovery, 280; number and designation, 281; brightness and visibility, 282; parts of, 283; forms of orbits, 284; significance of forms of orbits, 285; groups, 286; planetary families, 287; changes in orbits, 288; changes of appearance, 289; jets and envelopes, 290; tails, 291; companion comets, 292; constitution, 293; evolution of the tail, 294; types of tails, 295; mass and density, 296; light and spectra, 297; fate, 298; superstitions, 299; collisions, 300.
Common, A. A., his large reflector, 43.
Conic Sections, 284.
Conjunction of planets, 188.
Constants, list of, 471.
Constellations, defined, 1; names of, 9; how to find, 10, 11; history of, 340.
Constitution of the sun, 88.
Contraction of the sun, 86.
Copernicus publishes his great work in 1543, 473.
Corona, appearance of, 80; Schæberle's theory of, 81; nature of, 82.
Corona Borealis, 426.
Coronium, 82.
Corvus, 427.
Crater, 428.
Craters on the moon, 157, 158.
Crescent moon, 150.
Cygnus, 429.

330 INDEX.

Data, planetary, 472; historical, 473.
Date, change of, 133.
Day, length of, 103–105; mean and apparent solar, 125–127; sidereal, 128; civil and astronomical, 129.
Declination, defined, 122.
Deimos, 221.
Delphinus, 430.
Designation, of asteroids, 229; of comets, 281; of stars, 341; of double stars, 366; of variable stars, 373.
Dimensions, of comets' tails, 291; of stars, 348.
Directions for finding an object by means of an equatorial telescope, 468.
Disk of a star, 348.
Dispersion of light, 37; corrected, 38.
Displacement of spectral lines, 360.
Distance, of the sun, 49; determined by parallax, 123, 351; of the moon, 145; of the stars, 349; of the nebulæ, 386; of each planet, 472.
Distribution, of the stars, 346; of the nebulæ, 386.
Double Stars, appearance, 364, 365; number and nomenclature, 366; optical, 367; physical, 368; spectroscopic, 369; Sirius, 370; planetary systems, 371; evolution of, 397; list of, 469.
Draco, 431.
Draper, J. W., in 1840, first photographed the moon, 473.
Dumb-bell Nebula, 391.
Duration of human life on the earth, 87; of eclipses, 179.

Earth, dimensions and shape, 90; diameter, how measured, 92; latitude and longitude on it, 93, 94; variation of latitude, 95; the orbit, 96; the ecliptic, 97; the equinoxes, 98; the solstices, 99; zodiac, 100; length of the day, 103–105; midnight sun, 106; seasons, 107, 108; equatorial ring, 109; precession explained, 109–111; effects of precession, 112; different kinds of years, 113; Julian calendar, 114; Gregorian calendar, 115; aberration of light, 116; atmospheric refraction, 117; twilight, 118.
Earth Shine on the moon, 151.
Eclipses, the one of April 16, 1893, 81; of the moon, 170–172; cause of solar, 173; varieties of solar, 175; partial and annular solar, 176; total solar, 177, 178; duration and number of, 179; of Jupiter's satellites, 246.
Ecliptic, defined, 97; fixity of, 102.
Ellipse, described, 96; a conic section, 284; changed into a parabola or hyperbola, 288.
Elongation of a planet, 188.
Encke discovers a division in Saturn's rings, 258.
Envelopes of comets, 290.
Ephemerides of asteroids, 228.
Epsilon Lyræ, 372.
Equator, Celestial, defined, 20; fixity of, 102.

INDEX.

Equatorial Mounting, explained, 44-46.
Equinoxes, defined, 98; precession of, explained, 109-112.
Equuleus, 432.
Eridanus, 433.
Essays, topics for, 474.
Evening Star, defined, 191; Venus, 201.
Evolution of double stars, 397.
Eyepieces, their action, 33; achromatic, 40; negative and positive, 40.
Examinations, queries for, 475.

Faculæ, 54.
Families of comets, 287.

Galaxy, 338.
Galileo, discovers the phases of Venus, 205; thinks Saturn triform, 257; notices the vibrations of a pendulum in 1583, 473; makes a telescope and various discoveries with it in 1609-1613, 473.
Galle discovers Neptune, 271.
Gauss computes the orbit of Ceres, 225.
Gegenschein, 334.
Gemini, 434.
Gibbous moon, 150.
Gravitation, law of, 183; universal, 368.
Great Circles defined, 120.
Great Dipper, 20, 359, 369.
Greek Alphabet, used in naming stars, 341; given, 405.
Gregorian Calendar, 115.
Groups of stars, 359.

Habitability of Mars, 222.
Hale, Geo. E., observes a solar disturbance, 61.
Hall, A., discovers the moons of Mars, 221; monograph on the moons of Mars, 222, note; determines rotation of Saturn, 254.
Halley, his method of observing a transit of Venus, 204; his comet, 299, 301; in 1705 predicted its return, 473; in 1731 invented the sextant, 473.
Heat, of the sun, 84; produced by contraction, 86; of the moon, 165.
Hercules, 435.
Herschel, Caroline, 265.
Herschel, Sir John, makes a prediction about Neptune, 271; star-gauges of, 346.
Herschel, Sir William, discovers Uranus, 265; star-gauges, 346; in 1803 publishes his discovery of binary stars, 473.
Hesperus, 201.
History of astronomy, 473.
Hodgson, observation of the sun, 60.

Holden, E. S., opinion of the polar caps of Mars, 213; finds motion in the trifid nebula, 387; investigates spiral nebulæ, 392.
Holmes discovers a comet, 306.
Horizon defined, 21, 121.
Horizontal parallax, 123.
Hour Angle, defined, 122; of a star at any instant, 466.
Hour Circles defined, 122.
Huyghens, discovers the rings of Saturn in 1665, 257, 473; made the first pendulum clock in 1656, 473.
Hydra, 436.
Hyperbola, a conic section, 284; a comet's orbit, 285.

Image, formation of, 32.
Inertia, 184.
Intra-Mercurial planets, 178.

Japetus, 263.
Jena glass, 39.
Jets from comets, 290.
Josephus mentions a comet, 299.
Julian Calendar, 114.
Juno discovered, 226.
Jupiter, occulted by the moon, 162; may have disrupted the asteroid ring, 232; distance and diameter, 235; revolution and rotation, 236; appearance, 237–241; satellites visible with the naked eye, 237; belts, 238, 239; great red spot, 240; other spots, 239, 241; atmosphere and spectrum, 242; light and heat, 243; physical condition, 244; the major satellites, 245; eclipses, occultations, and transits of the satellites, 246-248; markings and rotation of the satellites, 249, 250; the fifth satellite, 251; observations of the moons give the velocity of light, 252; gathers a family of comets, 287; disturbs Brooks's comet, 292.
Kapteyn, J. C., investigates the form of the stellar system, 357.
Keeler, J. E., discovers a division in Saturn's rings, 258; determines their structure, 261; determines the motion of the nebula in Orion, 390.
Kepler, his speculations on lunar craters, 157; his laws, 185; guesses the number of moons of the planets, 222, note; his opinion about comets, 281; publishes his first and second laws in 1609, 473; discovers his third law in 1618, 473.
Kirchhoff's Laws, 73.
Krakatoa, eruption of, 324.

Lacerta, 437.
Landmarks in the history of astronomy, 473.
Langley, S. P., estimate of work done by the sun's heat, 84; observations of Mars, 215.
Laplace suggests a name for Uranus, 265; his nebular hypothesis, 395, 396.

INDEX.

Latitude, of terrestrial points, 93, 94; variation of, 95; method of determining, 141; of a ship, 143.
Leap Year, 115.
Lenses, 30.
Leo, 438.
Leo Minor, 439.
Leonids, 327–329.
Lepus, 440.
Leverrier computes the orbit of Neptune, 271.
Libra, 441.
Librations of the moon, 149.
Lick telescope, 48.
Life on the moon, 167.
Light, of the sun, 83; velocity of, 83; of the moon, 165.
Light Ratio, 343.
Light Year, 349.
Lists of telescopic objects, 469.
Local Time, 130.
Lockyer, J. N., his theory of variables, 382.
Longitude, of terrestrial points, 93, 94; determined by telegraph, 142; of a ship, 143.
Lowell, Percival, 219.
Lowell Observatory, 218, 221.
Lupus, 442.
Lynx, 443.
Lyra, 444.

Magellanic Clouds, 393.
Magnetic Storms, 65–68.
Magnifying Power of eyepieces, 36.
Magnitudes of stars, 1, 8, 342, 343.
Maps explained, 8.
Mars, distance and diameter, 209; revolution and rotation, 210; appearance, 211, 212; phases, 212; polar caps, 213; seas, 214; continents and islands, 215; clouds, 216; atmosphere, 217; canals, 218, 219; colors, 220; satellites, 221; habitability, 222; Hall's monograph on the moons, 222, note.
Mean Solar Time, 130.
Mercury, distance and diameter, 195; revolution and rotation, 196; transits, 197; appearance and phases, 198, 199; physical condition, 200; perturbs Encke's comet, 302; transit first observed in 1631, 473.
Meridian, terrestrial, defined, 94; celestial, defined, 121.
Meridian Circle, described, 136; used to determine time, 137–138; used to determine latitude, 141.
Meteorites, past appearances, 309; Ensisheim meteorite, 310; Kiowa County, Kansas, meteorite, 312; in flight, 313; path and velocity, 314; light and heat,

INDEX.

315, 316; meteoric stones, 317; meteoric iron, 318; elements found in, 319; Canyon Diablo, 319; origin, 320; observation of, 321.

Meteors, defined, 6; two classes, 308; a detonating, 311; path and velocity, 314; light and heat, 315, 316; meteoric stones, 317; meteoric iron, 318; elements found in, 319; origin, 320; observation of, 321.

Midnight Sun, 106.

Milky Way, 338; tree-like structures in, 339; shape, 356.

Minor Planets. (*See* **Asteroids**.)

Mira Ceti, 376.

Mizar, 369.

Monoceros, 445.

Month, sidereal and synodic, 146.

Moon, distance, 145; diameter, 145; orbit, 145; nodes, 145; periods, sidereal and synodic, 146; meridian passage, 147; rotation, 148; librations, 149; phases, 150; earth shine, 151; occultations, 152; appearance to the naked eye, 153; telescopic appearance, 154; topography, 155; the plains, 156; craters, 157, 158; mountains, 159; rills, clefts, and rays, 160; changes, 161; atmosphere, 162; spectrum, 162; water, 163, 164; light and heat, 165; temperature, 166; life, 167; effect on the weather, 168; worth to man, 169; eclipses, 170-172; mountains visible in a solar eclipse, 176; duration and number of eclipses, 179; origin of its features, 400.

Morning Star, defined, 191; Venus, 201.

Motion, daily, of the heavens, 13, 17.

Mountains, lunar, 159; terrestrial, 400.

Mount Hamilton, clouds visible there, 238.

Mounting, equatorial, 44-46.

Multiple Stars, 372.

Nadir defined, 23.

Nebulæ, defined, 7; various forms, 385; number, distance, and grouping, 386; sizes and changes of appearance, 387; spectra, 388; nebula in Andromeda, 389; nebula in Orion, 390; other notable, 391; real form of spiral, 392; Magellanic Clouds, 393; the nebular hypothesis, 394-404; list of, 469.

Nebular Hypothesis, general statement, 394; Laplace's theory and its modifications, 395, 396; evolution of double stars, 397; testimony of the nebulæ, stars, earth, moon, planetary systems, and sun, 398-402; its probable truth, 403; future of the universe, 404.

Negative Eyepieces, 40.

Neptune, does not conform to Bode's law, 223; discovery, 271; distance and diameter, 272; revolution and rotation, 273; appearance, 274; satellite, 275; physical condition, 276; captures comets. 287.

Newton, Sir Isaac, law of gravitation, 183; published the Principia in 1687, 473.

Newtonian telescope, 41.

Nodes of the moon's orbit, 145.

Nordenskiold finds supposed dust of shooting stars, 324.

INDEX. 335

North Polar Distance defined, 122.
Nova Aurigæ, 381.
Nucleus of a comet, 283; changes of, 289.
Number, of eclipses in a year, 179; of asteroids, 230; of comets, 281; of shooting stars, 322; of fixed stars, 336; of double stars, 366; of nebulæ, 386.

Object-glass, use of a large one, 35; achromatic, 39.
Oblate Spheroid, 90.
Obliquity of the ecliptic defined, 97.
Occultations, by the moon, 152; of Jupiter's satellites, 247.
Omicron Ceti, 376.
Ophiuchus, 446.
Opposition of a planet, 188.
Orbits of the planets, 181.
Origin, of the asteroids, 232; of meteors, 320
Orion, nebula in, 390, 447; constellation, 447.

Pallas discovered, 226.
Parabola, a conic section, 284; a comet's orbit, 285.
Parallax, defined, 123; horizontal, 123; equatorial horizontal, 123; stellar, 350, 351; of nebulæ, 386.
Paré describes a comet, 299.
Pegasus, 448.
Pendulum, compensation of, 135.
Penumbra, of a sun spot, 55; of a shadow, 170.
Perihelion explained, 96.
Periodic Comet defined, 286.
Periods, sidereal and synodic, of the moon, 146; of planets, 192.
Perseids, 326.
Perseus, 449.
Perturbations, 186.
Phases of the moon, 150.
Phobos, 221.
Phosphorus, 201.
Photographic Congress in 1887, 473.
Photographs, of faculæ, 54; of a solar disturbance, 61; of the corona, 81; of the moon, 161; of asteroids, 227; of an ultra-Neptunian planet, 277; of comets, 280, 305, 307; of shooting stars, 333; of the Milky Way, 338; of stars, 345; of clusters, 347; of nebulæ, 389-391.
Photosphere of the sun, 52.
Piazzi discovers the first asteroid, 224.
Pickering, E. C., estimates diameters of the moons of Mars, 221; plans star charting, 345; views of stellar spectra, 354; announces the duplicity of Mizar, 369.
Pickering, W. H., opinion of the water area of Mars, 214; observations of

the canals of Mars, 218; observations of Jupiter's belts, 239; observes Jupiter's satellites, 250.

Pisces, 450.

Piscis Australis, 451.

Planetary Data, 472.

Planetary nebulæ, 385, 398.

Planets, defined, 2; orbits, 181; motion, 182–186; two classes, 187; aspects, 188; apparent movements, 189-190; evening and morning stars, 191; periods, sidereal and synodic, 192; two groups of, 194; Mercury, 195-200; Venus, 201-208; Mars, 209-222; minor planets, 223-232; Jupiter, 235-252; Saturn, 253-264; Uranus, 265-270; Neptune, 271-276; beyond Neptune, 277; testimony for the nebular hypothesis, 401; data concerning, 472.

Pleiades, 347; proper motions of, 359; nebulous matter in, 386.

Plumb-line, direction of, 91.

Pointers, 18.

Pole, location of the north celestial, 18; fixity of, 101; precessional motion of, 112.

Positive Eyepieces, 40.

Præsepe, 347.

Precession, explained, 109–111; effects of, 112.

Prime Vertical defined, 121.

Prominences, Solar, quiescent and eruptive, 77; seen with the spectroscope, 78; associated with magnetic storms, 79.

Proper Motion of the stars, 358, 359.

Ptolemy, revises the scheme of constellations, 340; his work, 473.

Pupin, M. I., electrical discharges, 82.

Pythagoras, theory of the daily motion of the sky, 13; his teaching, 473.

Quadrature of a planet, 188.

Queries for reviews and examinations, 475.

Radiant, 325.

Radius Vector defined, 181.

Ranyard, A. C., his theory about clusters, 347.

Red Spot on Jupiter, 240.

Reference Books, list of, 476.

Reflecting Telescope, 25; explained, 41; Newtonian, 41; comparison with a refractor, 42; noted ones, 43.

Refracting Telescope, 25, 34; comparison with reflector, 42; invention of, 473.

Refraction by a prism, 28; atmospheric, 117; effects in total lunar eclipse, 172.

Reticle, 136.

Retrograde Motion of a planet, 190.

Reviews, queries for, 475.

Rice Grains, in the sun, 53.

Right Ascension defined, 122.

Ring Nebula, 391, 444.

INDEX.

Rings of Saturn, 257-262.
Roberts, Isaac, photographs of nebulæ, 389, 391.
Rœmer determines the velocity of light in 1675, 252, 473.
Rosse, Lord, his great reflector, 43.
Rotation of the sun, 58.

Sagitta, 452.
Sagittarius, 453.
Satellites, attending upon stars, 371; of the planets, 472.
Saturn, distance and diameter, 253; revolution and rotation, 254; appearance, 255, 256; discovery of the rings, 257; divisions and dimensions of the rings, 258; disappearance of the rings, 259; the dark ring, 260; structure of the rings, 261; stability of the rings, 262; the satellites, 263; physical condition, 264.
Schæberle, J. M., theory of the corona, 81; theory of the markings on Mars, 215; observes Jupiter's moons, 249.
Schiaparelli, determines rotation time of Mercury, 196; determines rotation time of Venus, 203; discovers canals of Mars, 218.
Schott, Doctor, 39.
Schwabe, observations of the sun, 59.
Scintillation of the stars, 337.
Scorpio, 454.
Screen, used in solar observations, 51.
Sculptor, 455.
Scutum, 456.
Seasons, in middle latitudes, 107; at the equator, 108.
Secchi classifies stellar spectra, 353.
Secondary Circles defined, 120.
See, T. J. J., investigates the origin of double stars, 397.
Serpens, 457.
Sextans, 458.
Sextant, 143.
Shadows, of the earth and moon, 170, 174; shadow of the moon visible, 177.
Ship, the position of, determined, 143.
Shooting Stars, described, 308; numbers, 322; paths and velocity, 323; masses and constituents, 324; radiant, 325; the August shower, 326; the November Leonids, 327-329; the Bielids, 330; orbits of, 331.
Shower, Meteoric, at L'Aigle, 309; the August, 326; of the November Leonids, 327-329; of the Bielids, 330; orbits of, 331; how to observe a, 333.
Sidereal Time, 130, 131, 466.
Sidereal Year defined, 113.
Signs of the zodiac, 100.
Sirian stars, 353, 354.
Sirius, its distance, 349; color, 352; spectrum, 353; double, 370, 417.
Small Circles defined, 120.

Solar stars, 353, 354.
Solstices defined, 99.
Spectra, classes of stellar, 353; of the nebulæ, 388.
Spectroscope, description of, 69–72.
Spectrum, the solar, 74.
Spectrum Analysis, the laws of, 73.
Sphere, the celestial, 15–17; position of points on, 120.
Spica, 369.
Spiral Nebula, 391; real form of, 392; location, 416.
Square of Pegasus, 448.
Stability, of the planetary system, 186; of Saturn's rings, 262.
Standard Time, 134.
Star Finder, 465.
Star Light, 355.
Star of Bethlehem, 201.
Stars, fixed, defined, 1; morning and evening, 191, 201; number visible, 336; scintillation, 337; Milky Way, 338; tree-like structures, 339; constellations, 340; names, 341; orders of brightness, 342; magnitudes, 343; catalogues, 344; charts, 345; distribution, 346; clusters, 347; dimensions and nature, 348; distances, 349; parallax, 350, 351; colors, 352; spectra, 353; of different spectral types, 354; light and heat, 355; the stellar system, 356, 357; proper motions, 358; groups, 359; motions in the line of sight, 360; the system of, 363; double and multiple, 364–372; variable, 373–383; nebulous, 385; hour angle at any instant, 467; list of double, 469; list of variable, 469; list of colored, 469; proper names of, 470.
Stationary Point of a planet's path, 190.
Structure, of the Milky Way, 338; of the stellar universe, 356, 357.
Structures, tree-like, 339.
Sun, distance and diameter, 49; how to view, 50, 51; photosphere, 52; rice-grains, 53; faculæ, 54; general appearance of a spot, 55; changes in appearance of spots, 56; dimensions of spots, 57; rotation, 58; periodicity of the spots, 59; observation by Carrington and Hodgson, 60; disturbance on July 15, 1892, 61; cyclonic motion of spots, 62; nature of spots, 63; causes of weather changes, 64; magnetic storms, 65, 66; the storm of February, 1892, 67; frequency of magnetic storms, 68; the solar spectrum, 74; constituents of, 75; chromosphere, 76; prominences, 77–79; appearance of the corona, 80; Schæberle's theory of the corona, 81: nature of the corona, 82; light, 83; heat, 84; causes of radiation, 85; contraction theory, 86; past and future, 87; constitution, 88; the midnight, 106; enters Aries, 112; the mean, 125; cause of eclipses, 173; varieties of eclipses, 175; partial, annular, and total eclipses, 176–178; duration and number of eclipses, 179; its path, 361; testimony to the nebular hypothesis, 402.
Sun Spots. (*See* under **Sun,** 55–64.)
Superstitions about comets, 299.
Synodic Period, of the moon, 146; of a planet, 192.

INDEX. 339

System, stability of the planetary, 186; of the stars, 363; systems of planets attending upon stars, 371; planetary, 401.
Swift, Lewis, claims discovery of intra-Mercurial planets, 178; his bright comet of 1892, 305.
Swift, the satirist, writes of the moons of Mars, 222, note.

Tails of comets, 291; evolution of, 294; types of, 295; of Swift's comet, 305; of Brooks's comet shattered, 307.
Taurus, 459.
Telegraph, used in determining longitude, 142.
Telescope, management of, 47; reflecting, 25, 41, 42, 43; refracting, 25, 34, 42; equatorial, 44–46; Lick, 48; invention of, 473.
Telescopic Objects, 469.
Telluric Lines, in a spectrum, 75.
Tempel's comet, 332.
Temperature at the moon, 166.
Temporary Stars, defined, 374; Tycho's, 375; Nova Aurigæ, 381.
Terminator of the moon, 154.
Theta Orionis, 372; condensed from a nebula, 386; spectrum, 398; position of, 447.
Thomson, Sir William, on the future of the sun, 87.
Tides, 169.
Time, the years, 113; the calendars, 114, 115; mean and apparent solar days, 125; inequalities of apparent solar days, 126, 127; sidereal day, 128; civil and astronomical day, 129; mean solar and sidereal compared, 130; relation between sidereal time and right ascension, 131; longitude and time, 132; where the date changes, 133; standard, 134; determination of, by a meridian circle, 138; sidereal at any instant, 466.
Tisserand, investigates comet groups, 286.
Titan, 263.
Topics for Essays, 474.
Total Eclipses, lunar, 172; solar, 177, 178.
Train of a meteor, 313, 315.
Transits, of Mercury, 197; of Venus, 204; of Jupiter's satellites, 248.
Triangulum, 460.
Trifid Nebula, 387, 391.
Tropical Year defined, 113.
Tschermak, theory of the origin of meteorites, 320.
Twilight, 118.
Twinkling of the stars, 337.
Tycho Brahe, his star, 375.

Ultra-Neptunian planets, 277.
Umbra, of a sun spot, 55; of a shadow, 170, 174.
Universe, future of the visible, 404.

Uranus, discovery, 265; distance and diameter, 266; revolution and rotation, 267; appearance, 268; satellites, 269; physical condition, 270; captures the Leonids, 329; captures Tempel's comet, 332.
Ursa Major, 10, 406, 461.
Ursa Minor, 10, 406, 462.

Variable Stars, definition, number, names, 373; classes, 374; temporary stars, 375; Mira, 376; Class III., 377; Beta Lyræ, 378; Algol, 379; Y Cygni, 380; Nova Aurigæ, 381; causes of variability, 382; how to observe, 383; list of, 469.
Velocity, of light, 83; of meteors, 314; of shooting stars, 323; of the stars, 360.
Venus, morning and evening star, 201; distance and diameter, 202; revolution and rotation, 203; transits, 204; phases and maximum brightness, 205; telescopic appearance, 206; atmosphere, 207; physical condition, 208; transit first observed in 1639, 473.
Vernal Equinox defined, 98.
Vertical Circles defined, 121.
Vespasian jokes about a comet, 299.
Vesta, discovered, 226; diameter, 230.
Virgo, 463.
Visual Angle defined, 31.
Volcanoes, lunar, 157, 158; terrestrial, 400.
Voltaire writes of the moons of Mars, 222, note.
Vulpecula, 464.

Watches, 135.
Water on the moon, 163, 164.
Watson, J. C., claims discovery of intra-Mercurial planets, 178; leaves a fund for the computation of the orbits of asteroids, 228.
Weather, changes due to sun spots, 64; effect of the moon on, 168.
Wolf, Max, photographs tree-like structures in the Milky Way, 339.
Wolf-Rayet Stars, 353, 354, 399.

Y Cygni, 380.
Years, different kinds of, 113.
Young, C. A., theory of sun spots, 63; observation of prominences, 79; opinion about the collision of a comet with the sun, 300; estimate of the light of the stars, 355.

Zenith defined, 22.
Zenith Distance defined, 121.
Zeta Cancri, 372.
Zodiac defined, 100.
Zodiacal Light, 334.

www.ingramcontent.com/pod-product-compliance
Lightning Source LLC
Chambersburg PA
CBHW030304240426
43673CB00040B/1051